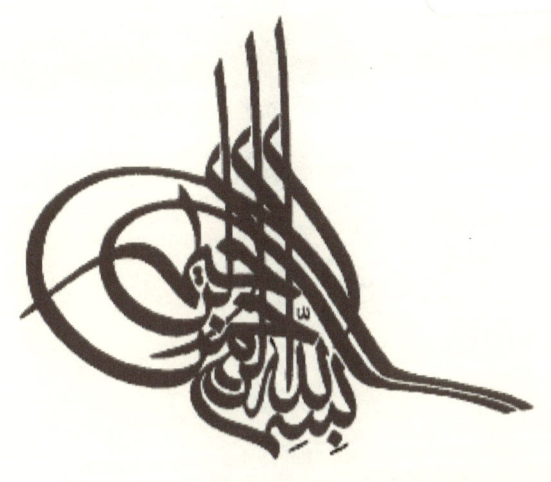

In the Name of Allah,

the Compassionate, the Merciful

The Life of Imam Khomeini

By Dr. Sayyid Ali Qadiri

Detailed Table of Contents

iv

PUBLISHER'S PREFACE

"Contraries Have Been Gathered in Your

Attributes..."

In the calmness of love, delicate as a breeze, free like waves, more blooming than spring, more shining than the sun, firmer than a mountain, bluer than the sky, greener than the jungle, whiter than white and clearer than water, a man calmly passed by us, a man who was history itself. The waves which were caused by his hands crossed the frontiers of the earth and joined the orbits. After him, the earth, too, got the smell of the heaven. Much has been said about him, still being said and will be said, but:

Whatever I may say in explaining love,

I get ashamed of it when I come to love itself.

The greatness and the reality of men like the late **Imam [Khomeini]** can never be described as they really are. His personality is the likeness of the sun when it hides its face for a while behind the curtain of alienation.

This which is in your hands is a discourse about the life and the memories of the Imam originally intended to present a new suggestion in this respect. The writer tries to get nearer to the depth of the Imam's personality, to explore, in a parallel movement, this holy life, and to study it exactly where it had been developed, i.e. within its chronological sequence, although his and our silent tongues repeat this verse of **Mawlana**:

Though the water of the sea is not drinkable,

Yet it must be tasted to quinch thirst!

Bruce Mazlish, a contemporary Western writer and thinker, in his book *Khomeini the Hidden,* writes: ―Two things have made **Imam Khomeini** what he is: one, his love of the Family of Revelation, and the other, his particular spirit of gnosticism."

The prismatic personality of **the Imam** and his prophetic appearance were glad tidings of security and faith, in the middle of an age which was about to get used to ‗ungodliness'. **The Imam's** appearance and presence caused the nations to enthusiasm and to try to resurge before the

Resurrection. Hence, immediately after the start of the **Imam**"s prophetic movement, there rose successive great movements, not only in the Islamic countries, but also in the countries where there still was a remembrance and a name of God. The original objective of these tempests was to smash the idols of disbelief and polytheism all over the world. It was a movement in the name of God along time.

Years before, the informed and the priests of the temple of human thought had predicted this appearance and presence. The late **Jalal Al-e Ahmad,** in his book under the title *Service and Betrayal of the Enlightened,* quoted the speech of the informed sunny old man of Qum, who, in the dark night of the ignorance of the Time of Ignorance, rose his voice calling the world to light. Now, a prompter has raised his head out of the fetters, free like a whirlwind, inviting the world to wakeness, and entrusting the fire of gnosticism, love and spirituality to the long-nighted ones of the earth.

The late martyr **Murtada Mutahhari,** by way of depicting **Ruhullah**" [the spirit of God], says that he was the extract and digest of faith. It was this very faith which, bravely and intuitively, spoke of the decline of Communism, and of the need of the contemporary critical world for a gnostic spirituality, the spirituality which he himself was its actual personification and crystallization. **The Imam**"s message to **Gorbachev** was not a small one. It was the message of a man, who, after centuries, like a spiritual leader and an internal guide for his era, called out to the new Caesars and Khosroes to submit to the truth, the wonder of innateness and the conduct of love and faith. The world has heard, and it will also hear, his voice. Egypt, Algeria, Afghanistan, Pakistan, India, Arabia, Iraq, Lebanon, Syria, France, South Africa, America, England and tens of other small and large countries in the world testify how great the holy voice of that old spiritual man in its effect was, and how blessful! If only man knew that bread-tables are in need of the blessing of faith!

The important subject about this godly personality is his Shiite bringing-up. Shiism was like an arena for the manifestation of the truth of Islam in the whole of his historical presence, brandishing the standard of justice, and asking for a hatchet to let his Ibrahimian appearance and existence smash the idols of power, gold and dissimulation. It is a chain which, along history, uninterrupted, like successive waves continually struck at the cold and rocky shores of injustice, until they were broken and driven away, though through this conflict it, too, received slaps. The special movement of **the Imam** in his religious understanding and holy presence was based on prophetic and Alawi invitation to the truth of revelation, the law of justice and the path of love.

2

All of these are the spiritual heritage of Shiism which **the Imam** presented to the contemporary humanity. If only man could understand the secret of the greatness which is deposited in this great heritage—the secret which **the Imam,** in his final advices, expressed in the form of his belief in the **Thaqalayn**.

The other subject which has no less importance is **the Imam's** gnosticism which was manifested in his high and heavenly soul, and disclosed existence in a holy witnessing. A refined soul which, with the grace of his pleasant breaths, filled the surface of the earth with the scent of his godly presence, and left signs of deliverance on whatever place he passed by. Ascetic at night, lion at daytime, had the old man received no light and no luminousness from the Truth of existence, he could not have lighted a torch along the path of the night-stricken humanity:

—Whoever kindles fire in himself is the light of the meeting!"

In the book *Service and Betrayal of the Enlightened* a chapter is devoted to **the Imam's** speech in the year 1342. **Jalal** stresses in this discussion that at a time when, in certain words, —the sky-beating fists of power are disclosed and throughout disgraced" and have taken to flattery and begging at the doors of gold owners, the powerful and the masters of dissimulation, the Shiite authority is still wakeful, and remains raising the banner of fighting fascism and imperialism. Later on, **Shams,** quoting **Jalal,** said that during **the Imam's** visit to Qum, he saw in his hand the book *There is Nothing in the West,* and, quite astonished, he said: —The authority who reads the newest books of the westerners is a man of insight and one must endeavour to entrust one's heart to him and follow him."

The Imam is the announcer of monotheism in the contemporary era. A great thinker, in the middle of the new century, said: —At a time when men of religion are empty-handed, what can the poets do?"

This talk comes true in respect of everybody who, in a time of difficulty, tries to undertake a great job. Undoubtedly, **the Imam** enjoyed the flow of the holy spirit of the **Christ's** breath, and thus he could breathe into the dead body of the new century the spirit of faith and love, and to historically carry out the desire of all the prophets. He used his strongest power against history in order to deny the empty-handedness of the spirit of the present era. It is these particularities which distinguish **Imam Khomeini's** revolution from other contemporary revolutions. **Teda Scotchpel,** the prominent contemporary sociologist, in his book dedicated to sociologically studying Iran's Revolution, states all the theories of revolution about the Islamic Revolution of Iran and discusses them, and then concludes that none of those

3

theories can sufficiently analyse this Revolution. The Islamic Revolution is a separately spun texture which must be separately studied.

The age of united disbelief is over, and now it is time for monotheism and a new era is starting. **Imam Khomeini** gave everything the color and smell of holiness. The earth got a heavenly appearance, and the soil got the color of the orbits. Literature had also a share of his presence and existence. Language, which formerly belonged to the multiplicity and used for tumult, got a divine color, turned towards unity and was used for innate disposition.

Literature has a great power. This deep and astonishing power effectively participated in the bringing about of some contemporary schools of thought. In fact, if a school does not make use of literature for transmitting its ideas and teachings, it has actually done a great injustice to itself. Imperialism and Communism—the two sides of the coin of the Western culture—tried to make use of the naked visage of literature to their own interests by reflecting it on the mirrors of minds. Now it seems that from that coin only one side is surviving, and that is the ugly visage of profit and capitalism, which kindles the fires of envy and greed in the souls of the people, and turns the people's lives and existence into dust and ashes. **The Imam** breathed a new spirit into literature. He regarded the language of poetry to be the loftiest and the most agreeable of languages. This was not just a complement. It was a contradiction to the contemporary definition of literature. On the other hand, it was the climax and the rise to which literature, in its true sense, can reach. The literature of the innate nature, the literature of the truth and the literature of humanity and justice were becoming strange to themselves. **The Imam** very well was aware of the fact that if a school of thought could not correctly and eyecatchingly make use of literature, it would face difficulty in carrying out its objectives. Is it not that the miracle of the Sealing Prophet was a verbal literary one? The Quran's inimitable literary structure showed that man, in his mental and moral maturity, attains to eloquency, and before this astounding geometrical construction of words and meanings, he has but to bow in homage. *Nahj al-Balaghah,* too, shows the way to the wonderful literary maturity and eloquent speech.

The new age, which has brought a hundred lights,

Has opened its eyes in his lap.

When the late „**Allamah Iqbal** of Lahore was reciting this verse, probably it did not occur to him that after half a century a man would rise and he himself would give to the new age hundreds of moral and divine luminous lights. With his special literature, which was his eminent, inimitable simple style, **the Imam** established a new ultra-way other than that of ordinary literature and men of letters. Literature, thenceforth, was no more a mere art, but a need. **The Imam's** attachment to the great men like **Sadi, Mawlana, Hafiz** and other great gnostic poets, caused him to pay special attention to the Persian literature and the literary men of the land of illumination. His part in spreading literature was kneaded with the part of literature in spreading his objectives, and hundreds of thousands, nay, millions, of pages of matters, writings, poems and articles, were penned about him in literary form.

About **the Imam** plenty has been written and said. But those which are more important out of them, and historically survive longer, are the speeches and writings which have a deeper literary color.

As it was already said, any school of thought which disregards the part of literature in spreading its ideals and teachings, will remain behind in the speedy literary contest, and will lose its addressees to the enchanting and attractive words of its opponents. The saying that the world of today is like a village, refers to this concept. Under the hegemony of technology and of the media, and by imposture and forgery of propaganda and the magic of words, the ideas are deformed and bewitched, and they find no way to a seclusion except through tricks and Babylon confusion.

Nowadays literature and men of letters are to be thought of once again and literature is to be taken seriously, because the enemies are taking it seriously, too. The importance of any piece written about **the Imam**, his ideals and his aims, increases when it takes a literary tint. This text, at your disposal, has such an importance. This written piece tries to draw a literary, biographical holy picture, and, by using the approved aspect of language, it is to show a beautiful readable text. Neglecting the historical share and the beauty of language is a neglect for which no generation and no age would forgive us.

Our sage men believed that one must be at the service of those words which kindle fire, not of those which pour cold water on the sparks of thoughts.

Basically, language is informative. This characteristic, due to its direction, is capable of being constructive or destructive. **The Imam** gave a constructive visage to literature, and tried to let it find, through making peace with innate disposition, a direction of humanity and unity. Now, if we are to move along with **the Imam's** desires and the values which he introduced to the contemporary history, we must regard important that which he stressed and confirmed, and follow up the same direction.

We have to try new borders in language, and to step into new valleys and practise new experiments which will increase our scientific and technical ability, and grant us success in the beauty contest.

In this work, **the Imam's** life is reviewed, from beginning to end, with a new attention and method. This review is twin with love and devotion. It is the pen of longing that, on the rug of separation, illustrates the historical fate of a loving people together with the object of their love. It is not a dry narration of history before you. It is the narrative of the consternation and love of a people who lovingly presented their full attachment, with complete sincerity, to the holy threshold of a spiritual old man, and manly and uprightly, they stayed constant in respect of this sacred allegiance. The sunny name of **the Imam** was brightly written on the forehead of the fate of this land. Now, this book, though small, is a mirror in front of the sun in order to have a suitable share of that everlasting radiance for the coming generations.

The writer tries, in a parallel movement, to relate how the stature of the young tree of **Ruhullah** became proudly fruitful in the body of the contemporary history, without any decrease and deduction. Truly, he has been accompanied by success in this work.

If we talk according to the new criterions, this work can be taken as a kind of historical novel: The plan and the prose are those of a novel, and the truth and the authority are those of history.

This writing, by returning to the time of beginning, takes care of the biography of **the Imam's** ancestors, with an insight in the picture and conduct of the existent men and women who, like pearls, opened to breed in them- selves the pure jem of that divine being with the grace of the Holy Spirit, and to be a new and different starting point in history.

After a long introduction, we come to the first chapter of the work. It starts with a detailed description of the historical situation of the town of Khomein, and how **the Imam's** ancestors settled there. Unlike a mere novel, here, all the narratives and episodes are documented, and only few signs and tidings have worn the apparel of mere written pieces lacking documents.

If the family of that great man, by the felicity of their truthful hearts, could prevent distortion and reduction in the *Shariah,* and presented a luminous picture of the holy truth in the clear mirror of their works, **the Imam,** on the same way, not only could, with his pen, guard that eternal epic, rather he started an event which, like a star, would remain evershining, and never decline from the sky of man's fate—The great act which God never bestowed the grace of performing its like upon any wise and learned man in all the history.

It is quite natural that there may be deficiencies in the text, which are not denied, but, as the Khwajah of Shiraz, **Shamsuddin Muhammad, Hafiz**—the gnostic man who was greatly respected by **the Imam**—had said:

—Consider truthfulness and affection, not the defects of sin,

As whoever is artless only looks at defects.

The key to the treasure of happiness is accepted by men of heart,

Let nobody get any doubt about this point."

It is hoped that those who are eager for the truth, and the insighted people, may look with the eye of care and kindness at these drafts, and generously remind us of any deficiency they see, so that once again this book may appear freer from defects, better revised and with clearer arrangement, and stand upright in an apparel of better printing.

14/3/1378

INTRODUCTION

"The Entire Arch of Existence Is From Allah and to Allah"
Imam Khomeini (*s.a.*)

A golden dome with four tall minarets, in the bounds of an area six million times less than the Iranian territory, in the south-west of the city of Tehran, can be seen from a distance. Under this dome is buried a man named **Ruhullah,** whose tomb is an exhilarative visiting place. He is the most renowned personality in this century, and he is the hero of our story.

When it was suggested to me to write the story of his life for those who do not know Persian, I hurried to visit him to get his permission. Under that dome, in front of his shrine I sat for hours thinking about him and how I should start and wherefrom.

I asked him: ―If a brush was given to you so as to paint yourself, wherefrom and with what color would you start?"

I waited for an answer. His collection of poetry was with me. I began turning its pages, telling myself: Probably I will find my answer in one of his odes. In the second line of the first ode offered to the public, I read:

I got free from myself and beat the drum of *anal-haqq* ' (I am the truth),
Like **Mansur,** I became purchaser of the gallows' top.

Through this line I heard him say: ―I would dissolve myself in the cream of the pen of creation and with it I would paint the sky in blue color, just like the reflection of the sea in the mirror of the sun. I would paint the night black so that the stars may not be strangers. The buds I would paint, at the beginning, grass-green, and in autumn, in all colors. On the stem of the sweetberries I would set an orange shoot. A quince flower I would keep for the bud of a tree which bears quince. To the ruby I would say: ‗Be in the color of the seeds of Saweh's pomegranate!' To the snow I would say: ‗Rain down white like stars and remain white, and run along whenever it is not winter.' The countryside I would divide in two with a river, then with a bridge I would join them. To the river I would say: ‗Roar such that when you run breathlessly they would not be able to swim into you twice.' To the fish I would say: ‗Swim up the stream to its spring.' The mountain I would order:

_Pour into the sea, but so slowly that the thunder thinks you are erect as a mountain.' In the grove I would invite the gazelle to fresh grass, then send the lion after it to hunt it. On the frog's tongue I would pour glue so that the mosquitos may not throng the jungle, and the frog I would insert into the snake's stomach so that the stork chickens, which are waiting for the worms, may not be hunted. To the eagle I would give a heart as vast as its wings so as to perch on the head of the viper. The butterfly I would fly with a breeze from a branch to another, and I would create so many sparrows and turtledoves that the jungle becomes full of songs...

When it is man's turn I would mix all the colors and knead them for forty years to become a thousand colors and _to come out in a hundred thousand displays so that I may see them with a hundred thousand eyes.' I would leave him free to settle wherever he likes, or to step outside my painting and to scratch the orbits with his head, and I would instruct the angels to spread wings so that when he gracefully walks he may not step except on angels' wings..."

All these he said in the first hemistage. As to the second hemistage, how fearful it was! At the top of each stout tree in the tumultuous jungle they had set up gallows.

The second ode, in which I found, in a way, my answer, was:

> Though from both worlds our gain was nothing,
>> No care is there, as Thy love is in our heart;
>
> The entire universe is a reflection of Thy Face,
>> It suffices us, then, to have the entire universe as our gain.

I wish I could pour a measure from the cask of this perception into the cup of my heart and make all my cells taste it drop by drop, and, when my fingers get drunk I would portrait the face of the beloved in the dawn dew, and paint the dew on the leaves of wild adonis, and baskets of tulips in the plain of the eye, and name it: _The image of his visage in the profile of the beloved.'

Such fancies warmed me, but they were not what was wanted from me. They wanted me to write something about the life of a man whom we know and do not know: When was he born? Where did he study? How did he choose his wife? What did he put of his mind and heart on his tongue such that he became the leader of a great Revolution? When did he, with a calm heart, and the waves of the arms of millions of lovers, go towards the earth?

How incapable I was of performing what many are capable of! I was at times coming to myself and at times forgetting myself. My imagination would enter through the windows inside the shrine and through the grave to where I could indulge in a conversation with him.

I said: The philosophers say that the original topic of philosophy is ‚existence'. Asked: ―What is existence?" They say it is ‚an axiom'. If you are asked: ―What is existence, and at what part of it are you? What would be your existence-giving answer to this existence-raising question?" I heard hundreds of answers, and before and after each, this sentence of his, like a tableau, was before me: **"The entire arch of existence is from Allah and to Allah."** Many times I had contemplated this sentence. I knew that it represented both the foundation and the objective of his thought. But that night for the first time I felt trembling at its appalling presence, because this saying means, too, that the sayer has ascended to the arch of existence.

The cup of certainty I assuredly brought to the effect that nothing less should be said, since it is backed by more than a hundred of verses and a thousand of *hadith*s. In the philosophic thought there are no words beyond these words.

I demanded permission to weave the calico of my painting myself—a painting as long as his age and as wide as my understanding. With a heart full of love, and wih a stormy mind and trembling fingers I drew in that imaginary painting a picture which started ‚from Allah" and was to continue ‚to Allah".

It was an ambiguous picture, because I had summoned „from Allah" from the darkness of nonexistence, whereas „from Allah" is the very existence itself. It was easier to interpret it like this: ‚From the Absolute Existence [*hastiy-e mutlaq*] towards the Absolute of existence [*mutlaq-e hasti*]'. Although this explanation could, to some extent, add transparency to my picture, particularly if I could understand the ‚absolute', but the problem of his birth would not be solved. Concerning the time in which he was born, had he come from nonexistence or from existence? If from nonexistence, my picture would be a spontaneous creation, but if from existence, what could be his former existence? Then, when he was no longer there, was he really no longer there?

The theologians have solved the problem by dividing life into this world and the world to come. So, if we say that he was born in the year so-and-so, we will not be saying: ―He came from nonexistence," and if we say that in the year so-and-so he played the tune of departure, we will not be saying: ―He hurried into nonexistence." Nevertheless, this would not solve the

11

original problem, because, explaining life by dividing it into this world and the hereafter does not fit only into the science of theology. The gnostics did not divide life into this world and the hereafter. They see life, at the beginning, as two sides of one thing, then as one side of all things. Then, in another stage, ‗all things‗ get a single meaning. He was a great gnostic, and if they say nothing of his gnostic life, then whatever they say, it will not be he himself.

How difficult it was to start portraying a sublime soul in a painting so short that it was as long as a single century, and as wide as the width of no more than the thickness of a thin thread. As such I had but to start from somewhere and to liberate myself from this uncertainty, especially that I had the feeling that among all peoples there were groups who were waiting to know about him a little more than what they had heard. In an afternoon connected to night, I once again had carefully read his will. He said: ‒What I have to refer to is that my political-divine will is not confined to the great people of Iran, rather it is a recommendation to all the Muslim nations and to the wronged people of the world of all nations and religions." When I paraded these expressions in my mind, I thought that millions of men and women, young and old, literate and illiterate, hungry and satisfied, rich and poor, from the north to the south and from the east to the west of the world were parading before my eyes. Most of them were those who kept hearing his name in the news headlines for ten years, and wished to know more about him: Where did he come from? Who was he? What did he want? What message did he have? Once again I felt embarrassed. I did not know what I should do with all those different peoples, and with what language I should talk to them.

I stared at the mouth of those who say: ‒The sun rises first from our land," to know what they want. Is it more important for them to see his life in the form of a calendar, or in the form of the stature of a culture? Do they prefer to know when he was born, or how he looked at Buddha, how he guarded the traditions, or how and why he broke traditions. To imagine that from among this row, a generation whose principal question was about business, stock exchange and interest rate, and wanted to know how much value he gave to the bourse stocks, was like the cold water of disappointment being poured on my head.

Originally the Chinese seemed to be of the same features. But when I gazed at the depth of their rows, I noticed aged persons of six thousand years old, mocking at the one thousand and four hundred years of this gnostic old man. I thought if I say: ‒Count his age from the creation of Adam," these would understand the meaning of the talk better than those whose connection with history had been severed. I had seen a group of the Chinese Muslims whenever his name was mentioned they would immediately stand up errect, and now they were waiting in a pressed row burning for hearing once again new things about him. I was telling myself: The Chinese, as their long history shows them, are a people of forbearance, so they may be talked to in details. But what should I do with the speed-addicted addressees, who have no patience for detailed readings?

When the Indians came, they had questions as many as their number. They mostly asked: —Considering his grandfather, wasn't he an Indian?" If I had answered that, considering his great grandfather, **the Prophet (s),** he was an Arab, I would have been in trouble with the European and the American Muslims, who know better than some Arabs, that men of **Allah** may be chosen from a particular clan, but they never remain confined to a race, a clan or a nation. To the Indians I replied: Yes, he was. To the Iranians I said: Do not quibble over the fact that his grandfathers had migrated from Neyshabur to India. To the Arabs I said: His grandfathers came to Iran so as to pour light on this land. But I knew that such a discussion in this way would be a barrier against understanding the depth of his thoughts. [1]

India has already experienced **Gandhi** the Great. So, the people who have seen a man who could, despite the common methods of struggle, present a different design, are easier to be talked to than to count the uncommon methods of **Imam Khomeini (*a*)** in his struggle with the political East and West, for the peoples who have no such experiences.

The Pakistanis paraded in four rows, and I saw four journalists standing at the head of the rows. I felt ashamed of them, because I noted that they knew of him more than I did, and to introduce him to their society they devotedly used their pens, let alone their scholars. One of them showed me a series of articles which would have taken three months to read, if I wanted to. I asked myself: —What can you write which they do not know? Will your scripts not be like carrying coal to Newcastle?"

When it was Afghanistan's turn, I remembered a corpulent man who, in the early years of the Revolution, so hurriedly descended into a sewage well to save the life of a well-digger such that I thought he would not come back again. When his self-sacrifice braided a thread of friendship between us, I understood that he had a doctorate in literature. Sometimes he would go to his country to fight and sometimes he would come back to Iran to work. I used to see him, till a part of night, wearily reading the newspapers, listening to the radio and, while reading his loveable books, he would be overcome by sleep. At times, in the middle of the night, while strolling along the veranda of a holy shrine, he would use his pen, compose poetry, write articles, and he knew very well when **Ruhullah** would get up at dawn for supplication. He even knew the dates of the birthdays of the children of his Imam. I asked myself: ―For these people what have I in my bag of thoughts which they have not?"

I was telling myself: If this golden dome is the axis of the world, what kind of divisions would this world have? From its east came the smell of **Ishraq** to my nostrils, and its west took the color of a declining civilization. Its north resembled an intense cold in which life freezes. Its south was like a hell submitted to injustice. But a moment later, by discerning things, apparently ordinary, my feelings changed.

I saw an old man from Azarbayjan who had come to visit him. He was so eager that he was weeping with the full width of his face. An old woman unknotted a handkerchief, brought out a banknote and dropped it inside the shrine. A newly wed young man, nodding with his head and eye to his bride, permitted her to throw her wedding ring into the shrine. A boy climbed up the shrine so as to empty his box of savings into the shrine. A disabled ex-warrior, who had only an elbow left from his four limbs, creeping on his chest, circled the shrine, with a smile of content on his lips. A tall woman who had brought her invalid child, with the hope of being blessed, brushed him against the shrine. A middle-aged man opened the supplication book and with an affable singing recited a supplication. A man had vowed to recite a section of the *Quran* beside his shrine everyday. A girl, who, I think, had come from Turkey, with incomplete *hijab,* was bitterly crying and, fearing no notification, hugged the shrine and earnestly was demanding something.

A number of Afghani workers were scrupulously cleaning the corners of the windows with handkerchiefs, while a caravan of Pakistanis were indulged in zealous mourning rituals in a corner of the place. Two blacks, whose nationality I could not guess, circled the shrine more than thirty times. Visitors from central Asia, on their arrival, all in a single row fell on the tiled floor and kissed it.

White-dressed people from Kuwait, U.A.E. and Oman were also seen among the crowd. They were performing the *salah* with their arms folded on their chests, and also with their folded arms recited a supplication text near his shrine. I remembered other nights, when men and women from England, Holland, Germany and America, a group with folded arms and a group with dropped arms, courted the shrine.

At that night hundreds of people stood in the *salah,* and tens of men and women dispersed and stretched here and there in the place closing their eyes for a slumber. Children of four and five freely leapt and gambolled around. A number of boys were sliding on the smooth, glossy tiles of the place. Noticing that no one prevented them was reflected in the boys' merrymakings which gave me a vernal feeling to the deepest of my soul.

A young man, absorbed in his dreams, was leaning against a thick column of the dome, and occasionally applying his pen to paper to scribble, with his left hand, some expressions which he audibly uttered. I was leaning against another column, looking at him. At times, when my eyes met his, he shyly lowered his eyes to his notebook. This shyness of his made him more amicable. I guessed he was composing poetry. I went up to him. He closed his notebook. He liked his poetry to be read, yet he was shy of his notebook being inspected. I read, and read again, but I got inspiration more than pleasure. His start was: ―If it were not for you, which column could I lean against?"

On bidding him farewell, his severed right hand answered my question about his writing with the left hand.

The poetry of this Iranian young man, the effort of the Turkish girl, the fervor of the Pakistanis, the longing of the Azari, and the mysterious feelings of the blacks whom I did not know where they had come from, were all a blissful manifestation carrying a message as clear as limpid water, allegorically telling: ―Whoever puts his foot in this holy place, without quitting his own culture and traditions, is its close intimate." Just then I realized who my addressee was and what he wanted from me.

Two hours had passed after mid-night, yet the shrine and the yards around it were as noisy and crowded as they were in the day and also as quiet as at night. It was a strange night. When I returned home with a saddle-bag full of inspirations, the cocks were heralding the morning *salah* with their crowings.

Before writing the biographies of great ones, the ancients had the tradition of performing a *ghusl.* But the moderners regard this to be an innovation. I did this innovation, and the water of the *ghusl* dismissed sleep from my eyelids and bestowed upon me the enthusiasm, the joyful activeness and the energy of the youth. Up till the *adhan* of the *maghrib salah,* the primary draft was prepared, and I took it to mean permitting me to start writing.

Inspired by the visitors of his shrine, I, accordingly, addressed all the people in general, since no one is stranger in this small sanctuary which is inspired by the big one.

The draft was sent to _The Institute for Compilation and Publication of Imam Khomeini's Works' (ICPIKW). After a few days the answer came that: ─All those who read the draft approved of it, particularly the late **Haj Ahmad Aqa** [the Imam's son] who was then still among us.

It is said that whoever was honoured by going on *hajj* and stood beside The Black Stone and asked **Allah** something, let him never doubt it that his demand would be granted. When I had the honour of touching The Black Stone, I asked seven demands: First, forgiveness for my past and future sins, and seventh, making my serious duties in life coincide with my high flying ambitions. The theologians say of the second part of the first supplication that it is invalid, yet a witty person said: ─It is a cunning supplication." But I see that my writing down the Imam's biography denotes granting the seventh demand, because when the draft was completely accepted, without any alteration, note or reminder, my breath came round and flew joyfully, and, at the same time, anxiety and mirth knotted together into a heavy burden which weighed on my shoulder. Actually, before writing the draft, I did not take the suggestion to be serious, and I wondered: ─Are writers so scarce?" When I heard the reasons for choosing me to stoop under such a burden I felt a shock, but I did not break my pride by saying: ─No!" I accepted the task under two conditions, after relying on **Allah**: First, to be completely free in what I write, with no remark whatsoever. No one may show his viewpoint, and no one shall alter my writing, even for a single word.

The second condition was that those who have suggestive proposals may not deprive me of their frank and most merciless and rude criticisms, as well as of their kind opinions. As regards the first condition, it was treated so simply that I doubted whether they had understood what I said, but in practice, it appeared that they complied with it. As regards the second condition, at first they took it to be a kind of flattery and courtesy. But when they realized that I was realy thirsty, they gave me gulps out of the treasures of thoughts, even more than what I demanded. Obtaining the needed documents and memoirs naturally encountered many obstacles through the crooked and twisted lanes of administration, to the extent of despair, as a result of the chronical disease with which most of the country's organizations and establishments, are afflicted, though, I am sure, not on purpose.

The first condition I did not impose for evasion nor to examine the orderers either, nor did I want to be pretensious as a writer. In fact I

16

positively believed that the hero of my story completely belongs to me. He had his Revolution in my country, my friends went to the warfront at his orders, he changed the world outlook and the behaviour of the society in which I live—not only I, but also my family and the generation of my offspring, all of them would harvest what he had sown. I had known him according to ideas of my perceptions, and I loved him within the limits of my understanding. So, what I am going to write will be based on my love, and a part of my life, particularly the moments of my leisure time, which I am to spend with myself, I will spend with him. Thus, it is unkind to myself if I am to write the talks of the others, to have the notes of the others and to think about the interests—and I do not know whether they are really for or against the interest—which are to be dictated by others and I have to write them.

The second condition was because I was asking myself: —Is he yours alone? Before you open your eyes to this world there were others who, in his class of philosophy, had drunk from the cask of his speeches the wine of gnosticism. Your grandfather was born when he was being weaned. Some of those who had seen in his seclusion the manifestation of grandeur are still living. Do they or you, know him better? That fifty-years old woman, who, after the martyrdom of her husband, sent her three young sons to the warfront, and now she appears like an eighty-years old woman on whose face loneliness drew deep wrinkles, yet every month she stands under that dome in order to present a part of her pension to her beloved. Who is more lovesick, she or you? So, who are you, what are you and how much do you worth that you want to be completely free, so as to boil in your opinion's pot whatever you like, making a paste out of it and make others taste it?

Are you capable of pushing his cloak aside to see his naked gnostic stature and accuse him not of heresy?[2] Do you know of philosophy as much as to perceive that —The legs of the rationalists are wooden?" Is morality in you so tall as to allow you to move your head above your wall? What do you know of *fiqh,* and how do you see politics? Aren't you afraid of drawing of him a picture which will be alien to him? Have you no fear of flinging those who read about his life, for the first time, into a wilderness?"

These multi-answer questions assaulted my soul like a storm, and the heart and reason judged that absolute freedom in writing makes me absolutely attentive to whatever anyone may say, not by my ears, but by the ears of my soul, and wait not for the acquaintances to tell their views, but to try to get to know the covert opinions of the friends and the strangers. Furthermore, from the time I started reading some books, which I did not approve, till now there has been a scuffle between me and a contradiction.

During my argument with that contradiction, sometimes my handwritings were torn to pieces. On starting this work the said contradiction showed itself in a more justified manifestation. On one side I firmly believe that a writer must be free. This I do not regard as a right, but as a duty. I am annoyed with those who take it only to be a right and not a duty. On the other side I admit for the reader a right wider than that of the writer. The writer knows what he is writing, while the reader knows nothing of it before reading it. Sometimes the writer consciously intends to capture the reader in his net and to deprive him of the right to choose and the cleverer the writer the stronger the net which he pulls over the reader's thinking. It was such that, while searching for a way to solve this contradiction, I found a term which may not be so expressive in any language as it is in the Persian and the Arabic languages: _Freedom' in lieu of _Liberty', as freedom is absolute liberty but under obligations and commitments.[3] To some extent, I had made the alphabet of freedom of the original religious literature. I had to do my best to practically try it. The requisites for practice were:

First, not to start writing without performing the *wudu* in order to remember that writing is a devotional, not a whimsical, act.

Second, not to have in the writing any partner, except **Allah,** in order to acquire the courage of writing what must be written.

Third, to make the *ayah:* **"... Give good tidings to my servants"** a fixed tableau in my mind, and not to regard any talk worthless, even the talk of an adversary. Likewise, not to be afraid of any modernist who may accuse me of bigotry, nor to be afraid of what the judgments of the bigoted, modernists, politicians and tasteless parties and groups may be. Furthermore, I may not act limply or undisciplined. In selecting a subject I should aim at an objective, and not to invite the reader to soliloquy, but if I could not give up this soliloquy, I may not, at least, conceal it.

Before writing down my primary draft, the ICPIKW had put at my disposal an outline as a source which was the result of the efforts of the researchers at that office. It was a valuable source for a start.[4] The news about my undertaking such a momentous task quickly spread among my friends and acquaintances, and whoever smelled of acquaintanceship put whatever he had in his bag of thoughts in a tray of loyalty and presented it to me, such that during most of the day caravans of news and memoirs ran down upon me. Each caravan brought me generously original gifts such that the size of my heard information increased so much that I was drowned in them, and much as I tried to classify them, I was incapable of arranging even a simple classification. When the flood of recounting of the memoirs subsided, the pen ran into the inkpot and from those mingled sources took its ink and paddled and galloped to write fast.

Fifty pages were quickly prepared. It was my hope that the book would not exceed two hundred pages. I asked a number of my friends to mercilessly criticize it. The first objection happened to be like this: The emotional load of the words and sentences is such that translating it into some foreign languages is improbable. I had in my mind to ask fourteen persons to read it. Not all of them were thinking as I did, but they were acquainted with different cultures. I knew that if there was any diminution in what I want to write, they would remind me of it. Some of them confirmed that turning some of my expressions into some other languages is impossible. My first limitation in writing became visible, that is, I should have avoided multi-sided phrases. This confinement would have increased the volume of the writings and decreased their depth.

When the number of the readers exceeded fifty, continuing the work became quite difficult. On one side I myself had wanted them to be merciless in their surgical operation on my writings, and, on the other side, each surgeon, taking into his consideration the safety of all organs, used his knife on an organ.

A friend underlined the paragraphs which spoke of: ―In his boyhood his financial condition was good," then, with a pencil annotated in the margin: ―Is this necessary to be written, particularly that he spoke much of the bare-footed, the cottagers and the oppressed?"

Another one annotated in another place: ―Don't you think that repeating the witty stories of his marriage would abate his leadership dignity?"

A third said: ―It is true that he said: ‗I had a rifle in my childhood and I used to fight against the wicked men, but the terrorists who try to find an excuse will find in this an excuse to murder his personality, which they actually did'."

Someone asked: ―Does not the story of the father's martyrdom incite the sick-hearted psychiatrists to psychoanalyse him?"

One said: ―Won't a loveless person laugh when he reads: ‗The breeze of the angels' wings wound in the orchard, and threw a line on the mirror of water so as to eagerly prostrate on the dust which was passing through the moments of another creation'?"

Another one asked: ―Is there any necessity for repeating his recitation of the *Shahnamah*, especially that there are many who still do not know what the purport of the *Shahnamah* is?"

19

There was a quotation by his brother from somebody whom he described as _the late'. One of the respectable critics underlined the word _the late', annotating to the effect that the deceased did not deserve the epithet.

I arranged the operated organs together, and there was _a lion with no mane, belly or tail'. There remained only the title and nothing more. On the other hand, the said operated organs were samples from reading which the other surgeons had derived much pleasure. An annotation said that it was good to say: ─His financial status was good," since it would confirm that his unrestricted protection of the deprived classes did not stem from a class basis, rather he reached at that attitude on an ideological basis. Another one said: ─How wonderful his choosing his wife was! I wish there were more details so that his followers might know how getting married should be." Concerning his recitation of the *Shahnamah,* someone said: ─He was a goldsmith who knew the value of gold."

Somebody believed, for some reason, that retelling a certain incident was not necessary, another one, or other ones, appeared eager to make me to handle that very incident with more details.

All of a sudden I encountered a pair of contradictions. On one hand I had to respect both parties who had obliged me by their suggestions of addition or omission, as caring for the opinion of one side meant neglecting the opinion of the other side, and, on the other hand, by firmly confining myself to make use of the viewpoints of my acquaintances, I had placed myself on the opposite side of my absolute freedom. Before finding a moral way for solving these contradictions, I suddenly saw myself face to face with a principal question—a question whose answer had always been with me, but due to its continual manifestation, it was hidden from my sight. The question was: ─Who is my addressee?" To say that he was general, not an Iranian, since all were his intimates, was not sufficient. Someone said: ─As regards the Muslims who have suitable information of the Islamic history and knowledge ,suffices them to have some hints, but those who have no Islamic knowledge whatsoever, what should they do?" It was a proper reminder. To redress this shortcoming there were two ways before me: One was to fill it up in the footnotes. The other was to insert in the text whatever is to be said in one way or another. The second way seemed more proper, because continually referring the reader to the footnotes is boring, and, moreover, it breaks the thread of talk. But what was more important was that **Ruhullah** minus Islam leaves nothing for him. As a matter of fact, his biography would be a real one only when seen through Islam. Thus, there is no way but to use Islam as context and see him through it.

20

Those who are attached to him know very well that his thoughts are transnational, yet they know that he was born in Iran, exiled from Iran, returned to Iran and from Iran he attacked the Western and Eastern politics and ideologies, and that the bulk of his speeches and writings was in Persian, and many of his hinting lessons refer to the history of Iran. Therefore, one cannot easily say that knowing, though briefly, the history and the culture, which irrigated the seeds of his thoughts, is not necessary.

Thus, the said fifty pages were multiplied by eight, but I kept the same structure which I had planned in my primary draft. For those who are not quite familiar with Iran's culture and history, I went on elaborating my work.

When he was still living, every day numerous letters used to reach his office from all over the world. Probably no office of a leader had ever received as many diverse letters as his. But alas! If answering all of them was theoretically possible, practically it was impossible. The International Affairs Department at the ICPIKW has translated a good number of those letters into Persian. I read a number of them carefully and classified them so as to know the addressee better. Formerly I had seen many letters sent by Embassies to some ministries. The contents of the letters had their places under seven general titles:

1. *Fiqhi* Questions: Most of the inquirers were from professors and students of Islamic knowledge. They wanted to have more information about his *fiqhi* ways, not the very precepts themselves. [5] Some of them wanted to know: Does he admit any separation between the political *fiqh* and the devotional *fiqh*? Does he take intellect to be a source of *fiqh*? Or does he regard intellect to be the essence of the principles? Does *Wilayah al-Faqih* stem from his *fiqhi* methods, or has it a root in his political philosophy? Has he created a connection between philosophy and *fiqh,* or does he regard each one of them to be a separate knowledge? What position has the *fiqh* of the Sunni sects in his point of view? These questions included some recommendations, such as concerning the *hijab* of the followers of other divine Books, accepting peace and permitting alcoholic beverages for the religious minorities.

2. Philosophic Questions: Some had heard that he was a teacher of philosophy, and some had reasoned that he was a philosopher. Consequently, many of the received questions discussed philosophic categories. Some questions had the required maturity, while other questions showed that the questioners were not professionals.

These non-professionals became my addressee, because the professionals, however, can, with more effort, attain to first class sources, and from among his speeches they can open a road to his philosophic principles, whereas the non-professionals do look for the truth, but they are engaged in other pursuits, and their philosophic questions are not a continuation of their business, though these were their real intellectual conflicts. It was clear that reading philosophic novels did not quench their thirst. Their natural dispositions to search for the truth incited them to resort to their pens and examine his philosophic answers, too.

3. Political Questions: This section had its particular complication. Repeating studying them changed my doubt into certainty that a group were in need of his answers for administrative, political and informative ends, yet it was obvious that others were in quest of more than that. They wanted to really know whether he was a religious leader, or a political leader clinging to religion. Most of these groups were those who believed in the intrinsic separation between religion and politics, and thought that mixing them was a thought from the middle ages. Some of the questions and criticising prejudgments were so daring that they hurt the translators. These, too, became my addressees, because I know my beloved liked the daring truth-seeker critics more than the sincere coward friends.

4. Psychological Bombardment: It is an old tradition that when a country is subjected to a military attack, other plans are laid to break down the resistance of the leaders and the people. Some of the mass media of the West and East spared no effort in psychologically bombarding this nation. Yet, although these bombardments mostly had reverse effects, this is something else which will be referred to when talking about its reasons. In this connection, one of the psychological bombardments which started after the occupation of the American Embassy and continued till the end of the war, was that his office every day received countless letters by unknown senders; with the hope that, if he himself was firm like a mountain, at least, the readers of the letters would bend their backs under the bombardment of abuses and uncertainty. Maybe one of their other objectives was to do away with the possibility of answering the serious letters. Looking into these worthless letters and analysing them are, in some way, worthy. At least, he could detect, from these letters, the weak points of the enemy [6] .I read some of these letters in order to recognize the daring addressees, whose minds were question -inciters, and they had no tranquillity nor calmness, and also to distinguish those who used vocabularies which, at first glance, seemed impolite, from those who sharpened their pens to sting.

5. Affable Letters: When I was reading some of those letters, it seemed as if the tubes of my tear-glands were connected to a water-skin. Isn't it nice that an old woman from Neauphle-le-Château writes: ―When you came to our district, blessing came to our house? I am passing through the last days of my life. Send me a sock, a handkerchief, anything to have it put in my coffin."

Tenors of other letters from other parts of the world:

* ―. I heard that when you speak, your hearers shed tears. If you have enchanted them from near-by, I am enchanted by you from far away."

* ―. When I see your face in the TV for a short moment, the depth of my soul fills with joy and I shed my tears of longing. I believe you are a man of God. I have two children, one was born blind and the other suffers from a heart disease. Invoke God to cure them."

* ―No leader is prepared (unless he is forced) to confess his mistakes. But I hear that you voluntarily admit your mistakes. Thus, one may believe that you have come from heaven. I implore God to illuminate our dark world with the speeches of men like you."

* ―Every information I hear about you I feel it to be smeared with deviation. A man, who talks with his followers, lowering his eyes all the time, cannot be a man of adventures, especially in old age. Talk to me, write to me: Where have you come from? What do you want? What message do you sense? Write to me, maybe God makes me, too, one of your disciples."

* ―When I read the history of the prophets I notice that they were encountered by persons with Satanic conduct. Now, you, who want to acquaint your people with God, the Satanic powers are challenging you. The prophets feared nobody. You, too, are afraid of no power. I have not so far heard that you claimed to be a prophet. Say, then, what is your claim? Are you Socrates? Are you a disciple (of Jesus)? Who are you? Whoever you may be and whatever your claim, I know your claim is right, because when disbelief covers the whole world, God sends a man to guide the people. You are now the very man who was expected to come. Alas! What separates between me and you is not merely the frontiers, the distance of language is a farther distance.[7]"

* ―I hope that your speeches, which are not related to power, war or politics, would soon be translated so that whoever was tired of the violence of this speedy civilization might be acquainted with your heavenly opinions."

* ―The streets of my country are full of light, its shops are full of commodities, its custom houses are active. We are short of nothing except a sacred soul. I wish you were born in my country so as to give to all these activities and commotions a supreme objective."

* —Why do you never speak of my country? Say something so that I may pen it with the most beautiful penmanship and put it in my working room and boast that a man from beyond has also spoken of my country. I hope the sentence which you are going to say will not be a curse!"

* —Lenin was a beloved leader. Hitler was so loved that he could muster a nation to commit suicide. **Gandhi's** livableness spread beyond the Indian borders. But I like to present my most cordial feelings to a man whom I do not know well, and of the past and the future of a revolution led by him I have no clear picture. Yet, at reading an article against you I am so annoyed that I cannot conceal it. I think you had stated that, _Even if this war lasted for twenty years we would remain standing firm,' and you had announced continuing the war till abolishing sedition from the world. But, strangely enough, you accepted peace and left the world in stupefaction. As you had said you drank the cup of poison. By this ingenious statement, without annulling the sacrifices of your followers, you showed a new path to your people. This artistry was so great that even after a hostile analysis its fineness cannot be denied.[8]"

The number of the amicable letters were so numerous that undoubtedly his office had no enough time to translate even a small number of them. But I found the opportunity to read a lot of those affable letters so as to know the needs better as well as the intellectual and sentimental conditions of the addressers. If the impact of some of my sentences is such that it seems out of the norm of biography writing, let those who are accustomed to conventionality accept my apology on behalf of those who discarded conventionality and dragged me bare-footed till *Arafat.*

6. Request for Knowing His Private Life: No great leader has a private life. If he has, he cannot conceal it. If he apparently can, there will be people who, for diverse motives, do their best to uncover it. The greater the leader and the wider his message, the more light thrown on the corners of his life. If in some time, no, in some other time, yes.[9] This is for granted and unavoidable principle, not dispraised, rather praised. Had it been dispraised, the Glorious Quran would not have let history disclose what the **Prophet (s)** wanted to conceal even from his wives. Undoubtedly, one of the secrets of this exposition is to confirm that knowing the private moments of the divine leaders, even if they do not like it, for their followers, is necessary, especially that knowing their most private affairs is, in itself, a way to a heavenly life.

As to why people like to know the most private moments of the leaders, many reasons can be noted. One of them is the instinct of curiosity. So, even if some persons, out of this instinct, asked him to write to them of the tiny things of his life, they have not asked something against this instinct.

A number of the people liked to know: What were his forefathers' occupations, ranks and professions? What is his order among his brothers and sisters? Has he brothers and sisters? How were, and are, his connections with his relatives? What is his education? Where was he born? How did he choose his wife? Isn't he afraid of rocket-attacks? How about the Day of Resurrection? How much does he love **Jesus?** What is his opinion in respect of **Zoroaster, Buddha** and **Confucius?** Does he think he is successful in his leadership? Does he fast? Does he kiss his children? What is his opinion about a sinner? Which food is palatable to him? Which kind of flowers does he like? Which color pleases him? Does he help his wife in her housework? Does he brush his teeth? What perfume and eau de cologne does he prefer? How many times does he take a bath per week? How does he spend his leisure time? Which sports does he like? etc.[10]

Years ago caring for such simple matters seemed to me meaningless, but now I believe that answering these negligible questions is a way to a sound and resistant life.

I tried hard, and I will try harder in another volume, with the help of Allah, to increase my efforts so as to answer all these questions, and, in answering such questions I do not think I am doing wrong.

7. Letters Apparently Nonsense: Some letters were apparently nonsense and could not be understood. Why did the writer bother to write and mail such a letter? From some expressions in the letters one may gather that some of their writers suffer from loneliness, and, under the pressure of nostalgia, they were driven to chew the cud with somebody. But why from a distance of hundreds of miles, and why with him in particular?

By casting a general look at all the letters we realize that they cover a wide range in which everything can be found: Letters astonished at the original theoretical gnostic discussions. Serious and deep, and sometimes superficial, philosophic discussions. Official political letters from the leaders of some countries. Letters from the leaders of liberation uprisings requesting guidance. Religious questions. Letters showing love and affection, as well as tender and kind letters. Also letters asking monetary help to improve a poor living, or requesting invocation for curing invalids. Incoherent letters without definite beginning or end from persons who do not know him well, but think he would probably read them. Also bombardments of abuse from knowing individuals, or from unknowing wronged ones. All these mean caring for a personality who did not exclusively belong to a particular nation, nor was he contained into the mould of a single subject. His declaration in his will that: **"... my political-divine will is not exclusively confined to the great nation of Iran, rather it is addressed to all the Islamic nations and the wronged people of the world from any clan and religion,"** is an evidence that there was a reciprocal connection between him and his addressees. Even the different religious beliefs, which are mostly the strongest fortress separating the followers of different religions, acted, in his respect, as a factor for removing other barriers, too.

On the other hand, age, education, nationality were also negligible by all the classes who used their pens and talked to him. Doesn't a look at these letters speak of the fact that we should talk to general addressees and not to confine ourselves to any particular class or age?

So, in retelling this biography I speak to a general addressee, exerting great effort to answer the answerable questions which found no answer. If a needful is longing to know whether the Ten Categories have also been unified by him, or whether they are still ten, I will try to consult the relevant experts and then to say yes or no. Further, if the mind of somebody is anxious to know whether the flowers of the garden were irrigated by him in person or by someone else, I will try to take it to be serious. Other than this, I also do not regard his biography to be his real biography, because he is in theory the same as he is in practice, and in decomposition he is not the same as in composition. If I talk of his philosophy and not of his gnosticism, of his *fiqh* and not of morals, the result, though appears to be researching and deep, yet it will not be himself. More important than that is the fact that if all of his dimensions are discussed mingled together, still it will not be himself. Therefore, I apologize to the specialist addressee, who is keen on strictly following his subject, regarding everything else out of the question, and ask permission to take into my consideration all the corners and to see him in composition. In fact I do know I am alleging a big claim, and if this allegation is caused by drunkenness, then let me have another drink and nakedly say that I go, camera in hand to take photographs of him in his covert and overt. But I do not stick them in an album for display, as I have dipped my pen in the extract of my soul so as to draw on the draft of the photos a big spirit within a small frame.

If my distance to gnosticism is like the distance between the earth and the Canapus, if of philosophy I do not know even its spelling, and if I am not neigbouring *fiqh,* he will cavil. You will have to lower your expectation from the writer, and take this work to be a snap of the sun on the folds of the waves of a pool.

If I was able to impart what was my objective and topic in this writing, and to tell who my addressee is, there remains for me to say what my method in researching and writing is.

In the year 1365 (1986) I was in charge of a research team working on the basis of the foreign policy of Islam. I had but to seriously concentrate on the political ideas of a person who built the Islamic Republic on a deep-rooted foundation, though in a new expression. This responsibility prompted me, besides reading his published works, to lend my ears to the affable, neutral and hostile expressions of the others. His political ideas were worked upon abroad more than inside. Every person and concern was motivated by an object, such as to have an example, or to face the Islamic fundamentalism. I read the results of the studies of the others as much as I could. Hundreds of questions had sparked in my mind. I had discussions with tens of experts, and gradually it became dubious as to whether I have been acquainted, to some extent, with his political ideas. The product of those studies was about fifty lectures and ten essays on some dimensions of his political ideas. Perhaps it was this background which prompted the International Affairs Department at ICPIKW to suggest to me to work out a draft of my finding and to write down his biography for those who do not know Persian and have no Persian sources within their reach.[11]

Those who are acquainted with discussing political ideas know very well that the political ideas are the most complicated section of the philosophic issue of every revolutionary theorist or social reformer. In our country, understanding the political opinions of the thinkers is double complicated, especially if we try to discover them through classical methods, because religion is not beside life, rather it is always the life itself, and the impressions from the spirit of religion are as numerous as the breaths of its followers, though it rules equally in implementing the precepts. Consequently, understanding the spirit of the religious beliefs of every political thinker has priority over understanding his political opinions. Knowing generalities of religion, or even some slight parts of it, cannot explain all the aspects of the ideas of a political thinker. For example, if somebody has studied the ideological bases of all his contemporary *mujtahids,* and thinks that he has become acquainted with Shiism, and able to picture his opinion, on the basis of his own thought, has gone the wrong way.[12] Naturally, knowing the generalities of the principles and branches of each unanimously accepted knowledge, is the first step to every knowledge, which, if neglected, leads to double ignorance. This first step does not negate the above statement.[13]

On the other hand every idea which leads to a new plan is not spontaneous; rather it has its root deep into history, culture and literature. Our past literature is full of diverse political ideas, though with philosophic quiddity, but it was not, and is not, known under this name. The main reasons were that the term _philosophy', in its specific concept, became obsolete, due to the traditionalists' trends, or due to the establishment of *sufism*, or due to the high flying of the gnostics. Even **Mulla Sadra**, the celebrated philosopher and the discoverer of the trans-substantial motion, because of his *fiqhi* personality, was the centre of the *ulama*s attention, and because of his philosophic personality he was subject to the uninformed slanderers. Of course, theology, which was used in the arguments with the different Islamic groups, or with the People of the Book and the atheists, was also a reason for caring less for philosophy. Nevertheless, I repeat that our literature is fraught with deep philosophic researches and political philosophy, though not under the name of philosophy[14], sometimes nameless, sometimes under the names of wisdom, admonishment and ethics. Furthermore, the oldest classification of the secondary principles of religion, whose precepts the *fiqh* takes care to explain, had so well shown its effectiveness that most of the *faqihs* found themselves in no need of a congruous political thought, regarding the *fiqhi* method sufficient to administer all the affairs of the society.[15] **Imam Khomeini (a),** along the erection of the structure of his political thought, paid close attention to revive religious jurisprudence which is connected to all the social affairs. He also unified that with his philosophy and gnosticism.[16] So, if we want to deal with his political thought, we cannot disregard his *fiqhi* point of view, and likewise we cannot keep away from his gnosticism.[17]

Certainly, such discussions should not hinder the non-Muslims and the uninformed about the topics of *fiqh* from trying to know his political thought. Discussing such questions separately is difficult and tiresome to the unexperienced persons. But if it is pictured in a biographical story, understanding it will be as easy as drinking a glass of cold refreshing water in the hot noon of a summer day.

In understanding his political thought, deeply and purely, there appear many other difficulties. One is mental prejudgement.[18] The other is that before writing down his political thoughts, as men of pen do, he used to talk with the people. So, his political thoughts are mostly to be looked for in his statements and talks with the people, rather than directly in his writings. Of course, the people who were not contaminated with the common methods of thought-investigators, it was easier for them to understand him by means of their instinct and disposition, than for the experienced politicians and the curious researchers who are accustomed to the classic methods.[19] On the other hand, it is natural that digging out, and searching through, speeches, which accompany time, place and the addressees in particular, are much more difficult than doing so through his written works which either observe these three in general or are void of them.

The third difficulty concerns most of the political thinkers who create it when they become political leaders, i.e., usually their political opinions mix with their political thought, causing a sort of conflict. **Gandhi** is a prominent example of such conflict. But the political thoughts of the **Imam (a),** according to researchers, are more mistaken with his political opinions than **Gandhi's,** for many reasons.

To solve this problem I divided the ‗political knowledge' into five sections defining each one of them. I think I could, to a large extent, make a distinction between **the Imam's** political thoughts and his political opinions and views.[20]

Before becoming aware that the ‗political knowledge' should be divided into separate sections so as to recognize the thought from other topics of the political knowledge, I was encountering another problem, i.e. most of the political leaders, while talking to their addressees, think that they already know their theories, and the more the leader is popular and loved, the commoner this condition. Of course the addressee would immediately and unconsciously understand them, but if the researcher is not in the row of the addressees, in his research, he will be involved in contradiction or in simple-mindedness.

Most of the leaders, particularly the leaders in the years of maturity, utter a minor, and, without stating its major, derive the conclusion.[21] If we make a space between the minor and the conclusion, and try to look for the omitted majors, they will be quite valuable, because the concealed theories of any scholar together with his uncovered ones would make the basis of his real thought. I named this method ‗logical display', and in this story, besides his uncovered theories, I tried to extract his concealed theories by means of a displaying method. For example, in respect of the position and originality of consultation and council in his political theory I displayed some two hundred sentences. Of course, I will not take the reader behind the scene of display so that he may not get tired of the crowded work. Instead, in any occasion on which a statement is quoted from him, I tried to have the most comprehensive one and to be in conformity with his concealed and uncovered theories, even if it was not the most beautiful one.

Before being a scientific branch, history is a current event. A considerable part of every person and personality is formed by his historical identity. Language, culture, knowledge, philosophy and art have come from the depth of history and were bestowed upon us as a gift. Great personalities, who had been born thousands of years ago, are now present in every moment of our lives.

The Buddhist, who does not keep the picture even of his own father, keeps the statute of **Buddha** on the shelf of his house. There are many people who have lost their families, but they take **Mary** as their mother and **Jesus** (*a*) as their intimate companion. The Muslims, before naming any of their relatives, they name **Muhammad** (*s*) in their *adhan* and *salah* with respect every day. We mourn over our dead relatives for few days, but time gradually washes away our sorrow. Yet whenever the Shiite hear the name of **al-Husayn** (*a*), the flower leaves of the red poppies set pure dew drops in the sky of their eyes, as if his blood is still gushing out in his site of murder. It is such that the positive and negative historical personalities transmigrate into us and we are with them and cling to them. Of course we regard some of them to be Satans and we are hostile to them and detest them and are disgusted with them.

To understand a personality and the depth of his thought, besides knowing his biography, knowing those with whom he lives, and has in his heart, and mind close connections with them seems quite necessary, because a considerable part of the identity of his thought is made by personalities who are mostly real, though at times fantastic. With this point of view, how much of the country's history and of the biographies of those he loves and hates, one has to know? If we want to know him as he was, everything must be known—a fact which is impracticable, since it requires a mouth as wide as the sky." So, we are forced to be satisfied with the least.

Choosing the leasts brings about a difficulty, that is, on what basis one is to choose a subject and leave another? If it is said that to choose the most important events and the most famous historical personalities would be sufficient, the same question would remain there in another way, as it is not easy to decide what is the most important. Did the World War II, with all its events, play a more effective role in the process of forming his thoughts, or his childhood conversation with a rifled shepherd who jokingly told him: The foreign rifles and bullets do not kill the foreigners?"

It is also naivety to think that the events which we think to be important were also similarly important to him. For example, one of the most important days of our country's history was the day of his return to Tehran from exile, and the nation displayed a most sensational, magnificent and historical reception of their leader. But when a reporter asked him while still in the plane: ─Now that you are returning to your country, what do you feel?" His reply was: ─Nothing." Certainly, if that day was to him a little more important than the day before, instead of the book which was summarized in the flowery term ─Nothing", he could have used another expression so as to manifest the importance of that significant meeting from his own point of view.[22]

The solution which occurred to me as suitable to lessen the interference of personal tastes in choosing the things which appear important was to search through his works to take notes of any name or historical event which we face and detect their importance from his speech. I did so, and I vowed to explain only the events and biographies of the personalities who have an effect in his works, and who are in a way important to him, not to me or to the others, or to the artists who take it to be more exciting in story-telling. Of course I confined myself to explain, and to expand on, only the part which pictures a generality for thought-making. If it seemed that in explaining some events I have exaggerated a bit, while I apologize to some readers, I have two reasons for thinking it to be necessary: One because I feel that sometimes generalization does not put the foreign reader in the very atmosphere of the event. Second in order to keep the _rhythmic beat of his talk'.[23]

In this biography I found it unfair to neglect the rhythm of the talk. The rhythm which I chose was, I think, in proportion to the topics. In some instances I give the reader a respite by offering little information in a paragraph so that he may mentally take in the former message. In other instances, I have a swift rhythm in a single sentence in which I arrange a number of messages so that the reader may not have to deposit all of them to his memory. I want him to hear and to quickly go past it. Also sometimes I would repeat a matter, but in two tunes so as to play the two sides of a subject, and to bring to harmony the rhythmic beat of his talk with the rhythmic beat of his life.

Accordingly I started writing. After a while I realized that the absence of some persons and events and details from the works remained from him caused some of the links not to join together. So, I began looking for the missing links of which there are apparently no traces in his works, and in the memoir unit, which is an oral history named _heart's treasury', some of the links are not found. I felt I am in need of second-hand stores in which I may find the missing links, if I search well. The defect of these second-hand stores is that they do not give out invoices, or if they do, and if I show them, they will lessen the prestige of the book in the eyes of the professional and classic researchers. Nevertheless, I provided many latches-and-catches from whole-salers.[24] Therefore; they will not have notes as references. For example, once I found that he had written an exciting notice on a packet of tea, which he had cut neatly and had written it with a nicer handwriting than usual, I wanted to know why. I was entangled in the question as to: Why did he waste his precious time to carefully trim the unwanted borders of a tea-packet in order to use it as a piece of paper, though a much better piece of paper he could have bought for only 10 *shahi*s? Did he want to practise economy? Did he want to allude to the fact that if we look around we will not see little the possibilities around us? Did he take the paper of the tea-packet as a living being which if he threw away, it would cry out his expatriation?

Except a few, most of the *faqihs,* politicians and socialists would not be prepared to answer these apparently valueless questions. I had to ask other people, those who were ecstasized by such questions and they uttered delicate things which were the key to the understanding of a thought. A grocer said: "It took me years to understand why he had the supplies for his house bought day by day." "What was the reason?" I asked. "It was," he replied, "if death came, his burden would be lighter." "Didn't you think that probably he wanted to know the prices everyday?" I put in. "In fact, this is more important," he said, "but I was afraid of saying it lest I would be mocked at. He also wanted to know the daily situation of the commodities, and at the same time, he had his supplies purchased daily in order to be informed about us every day." I said: "Please, say more, as it deserves hearing. What else?", "So that the retailer's hand may not get accustomed to wholesaling, and he may not ill-behave toward one who buys by retail," the man said, and he went on saying and saying, counting ten reasons, each of which was a wise one. I asked him: "How do you know that what you say is not daydreaming?" "For many years I listened to him lecturing the people from above his *minbar* (pulpit), relating many narratives quoted from the pure Imams (*a*), from which I understood the reason behind this and many others of his conducts," the man confirmed.

When he talked of what he had heard, I noticed that many of his notable students were present at those lecturing meetings, but their selections were different, and what he had heard they did not hear.

From a hard-working writer, who had written a lot about him, I asked: ―What was his opinion in respect of the *Nowruz* feast?" Quoting someone he said: ―I only know that on the first day of Farvardin (21st of March) [the *Nowruz* day], he drew his *aba* over his head and fell asleep." From the sweeper of his lane I asked: ―Have you ever seen him?" ―Only twice," he said, ―but my feast-gift used to reach me every feast day in a sealed envelope." I asked him: ―When did you receive his last gift?" A week before the *Nowruz,* with a letter which I had it framed, and a pair of stockings which I keep unused," he said. My missed link I found here, in how much value he paid to the national feasts. Going through his works I realized that this point had been concealed due to its being too obvious.[25]

Resorting to such a source, and in such a way, has a less documentary value, to some historians, than the oral history. But before estimating the documentary value of this writing, I evaluated the discovery of the essence of a thought which sowed its seeds in the deserted and crowded alleys of history, leaving a sign in the trunk of each sapling.[26]

At times I dipped my pitcher into the fountain spring of his talks, and at times I filled my pitcher at the shore of the wavy sea of the people, taking a cup from each wave. But alas? For some time I was unaware of a clear spring, and when I reached it, it was no longer running, just trickling, and increasing one's thirst. This clear source that could portrait the first twenty years of the life of **Ruhullah** better than anyone else, is his brother, **Ayatullah Pasandideh,** who was born eight years earlier than he, and now while writing this, he has lived seven years after him.[27] I asked myself: Hadn't **Allah** created him earlier and granted him more years so that instead of looking a picture on the wall we could look into a mirror to see his memory of the moment, which cannot be seen in the bricks of the documents? On those splendid moments in which **Ruhullah** was born tens of people were present, but now there is only a single person who can tell us how it was. He knows about his relation with mother and relatives, food and clothes, the environment of growth and development, temperaments in childhood, going to school, the father's martyrdom, moments of seclusion in the house, till his leaving Khomein; he remembers all of them, but to draw them out of his memory is not an easy task. Many times he was interviewed, and the result was a booklet published under the title *The Memoirs of Ayatullah Pasandideh,* but more than that can be found by means of a different method. I chose this one and as much as I could I filled my cup from the trickling drops of his fall.[28] Having this source within my reach changed my method to some extent, as I realized that if I had no fear of writing much during the formation of the skeleton of the thought, neither I nor the reader would be dazzled, when I reach the period of his political maturity, by the plurality of the subjects and the crowd of the personalities, who enter into his life, especially that when this river reaches the expanse of the valley beyond the national society, it becomes so wide that I will not be able to embrace in my look all its meadows. This source inspired me not to easily pass by his periods of childhood and youth, and to use them as the basis of a thought, and to follow up in a line threading the trace of each event during these periods till his death. This will incite me that, in order to discover a thought within the period of politics, which is full of ups and downs, I must look for only what belongs to that period.[29]

In addition to this possibility which somewhat extended the periods of childhood and youth[30], by referring to other books which portrayed his life I realized if we regard his periods of childhood and youth less important than his years of maturity, we will not be able to easily show the swift paces of the development of a culture and the progress of the changing of a thought—the thought which led to a revolution which was against both the previous regime and the regimes before it[13] .

At the end of this part of the Introduction I deem it necessary to mention the following points:

* I decided not to state the references which are unlikely to be within the reach of the foreign readers. Nevertheless, for the benefit of the researchers, I had to mention some of them.

* If a subject was referred to in more than three references, and there was no objection against it, I regarded it as a _popular' saying and found no need to state their references. If there was any discrepancy in different sources, and although I chose the narration I thought to be the most correct, I stated the sources to compare the discrepancies.

There are two kinds of quoting from him: Sayings which are present in his works, and sayings which are quoted from other narrators. The word _probably', which is frequently occurring in this work denotes that the author is not sure of the compatibility of the subject with the real event, leaving open the door of reconsideration.

* I tried hard to look at things through his eyes, and to see the events, the personalities, and the topics as he used to see them, since I am writing his own biography. It is, thus, probable that the historians and the thinkers have a different look at some events, personalities, and topics. However, if there was a gross difference between his view and that of the majority of the thinkers, I had, as necessity required, to clearly retell the views of the others.

* At times I made use of second rate sources for two reasons: first, because I saw that matter, for the first time, in a second rate source, and, due to moral reason, I could not ascribe it to first rate sources. Second, because, probably some researchers may have no first rate sources at their disposal.

* In some instances I refer the reader to sources whose authenticities are doubted by the researchers. This is because I could not find the subject anywhere else. Of course, if I add no footnote to it, it means that I take it to be correct.

* In vol. I, from his birthday till his moving to Qum, the events are chronically well kept, but I confess that after his settlement in Qum, and while being after his lectures and teachings, I neglected to timely follow up the political events. I hope I would be able to make up for this shortcoming in vol. II.

* In quoting some events and memories, particularly concerning ethics and philosophy, I did not state the source for two reasons: first, because at times I interfere in the speech of somebody regarding the speech of somebody else, and I do not want to cause two or three of the great men face one another in this work. Second, I found, due to certain indications, that a single subject was seen by somebody from a particular angle and by another from a different angle, and the transmitters, whether by writing or orally, used to tint the subject with the color of their feelings.[32]

* The number of those who helped me in relating these memoirs and participated in my researches are beyond counting. Therefore, besides impracticability of stating their names, there are other reasons which prevented me from naming them. One is that a number of them in person asked me not to refer to their names.[33] Another is that at times I got from the narrations a mutual chapter, while the narrators themselves did not concentrate on a mutual chapter. Sometimes I concluded from a related sentence or an event a contrary to what the relater had said. Nevertheless, I ask permission to mention the name of the brother and friend, **Dr. Mahmud Burujerdi,** on behalf of all the friends who had helped me in this work, because, he was, unaware, the touchstone for many of my hearings and readings, besides his narrating many memoirs about the seclusion and manifestation of that beloved, which in fact were new and pure.[34]

* The last detailed talks in this brief are two soliloquies: The first I deem necessary to be disclosed to the intimate friends who themselves are biographers and have their own styles in writing. The second is for more familiar talks, talks which are penned only for the men of heart. But a strange feeling was prompting me to write them down. When I was writing it, the pen itself, as a released small boat, went ahead. I had the intention to summarize it and place the summary in the Introduction, but it could not be summarized, and so I decided to leave it unsaid till another opportunity.

The First Soliloquy

Ever since my youth I like to write the stories of great men for my coeval friends. This desire has become the queen of my heart. Whenever I get tired of everyday work, I sharpen my pen to aim it at a great personality, but I always find that my pen acts like an arrow, wounding the soul of my beloved character. At times, after a while the character of my story has appeared to me mean and we have parted half way. A number of bitter experiences prompted me to choose personalities, to imagine the separation from them is to imagine the drying up of a branch separated from a thicket. On this basis I found that only the prophets and the Imams of guidance should be in my consideration, such that if the heavy storm of the philosophic doubts break me, I will once again grow from the very root. With this thought, the prophets whose names are stated in the Quran became the heroes of my stories. Likewise, the house of **Master Ali (s)** became the arena of my desires for writing. But it always happened that, after a while, I tore whatever I had written in order not to see them any more and be ashamed, then started again with the same activeness. Once a publisher tempted me to hand him for publication the biographies of the _Five Prophets of Resolution'. When it was time for revising the first story, I hurried to tear it, because I realized that the writer is sitting outside the ship.

Ibrahim the Friend (a) had the most sensational gnostic life. When he was smashing the idols, I watched him from the window of the idol-temple. When he was thrown into the fire, I heard **Gabriel'**s voice hurriedly shouting: ―What is your need?" He heard the answer: ―Do not be a barrier between me and my Lord." When **Ibrahim** was hurled into the fire, I was among the audience. I cried bitterly, I shouted and I fainted. When I came to myself the fire had become a garden. I believed, but I had not been to the fire with **Ibrahim.** I asked myself: ―Is this the life of a looker on who has witnessed the sparking flames of the fire till the blowing of the breeze of the garden, or is it the life of **Ibrahim the Friend** who has been in the fire?"

When he left **Ismail** and **Hajar** in the burning desert, I stayed to see what would **Hajar** do in that alienation and loneliness. I could not accompany **Ibrahim** in his journey to see what he would do in his strangeness. Was this part the story of the life of **Ibrahim the Friend** or the life of **Ismail** and **Hajar?** This was also torn so that I may not be induced to publish it.

When **Moses (a),** the Interlocutor, was playing with **Pharaoh"s** beard, his foster-father, I do not know how he felt. Did he love him because he used to sit on his lap, smiled at him, filled his stomach at his table and called him father? Or, because he was to become a great Messenger of Allah in the future, in his childhood, too, he was disgusted with arrogance? When **Moses** put fire in his mouth, I felt my tongue blistering, but my pen did not stammer, as all the stammerings were in the past. When **Moses,** the Interlocutor, accompanied the holy man in his journey, and could not bear seeing the ship being pierced, a boy being beheaded and, despite the pains of hunger, building an unpaid-for wall, I was loosing my patience because of **Moses** _loosing his patience, and I was on the side of the holy man. But when I read the story once again I felt ashamed of **Allah"s** great Prophet, and before wiping my sweat off my forehead, I tore my paper-pieces, though I grant **Mawlawi Rumi** the right to sing the story of *Moses and the Shepherd,* since he is like an eagle which spreads its wings and, dancing, flaps high away, or at times dives down, turning some of its seeings into hearings.

The attractive *ayahs* of the *surah* of **Maryam** maddened me, and when **Jesus (a)** said: ―**And peace on me the day I was born, and the day I die, and the day I shall be raised alive!**" (Quran, 19:33), the resonance of his voice resounded in my ear, but my pen did not act like the string of a guitar to make the reader hear what I was hearing, too.

Thus, I knew, and now I know very well, that I am too small to write the astonishing stories of great men. Of course I regard this worry of mine praiseworthy, while for some others it is dispraise because if all become so irresolute, the godly men will be left with no biography.

Even though I resemble a young pigeon not yet shaken off its fluff and unable to fly in the atmosphere of the lives of the prophets, yet I wish that the eagerness for flying in the skies would remain with me, so that I might not be heavy like a domestic hen, nor should I get accustomed to eating the leftovers. This desire has so far done as I wished. On one side, my feeling of smallness took away from me the courage of writing about the moment in which the small hands of **Ali (a)** rested in between the warm hands of **Muhammad (s),** willingly giving his allegiance to the Beloved of **Allah,** and how the contents of the two hearts flew on one another, and how the whole existence danced in the ecstasy of this union, and, on the other side, I find myself bigger than to write, independently, about the personality of one of the contempo- rary men of politics in my country—the men in the description of their best a contemporary poet said:

Plant trees in the place of men of politics, so that the air may be fresh.[35]

But **Ruhullah** was neither a prophet, since **Muhammad (s)** was the last of the prophets, nor was he in a position lower than those of some of the past prophets, as the last of the prophets said: ─The scholars of my *ummah* are preferable to the past prophets.[36]" It was this that I dared to pick up my pen. Nevertheless, had I not given my word, and had it not been for those who were waiting, this work would have also been torn to pieces, because I still find my instruments for carrying out this heavy task insufficient. But what could I do? It was a moral promise which I gave.

By this statement of mine I dragged the reader to an unpleasant prejudgement. That is, from the beginning they will accuse me of partiality. They will say that I have raised his position so high as to make him the complete evidence of that noble *hadith*. So, if they say: ─The author is a lover whose book is an excuse for his love, and has no creditability more than that, as he himself admits it," they will not be saying anything other than the truth. This is an accusation for a part of which I would give my life, and on another part of it I have a note. I expect the reader to consider this note. The part which I accept is that I am, in fact, a lover, and I am ashamed of myself because my love did not put me aflame to the extend of burning off my existence.[37] But before being a lover I am fond of him, and fondness is superior to love.[38]

Now to my note. Love and hate are the two sides of one spectrum, as are all the contraries.[39] Do we know anybody who chose a subject without having any feelings of love or hatred towards it? If supposedly this is not impossible, though it is, how, in practise, can one choose something and claim to be impartial towards what he chose? At most he may claim to be standing in the middle.

Probably they may say it is a confusion of subjects, because being attached to a particular branch and being attached to the subjects contained in that branch are not the same. History is a thing, and historical personalities are something else. A historian cares for history, not for all the historical personalities. Apparently the objection is proper, but not deep, because the sayer looks at the middle of the event. If he looks at the beginning he will see that loving history springs from the loved or the hated personalities of history. To be short, as this discussion is lengthy, and frankly speaking: The one who does not take a personality to be hateful and picks up his pen, his sensitivity is not sufficient enough to take him to the threshold of a stimulation causing him to be in conflict with the common beliefs of the others. Likewise, the one who is not in love does not know what to look for to add as firewood onto the kiln of his love. That is why I am sure that love and hatred are not the blight of knowledge, rather they are stimuli. Whoever is more in love has a deeper insight, and whoever hates more, also sees deeper.[40]

What I believe to be the causes of insufficient knowledge are three:

* Adopting the easiest and weakest methods of attaining to complicated and difficult facts.

* Endeavour to confirm prejudgments.

* Starting the research in the absence of love or hatred.[41]

In this book I tried hard to adopt a formal method in finding out facts so as to have the infiltration of taste the least possible. Since I write with sincere intimacy, I do not consciously have more than a single prejudgement, which is to regard what is connected to him as ponderable, and not to neglect anything as to be commonplace or clamourous. This in itself was a merit which I encountered while investigating so many questions, and which disrupted my mental anticipations.[42] If I conceal my love for the beloved whom I am writing about, the reader will immediately discover it in the very first pages. So, much better to confess it myself beforehand [43], and to add that writings of the loveless writers are worthless to me, particularly if the writer has written about a personality of fame.

Besides the above-mentioned questions, inspired by the stories of the prophets in the Glorious Quran, I have found a solution for the contradiction between _perfect impartiality', which is the worry of the scientific work, and the argument of _love and harted', which is said to be the plague of knowledge. Now I believe in its correctness, and I have to refer to it, after a brief introduction:

The *ayahs* of the Glorious Quran include both contexts which throw light on a number of subjects, and show methods of handling the subjects, which are not less important than the handling of the subjects.

The biographers of the early centuries of Islam used to take their subjects from the Quran, as well as the methods of handling them—the way which led them to the truth and reality. Nowadays, mostly the subjects are handled, while the methods are neglected. Hence, the biographies written by the earlier writers are generally more readable and exemplary than the biographies which are written today.

The method of writing biographies, which was inspired in me by the Quran, can be summarized in the following:

1. Each chapter of the story is to be an exemplary, not for amusement.[44]

2. Being an exemplary does not mean that the stories of the Quran engage only the mind, not the heart.

3. Miracles and the supernatural things are to be related, though some people may not believe in them.

4. Every subject has an exterior and an interior. The exterior is for the primary contact, and the interior is for the later successive perceptions.[45]

5. It does not make everything like _Turkish delight'. It incites the reader to ponder so as to solve some of the contradictions himself.

6. In the *ayah* unit it talks in brief, and in the Book, in detail.

7. It does not let the subject go, and in some farther *surahs* shows other aspects of the subject.

8. It is not satisfied with generalization, but goes into tiniest details if needs be.

9. It exposes the hidden secrets of the hearts.

10. It takes the readers in general, hence, along with beauty and simplicity surges fluently throughout the *ayah*s, leaving in each *ayah* a trace for the experts to follow-up deeper questions in it.

11. No one is alien in the Quran, neither the people of the Book, nor even the polytheists and the disbelievers. Moreover, it contains no instruction that it should be put at the disposal of only the Muslims.[46]

12. It avoids no subject on the pretext that it may displease a reader, yet , the vocabularies it uses do not cross the borders of chastity, rather it goes to say that a scene can be incarnated without having to use words devoid of elegance.[74]

13. If necessity decreed that a subject must be related to throw light on a topic, even if it might hurt the holiness of the prophets, in the opinions of the exterior theologians, it would relate it so that the prophets may not become legendary and unfollowable. On the other hand, it shows that the values in the laws of existence are not those which men, in a particular time, depend upon together with their own cultures and values.

14. Whenever actual events could not reflect the appearances of all the facts, it resorts to the language of symbolism and metaphor.

It is evident that if men and jinn cooperated and tried to form a *surah* like the *Quran,* they would not be able to make it. But if any man, with whatever knowledge, takes the *Quran* to be a Book of guidance, he may also be inspired by it. Being thus inspired by the *Glorious Quran,* I chose a style which I think would not only regard my prejudice and love of my beloved not to be a plague against knowing him, it would rather display my perfect impartiality in a better manifestation.

Thus, if I realize anywhere the hero of my story judges and openly says: —I am wrong," I will not evade saying it so as to show that in his political thought confessing a mistake, is a principle, and it is such a thought which makes him lasting.

The early biographers wrote that **the Prophet** set up his tents behind the wells of Badr. A nameless soldier said: —If this place which you chose is not revealed to you, the rules of war demand that the wells should be in the back." **The Prophet** followed his suggestion. No body objected to the biographers that reporting this incident would injure the infallibility of **the Prophet (s)**. Hence, in the imposed war, if I see that somebody had a viewpoint different from his, I will not be ashamed of relating it.

If I find somewhere that he had said: —I never touched my wife without performing *wudu* (ablution) first," I will also take it to be within the norms of politeness. This artistic manifestation of godly men, who are able to turn worldly pleasures into heavenly ones, too, I will not keep hidden for fear of the narrow-minded, because I have learnt from the early biographers, who had learnt from the *Quran,* that it is not unbecoming, rather a good deed, if the **Prophet (s)** had once said to one of his wives: —Talk to me, O Humayra'."

Somewhere I wrote: —In the *andarun* (penetralia) **Hajar** was restless by the pain of separation." Somebody noted that it is possible that some of the _ironed' ones would object that it was out of elegance. I reminded him that **Allah** has related the story of the childbirth of **Mary (a)** in this way:

"And the pangs of childbirth drove her to the trunk of the palm tree. She said: Would that I had died before this and had been totally forgotten!" (19: 23). Considering the *ayah,* the critic withdrew his other four objections.

I have found in the *Quran* more than a hundred points taken out of deep and beautiful stories, which, as **Allah** says He protects them against distortion and omission, have been protected, or else, according to some of the biographers, they must be omitted or redressed due to moral, political and taste interests. Have a look at the following examples:

In the *Glorious Quran* the first prophet is **Adam (a)** who became **Allah"s** vicegerent. At the beginning he settled in Paradise, tricked by Satan, disobeyed and was sent down. Should not these sentences about the **Prophet** of **Allah** be omitted?

One of **Adam**'s sons (**Cain**) killed his brother, and **Allah** exposed it to the public openly.

The first of the *ulul-azm* prophets, **Noah** (*a*), had a son who was not worthy getting on board of the ship and was drown in the flood. His father mourned for him. This prophet's wife met the same fate as her son, and **Allah** described her in the *Quran* as disloyal. Is it not bad to say that the son and the wife of a prophet of **Allah** were disloyal?

The second of the *ulul-azm* prophets, the hero of monotheism, was **Ibrahim**, the Friend of **Allah**.

The great hero of monotheism, who entered the fire and came out proud, has somewhere said: ―My Lord! Show me how you give life to the dead." He said: ―Have not you believed (yet)?" He said: ―I have, but just to set my heart at ease." **Allah**, by giving life to the four birds, which he had crushed in a mortar, showed him how He gives life to the dead.

When four angels became his guests, but did not eat from his food, he was afraid in his heart. The angels told him not to be afraid, and they gave him the good tiding that he would be given a son. They told him they were going to the people of **Lot** to destroy them. He had wishes which **Allah**, with the most charming expression, called _argument'.

While he was taking **Ismail** to the sacrifice place, **Satan** was coming on him, and he was throwing stones at him, and **Allah** had no objection that some may say: ―Therefore, it is clear that **Satan** had the desire to deviate even the hero of monotheism.[48]"

Before **Moses** being born, the bellies of the pregnant women were cut open, by **Pharaoh**'s order, so that **Moses** may not be born. When he was born, **Allah** arranged things that **Moses** should be brought up in **Pharaoh**'s palace. In his childhood he put fire in his mouth and thus his life was saved.

In his youth he killed a Coptic and ran away from the town.

When he threw his stick down and it became a serpent, he was afraid. **Allah** said: ―Do not be afraid."

When he spent forty nights in the mountains and came back found his people deviated to calf-worshipping. Vexed, he took his brother, **Aron**, by the collar, though he was another prophet, and quarrelled with him.

When he accompanied the godly man in his journey and witnessed strange incidents, he could not bear it and at each incident he uttered his objection until at last the godly man quitted him.

Yunus (*a*), too, was angry with his people and he was sentenced to imprisonment in the stomach of a fish for seven years.

Allah described the story of **Joseph** the best of stories. He speaks of the handsomeness of a man, of his truthful dream, of the envy of **Jacob**'s sons, their crime and lying, of selling him in the market, of his period of servitude, of the disgraceful love of a flirt, of **Joseph**'s chastity, of the argument of Egypt's ruler with his wife, of relating the beauty of a face which made the women enchanted and caused them to cut their hands, of his imprisonment for a crime which he did not commit, of imploring his released cell's mate, of a moment's negligence of remembering **Allah** and his remaining seven more years in the prison as a punishment, of interpreting another dream and his coming to power in Egypt, of the story of putting the (measuring) cup in his brother's belongings, of the curing smell of his shirt for his father, and of hundreds of other general and particular points. Are not all these a proof that in respect of the great men of religion there is nothing concealable, and whatever is there, is utterable? But what kind of utterance it is which makes the story the best of the stories![49]

On discerning these stories in the *Quran*, I noted that as far as the lives of the great men are concerned, one has to be on the alert so that nothing may be cut off by the razor of censorship, and that loving them may not prevent one from keeping unsaid what had actually been said. From the amazing *ayah:* —**Allah is not ashamed to set forth any parable (that of) a gnat or anything above that.** (26:2) —. I took the limit of the unutterable things to be those which do not fit into my writings. Therefore, if I was forced by necessity to name anyone of his relatives who did not come in the way of his aims, I would regard nothing in writing about him, because the *Quran* says that **Noah**'s son was no good, disregarding his father. If he had somewhere said: —I was mistaken," and somebody said that this should not be retold, I would say that the **Prophet Jonah** said: **"... I have been of the wrongdoers,**[50]**"** which is more than that.

So, to observe impartiality, which is a requisite for research, I realized that nothing may be neglected if it is needed in portraying a soul, and not to be affected by any expediency. I have kept this type of impartiality, and believed in the correctness of this view by going through the stories of the *Glorious Quran.* Nevertheless, certain considerations forced me to be cautious in choosing the events. At times I was so cautious that I felt I was somewhat scrupulous. Despite my belief that what is to be said and fits into my work, must be said, my problem with certain secondary personalities could not be solved by saying or not saying. Many a time I asked myself and experienced people what should I do with secondary personalities?

We do know that **Allah,** who is the knower of all secrets, considers all aspects in disclosing any matter, but was man given such a right? Most historians say yes, because the task of the historian is to discover the events and their causes, and if there appear some observations, this science will be filled with unutterable talks and observations. But, on the other hand, there are in all religions red lines which are not to be crossed and enter into the individuals' privacy, as the said *faqih* himself, in his 8-point declaration, said: ―If a person entered a house according to a permission from the public prosecutor, and saw that the people of the house were in privacy doing irreligious acts, he would have no right to disclose their acts in public.[51]‖ Thus, whatever one knows of the others, one has no lawful permission to disclose all of them in public. So, if I say something about the one who is no longer living and cannot defend himself, while I know if he were living he would not allow me to disclose it, the sin of backbiting would be doubled[52], especially that one of **Allah**'s attributes—which man is advised to adopt—is to be ‗Coverer of Faults'.

The absolute good and bad are not discussed, since judging them is religiously and logically permitted. The discussion is about the evildoing of the good ones or the conducts of those whose badness and goodness cannot be easily judged. The historians, with utter naivety, found a way to solve this problem. They say: ―We look for the events and the peoples' conducts void of values, therefore, goodness and badness, which are categories of value, have no way into the arbitrations." Despite this permission the problem remains intact, because this way is applicable only after choosing, while the earlier stage, which leads to choosing, is not void of values. As we see, protecting the national advantages and political interests has its effect, as fixed values, on publishing, or not publishing, the secret documents in all countries. If a foreign enemy demands from a patriotic researcher to study the happening of an event, the researcher will not give a positive answer. If the national advantages and the political interests are a factor deterring uncoverings, why should we not leave the curtains uncleft due to moralities?[53]

The answers given to this question apparently are not immoral, but they have no depth, either, as if they are uttered and repeated only to calm down the conscience. What is common among them is: ―Everybody has his individual and social identities. His individual identity cannot be disclosed, except within the frame of law, but his social identity can be. Furthermore, everybody has his present identity which is changed to a historical identity after his death. If his identity of the day cannot be exposed, his historical identity can be."

Of course, what has been said above was due to the fact that the rights were regarded to be short-scoped, while religion gives man rights which death does not bury all of them with his body.

The cotton of such discussions had centuries ago been carded. Today, the historians are not hindered by such worries from surveying. But regarding the biography of a man who had a great share in reviving the belief in religion, neglecting such concepts brings his ultrabiography down to a daily level. He started leading a revolution which took religion to be the guideline and the axis. So, it would be rude to him and to the revolution to make use, in writing his biography, of such method which does not coincide with the religious ethics on the pretext of being scientific.

If the short-sighted impressions of the science of history give permission, on the basis of documents and evidences, to expose the conduct of every person and personality and to judge his function, yet it is not certain that religious rights and ethics give such permission, too.[54]

Someone talked about another who used to impede the progress of the uprising. I decided to get acquainted with the intricacy of his work, so as to know why and for what purpose. He resisted talking until at last he was taken by surprise. He realized what I was after. He said: ─I have repented and I am sure the Imam has forgiven me, and I have hope in **Allah**ʻs generosity. In order to have my repentance accepted, I do not fear worldly degradation. But what to do with my children who would be disgraced in the society at my confession about my past? I ask you and the one who introduced me to you: If **Allah** has forgiven me, would it not be a sin upon you to disgrace me in the eyes of **Allah**ʻs creatures?[55]"

The type of impediment is important, and the type of offsetting it makes the conspiracies more important, and I think the very retelling it throws light on a dark corner of the history of the uprising. But he did not allow me to relate—even without naming any body—examples of how the impediments were done, as he thought that he would be recognized in this way, too.

I was perplexed at this situation: Is it right to think that to throw light on a dark corner, permits you to darken a life, or even a moment of it, in the eyes of a family?

To solve this problem I referred once again to his works in order to know whether he himself had experienced such worries. I noted that he had, as he referred to unpleasant incidents, but he mentioned no name at all. Much as he moaned of the sanctimonious, the irreligious and the hypocrites, nobody had heard him refer to any person by name, unless that person had already been famous for that.

In short, I do not know still the limits for disclosing the names of the secondary personalities who played a negative role in his life. I even do not know, at times, if the role which I regard as positive, does the concerned regard it positive, too?[56] Therefore, I will tell whatever is utterable about him. But as to the secondary persons, I will be satisfied only with what they had already published in a book or in an article, or that for the disclosure of which I find a permission in his works. At times I relate an incident without mentioning its participants.

Nevertheless, if unknowingly I related some events or memoirs in such a way that I trespassed the limit and disregarded a right, I implore the concerned persons to cordially forgive me.

Under such conditions and worries, there are many kinds of memories and events which cause one to penetrate, to some extent, deep into his political ideas and thoughts, but at present I refrained either from relating them, or from mentioning the names of those who participated in their make.

1. Instances which are related to the national security, and relating them at present is more in the disadvantage of a nation than to the advantage of the reader. Of course, such matters are temporary and will be disclosed later.

2. The memoirs which hurt the social, scientific, religious or political prestige of somebody and cause to lose the rights of others, or register somebody's name in the black lists of the terroristic groups abroad.

3. The affairs which, due to lacking authentic documents, I could not card, and still I do not know what was the reality of the cases.[57]

4. Relating cases in which some persons ill-treated him, and he forgave them. Hence it is not allowed to relate a memoir from them, except in a way they cannot be recognized.

NOTES ON THE INTRODUCTION

1. A year before the victory of the Revolution, there appeared, at the instructions of the SAVAK, an essay in *Ittilaat* newspaper, with the aim of defaming him among the people, by saying that his forefathers lived in India. But it increased his popularity. After the Revolution there also was among the Pakistanis propaganda that if he is a *Sayyid*, then he is an Arab, if he is from Khomein, then he is an Iranian, and if his forefathers were Indians, then what has he to do with you that you back him so much? **Hasan Yusuf Ahmad** wrote a poem in Urdu in answer to such doubt castings. Hereunder is the translation of a part of it:

From the earth to God

Which earth?

The earth of Arafat, where **Adam** knew **Eve,**

The earth of the *Qiblah,* where **Ibrahim,** with the hands of

Ismail, built a House

So that **Ali** the **Murtada,** would be born in it.

The earth on which **Husayn**'s blood was shed so as to grow the fragrant tuberoses.

The earth of the heroes land, the most famous champion, **Rustam** of **Dastan.**

The earth of Neyshabur, where **Attar** used to pick curing

herbs from its desert.

The earth of India, which **Gandhi** took to be his land, and **Jinnah** his.

... **Iqbal** said: ―From India, Samarqand, Iraq and Hamadan rise up. Now you have risen from everywhere, from every land you have a handful earth.

Now nobody has an excuse to say you are not of his land,

Even Neauphle-le-Château gave you apples."

2. Among the close Companions of the **Prophet (s)** there were two of the great ones who had quite amazing lives. One was **Abu Dharr** from Ghaffar, the deserts near Mecca. He was of the ‗outstrippers'. The other was **Salman,** an experienced old man from Iran. Both lived, for some time, on the *suffah,* and after the **Prophet (s)** both became of the faithful supporters of **Ali**

(*a*). But the **Prophet** had said: "If **Abu Dharr** knew what was in **Salman**'s heart, he would accuse him of disbelief."

3. The word _free', which is equivalent to the Arabic word _hurr', denotes one who is not enslaved by anyone or anything, yet he is not undisciplined. The freemen cannot be ensnared except by love, nor can they capture anybody except by generosity. That is why I guess that the message of men of pen is freedom, being more general than liberty, i.e. Liberty is a part of freedom.

4. After few months, *Hadith-e Bidari* [The talk of wakefulness], by Mr. Hamid Ansari, based on those sources, was sent for print. I got information that it was being translated into the Arabic language. The printing of that book lifted from my shoulder the psychological pressure of having to make haste in writing.

5. Generally, his *muqallid*s knew how to present their religious questions to get their answers. A number of *faqih*s had always been present in his office to reply the religious questions coming from inside and outside the country.

6. The late **Haj Ahmad Aqa** said: "Within the very first days of the victory of the Revolution, **the Imam** told me: _How is it possible that somebody undertakes the responsibility of an uprising, and yet nobody abuses him? So far I have not seen a letter which abuses me.' I shamefully said; _The letters are read first, and the ones with nonsense talk are thrown away.' **The Imam** said: _From now on let me see a number of them so that I may know the weak points of the enemies of the Revolution.' Answering the question: Is it also possible to know, from such letters, the weak points of the authorities? He said: _Yes, both their points of weakness and strength'."

7. The answer is given by **Mawlana**. He said: "Sympathetic concurrence is more pleasant than talking the same language."

8. Now that I am writing these words, the relevant texts are not within my reach; therefore, I depend on my brief notes and my memory. If I am weak in conveying the nicety of these samples, I apologize to their still living writers, and concerning the truth-seekers, who are no longer in this world, I request Paradise for them.

9. The world has become as if it is made of glass. And, according to a joke, which is not far from taking place in one's mind, it is said: If the right hemisphere of the brain wanted to transfer something to the left hemisphere, the satellites would photo it. Probably in the near future both the research softwares and the hardwares would be so efficient that one may claim that

whatever is in the world of visibility can easily be exposed, even if it were in the dark depths of history or in the dreams.

10. Of course, such questions are useful to the political analysts, but it is pessimistic to think that such questions are tabled only for planning conspiracies. Likewise it is too optimistic to think that some politicians wanted to know his tendencies so as to send him gifts. Probably some of them wanted to study the secret of his being loved. This pretext, for the pure souls, is a good start to conversation.

11. Before becoming a political leader, he was a *marja* of *taqlid* for a great number of the Shiite, both for Iranians and non-Iranians. But the people of the world knew him only when his name came at the head of the political news. So, it was more correct to start the talk with the non-familiar people about his political ideas. The experienced people, of course, know that the political ideas are not talked about through political subjects.

12. For example, if somebody tries to uncover the bases of Absolute Guardianship—which has its root in understanding monotheism, the objective of the prophets, the position of guardianship, the ultimate aim of creation and man's message—and, by comparing the perceptions of others of his contempo -rary religious authorities, tries to understand why he has arrived at such a belief, he will be covering a part of the road. But to uncover the bases of such a belief one has to look for his personal understanding in the said categories.

13. He himself says [in poetry]:

Fati! You and the true knowledge, what does it mean?
Knowing the essence with no quality, what does it mean?

Unread A no way to Z you will find,
Without spiritual travelling, what does talent mean?

14. One of the great political scholars is the *hakim* **Abul-Qasim Firdowsi,** who inspired by the Shiite teachings, could, in a very complex and skillful way, separate the Arab, the Turk and even the Persian nationalism from the spirit of Islam, but he is more famous as a national epic poet and a mythologist than as a political thinker, though he is called *hakim.* Today it has been forgotten that *hakim* was an epithet indicating a thinker, including philosophy, and sometimes denoting a physician, too. This is also an evidence that the past epistemology of Islamic world was not so strict about the limits between the experimental sciences and the humanities.

15. The secondary principles of religion are divided into three sections:

a. Devotional Acts: They cover: the *salah, fasting, khums, zakat, hajj, jihad*; bidding the good and forbidding the bad. (A number of the scholars add to them *tawalla* and *tabarra).*

b. Transactions: Covering contracts and agreements.

c. Precepts: Covering the rights, blood-money and punishments. This type of classification of the secondary principles of religion, which handles thousands of general and detailed matters (covering even the supererogatory practices, such as hair-dying, nail-clipping as well as what is allowed and not allowed in the wars with the enemies), induced many thinkers to say that the society in practice is not so much in need of researches concerning political thoughts.

16. Concerning those who use the term _inquiring *fiqh* against _traditional *fiqh* _he said: ⎯No, only the **Jawahiri** *fiqh,*" by which he referred to the *fiqh* which is connected to all the individual and social affairs. Most of the *faqihs* also tend to the **Jawahiri** *fiqh,* but their impressions are not the same. Some of them regard only what is written in the book of *Jawahiri* to be the **Jawahiri** *fiqh,* while he regards its general outlook as the **Jawahiri** *fiqh.*

17. For example, many of the *faqihs,* who have nothing to do with philosophy and gnosticism, in their instructions concerning commencing the *hajj* rites say that the intention is to be recited correctly, while he does not regard it necessary to be articulated. But in respect of *tawaf* he says if the performer of the *tawaf* feels that he has done a part of it not for the sake of **Allah,** he will have to repeat that part. In this way philosophy and gnosticism spread their shadow on the delicacies of his *fiqhi* judgments. The contrary is also true. For example, the Sunni and Shiite *faqihs* unanimously judge that the one who curses the divine prophets is deserving death. Thus, sentencing **Salman Rushdi** to death was based on this precept, and no political interest can cancel it. (Naturally, the foundations of such unanimity were not, at the beginning, void of political observations, therefore, this type of judgments, in an aspect, falls with the frame of political *fiqh).* Of late, a number of thinkers admit separating the political *fiqh* from the devotional *fiqh,* or, at least, for teaching purposes say that this separation is necessary. But in the works of **the Imam** no such separation is seen, or the author has encountered no such thing.

18. Before being worried about the prejudgments of others, I was, and am, worried about my own condition.

19. Very delicately, this can be a possibility for firm recognition of the perceptions and the explorations. As an example, I have but to state that

when the 3-membered Iranian delegation went to Moscow to convey the **Imam**'s message to **Gorbachev,** the society knew nothing of the contents of the message. Many of the expert politicians could only guess, but none of their guesses hit the reality. An old man, named **Naddafi**—who was then living and a pensioner working as a waiter in the International Political Studies Department at the Ministry of Foreign Affairs—was asked: ―What for was this delegate sent to Moscow?" He, positive and quite certain, said: ―It was sent to invite **Gorbachev** to Islam." It must be said that the principle of inviting to Islam is one of the most important principles of Islam's foreign policy, and it surely had its lofty position in the **Imam**'s political thought.

20. These five sections are:

Politics, knowledge of political events, political analysis, political opinion, and political thought. For the political thought I think the following definition is a comprehensive and preventive one: ―The group of the philosophic beliefs which are directly connected to administrating the society's affairs." It must be said that these five sections are mixed together, and separating them is theoretical. (Look up **Imam Khomeini** in *Five Sections of Political Knowledge*, a collection of essays on the Islamic Revolution and its roots, vol. 1, published by the Teachers' and Islamic Teaching Lessons Department, The Leader's Representation Office in the Universities, 1995).

21. Ordinary people also talk like this in their daily talk. For example, when somebody catches cold and is asked: ―How did you get cold?" The answer would in most cases be something like the following: ―The door was open and I caught cold," ―The cooler was high," ―It was hot and I dived into the swimming pool," ―I returned from the sauna bath without dressing myself well," ―I caught it from my mother," etc. As a matter of course these premises do not result in catching cold. What are omitted are the majors which are not uttered by addresser on the supposition that they are obvious.

22. In moments when significance, delicacy and beauty are manifested more, one becomes sensational. But if everything, at any moment, is significant, delicate and beautiful, what then? To our nation, the day when they could hug him was so significant, delicate and beautiful that they were utterly confused. They raised his car on their hands, such that the man, whose foot was mashed under the wheels of the car, did not utter the slightest cry of pain, due to his eagerness. But about him who, even during exilement, used to feel his people beside him and never felt being away from them, what can be said? When he uttered the word ‗Nothing' in reference to those significant moments, the one who is not acquainted with the depth of his feelings cannot

bear from this any impression except that he is an unfeeling man. But to those who know him well, it is not concealed from them that the significance of the midnight when they were asleep relieving themselves from the day's tiredness, was not less significant than the day they tired themselves in their coming to receive him. I hope to be able, along this biography, to acquaint the reader with the more important and complicated senses of the word _Nothing'.

23. I borrowed this term from a friend, instead of merely _rhythm', with the difference that if the unit of conveying a message is a paragraph or an expression, how much information can each unit convey to the reader? If much, the rhythmic beat will be swift or red; if little, the rhythmic beat will be slow, blue or grey.

24. Mostly, when I could find a matter outside his works, a trace could be found in his works. If not in his sayings and writings, then, at least in his collection of poetry.

25. For example: On the threshold of the *Nowruz* of 1342 (1963), by way of protesting against the policies of the Shah, he issued a shocking statement under the title _The *ulama* of Islam have no feast this year'. The political side of this statement was a veil against understanding that the national feasts were to him valuable. However, his collection of poems starts with an ode about the *Nowruz* feast. For ten years the TV used to begin the New Year with a message from him. When I was rambling through the lanes and alleys of memories I saw some eighty refreshing gardens with red apples so as to add color to _haftsin'* table which is spread throughout the plateau. A man, who, a generation before was a young man, said: —The last weeks of the month of Esfand, 1335 (1956) were very bad for our family. I had no father and my mother could not provide new clothes. On that sorrowful night somebody knocked at the door, and the light of joy in my mother's eyes illuminated the house. She opened the bundle which **Haj Aqa Ruhullah** had sent. He had sent clothes for all the members of the house. How beautiful they were! I hadn't before worn such a beautiful blouse and trousers like his gift."

To follow up the expanse and scope of leadership in his thought, we are very much in need of such tiny things. But it is clear that the memoirs, which artistically manifest themselves, rarely find their way into apparently serious books.

* *Haftsin* (Seven _S's): It is a Persian tradition to lay, on the *Nowruz* feast, the 1st day of the Persian new year, a table on which seven mostly eatable things whose names begin with letter _S' are set—the translator.

26. At the beginning history was not in written form, except a part which originally started with writing or picturing. Thus, the value of what is in the bosoms is not less than what is in documents and handwritings, though both have the same quality. But, under some considerations, the definition of the oral history is different from the written history; and some researchers take the oral history, compared with the written history, to have less documentary value. On the basis of my personal experience, I noticed that to discover the truth and what is behind the curtain, there was something more valuable than depending on the written and oral history, that is, when the narration of a narrator loses its dependability. When the pen rolls on the paper, tens of notes line up. When the cassette recorders and cameras are present, and when it is decided to register a name in a written work, the speaker conceals the secrets, sometimes, of course, because they are unimportant, not because anything else. But, in discussions without introduction there may be uttered talks which would not have been spoken, had an introduction been arranged. Many details I obtained in this way, and to some of them I attach great researching value. Of course, when the opening of my ear swallowed something coming out of the mouth of somebody, I did not digest it unless at last I found a trace of it in his works, even in a piece of a hemistage of a line of poetry. Whenever I could find no trace, but found it necessary to state it to complete the picture, I conveyed it to the addressee through the rhyme of talk.

27. Some coincidences are quite surprising. Now that I have brought the skeleton of this Introduction to an end, I came in my revision across the name of this great man. An hour before a friend had phoned to congratulate me on the occasion of the birthday anniversary of **the Imam Muhammad al-Baqir** (*a*), and now he phoned once again. My ear heard the name of a man my eyes were fixed at him in the papers. He consoled me on the demise of **Ayatullah Pasandideh.** It was a painful piece of news which he heard over the radio, and he knew what my feelings would be at hearing it. He repeated his apology many times.

Now as I am looking at this name, I ask permission to condole all the truthful and free readers on the departure of a person who was both the elder brother of the hero of our story and acted as his father and teacher. The author and the readers are greatly indebted to him. Had it not been for him we could never have found our way to what was not seen by others.

May his lofty and free soul be happy, as truthfulness, purity and clarity were running in his veins. If he knew anything he would not refrain from telling the details, and if he did not know he would not mislead by generalizations. Whenever he had something to tell he would summon the truth and let interest go. He was so broad-minded that his tongue would never utter but the right thing. He had attained to such a magnanimity that he had washed clean every tint of haughtiness and conceit. If you greeted him it was as if you had greeted a peasant, but if you sat to listen to him talking, you would find sagacity and ingenuity in his relevant answers. May his free soul be flooded with mercy and may **Allah** associate him with the saints and the Master of the freemen.

28. If we, with this generality, want him to tell all that he knows, he will fill a cup from the cask which he loves best. If out of what he has said we derive questions in order to hear more, again he will fill another cup from the same cask. But if we make a story out of the event whose generality we know, the story will press a fancy on the real memory. For example, describing **Ruhullah**'s guarding during World War I, I said: "Every night he used to ascent to the roof in order to guard his household..." He said: "This is not true. He ascended to the roof only few times to please his mother. Most of the time he used to spend in the trenches outside the house." This became an excuse for telling the detail. Another example: A number of contradictory pieces of news to the effect that after the Coup d'état of the 3rd of Esfand [22nd of Feb.] he left for Qum. His leaving for Qum I based on those hearings. He observed that it was not so: "He sent a letter from Arak that on the night of the feast he would come to Khomein." Asked whether he arrived in Khomein in daytime or at night, he pressed his mind then he said: "In the afternoon." Whether it was cold or mild, he said: "It was raining, and the coal-stove placed in the alley to receive him was sending its smoke in the mist..." He also remembered the color of the cloth in which he had bundled his belongings. He related detailed episodes about his visitors during the days of the feast.

29. I felt that in some topics I practised too much concentration on the analysis of his psychology. I apologize to his great soul, which cannot be contained in the chair of the common psychiatrists, and to the readers, too. But when I wanted to choose another expression away from the psychoanalysis and yet to expose the primary roots of a thought, a more suitable way did not occur to me. Of course, in order to renew my love of him, I pledged not to be sly in such instances, and show the analysis so clear that the reader may still doubt.

30. I haggled with myself: Was handling his childhood period really a selection out of consciousness, and was there no reason other than having a possibility provided for such research? The result which I gained was that

had it not been for that provision, this important matter would have been neglected.

31. As from late in Safavid days, when the international relations took a newer form, every revolution anywhere in the world, and in whatever dimension, had, more or less, a connection with the whole world. Any development, change, reform or revolution, directly or indirectly, was affected by, and had its effect on, the victorious regime. So, when I say: ―The previous regime and the regimes before it," I do not mean only the construction of the Iranian governments, nor is it only the political side of it. If we take the cultural, political and ideological characteristics before the World War I to be a system, the Constitutional Movement in Iran was not less effective than that system. If the end of the World War I is regarded to mark the beginning of another system, in which force was quite made, the Coup d'état of the 3rd of Esfand was the offspring of that system. The World War II represented a third system which placed two military, political and mental poles in the ruling position over the whole world. Although, from the political dimension, the world was never contained in the two victorious poles, and the uprising of the non-alignment, though weak, was the third pole, yet, Iran was placed in the penumbra of the Western Block. The Islamic Revolution took out Iran from the penumbra of the Western Block and changed the past solid order into a running one. I hope to be able to show some of the characteristics of this running order in the philosophic, cultural, ideological and political structure of the world in the biography of this great man who skillfully knew very well the essence of the international orders.

32. The reader must also be apprehensive about the writer who also tints everything in the turns of his method and perceptions. Naturally most of the writers think that they have discovered the truth, and this writer, accordingly, would not think himself exceptional. But as the hero of the story is a great man, the writer will always direct both himself and the reader twice.

33. Those who are not prepared to name them have their own reasons, which appears to some to be quite surprising. Some of them believe the nature of the work to be a kind of backbiting. These are two types: One type regards both praising and dispraising to be backbiting. They believe that even praising that beloved is not allowed if the praiser knows that the praised does not like it. These, however, did answer some questions, but they were afraid of generalization. Another group were those who thought that to repeat his praise for an event in which many personalities were present with opinions different than his, is in fact dispraising the others.

Others, by way of precaution, said that, due to weakness of their memory, it is possible that, in repeating some memoirs, the reality may mix with fancy.

A group said: Somebody has narrated the event differently, so it is not becoming to repeat it. This group may also be divided into three sectors. A number of them had moral observations, others had political observations and some others had personal observations.

There are others who find it menial to come down from generalities to particularities and have their names stated among the narrators of the particularities.

Such being the case, I thank all those who agreed to reply, for hours, my particular questions, which at times were more like investigation, and I hope they will forgive me if I heard in what they said something different by assaying them according to my criterions, and so, writing something else.

34. For a time we were neighbours at the International and Political Studies Dept., in two rooms with a door opening at each other. I am not exaggerating if I say we spoke almost everyday about that beloved. One day we talked about his relations with different people, on another, about his taste in respect of colors, on a third, about his joking with his friends, and at times the talk was about his serious political discourses.

Dr. Burujerdi is a man of good memory and sociable, and for every topic he has several memoirs in his bag. Some events he himself had seen, and some he had heard from others. The size of what I have heared from this generous friend exceeds the size of ten books, with more than a thousand subjects. Although at that time I did not know why **Allah** had brought him to this department and put him in a room next to mine, nor did I know to where repeating his memoirs would lead, but in my hidden conscience I was feeling that my unquenchable thirst, which incited in him the desire to talk, would one day be useful to me, one more serious day than those in which I was working on his political thought. If at that time I carelessly did not offer my thanks, I hope my thanks may not now decrease his reward.

35. By **Suhrab Sepehri**.

36. And also: ―The scholars of my *ummah* are preferable to the prophets of the Israelites."

37. A plant named *ashaqah* has presented the term *Ishq* (love) as a gift to the gnostic literature. It is a plant which grows in the shade and, searching for the sun, it climbs up the walls, and at the first meeting with sunrise it burns off. Thus, union (*wisal),* in the language of love, is to burn off, not to survive and get gratification.

38. *Hubb* (love) and *habb* (grain) are two roots of the same base. *Habb* is a grain that takes root within the earth and germinates. When enough sunshine reaches it, it gains strength and grows. But if the sunshine is not enough, it dies out.

39. The contraries are countless, such as the bad and the good, beauty and ugliness, knowledge and ignorance, heat and coldness, light and darkness, etc. The farther we get from the bad the nearer we get to the good, and the more we keep ugliness away, the more the beauty is manifested. With ignorance we come to this world and proceed towards knowledge. The hot and the cold merge together, and, although both are proportional, yet both are on the same spectrum. Although moderation is proportional, it gets its concept in the middle of a spectrum. When light comes, darkness loses color. Everything has in each moment its dark part. When the absolute light comes nothing remains except light.

40. In the sphere of gnosticism, principally love is both the cause and the means of cognition. The more the searcher is in love, the more he is gnostic. Similarly in the exact sciences, such as mathematics, the coefficients would not appear without love. In arts and the like, such as calligraphy and gardening, love, before being a motive to knowledge, is a kind of knowledge. As to the humanities, particularly history, tracing the effect of love upon knowledge is a bit difficult, because loving the personalities would be interlocked with the interests, ambitions, internal inclinations, wishes and values of the searcher. In this sort of knowledge it is wrong to say: ―Empty yourselves from love and hatred and then start searching." Such an instruction is useless and impractical. At most, the result would incite the writer to conceal from the reader his love and hatred, as much as he can.

41. I searched into the works of tens of writers to find out a specimen of whether it is possible to write about a personality without feeling love or hatred towards him. I failed in finding even a single sample (although in their introductions it is so claimed). But I, of course, saw those who started with hatred and ended with love, and vice versa. Even in the encyclopedias, where the number of the words are counted, and whatever is loaded with positive and negative sentiments are pushed aside, one, nevertheless, can inspect the spoors of the love or hatred of the writer and the editor as clearly as those of a walker on the snow. To these one may add the interest and the quest for benefits and ambitions.

42. Naturally there are prejudgments and mental anticipations which come from the unconscience on which the researcher has no control. More important is that it is not only the writer who has prejudgments and mental

anticipations. Likewise is the reader, too. In this work I had my experiment on no less than a hundred persons.

43. I openly say and am happy of my saying:

I am the slave of love and free from both worlds.

Nothing is on the page of my heart but the *alif* of the stature of the beloved,

What to do, my tutor taught me no other letter!

44. —I their stories there is certainly a lesson for men of acumen. It is not a forged talk, but a confirmation of what is before it, and a detailed explanation of everything, and a guidance and a mercy to the people who believe." (*Quran,* 12:111).

45. The literature which is inspired by revelation, such as the speeches of the great prophets and the pure Imams, and, on a lower level, such as the messages of **Mawlana, Attar, Jami** and **Hafiz,** they have similar characteristics and their interiors would not completely become manifest. The everlasting literatures of the exalted men also have degrees of depth which may be regarded as their interior.

46. It says: **"And We reveal of the Quran that which is a healing and a mercy to the believers, and it adds only to the perdition of the wrongdoers."** (**Quran**, 17:82). It also says: —No one is to touch it except the purified ones." (**Quran**, 56:79).

47. In explaining the psychology of some individuals it uses expressions with an exterior, while their interiors expose the limits of elegance. For example, it says: —So his parable is as the parable of the dog, if You attack him he lolls out his tongue, and if you leave him alone he lolls out his tongue." (**Quran**, 7:176).

48. The story of sacrificing **Ismail** and the coming of **Satan** several times to seduce **Ibrahim** (*a*), encouraged me to write: —The sapling, which he willingly planted and willingly gave water, he took to the sacrifice place for the pleasure of **Allah,** and **Satan,** sympathizingly, appeared to him and said: _Are you sacrificing —the national interests" for the sake of a belief?' He threw stones at him, and picked up the pen once again. Once again **Satan** came, asking this time a hurting question: _Which is more important, —the country's interests" or declaring a judgement?' Receiving the stones, **Satan** cried: _Alas! You do not know diplomatic etiquette,' and a bigger stone struck his head. In the third time, dressed in the apparel of Sufis, **Satan** began giving advices: _You have the snows of old age on your beard, do you want to have wider fame than what you have? Are you the only *faqih* and the others are not?' In another time and dress he said: _Let someone else issue

judgments so that the crystal of your enlightenment may not be broken... Isn't the country in need of tranquillity? If you do not care for your own reputation, then do remember the reputation of your culture and religion.' Do know and be sure that they will say: It was not he who had such cruelty; it is his religion which made his followers so cruel...' This time, too, he received such a stone that after it he could not rise up, and the pen ran into the inkpot and the judgement was issued... But **Allah** was not after **Ismail**'s blood, nor did He desire his national and his country's interests to be sacrificed. He wanted him to get nearer to **Ibrahim**'s position, and, nearer as he got, the interests of his country crossed beyond Iran's borders, and protected the other religions against the aggression of the irreligious ones, too."

49. **Allamah Tabatabai** wrote: —. So, the best of the stories means the best story and *hadith*, and it may be said that the word story also means narration... such as the story of **Joseph,** which, in the style narrated by the *Quran,* is the best narration, because, although it was a love story, yet it is told in such a virtuous and pure style that no better can be there." *Tafsir al-Mizan,* Marwi Printing House, vol. 21, p. 124.

50. **"And Dhun-Nun [Jonah, the man of the whale], when he went off in anger and thought that we had no power over him, he called out in the darkness that: There is no god save you. Glory be to you! I have been of the wrongdoers."** (21:87).

51. Quoted by concept.

52. Except in open debauchery if the debauchee does not care being exposed.

53. Probably because moralities are proportional. If this is true, then we must prove that the advantages and the interests are neither proportional nor conventional.

54. Those who did not want to talk in his praise lest it might seem in a way dispraising others, if they do it with conscious faith, not by way of seeking security seemingly to avoid backbiting, they deserve being esteemed.

55. He told me the following famous narrative to fillip my feelings: It is said that **Allah** releases the angels, who record the bad deeds, from their task five times a day. Then He would not send them to the same person till the end of his life, so that they may not witness the sins of his servants more than once."

56. One of today's *ulama* and students of yesterday demanded from him an *aba*' to be blessed by it. Now, he agrees to allude to that incident, and yet he believes that demands of this kind, even for blessings, are far away from

honourable prestige. It thus happens that the positive and the negative become arguable.

57. There is no such a case in volume 1.

IN KHOMEIN

Khomein is a town in the south-east of the Central Province of Iran. It is an old town, with some ninety surrounding villages. It goes back to more than 1500 years in history. It is said that **Huma**, the daughter of **Bahman Kiyani**[1], had built it. Its name, then, was Khomayhan, which is a combination of **Kho,** which means _good', and **Mayhan,** which means _a place', i.e. a good place, or a sacred place.[2] This town and its surrounding villages were called Kamareh, too. Anybody whose family name is Kamarei, it means that he, or his grandfathers, were born in this town or in the surrounding villages.[3]

The houses of Khomein, like the houses of the central towns of Iran, were built of sun-dried bricks and went up with clay and roofed with wooden beams. The facades were plastered with clay mixed with straw. There were, however, few houses in each quarter with baked brick facades. Some houses had slant gable roofs, protecting them against snow and rain. The general features of Khomein greatly resemble Golpaygan and Khansar, its two neighbouring towns. Its quarters, lanes and alleys are not so much different from those of other towns of the central province. Of course, its subterranean canals are mostly full of water and its plantations are prolific. There are many springs in Khomein with somewhat large orchards. In the past its plantations were more, and now its houses, like the houses of most of the other towns, are built of pressed bricks and iron beams or with concrete and earthen bricks.

The prospect of Khomein in spring appears attractive because the white crest of Alvand[4] Mountain can be seen from several miles, and the plain of red poppies with wild tulips and yellow lilies receive the passer-by. Although the town is sieged by thirty mountains, a vast plain has kept the peaks far away and has set them like fortresses which guard the town. Now, 149 villages in the five unbesieged[5] rural districts embrace the town. Nearly one hundred and fifty years ago there were some one hundred villages scattered around the town and a rural district was meaningless.

When the sun shines on the peaks and the slopes of the snow-clad mountains, the springs and the canals get full of water. The river of the town, which flows roaring with the spring time rain, runs down from high falls and twists through the narrow dales, sometimes deep but narrow, sometimes wide but shallow, until it comes to Golpaygan where it joins the river of that town, and in Khansar it concludes a contract with another river[6], wherefrom they run down breathless to Qum. Nevertheless, Khomein is not the most beautiful town in Iran, nor is it among the most beautiful ones. It has no particular distinction above that of similar towns. Its original distinction is that its lap brought up a man, who, in the autumn of life, when the politically distinguished persons become Sufis, became one of the most famous political visages. The name with which that great man was distinguished was taken from this town. So, in gratitude for the name it presented to that great man, even if it be effaced from the geographical maps, it will remain eternal in the historical map of the world.

Iran is an ancient country with its roots deep into the depths of time, witnessing so many springs and autumns. That is why its historical trunk is corpulent and adventurous. The history of a town like Khomein, which stems from a stout branch of that trunk, must also be full of events.

Whenever the central government was subjected to a storm, or went into the mid-day slumber, and became half-dead or out of breath, the wicked gangs got active and the local rulers had prosperous markets. At such times, the rascals, with the permission of the Khans' [the tribal chiefs], would climb into the houses of the people. From the houses of most of the Khans rose towers and fortresses. Compared with other neighbouring towns, Khomein enjoyed richer yields; hence its towers and fortifications were more.

A House with a High Tower

In one of Khomein's quarters[7] two towers or forts rose high from a house overlooking the town. The taller tower was on the eastern side of the house, and the other one was on its south. This house, at a river which was mostly full of muddy water during spring time, and with little water, or with no water at all in summer, belonged to **Muhsin Khan,** who, being afraid of the aggression of the wicked gangs, stationed several guards in each tower. It was built of clay, raw bricks and sizable wooden beams, in several stages. At first, there was a large yard with a number of medium size rooms for an ordinary family, then, in another yard they built several larger rooms and a hall, for a life of frequent coming and going. The two towers went up errect when **Muhsin Khan's** father died, and he became responsible to look after the farmers who worked for father. A select architect basically repaired the house several times and he joined the two buildings together and connected the corridors to each other in such a way that they seemed as if from the beginning they were a single one with two towers. He had the entrance wall built with bricks, with two stone-benches at the two sides of the front door, using lime-mortar so as to be endurable enough and the bricks may not become loose due to frequent usage.[8] **Muhsin Khan** had built this house for himself, and he continued to enlarge it along with the continual development of his social status.[9] Then he sold it to someone who was not a Khan, nor had he the disposition of one.

The one who bought it was a man whose pulse thronged with zeal, and the shelterless used to encircle him. He needed a fort to secure him against the wickedness of the wicked.

The doors of this house had two pegs on their chests. At down, when the two leaves of the door were turned open on their pivots till the night, the pegs never showed themselves face to face so that nobody might rob them with his hand, and if someone had a business or needed something, he would just knock with the knocker by way of asking permission, and, with a _Ya Allah!_' saying, he would, without any apprehension or timidity, enter the house, because it was the house of a man of a lineage of knowledge and action, and it is a shame on an active scholar to close his door, to break away from the people, to only fix his eyes onto books, to forget the people. When people pawn their heart with somebody and invite a scholar to their quarters, the scholar becomes an endowment for the people, so, it is not becoming of the house of an endowment to be locked, because only those who do not feel ashamed will knock at the door, while those who feel ashamed will not knock at a locked door.

Entering this house one would pass through a courtyard along one side of which there were lines of green summer vegetables used at the table of the owner of the house to serve his sporadic guests. At the end of the autumn they would be ploughed. In the lines of the greenery there were fruit trees, producing juicy fruits, and along the wall there was a row of trees which spread their shades in the heat of summer. On the other side there was a heart-shaped pool throbbing on the bosom of the courtyard, and, with a faint breeze, there would be tiny waves. The length and the width of the courtyard were almost equal, with an area of a little more than four thousand square metres, paved with bricks. As a matter of fact, it was a garden-like fortress with the name of a house, which, on the 15th of Rabial-Awwal, 1255 A.H., was sold at 100 *tuman*s, but today no one can afford to buy it. However, at that time a hundred *tuman*s was not small money. The marriage portion of the lady of this house, of which she owned a share, was twenty *tumans* in cash, and the carpet—which she brought with her as a part of her trousseau so as to be spread under the feet of the household and to give life to its artistic designs—had been bought at five *tumans*.[10]

The two joint buildings embraced the pool. In one building there were the rooms for the wife and the children. This building was called *andaruni* [the private quarter]. The guests' rooms were in the other building called *biruni* [the guests quarter]. This architectural tradition, taken from religious teachings, although sometimes served ignorant beliefs, and had the rotten smell of aristocracy which hurts the nostrils, yet, when the inside of the house is not polluted with luxuries, the connection of the architecture will be with the principle of practicality. This is because art mostly tends to fancy and is hostile to practicality. This architecture puts _chastity' and _freedom', which usually scuffle, hand in hand. The noises of the *biruni* would not deprive the wife from freedom, and the woman, flaunting with freedom, would not let chastity skip of her hands, rather she would learn that life is partly inside and partly outside, and both go side by side in a single unity. But the tumult of the outside should not subjugate the inside. Such was this house and now it is the museum of the same concept.

Today the rooms are intact as they were, but at nights, instead of the oil lamp, electricity lights them. Its doors, windows and walls have several times been repainted. That heart-shaped pool is still unchanged, except that it now takes its water from the town's pipe network. But it is regretted that sometimes _development' knows not what it does with the memorials. Development and widening the streets could not cope with the eastern tower and fortress, and the one which was knocked down in this contest was the tower.

The Visage of Sayyid Ahmad

If someone had the intention to meet the host, he would have to leave the pool behind, ascend an eight-stepped brick stairs without handrails. There he would be received by a middle-sized and middle-aged man, who with his warm reception, affability, agility and sharp look, mingled together, and, using the relish of familiar and intimate words, pronounced in the charming Kashmiri dialect, would spread the smell of close friendship and sincerity in the air. The guest in this house felt as if he were the host. He would pour a cup of tea[11] for himself, and might, at times, offer one to the **Aqa**, too. In his presence, he was called **Aqa**. In his absence, he was known as the „**Allamah Sayyid Ahmad Hindi**.

One of Khomein's villages is called Farahan, at half a farsakh from it and connected to it. **Yusuf Khan**, from this village, went to Najaf [in Iraq], sent by the people on the errand of finding a man who could satisfy the people's religious needs in Khomein. From among the religious scholars he selected the **Allamah Sayyid Ahmad Hindi,** who had the stamp of affection on his forehead, and had no fear of migrating to any country. His grandfathers were also messengers who immigrated from Neyshabur[12] to Kashmir so as to meet the questions of the believers in religion there with relevant answers. **Sayyid Ahmad"s** father, as a religious missionary, drank a cup from the pitcher of martyrdom, and his name, which was **Sayyid Din Ali,** was changed to **Din Ali Shah,** as in Kashmir the elite are called Shah[13], and martyrdom was an evidence proving **Din Ali** to be of the elite. That martyr, i.e. the father of **Allamah Sayyid Ahmad,** was a grandchild of **Mir Hamid Husayn** who wrote his book *Aqabat al-Anwar*[14] in India, where he died.

After the martyrdom of his father in Kashmir, **Sayyid Ahmad** travelled to Najaf so as to learn more, and he did learn that wherever his knowledge would be more fruitful, he must make his home there. So, Khomein was prepared to embrace the man with **Hindi** epithet and grant him the epithet of **Khomeini.**[15]

Muhammad Husayn Beig was one of the nobilities of Farfahan's village, but his nobility brought him nearer to the family of knowledge than to the elite of the town. He had two children: a boy named **Yusuf Khan,** who was an intimate companion of the **Aqa** in the *biruni*. The other, a girl, called **Sukaynah,** who became the **Aqa"s** spouse and inmate.[16] In this house she gave birth to three daughters, and the fourth was a boy. On a Thursday, when the sun was rising in the horizon, he, keeping pace with the sun, came to the world.[17] They took his name from the epithet of the last **Prophet (s)**, **Mustafa. Aqa Sayyid Ahmad** had two other wives, **Shirin,** daughter of **Abid Golpaygani,** and **Bibijan,** daughter of **Karbalai Sadr Ali Khomeini.**[18] One of them gave birth to his first son, **Murtada.** He studied and became a scholar, but, before finding the chance to marry, death opened its wings and took his soul, in the prime of youth, only one year after his father's death.[19] Thus **Mustafa,** the only son, survived until the blood of his father boiled in his veins. He, with his sisters grew in that house. Perhaps, sometimes he used to climb up the towers, sometimes he used to entrust his body to the water of the pool. **Sultan Khanum**[20] was the first sister, **Agha Banu**[21], the second. The third sister, **Sahibah Khanum,** had a strange fate. It was destined that a man from the Qareh Kahriz[22], near Aligudarz, with the name of **Shukrullah**

Khan, proposed to her. When she moved to his house, she dreamt that her husband's brother, **Karim Khan,** had fallen to the ground from a high tower. Not much later, in the war waged by the government of the time against Qareh Kahriz village, the tribe of **Karim Khan** and **Shukrullah** was so demolished that there remained no trace of that family. **Sahibah Khanum,** crying and with a burden of pains, returned to Khomein. Many years later she concluded a marriage contract with **Mulla Jawad Kamarei,** a wealthy man from Khansar. She did not conceive. Many years passed together, until grace helped them and, instead of her own child, she could, by smelling her brother's son, pour water on the fire of longing for a child—the fire which is kindled in the heart of every woman. Yet, at this time another heart-rending incident brought her so much grief so as to put to full trial her endurance ,and to teach whatever she had learnt of patience and forbearance to her niece dearer than her life—I wish the name of this lioness were **Zaynab!**[31]

Every Muslim is allowed to give all his wealth to charity establishments, or to anybody he likes, after putting aside the expenditures he needs for his family, and after settling any debt he has to pay. But if during his life he did not do it, after his death the inheritance law would be enacted, and his right to dispose of his wealth would be confined only to one-third of his left wealth according to his will. All the heirs are to respect his authority over this portion of his original wealth. If the will covered more than one-third, it would be up to them to comply with his will or not. Those who possess considerable wealth, in order to prevent any possible dispute among their inheritors over the more required items after their death, transfer their wealth to the inheritors of tomorrow. So did **Aqa Sayyid Ahmad.** He, according to the inheritance law, gave to every one of his sons two shares, and to every one of his daughters one share. He kept a portion to be given to an expected child to be born shortly, should there be any, if not, it would be spent on his shrouds and burial. The house in which he used to live was **Mustafa"s** share, a share of which already belonged to his mother. It was written in his will that when he closed his eyes; they should take him to Karbala to bury him adjacent to the **Master of the Martyrs.**[24]

His Visage Was the Light of the Town

In late 1285 or early 1286 A.H. he closed his lips forever. The people carried the coffin on their hands to the gates of the town. Then, on mules and horses, they galloped from Khomein to Karbala, all days, lest the body might get rotten. Despite the fact that the distance was too long and the caravan was on the road for no less than a month, all the travel's expenditure did not exceed ten *tumans*. As to the expenses for *salahs* and fastings, which he had bequeathed to be paid for, they were 23 *tumans*. It seems that he had willed that the *salahs* and fastings of his whole life should be repeated. This was a tradition with those who were uncertain and afraid lest their devotional deeds should not be acceptable to **Allah,** the Exalted.

His visage was the light of the town now going away from among the people, and the features of the town took the signs of sorrow for being bereaved of him. The girls came back home with swelling eyes. **Mustafa,** who was only eight years old, had not the feet to carry him to the house which his father had left. **Murtada** could not stay more than a year. He, too, left this world.[25]

The celebrated lovesick of the town stayed in Khomein thirty years, from youth till old age. [26] He visited all the surrounding villages, giving knowledge to the ignorant, and to their scholars he taught action, and with their acting scholars he was sociable. As much as he could, wherever he found a waste land he bought it and had it cultivated, and as much power he had in the finger-tips of his faith, he offered his thanks in the form of creating habitable and flourishing hamlets. Within eighteen years[27], in the three villages of _Shahin', _Aswaran' and _Nazi'[28], which were not so much far away from the town, he established several plantations.

In Khomein he arranged a large fruit orchard and made it like a paradise. He bought a caravanserai in order to receive the caravans as his guests. His income exceeded one hundred and twenty *tumans* a month, from which he did not expend more than his family's expenditure. The poor got a share in his wealth so that no hand should be extended towards the Khans. The religious scholars were exempted from paying income tax, but those of them who got rich used to pay taxes. He paid taxes and was in no need of the religious taxes the people used to pay to the religious scholars. The unfair landlords usually took two-third of the yield, and the fair ones took half of it. The pure-natured took one-third of the water-irrigated cultivation and up to one-fifth of the dry farming yield from the farmers. He was of the last category. When wisely settling cases of arbitration, he used to take any case, by himself, to the court, if necessary, for settlement. He never confined himself to laziness, and as he took his mind to knowledge, he took to give strength to his body by sports. One day he heard that the soldiers of the government had assaulted a young boy. He did not ask help from his friends, so that he may not cause contention. He took his sword and rescued the youth from their clutches by the strength of his arm. To the people he was a man descending from the pure progeny [of the **Prophet (s)**], in whose eyes the love of the people waved. Courage resounded in his speech, his heart throbbed for **Allah,** and the fate of the people occupied his mind. Knowledge and action were mixed in him and both his outward appearance and inward disposition were praiseworthy. It seems that when he came to this region blessings have also come with him. Although he is no longer in Khomein, as he is buried in Karbala, yet the blessings are still there. Perhaps in their inner inside they knew that in his loin there was a man who would come, and it was because of this that the blessings were still pouring down.

Sufrehs Spread in Years of Famine

Two years before closing his eyes, a severe famine digested the people of the country.[30] The modest poor used to hide from the eyes of their dear relatives so that they might not witness them dying. A pat would be put on the fire boiling for hours on end so that the pieces of hide may give out some of their grease, and the warm water which the children drank as a soup, might keep them alive for another day. Some ignorant people used to store the grains in their granaries so as to sell them at the cost of all the existence of a family for a meal. Had it not been for them, famine would not have opened its jaws so wide to swallow the lives of the people. Other wealthy persons did open their stores to the people, but not so emotionally. They were wise enough to cook soup and steam-cooked rice and invite the people of the district to it. The popularity of **Aqa Sayyid Hindi** during this year of famine doubled, because he had written the names of all good wealthy personalities in a notebook, and with their cordial cooperation famine in Khomein had only few victims. In that year the doors of his *biruni* and *andaruni* were never closed, and the *sufrehs* were taken away only to be washed and respread. It was quite surprising that when the famine closed its mouth, the stores were not swept clean. In this year the people of Khomein could well understand the meaning of the noble *ayah:* **"The parable of those who spend their wealth in the way of Allah is as the parable of a grain growing seven ears, in every ear a hundred grains, and Allah multiplies for whom He wills, and Allah is All-Embracing, All-Knowing."**[31]

With his death, silence cast its shade over the lane, and the door-knockers began to face the guests. The *biruni* lost its former animation, and spiders started stretching their networks in the ceiling's beams. **Murtada,** his oldest son, fell ill, and after a year he burnt his mother's heart by his leaving her for ever. **Mustafa,** who was then eight years old was too young to be able to enliven the *biruni.* When he grew older he had to leave for the scientific *hawzahs* in Isfahan and Najaf for further studies. He used to visit home once or twice a year, or even once every two years. But the *andaruni* remained as it was, with the relatives and the friends frequenting the house.

Twenty Seven Years Later

After twenty seven years, the *biruni* flourished once again. Now a tall, middle-aged man would sit on the veranda gazing at the pool, the heart of the house, wherein water rolled on. The trees grew bigger, the summer plant-strips were still there, but the tiles of the yard cracked due to the winter snow, the clay walls were washed by the autumn rain. The wooden beams of the room on the second story, near the tower, could not endure the weight of the winter snows and broke to pieces, the forts slowly fell down, the guards were sent away, but outside the house the tumults of the Khans are still practising aggression.

The central government was in the incapable hands of one of the most capable kings of the Qajars, **Nasiruddin Shah,** who was in those days, celebrating his sixty-seventh birthday anniversary. [32] He was the same king who ruled for some fifty years[33], and who, prompted by the enticement of his mother, who had a power over him, ordered the main vein of the wrist of his political teacher, his first grand vizier, to be cut with a razor and to put an end to his glorious life.[34] The only purpose of this pleasure-seeking, ignorant of the time, was just to preserve tranquillity in his Dar al-Khilafah, Tehran. Even the large cities were not secured. In small towns, his disciplinary officers were either at the service of the landlords, or they themselves were the cause of disorder. The wicked were armed with rifles, the Khans hired riflemen, and the defenceless waited to see if the fortresses would rise again.[35]

Delay was not allowable. Within few sunrises and sunsets, the workers alongside the builders and the houseowner and everybody who smelled of friendship put hand in hand, and the house was renewed as it had been thirty-four years before, where its present owner was born.

Nowadays, a man of thirty-four sits in the *biruni,* and whoever wants something from him would also go past the pool, leave it behind, ascends the eight railless steps, and then this man, like his father, would open his arms to him. Winter drives him into the room, and in summer he spreads a rug and pillows in the veranda, and, after asking about one another's health and affairs, he sits, with the softness of the dancing of a fish in the clear water, leaning, with the firmness of an eagle, on the pillow, yet, like the pupils in a schoolroom, listens attentively to the visitor's need. Most of the visitors come with religious questions or scientific problems. He calmly parts his lips and gives simple answers. He bewilders nobody with his answers. Once a woman came to him and said that her husband gave her such a slap with his heavy hand that her cheek turned red. He summoned the husband. If he would not come he himself would go to him, look him in the face, and what he saw in his complexions would decide the tone of the talk. If he was to use a commanding tone he would use it as in forbidding the bad. Yet, his spiritual appearance would be sufficient, and the tone of the speech would mostly emit the scent of advice. From then on the wife would never be slapped any more, and this generosity is not below the expectation from a religious man.[36]

Sayyid Mustafa in Place of His Father

In his presence people used to call him **Aqa,** at his absence he was called: **Aqa Sayyid Mustafa,** and sometimes: **Aqa Musawi** or some call him: **A Sayyid Hindi.** If this is to be translated into Arabic, it should include the attribute _Sayyid" twice: One for **Aqa,** which means **Sayyid** or **Mr.,** and the other is because every offspring of the **Prophet (s)** gets the attribute of **Sayyid** before his name. **Aqa Mustafa** was a **Sayyid.** Any **Sayyid** whose family-tree is a branch of the sturdy trunk of the progeny of the **Imam Musa al-Kazim (a),** the seventh Imam of the Shiite, can be called **Musawi.** So, **Aqa Sayyid Mustafa** was **Musawi.** Inside the house he wore a white cap on his head, but in the outside he wore a black turban. The black turban is worn by the **Sayyids** as a sign of permanent mourning over the martyrdom of their grandfather, **al-Husayn (a).** Even in marriage ceremonies they would not take it off. Some of them use a green shawl or turban, which was the head-cover for most of **Sayyids.** However, those who study religious knowledge, which, in its preliminary stages, equals today _B.A.', and the advanced stage sometimes equals _M.A.', are entitled to officially preach religious topics. If he, in a special ceremony, wears the *labadeh* and puts the _aba' on his shoulders, and the turban on his head, he will be called **Hujjat al-Islam.** **Aqa Sayyid Mustafa Musawi,** at the beginning studied a little of the preliminary books in Khomein, then he left for Isfahan where there was an active seminary. There he became a **Hujjat al-Islam.** Then he travelled to Najaf in order to take lessons in *fiqh* from the late **Mirza Shirazi** who was the Shiite authority.[37] Whoever comprehends the *fiqh* such that in understanding the precepts of the religion he would not need to imitate another authority, he is called *mujtahid* and is given the attribute of **Ayatullah,** which today equals _PhD'.[38] Now, **Aqa Sayyid Mustafa** was a scholar called *Ayatullah.* He was so brilliant that the elites of Khomein named him *Fakhr al-Mujtahidin.* The people had waited twenty-seven years for him to come back to them and take the place of his father. When the invitations became official and were repeated, he was too modest to refuse, and thus he came and remained in Khomein for eight years, in the same house where he was born, grew and had childishly played around.[39] He stayed and probably he undertook the chairmanship of the religious schools in Khomein.[40] The people believed him, and he loved the people with all his heart.

A Fruitful Marriage

Fate predestined that he should marry a girl who, respecting knowledge, and having a pure emulsion of spirit, would bestow purity on her children when they put their lips at her breasts. The proposal to **Hajiyah Khanum Ahmadi,** daughter of **Aqa Mirza Ahmad,** the *Mujtahid* of Khansar had a positive response. This girl was a granddaughter of **Haydar ibn Muhammad Khansari,** the author of **Zubdatut-Tasanif,** who became among the elite class of the authors.

Past Memories

Now his home is warm. He had enough experiences of being away from home for years. Now he wants to stay in this town always. Sometimes he remembers his bitter and sweet memoirs. He recollects when he followed his father's coffin with tears; he had finished the primary schooling. Perhaps he liked to replace his father, maybe he did not know what he had to do. However, it was a custom among the families of religious scholars to send their clever sons to study in the theological teaching *hawzahs*. Even if they were not so clever still those *hawzahs* would attract many of them, though to no avail, wasting their lives in learning nothing. There was no other alternative. The first person undertook his teaching was **Aqa Mirza Ahmad Khansari,** son of **Akhund Mulla Husayn Khansari.** He opened to him his house in addition to his room. He soon realized that this orphan boy of eight years would take in the preliminary lessons in less than eight years. Now this teacher sporadically visits him, and sometimes he, his wife and son visit him. On those days when he used to go to his teacher's house, neither he nor his teacher knew that when both were sitting in the veranda or relaxing under the *kursi,* reviewing the lessons, and when **Hajiyah Agha**, the small girl, on hearing her father's voice, creeps on her four out of the adjacent room, goes round the pupil and sits on her father's knee and leans on his warm chest, and, while fingering her father's beard, draws the picture of the blissful complexions of this boy, on which settled the temporary dust of grief for his

71

father's death, no one knew that the affection melody of this pupil would, years later, be a reflection of a proposal tune.

As the preliminary lessons came to an end, not only the *biruni,* but the *andaruni,* too, came under a silence caused by his travel to Isfahan. In those days, the theological hawzahs in Isfahan embraced a number of famous scholars. It was at this time that the desire to marry started boiling in his veins, and there was none to knock at the door of his heart except **Hajiyah Agha,** whom he had not seen for years, though he knew that she had grown tall like a cedar tree. When he sent his proposal message and received positive reply from both the father and the daughter, he went back to Khomein, where he _spread the carpet of wedding'. The wedding ceremonies were splendid, and almost half of the people of the two quarters of Khomein were invited to his table. The bride's father was from Khansar; so many Khansaris were invited, too, in order to give more warmth to the party. **Aqa Mustafa** had the courage to ask his wife to change her name from then on, to **Hajar,** and she liked the name. A week later he said farewell to his relatives and left for Isfahan with his wife to live there.

Hajar Khanum, who was experiencing the custom of marriage life, was living in a rented house in Isfahan, waiting for her husband all day, rubbing her hands together, until their first child, **Mawlud Agha**, came so as to keep company with **Hajar** during the absence of **Aqa Mustafa.**[41] One day he took **Mawlud** in his arms and with **Hajar** left for Najaf so as to benefit by the knowledge of great scholars in that *hawzah.* No one had registered the day, the month or the year, but what is doubtless is that he did not stay in Najaf for more than five years, and, at the invitation of the people of Khomein he returned to his birthplace, settling in his father's place.[42]

A while after returning to Khomein he married a woman, named _**Shahzadeh Gawhar Maliktaj Tehrani. Hajar Khanum** magnanimously tolerated this woman who had not many relatives in Khomein. **Gawhar Khanum** for a while lived with her rival wife[43] and sat at the same table at which the other members of the household used to sit. But she bore him no child, nor did she leave any lasting memoirs. Probably it was for this reason that she created no unexpected event, committing herself to a calm, brawlless life, since she was a stranger whom fate had dragged from the capital to Khomein, and placed her among the members of a house very much frequented by visitors. She merged into that environment.

His House a Court of Justice

It is in the fate of every great man to emigrate and leave his home so that he may not be brought up slowly and calmly like chickens. The cold and heat of other lands and the difficulties of the time are necessary to put hand in hand so that the one who wants to become a scholar may not remain ignorant of what is going on around one in the world. Now that he had known other towns and got acquainted with other cultures, had completed the high level studies in another country, had followed up the news of the world and got their lessons he realized that the way of propagating the religion was not merely by explaining religious questions. The people have thousands of questions all of which are religious, but most of those who explain such questions regard only a part of them to be related to religion.

If a Khan took a young beautiful girl out of a village-house by force, compelled her to wear the wedding dress, while the girl, trembling for fear of him, said: ‗Yes‗ to the agent, what would the religious judgement in this case be? A hectare of land gave three tons of wheat. If its owner died and his three children became orphans, that land would meagrely stay their stomachs for a year. If a landlord should like to buy that hectare, too, and pay for it, in installment, two bags of flour per year, who could be so daring to invalidate that transaction?

Had the government sent a judge, he could judge. If no judge was sent, the arbitration would have become the duty of the town‗s *mujtahids*. The *nazmiyyah*[44] would, then, carry out the mujtahid‗s judgement as long as it did not contradict the interests of Khans and the Court. This town had no official judge, and, like Khansar, it was administratively annexed to Golpaygan. So, consequently, it had no strong *nazmiyyah,* and thus, the riflemen of the father came again. Those of them who had got old sent their sons. The armed merchants offered to serve him, that is, to send their armed guards to protect the town and their properties under his leadership.[45] Now, this house has become once again a House of Justice. Some would come to take lessons and to reiterate what they had learnt before. But people mostly came to discuss with **Aqa Mustafa** the problems of the town and the surrounding villages, and he, quite manly, tried not to stoop before any problem. In case he could not alone solve a problem, he would seek the help of other scholars in the town. Of course sometimes he would feel weak before the wickedness of some Khans, but never powerless. One day, **Hishmatuddawlah,** one of the Khans of Khomein who had his own servants and retinue in the town and in the village of Hishmatiyyah, one farsakh afar, resisted his judgement and ordered the **Aqa** to be arrested, and imprisoned him in one of the dungeons of Hishmatiyyah. But **Haj Sayyid Rida Rayhani,** who was a friend of both of them, and he, too, had his considerable retinue and riflemen, warned **Hishmatuddawlah** against the consequences of his procedure. After his release there was some reservedness between the two. At that time each part of Khomein was administered by a Khan, and, strange enough, some of the big Khans did not live in the town, as their forts were standing high in the villages outside the town. Some did live in the town, running several villages. Some villages had the landlord and farmers together. However, if deserts separated the towns from the villages, between this town and its villages there was no desert to be seen, because most of the town's population were the villagers living in the nearby town. Sometimes non-relative marriages used to connect families from a village with families from other villages. In some instances the Khans and the landlords ran the town, and in other instances the town-dwelling Khans ruled one or more villages. That situation caused the problems of all the villages to mingle with the problems of the town, and the unofficial ruler and judge of the town and the villages would not regard themselves confined to their own quarter and town. It was a complicated state, more complicated than today's division of the country, because although feudalism, Khanism, the landlord-and-peasantry system, are repulsive terms reminding one of barba- rism, yet, despite their negative impact at present times, at their own time they had deeper meanings. A Khan or a landlord was not merely a name; it was an economic unit taking the place of small political units, working like a party. In some instances it might take one to the post of chancellorship, and in other instances it might knock one dawn such that one would not be able to rise again. A part of commerce was knotted to their needs, and culture was turned ugly or beautiful by their conduct. Which government could govern the vast lands of the country? Which structure could arrange social relations? This system, which was an economic-political structure, in local attacks and retreats, in permanent friendships and competitions, could give better management to the social relations. It supplied the kings in their wars with soldiers. Of course, it mostly interpreted justice as it liked, and at times it brought injustice to its ultimate end. In such cases, the farmers would not keep silent. A Khan might be strangled and they might strike their spades into the land of another Khan. At times, several generations of the farmers would protect several generations of well-behaving landlords with their lives. So, that system, natural, unpraiseworthy and disorderly as it was, had serious participa- tion in managing the estates.

The Khans of Khomein

At that time the Khans of Khomein were more than twenty, who, in three rows, were contesting with each other. A group of them was led by that same **Hishmatuddawlah,** and the range of his power covered Kamareh and forty villages. Another group of Khans were those of the Qalah, the most famous of whom was named **Aliquli Khan,** who ruled over fifteen villages. A third group was the Dalaiys who ruled about ten villages. **Haj Abbasquli Khan and Haj Jalal Lashkar** were two of the harmless Khans of the Dalaiy who visited Mecca and apparently performed the *hajj* rituals and gave out food. But before being benefited by the income of their properties, they filled their stomach with usury which was disguised under apparently *halal* religious cover.[46] Other villages had weaker Khans, or had no Khan. Some twenty percent of the population of the town served the Khans. In some villages all were their servants. The balance of power between the independent Khans and those three competing groups was established, therefore, few contensions used to take place between them, but the other eighty percent of the population never were secured from their occasional aggression. Although the name of Khan coincided with some of them, as they kept feeding the hungry and gave shelter to the weak, but the fuss about Khanism in the history of the country was serious, and changed, in the Qajari rule, into severe astonishing injustice, depriving the town of security, and the eyes of sleep.

Now **Aqa Mustafa**'s monetary situation was good. When the farmers discussed with him their economic problems, he used to give them out of the fund of the *khums* and *zakat* which are obligatory. In case there was nothing in the fund, he would offer from his own money as a supererogatory expenditure for necessary occasions. Notwithstanding this, his economic method exposed the landlord and peasants system of Khomein to a notable threat, causing the other peasants to be impudent and to revolt against the Khans and landlords. Some of the Khans might sometimes blame him for his method. He would answer: ―Allah observes our deeds and knows if we pay what is due to the peasants or not. If we pay, the peasants would cultivate more delightfully and our money would grow, but if their children's due was swallowed by our children, they change into *haram*—eaters who would exonerate the bastards."

In Aliquli Khan's Fort

One day **Aliquli Khan** invited him to his fortress and laid for him a fantastic table so as to bind him by breaking bread with him to convince him not to be

75

so enthusiastic in defending the farmers. **Aqa Mustafa** accepted the invitation and took with him a number of his friends and peasants to the party. **Aliquli Khan** had the table laid for the **Aqa** and some of his companions in the hall of the fortress, and another table he laid in the yard for the servants and the riflemen accompanying the **Aqa**. **Aqa Mustafa,** holding **Murtada** by the hand, entered the hall followed by his company of merchants, businessmen, servants, riflemen and peasants. All entered the hall. Embarrassed, **Aliquli Khan** sent for his own servants and farmers, inviting them to the party.

The muddy shoes of the peasants were taken off at the gate of the fortress. **Aliquli** had sent orders that they could enter the yard with their shoes on, but his peasants thought this to be a test, and thus they dared not to obey it. He ordered the bewildered peasants to enter the hall, but no one of them had the courage. At last he had but to shout at them to enter. A number of the more daring ones went in at the second shouting, then the others, with their heads hanging down and their faces red with shyness, murmuring words of greeting, followed suit and sat in the nearest place. **Aliquli** ordered longer table-cloth, which usually was a length of cloth, to be spread for the large group, while his neck-veins swelling out because of blood pressure, and arrogantly issuing his orders. He then turned to the **Aqa** and said: ―You are welcome, but what wrong was there in our being together ourselves, and the peasants being together themselves?"

Aqa's Peasants Are Gentlemanly

Aqa Mustafa knew that it was a long story. He smiled by way of an answer. But one of his companions naively uttered first what he should have uttered last: ―**Aqa's** peasants are gentlemanly!" **Aliquli,** who was already nervous and would burst at the least irritation, proceeded towards the man, raising his hand to retort with a slap, but the **Aqa's** majesty prevented him and let down his hand, and without knowing what he was to say, he said: ―*La ilaha illallah!*" [There is no god save Allah!]

The Layout after Lunch

After lunch they brought in fruits, tea and hookahs. **Aliquli** asked the **Aqa** to come with him to the next room to have a friendly talk. **Murtada** did not leave his father. A number of the companions went in with him. Glowing embers were ablaze in a brazier, two *wafurs* with large heads, and a quantity of pure opium, were put in a tray. This was the souvenir of the British who offered it to the people of Iran. At the beginning they were buying the opium residue at high prices in order to make opium-smoking benefitial and, thus causing many people to become opium-addicted. Then they began selling the opium at high prices and no longer bought the opium residue. They leased the lands cultivated with sugar cane and wheat, and planted them with poppy. An important reason for abolishing the sugar-cane plantations in Iran was using their lands for poppy planting. Before the British bring in and spread it, the opium residue was bought from the herb-dealers as medicine. But during those years it became plentiful everywhere in most houses and tea-rooms, like sweets. **Aqa Mustafa** pointed out to **Aliquli** that he was not an opium-addict and that he did not want to let his son be a witness of his companions' opium-smoking. Talking about the characteristics of opium brought in other subjects, **Aliquli** said that he had planted some poppies, but the opium of Luristan was better. The **Aqa** said: ─A yellow dog is a brother to a jackal." The answer was: ─It is the cure for every pain." It seemed that most of the companions of the **Aqa** were opium-addicts, as they sided with **Aliquli** in respect of the exclusive characteristics of the opium. One said: ─It is the best cure for ear-pain of the children." Another said: ─For the pains of the leg and back nothing is better than opium." A third said: ─It causes constipation, but this is nothing compared with its other thousand advantages." Another said: ─I have, of course, heard that it creates bashfulness." **Aliquli** said: ─You talk of yourself!" Meanwhile the *wafur* was going round from hand to hand. **Aqa Mustafa** was somewhat surprised to see how addiction turned some serviceable people into inconsistant ones. He raised his hand to his mouth and took out of his pocket a large handkerchief—which most men used to carry in their pockets, and which was mostly hand-woven by the women of Yazd—and held it under **Murtada**'s mouth, and both hurried out of the room. A quantity of lemonjuice was poured into a glass and was given to him to drink. After few minutes, when the opium equipments had been taken out, they returned to the room. But blood had not yet reddened the pale cheeks of **Murtada.** Gradually more serious topics, for which the party had been held, were handled.

Ears Hear Threatening Sounds

Murtada was pricking up his ears, sewing his eyes to the lips, feeling afraid of the apparently friendly idle-talk going on. He threw himself on his father's lap. The bits of the talks which remained in his memory are: ─O **Aqa,** you are a learned man, so, it is better to entrust your riflemen to us. We know the language of the thieves and the armed men. It is not becoming of you to meddle in the trivial affairs of the people. They pretend to be wronged and complain to you against us, and you, due to your innocence, believe them. These peasants are ungrateful. No sooner you turn your head than they steal everything. They eat from both the feed-bag and from the manger. Instead of teaching them about the *halal* and the *haram,* you treat them in such a way making them more daring and think us irreligious. We do perform our *salahs.* I had the honour to go to *hajj* twice. As to my not fasting, I have my religious excuse for that. Concerning our preaching gatherings, you yourself had participated in them. I have heard that you say that marrying girls without their consent is *batil.* Are you against **the Prophet's** tradition? I think that everyone who does not like something attributes it to you. As regards your behaviour with your own farmers, I should say it is not right. They must be content with what they have. If they get more, they will grow tails and start kicking. Considering my good attachment to you, I have said what was necessary to be said. Others may give annoyance to you."

Aliquli's talking lasted for more than an hour. **Aqa Mustafa,** sat with his legs folded under him, lending his ears to **Aliquli.** Finishing his talk, **Aliquli** said: —Let us now go to see our guests to the door." The **Aqa** said: —I thought I, too, had my turn to say something," and he began talking: —Let us start from the last thing you said. Am I a little girl to be afraid of being annoyed?" **Murtada** noticed that his father's tone of voice was beating the drum of argument. He felt more afraid and pressed a corner of his father's *aba'* in his fist. The **Aqa** went on enthusiastically: —As to your hearing of my saying a girl cannot be married by force, it is the judgement of Allah, but to say I forbid temporary marriage, who am I to do so? The *halal* and the *haram* of **Muhammad (s)** remain so till the Day of Resurrection. [47] As regards your preaching gatherings, *salah* and *hajj,* they can be accepted by Allah only when they are done sincerely and out of faith. I must tell you that if there is even a thread of the peasants' rights in the clothes you wear, your *salah* and *hajj* are *batil.* Regarding the rights of the peasants, they have a right and the landlord has a right, too. When some gentlemen start preaching the people, they think that it is only the peasants who are to be preached, and that the landlords need no preaching. I think all people need to be preached, particularly the landlords, because they have more gold and jewellery, and Satan more lurks behind the wealthy. But if you think that giving the peasants their right in full would grow tails and make trouble, I must say if the other name of one's prestige is tail, I and you must have had our tails much earlier. [48]"

On his way home, **Aqa Mustafa** was absorbed in his thoughts and talked little. When he arrived home, repeated his *salah*s of noon and afternoon which he had already performed in the fort, and told **Hajar Khanum** to pay charity in atonement for the food they had in the fort.

The Creator is Busy with another Thing

Such are his thoughts and conduct. Moreover, modesty and politeness have made his complexion heavenly. Knowledge and insight have a tone in his voice. Magnanimity and courage are heard in his firm steps. All these have put hand in hand to make him more loved by the people in their heart and mind. But the Creator, away from the eyes of the creatures, is busy with something else. He is keeping him busy with the worldly and heavenly deeds of the people, which he deeply loved, so that the blood boiling in his zealous veins, may portray his conduct, thoughts, faith and affection, and then to have those affable portraits offset on his genes, preparing them for an amazing sperm to come.

It is strange to note that the last child of **Jacob (a)** was **Joseph (a),** the last child of **Imran** was **Moses (a),** and the first man to believe in the last religion was **Ali (a),** the last child of **Abutalib,** and the daughter who became the spring of **Kawthar** was **Fatimah (a),** the last daughter of the **Prophet.** Probably, one secret of such coincident is that the sperm is maturable, too. Now, out of the progeny of those two first and last there should appear a man, whose zygote should clot in the years of the father's maturity. Probably the wisdom of the recommendation to fast and to breakfast with good food, to perform the *salah* before going to bed with your wife, is that perhaps these would work upon the genes to produce a sound and pious draft. Yet it is not a concealed matter that to observe these recommendations is a respect to the coming child, and that whoever observes them more will have a more respectful child. So, it is not concealed from esoteric hearts that the man who for more than thirty years continued performing the obligatory and the supererogatory devotional acts, his sperm must, inevitably, produce a potentially great man.

Waiting for a Great Event

It was around the end of the last week of Shahrivar, all the fruits of the orchard of the dynasty of **Aqa Sayyid Ahmad Musawi** are gathered in this very house in Khomein waiting for a great event. A *sufreh* is spread in one of the rooms of this house. All those who sat around it—except two of them— had one day opened their eyes to the world in this room, or, rather, this room had opened its eyes and its arms to receive them. The two exceptions were **Gawhar** and **Hajar,** the governor of the *andaruni.* **Aqa Mustafa,** the master of the house, himself, fourty-two years ago, opened his eyes for the first time in that very room. His three sisters, who were sitting next to each other, older than him, watching **Hajar Khanum,** all had been born in that room. **Aqa Mustafa** has now five children. They, too, were born in the said room. Probably, of course, the first, **Mawlud Agha**[49], was born in Najaf.[50] It is probable, however, that when **Aqa Mustafa** was studying in Isfahan, he brought **Hajar Khanum** to deliver her child in Khomein in order to be cared for by her people. The second child was a daughter, named **Fatimah**[51], who also drew her first breath in that room. **Aqa Murtada**[52], whose milk teeth were falling down, and his younger brother, **Nuruddin**[53], were also born in the same room. The youngest child of **Aqa Mustafa, Aqa Zadeh Khanum**[54], who was still expecting to get her milk from her mother's breast, got her first milk in that room.

Moments of another Creation

Now the beams of the ceiling of the room which, in the countings of the children at bed time, counted odd in a time, and even at another, are waiting for another birth to take place in the same room. All are waiting. **Aqa Mustafa** is thinking: If **Hajar** is to toil once again, the room will shake if it is not fit to see the face of the midwife one more time.

In the *andaruni* **Hajar** is writhing with the pain of separation. In the *biruni* people are coming to congratulate the **Aqa** on the feast of **Kawthar,** as the whole town is throbbing with celebrating the anniversary of the birth of the last daughter of the **Prophet (s).** The people in the *biruni* are noisy. In the *andaruni* there is another noise. Noisier than the *biruni* and the *andaruni,* is the inside of **Aqa Mustafa,** not by voices, but by the attack of the army of a stormy imagination. He cannot bear remaining in the *biruni,* and he is not admitted into the *andaruni,* as only women are there. If he wanted to go up to the roof, as he used to do when he could not sit still, to have a prospective scene of the town, how would he be able to leave the guests? If he stays with the guests some of whose wives are with **Hajar,** the thought of **Hajar** and her cries, which do not reach the *biruni,* but they wind in his ears, causing him to writhe restlessly would cause the guests to wonder. They know that there are things to happen in the *andaruni,* but they know nothing of what is going on in his *andaruni,* his inside. He sends a servant to the *andaruni* every now and then, and the servant comes back signing: "No, not yet."

To be kept waiting causes him to become restless. Eagerness and enthusiasm are maddening him. Anxiety joined expectation to double his restlessness. He does not know why his heart is throbbing this time harder than the past five instances. Probably it is because this time this expected new comer's visit coinsides with the anniversary of the birthday of **Fatimah** (*a*). If the baby is a daughter her name will certainly be **Zahra**, because his second daughter had already borrowed the name of **Fatimah** (*a*).

From the World of the Womb to the Outside World

Suddenly the breeze of the angels' wings blew in the orchard, and threw lines on the mirror of the water, and the angels vied with one another to eagerly throw themselves in prostration on the clay passing through the moments of another creation, reciting: **"Blessed be Allah, the best of the creators!"** Before the coming of the page hurriedly from inside to give the good tiding and ask for the usual tip, **Aqa Mustafa** received his tip from his own heart, as the storm in his heart subsided and calmness was setting up its tent in its place. He was summoned to the *andaruni* to take his child into his arms, and to grant a coin to the midwife by way of being kind to her. When the sister was taking the baby from its mother to hand it to its father, the **Aqa** cast a glance at **Hajar**'s face to enjoy seeing the effect of those great moments of heavenly grace, as a mother's feature, after delivery, acquires the complexion of innocence like that of **Mary** (*a*), and the blossom of a smile on the lips of the wife penetrates deep in the heart of the husband to turn it into a blossomy spring. Without having to open his lips to ask, **Hajar** answered his unspoken question: ─I'm all right!" The midwife said: ─It took a long time." **Sahibah Khanum** finished: ─Hajar Khanum has a high fortitude!"

The newborn, which was wrapped in white diapers, possessed a magnetic field that when it was placed in the arms of somebody, it was difficult to separate it from them. **Murtada** was firmly holding the baby into his arms, pressing it to his chest and preventing the father from smelling it. **Nuruddin** was raising himself on his toes to kiss its cheek; the sisters were snatching it from one another. But the father, who did not want to let the throbbing of waiting break his dignity, endured the moments in which the baby was passed from hand to hand, lasting for a time. At last the wrapped baby was placed into the arms of the father. He gazed at it for a moment, and the magnetic field worked its effect on the father and forced him to bend his head to print with his lips a kiss on the baby's crimson cheek. The father's lips used to be rounded such as to suck in the soft rosy cheek, as if he, with his soul's ears, could hear the secret whispering: ─And peace be upon the day on which I was born," as when he moved his head away to see better the complexion of his child, his tongue started uttering words of adoration: ─O my son, my love, my soul, my spirit, my **Ruhullah**!"

The mother had thought that as her name was **Hajar,** her son's name must be **Ismail,** but now she realized that **Aqa Mustafa** was preferring the name of **Ruhullah.** She immediately said: —What a good name!" Thus, **Ruhullah** became the name of the newborn boy, who, on Wednesday night or on Thursday[54/1], came out of the world of the womb into the outside world.

Although we do not know quite well that at that moment whether the moon was drawing its bow in the sky, or it was the sun pouring down its light on the earth[55], yet we do know that it was the first of the month of Mehr[56], and that the earth had went round the sun in the solar year 1281 times, and 1902 years before that, there had been born a child who, with his **Masiha** breath and by **Allah's** permission, breathed life into the dead bodies and became **Ruhullah.**[57] Nineteen centuries went by and on the 24th of September, this newborn came to breathe the spirit of life in the stone age of the twentieth century. The first **Ruhullah** brought message from the invisible world, and was a Messenger of **Allah.** The second **Ruhullah** was only the reviver of the religious values, as the Message had been completed by the coming of **Muhammad (s),** and humanity needed no new religion. But whenever the believers change from petrification to such hard rocks, and whenever the dust of disbelief covers the innate dispositions, there will appear a reviver. This newborn, carried now in the hands of **Aqa Mustafa** to give it a name, was given the name of **Ruhullah,** which was a coincidence between the name and the named. The body of the human civilisation is bulky but soulless. If it is acceptable that it is **Allah** who gives names, there is no doubt that He had chosen the name of this elite newborn without any intermediation.

At that time the dates of birthdays and marriages were usually registered according to the Arabic calendar. When the pen ran into the inkpot to inscribe the name of **Ruhullah** in a copy of a manuscipt *Quran,* the moon had gone round the earth 1320 years (12 times per year) after the *Hijrah* of the Prophet (s). The day was the twentieth of the month of Jumadi ath-Thani, smiling at whatever was obvious and hidden.[58]

The Milkful Breasts of a Brave Nurse

When **Ruhullah** was in the arms of his mother to be nursed, **Agha Bigum,** who was passing through her last months of breast-nursing, during which a child seems to become more greedy for its mother's breast, was enviously gazing at her mother's breast. It was a heart-rending scene and it had to be continued for few more months. Worse than that was when it was **Agha Bigum's** turn, as she would then suck all that was in her mother's breasts, and when it was **Ruhullah**'s turn, he sucked at her breast until he got tired, but never satisfied. An idea flashed in the aunt's mind. Nurse **Khawar,** whose husband was a rifleman working for **Aqa Mustafa,** had lost her child, **Muhammad,** sometime before, and though her heart still broken, yet her breasts were full of milk. The aunt took **Ruhullah** in her arms and went to her house and said to her: ―If you nurse **Ruhullah** you will be rewarded by **Allah.**" She, who could calm down her grief by holding another baby in her arms, immediately said: ―If I did, my breasts would not see the fire of Hell." She hurried to the yard, performed the *wudu,* recited the *surah* of *Ikhlas,* and put her milkful-breast in **Ruhullah**'s mouth. Afterwards **Ruhullah** was taken to her house for few days, then she herself began to come to the house of **Aqa Mustafa** to smell **Ruhullah** and nurse him until he was satisfied. She was like a lioness with heavily nourishing milk. **Aqa Mustafa** had accepted her nursing on the condition that she may not eat at any table except at his and except the tray of food sent to her house from **Aqa Mustafa**'s house.[59]

Birthday Party
A week later two big and two smaller pots were put on the stoves built of bricks and mud. Large, dry logs were put under them and fire was made. Near the noon two large trays full of glowing live coal were put on top of the two big pots so that the rice may cook well. In one of the smaller pots the *qimah* broth was being cooked, while in the other smaller pot soup was boiling, so that the relatives, the friends and the neighbours may eat at the same time on the two celebrating occasions: the birthday party and the circumcision party. It was still hot. On Thursday noon a long *sufreh* was spread in the yard for the men, and many smaller *sufrehs* were spread in the rooms for the women. After lunch, **Ruhullah**'s cradle was placed in the shade of a tree so that he may easily be seen by the guests, without having to carry him. On that day so much kisses were poured on his rosy cheeks and slim hands that his soft, tawny skin reddened and smarted. After few days he fell severely ill. His mother vowed for his recovery. What vow? The father vowed to fast for ten days. The nurse **Khawar** vowed to cook *samanu*[60], a vow which continued for many years afterwards. It was his severest sickness. In those days there were no vaccines. So, probably till the age of ten he got several illnesses, such as chicken pox, whooping cough and measles, all of which he easily overcame. Only the mumps—which is said that if a child gambols too much it will cause him to be sterile when he is grown up—worried his mother too much. He got it when he was five. In such an age, if

the child does obey orders from his elders, he cannot obey their orders to stay in bed and give up gamboling and moving.

The Identity Card

At that time no identity card[61] was known yet. The name of a newborn was written on a piece of paper, or on the inside cover of a book, mostly on the inside cover of the *Glorious Quran*. **Ruhullah's** name was written under the name of **Nuruddin** on the inside leather cover of a MS *Quran*. When the Statistics and Registration Administration started giving out identity cards, its officials thought that they could register the birthday date provisionally. Accordingly they wrote: 1279 solar calendar, without stating day or month. However, maybe it was not so, and they, out of kindness, registered him two years older, so that the Shah's recruiting officers may not come after him.[62] He was not the only one whose identity card did not tell the truth about the date of his birthday. Many others either bribed the officials or had some sort of relation with them. So, some such cards showed their owners older. But why did **Ruhullah's** identity card show another date?

It was in 1304 when he got his identity card. His brother, who used to register everything quite strictly, said: 1305[63] and the name of the official he said to be: **Jafari Nezhad,** in Golpaygan, which, actually, was correct. But the identity card which the Islamic Republic gave to him was signed by **Ali Akbar Rahmani,** the Director General of the S.R.A. of Tehran, instead of the usual official who must have loved to have that honour. This means that if the date of his life is to be written according to the registrars of events, whatever they may register, it makes not much difference, as whatever date was written in his identity card, it did not change the history which he inscribed. Even his not going to military service had nothing to do with the date of his birthday written in his identity card, as the law had exempted the *mujtahids* from the compulsory military service.

Family Name

Family name is current ever since the time of the identity card. Before that, one was known by one's father's name, or by the name of one's birthday place, or by one's dwelling place, from which the family name was derived.[64] Some authors who had a famous work, the title of the work gave them their identity name.[65] The high ranked governmental personalities received their titles from the Shah.[66] When the name of **Sayyid Ruhullah** was entered in the identity card, **Mustafawi** was chosen to be the family name, after the name of his father, while **Aqa Nuruddin** chose his grandfather's family name, Hindi[67], for himself. **Aqa Murtada,** the elder brother, chose the name Pasandideh[68] as his family name. **Sayyid Ruhullah,** who was 23 years old at the time of registering the document, ascribed himself to **Mustafa** in order to keep the name of the martyr alive. He could hear from the lips of his father the *adhan* only for four months and twenty days, and the lines of the complexion of his father in each one of his smiles were engraved on his clear mind, and sometimes he used to creep to his father's chest and got a lip-to-lip kiss. However, before being able to say Papa to hear from him: Dear, the father stamped his last kiss on his cheek before leaving for a journey, from which he never came back, because the Khans had done too much injustice and oppression against the people, and, consequently, **Aqa Mustafa** travelled to convey the cries of the wronged people in Khomein to other parts of the country with the hope to get some solution. But on the road to Arak he was martyred, and **Ruhullah,** while still at the beginning of life, became an orphan.

Destiny's Amazing Secrets

Destiny has amazing secrets! When **Muhammad** (*s*) came, his father was gone, so that he may taste the bitterness of being an orphan, because when he becomes a prophet, numerous men should guard the gift of religion with their lives, kissing the drawn swords. They should not bind their hearts to the future of their orphan children. They knew that **the Prophet** had from the beginning to bear the torment of orphanage, and he knew better than them what being an orphan means, and knew very well how to be a father for an orphan. **Ruhullah,** who was later on to brush the dust off **Muhammad's** religion, would need thousands of men to offer their pure blood to wash off the dust from the religion, and there would remain many children who would not close their eyes, waiting for their fathers, then, in the morning they open their eyes in empty houses where they see no father, cast their eyes every-where, on empty tables and foodless plates, and wither in the fate's strange coldness, and, like the leaves dried by the merciless windstorms of time, drop on the ground. **Allah** wanted to let him be acquainted with the difficulties of orphanage, so that neither through book, narration and tales, nor with the concentration of the mind alone, which are acquired knowledge, but also with zeal, resistance and life, which are intuitive knowledge, he may learn how to behave with the orphans of tomorrow, and when he speaks of the good servants of the people, says: ―Serving in *Bunyad-e Shahid*[69] [The Martyr Foundation] is at the head of services."

From the martyrdom of his father he also inherited another token, that is: persisting on fighting oppression. This he first learnt from his father. **Aqa Murtada,** the elder brother, who later compensated for the loss of the father and bore a part of the burden on his shoulders, after eighty years said: ―As from those first days of life he used to hear with his body and heart's ears that his father was the victim of his combat with injustice.[70]‖

Then, when he travelled into the history he read nothing but that religions came to teach thousands and thousands of lessons, and before, after and through comprehending *tawhid,* which is the first and the last lesson of the Ibrahimi religions, this concept is clear that with darkness and injustice there can never be any reconciliation at all. He so absorbed this concept in himself that even late in his life, when the snows of old age cool down most of the great fighters and tend them to Sufism, he, with the same enthusiasm and eagerness of his youth, said: ―To me, place has no importance, what is important is the struggle against injustice. Wherever this struggle takes place I will be there.‖[71]

Mother's Warm Bosom

Ruhullah now is a child who finds warmth in his mother's bosom, while his father's affection is in his subconscience. **Sahibah Khanum** is an affable, sociable and brave woman who was called ‗Khahar Aqa‖, i.e. Aqa's sister. She is **Ruhullah's** aunt. **Naneh Khawar** was also a jack-of-all-trades who came to this house to help the mother and the aunt in their housework, besides nursing. No doubt that his parrotlike imitation and repetition of words, and which afterwards decided Khomein's tone of his fiery speeches and charming words, were mostly borrowed from those three. It can be said that his earliest teachers were those three. It is also undoubted that **Murtada,** who later became his formal teacher at home, had put whatever he had on the tray of sincerity, with many stories of his father's arguments with the Khans. **Ruhullah** heard from his brother that his brave aunt, in the way of avenging his father, together with all the others—except **Ruhullah** who was still in need of his mother's breasts—and **Haj Shaykh Fadlullah,** his mother's uncle, and a servant, took the difficult road to Tehran. Two months she stayed in *Shams al-Imarah* and could force **Atabak Azam**[72] to punish the murderer[73], so that the Khans of Khomein, fearing punishment, would no longer spill the blood of the wronged and those who demand their rights. Sometimes in his youth **Ruhullah,** remembering his father and grandfather of his father, under some of his writings he signed Ibn ash-Shahid‗ [son of the martyr]. Patience, which is one of the key-words of religion and faith, he learned from his aunt, not in the meaning of keeping silent in the face of ugly events, but in the meaning of forbearing the calamities, being firm and truthful in encountering the inequitable, as his first lesson in religion and politics. The history of his grandfathers from Nayshabur to Kashmir was related to him by his aunt, and the other part, to Karbala, al-Madinah and Mecca, he himself followed up, and from there up to **Ibrahim (a)** he traced his grandfather, so as to know who they were, what they did, in order to know who he was to be and what he was to do.

The First Spring

The first spring, when the trees started budding, **Ruhullah** was six months old. The aunt, the nurse and mostly the mother, used to carry him in their arms and take him for a round in the garden. Early in spring, rain and hail gave no tiding of their coming. Sometimes the glowing of the sun was lowered down by the clouds, and a few moments later lightning flashed all over the sky and the veins of thunder, with a fearful roaring, threw light on the young quivering leaves. Commonly every child is afraid of such natural phenomena, but when an arm of the mother becomes a seat and the other arm becomes the back of the seat, and the child clings fast to the mother's collar, and presses his chest to hers, the nice tune of her throbbing heart changes the fearful noise of the thunder to a nice melody. The child fears, but a fear which entails childish joy. The eyelids press together so that the eyes may see nothing, then the eyes open heavily to see what mother is doing. If a smile of contentment adorns her face, such a fear of nature becomes mirthful. The memories of this vividity inspire poetic nature and, till the end of life, scent the art of living in beauty. The fear of nature, when the child is in the arms of the mother, and the mother is fearless, causes the child to be brave. **Ruhullah** spent two such springs on his mother's bosom, getting acquainted with the nature of spring. Later on he could sit in the veranda and witness the flash of lightning in the sky, the roar of the thunder, and then the flood-like rain pouring down, witnessing and hearing the signs of **Allah**[74], and feeling the pleasure of discerning the sky's effect on the earth and the veins connecting it to existence. How does rain run into the brooks? How does the dead earth derive life from water? It seemed as if during the first three years of his life the dam in the sky had broken and flood-like rains poured down, and lightnings and thunders were happening too frequently. There were lightning and thunder more than former years, and there were thunderbolts leaving their trace on the rocks or burning a tree. Rivers were brimful, fruitful trees grew tall, but the hail whitened the earth with their blossoms. In summer the trees were flourishing, but with less fruits.

In Solitude with Nature

The shovels, thick and thin, used for turning the soil, incited tendency to play with them. One of the pointed light shovels was a playtoy for **Ruhullah**. When it was sunny he used to till the land of the garden with it. He learned how to use the shovel from a servant who, after finishing his daily work, used to fallow the land with a shovel. Seeing the worms which sometimes came out and wriggled softly on the earth caused trembling, yet they, with their quick dancing, said that life had thousands and thousands of manifestations, and that in the black color of the earth, the red color of life was going on.

Mother used to leave him to himself to wonder in the yard and be alone with nature. When the *muadhdhin,* from the minaret of the mosque, called for the noon-*salah,* mother used to look for **Ruhullah** and call him. If she heard no reply she would call again, and if the childish naughtiness wished to tease her and keep her calling with no response, she would slowly and silently tiptoe towards him, but he, a brisk deer-like child, would flee away, sometimes a shoe might slip off his foot while running away, and he would fall face down, scratching his hands and knees. Mother, like a swift hawk, would arrive on the spot, put her right arm round the boy's belly, lift him from the ground, and, with her soothing words loved by children, would change his crying into a boisterous laugh of a drunkard ringdove, and she would soak him in her caresses and fondlings up to the pool, where she would sit on its edge and wash the slim hands of her son, removing the dried mud from them, cleaning his nails, throwing water on his face and wipe off the muddy water. She would immerse his face, and then both his arms till the elbow, into the pool to have them purified. In summer time his soaked face and hands would dry before reaching the room. In the autumn, she would dry them with a clean handkerchief, the face first and then the hands. Neatly folded clothes would be brought out of a chest and he would be clothed with them after taking off his morning clothes. It seems that this was a daily procedure that cleanliness became a part and parcel of **Ruhullah**'s nature, such that till the end of his life no speck of dirt could be seen on his collar. Before meals he used to perform *wudu,* and before the *wudu* he used to thoroughly wash his hands with soap. As a matter of fact, the practice of washing his hands with soap he learnt when he moved to Qum. Formerly soap was used only in the bath. Before learning *fiqh* he knew that the *wudu* would be *batil* if done with any intention except for **Allah.** However, there may be a rationale in every precept, so, one of the recommended preludes to *wudu* is washing the hands for cleansing purpose, and cleanliness is a divine precept. Once he said: ―If there was no prohibition and if it was not difficult for the others, I would have, changed the spoon after each time I put it in my mouth." [75] However, he did observe the common manners of the table. It frequently happened that he ate only bread and yoghurt, in which case he needed no spoon. But when there was salad or yoghurt as a relish with other dishes, he certainly used different spoons and forks for them. This he learnt from his mother, as when she spread the *sufreh,* she used to place a spoon and a plate for everyone at the *sufreh.* In those days this was not so much common. In most families it was common to place a large plate in the middle of the *sufreh* and everyone used his spoon, or even his hand, to eat from that plate.

This mother had allotted a separate bed for each of her children. No one had the right to sleep in the others' beds. **Ruhullah's** mattress, like the mattresses of the other children, had a white bedsheet, which was at the end of the weak washed in the *tasht* and spread in the sun to dry. In winter time, when the rainy weather did not allow the wet clothes to be spread in the open, a rope was fastened in a room from side to side and the washed clothes were spread on it, near a kindled fire, to dry. Sometimes the clothes got the smell of the natural scent of the smoke of burning wood in the stove.

Long Hair
Up to his fourth year he had long hair in the color of early night, and casting a bluish-green color on his ear lobe. While combing his hair and twisting it a little, his mother usually borrowed a kiss from his cheek, and loved to immediately pay back her debt. Probably it was the first time that **Karbalai Hasan,** the barber, cut that hair. Afterwards, up till his tenth year of age, the barber, instead of coming to that house once every two months, began to frequent the house once every ten or fifteen days to cut the hair of the boys. **Ruhullah** was the last to have his hair cut. He did not like the barber's manual hair clipper. When it was his turn, he would run away, but they would soon catch him and seat him on the four-legged chair of the barber. The first time he had his hair cut, the barber repeatedly said: ―Excellent! Excellent!" **Ruhullah** believed that he really became handsome. **Murtada** and **Nuruddin** used to go round the barber's four-legged chair and repeat: ―Excellent! Excellent!" Then he had to go to his room so that his mirror might confirm the barber's approval. But he jumped out with a clinched fist

and knotted brows, and directed his blows to those who had appreciated him. He loved long hair. It was instinctive in him. Later, when he read in the history that **the Prophet (s),** before performing his first pilgrimage, had long, curled, ever-combed hair, starting, like a fall, from the top of his head down to his shoulders, his love for long hair doubled. But it was, and still is to some extent, a tradition that a student of theology should have his hair cut short, or even razor-shaved from the butt. Ever since he wore the students apparel, he remained committed to that tradition.

After the victory of the Revolution, one of his closest relatives, a religious man, who accompanied him in privacy and in public, and intimately sharing his secrets, wearing the theologian apparel, with short-cut hair, shorter than the hair of the non-turbaned men, used to sit near his chair, and their pictures were seen by millions of people. Between these father and son there was an intimacy, deep as faith, and clear as crystal, to the extent that, not only in his speeches, but also in his written messages and writings, he was mentioned barely as _Ahmad". Nevertheless, he never reminded him: –Son, a student must observe all the traditions of studentship, especially if he is related to me!" This is because he believed that man's existence is not all for observing traditions. The wife and the children have their rights, too. If there is a contradiction, however small, between the rights and the non-compulsory traditions, reason and Islamic law judge in favour of the rights. There is no doubt that if his son's hair—which was visible from under the turban, and which millions of people used to see it on the TV of the Islamic Republic of Iran—was, in the father's eye, against studentship, he would quite seriously have reminded him of that. Probably he intentionally did not say anything so that he might reform a public custom, especially for the young students ,starting with himself. But as regards looking after his own hair, he was so serious and punctual that they used to say: –The barber could adjust his watch on his arrival." Even in his last weeks of life he was strictly punctual.

Swimming in the Pool

It was strangely wonderful to have a nap on the veranda on a summer afternoon. A rug was spread there. The children's pillows were placed side by side in a row. **Ruhullah,** the youngest, used to have his mother's arm as a pillow, and, while lending his ears to her lullaby, he tried to follow with his eyes the colorless breeze which, thinner than a ghost, passed calmly through the leaves of the tall aspens and poplars, combing the branches. He would look at the sparrows darting from branch to branch in the hope of finding a grain, picking at the large pieces of still green pomegranates. Suddenly an untimely cock would flap its wings and crow. When the calm and soundless sleep weighed upon **Ruhullah's** eyelids the mother would stealthily draw out her arm from under her child's head, and she herself would fall asleep. In most instances mother would get up earlier, but sometimes **Ruhullah** would get up, and without waking his mother, stealthily descend the steps to watch a butterfly, spreading its wings, opening and closing them like a book, over the Muhammadan roses growing near the pool. The water in the pool would sometimes attract him to draw near the pool. More than once he had fallen into the waters of that pool, and of his splashes in the waters mother would hurriedly jump up and run worried to the pool. Probably his first lesson in swimming he learnt was in this pool. When he became a *faqih,* he so earnestly recommended learning swimming as if it were an obligatory duty. One day, when the commander of a battalion, who was teaching his divers to swim for the purpose of crossing the Arwand river under-water to capture the [Iraqi] town of Faw, he rebuked them, saying: ─With such swimming you cannot conquer Faw. You must learn swimming like **the Imam [Khomeini].**" Hearing this, his men became so enthusiastic that they could no longer feel the coldness of the water and nose-dived into the river.[76]

Vague Memoirs

Memoirs are not always clear. Sometimes one would not remember what the incident was and why it happened. Children's memoirs are mostly of this kind. **Ruhullah,** too, had much memoirs of this kind. He was two years old, playing in a room. A stout man came in, sat down and indulged in conversation. Suddenly he turned to **Ruhullah** and asked him: ─What did **Sarim Lashkar** do to deserve flogging?" Asking such a question from a child could have no reply but to put his finger into his nose. But the man gave him no time, and, while **Ruhullah** had no escape from his eyes, he gave the answer: ─He had taken a morsel bigger than his mouth, so we flogged him." Well, what did **Ruhullah** understand from this? As a matter of fact, why did the man address him with those words? Who was he? Why did he address him so flatly? Maybe he spoke of someone to warn someone else. This can be neglected. But if one persists on knowing the reason behind everything, perhaps this meaningless show was to make **Ruhullah** think about this memoir and those words many times so that he himself may reach the conclusion that one's mouth is for big talk, not for big morsels. After the demise of **the Imam Khomeini,** out of thousands of worthier speeches, the story of this conversation came to the tongue of **Ayatullah Pasandideh.** The story went like this: **Sultan Khanum, Ruhullah''s** youngest aunt, married **Karim Khan Qalehi.** His name was **Karim** and his family name was **Khan Qalei,** as actually he was a Khan and his house was in a large *Qalah.* The fruits of this marriage were two boys and two girls. One of the boys, **Yahya,** went to Tehran and became a teacher of calligraphy. The other son had a name, a family name and a lengthy story: **Imamquli Khan Sarim Lashkar Biglar Bigi,** who had become one of the famous Khans of Khomein with riflemen, married the sister of **Jalal Lashkar,** another one of the Khans of Khomein. This marriage was fruitless. There was a dispute between his wife and her brothers on their father's heritage. **Imamquli** backed his wife and the conflict increased, and the riflemen of the two parties stood on alert facing each other. **Imamquli,** who was **Ruhullah''s** cousin, had his father's fort, which was a strong one. His wife's brother occupied the tower and the rampart of the house in which **Ruhullah** was living. At last, the force of the other side weighed more, and he was caught, tied to a tree in the yard of the house and was given a sound beating. **Ruhullah** had not seen that beating. Now he got its spark to know its story. **Imamquli,** with his riflemen and horsemen, moved to Kerman in order to live beside that district's governor, **Amir Mufakhkham.**[77] But he soon regretted that. On his way back to Khomein, near Nain, in an orchard of pomegranate, he died. It became known that the one who had addressed **Ruhullah,** was the brother of **Imamquli''s** wife, and who backbited a dead man, and by doing so he was praising himself, as it seemed that **Imamquli Sarim Laskar Biglar Bigi** was a warrior, a grandchild of the well-known **Abbas Mirza**, who had inherited fearlessness from his grandfather, but his Khanist inclination brought him up as a bully.

He had composed a poem, as ugly as his own character, in praising him:
If it hears the name of Biglar Bigi,
The mountain of Alborz becomes (flat) like a saucer.

Witnessing the First Power-Struggle

These tower and rampart are history themselves. A short time after this event, a man from Isfahan, by the name of **Nur Muhammad Khan,** was appointed by the governor of Golpaygan as ruler of Khomein. He leased the *andaruni* as the Government Office. **Haji Muhammad Aqa,** one of Khomein's rich men, let his house in the next lane to the ruler to station his riflemen there as a base. Another Isfahani man, by the name of **Sayyid Muhammad Sadr,** was appointed by the Government, as the head of the Justice Office. He, too, hired a number of the rooms in this house to be used as the court. He had a servant, a guard and a rifleman. **Ruhullah's** family transferred the furniture to the *biruni*. The *andaruni* and the rooms under the tower were handed over to the ruler and the judge.

Husayn Khan Qareh Kahrizi, a relative of **Shukrullah Khan,** the first husband of **Sahibah Khanum,** called one day on the ruler. We do not know what happened between them that the ruler ordered him to be imprisoned. However, **Husayn Khan** was the Khan of two villages, and it seems that he was an illiterate and unruly person. When they tied his feet to a *Khalili*[78] in order to jail him in a room under the tower, he told the boys to tell somebody to come and release him. **Sahibah Khanum,** who knew that it was an endless story and that it would cause disorder in the house, sent to the ruler to release the Khan, but the ruler, who could not estimate the force under his rule, nor the power of the Khans, did not comply with her demand.

One night, probably after midnight, many footsteps successively descended such that they wakened up the people of the house. **Murtada** peeped out and saw a number of riflemen standing in the corridor. Other riflemen were ascending a ladder to descend on the other side of the wall one after the other. A moment later there was knocking on the door of the *biruni*. **Nasr Abdul Hamad,** a servant at the house, went to the door. They said: ─Open the door; we want to ascend to the tower." **Nasr** said: ─There is no way to the tower from the *biruni*." They said: ─We know there is." Afraid, he opened the door. Armed men crossed the orchard, passed the pool, and occupied the towers. **Alijan Khan, Husayn Khan's** brother, ordered his men to shoot. The sound of the shooting broke the silence of the night in the whole town. The Qareh Surans (the gendarmes)[79], down the tower and the rebel riflemen in the towers, stood facing each other. The ruler brought out his rifle from the closet with a shaking hand, but he did not come out of his room. The rebels went to the small room under the tower, untied **Husayn Khan,** who cursed the ruler with bad words and ran away. But the rebels were not satisfied with the release of **Husayn Khan.** They demanded the ruler's blood. **Alijan Khan** told **Sahibah Khanum:** ─Surrender the ruler to us." She asked him to stop the shooting.

When the fingers were raised from the triggers, the aunt took **Murtada** by his hand and went to the ruler's room and told him to come out. The ruler, who used to address her as the children did, said: ─O aunt, they will kill me." The aunt said: ─As long as we are here they will not kill you." Then she continued: ─I told you. If one cannot do something one must not do it. Didn't I tell you to free **Husayn Khan,** why didn't you release him?" The ruler seized **Murtada's** hand and said: ─I won't let you take him. As long as he is here they dare not kill me." She snatched his hand from him, and he had but to leave the room. He had left the rifle and held a copy of the *Quran* in his hand. **Alijan Khan** took him to the yard, tied his hands and ordered the horses to be brought out of the stable, and to plunder his belongings. The plunderers said to **Ruhullah"s** family: ─Show out whatever is yours out of the properties." The aunt pointed to a room rented to **Aqa Sayyid Muhammad Sadr.** They did not approach it. When they took the ruler, with his hands tied up, to Qareh Kahriz, the same village in which the husband of **Sahibah Khanum** was defeated by the government's forces, he felt less afraid and started crying: ─You must surrender!"

This was the first serious show of power-struggle which **Ruhullah** witnessed in his childhood: A show of which no part was rightful.[80]

Tales in Snowy Nights

In winters, the season of coldness and snow, playing in the open nature becomes less frequent, and the *kursi* takes the place of the yard in occupying the thought. Sometimes the mother would enliven the stories of the ancient, local stories or the famous Iranian tales, such as the heroes of the Shahnameh or the tale of **Amir Arsalan.** The sweetest of all were the true historical biographies of the prophets, nevermind how many times you hear them. After lunch and dinner the children would relax under the *kursi* and stretch their legs, as the cover of the *kursi* would conceal the unbecoming stretching of one's legs at the presence of the elders. The cold of the yard outside and the warmth of the *kursi* inside, together with the luxury of relaxation joined to make the true stories of the men of truthfulness more interesting. Sometimes the aunt and sometimes the mother were the narrators of stories, causing the children to be absorbed in their visions. Which prophet's story was more interesting to **Ruhullah?** Nobody could discover this secret. But if we believe that everything everywhere in the world leaves its trace, then we may refer to his poetry, where there are words which come up from the subconscience. There is no personal interest in poetry, and one feels freer in constructing a line of poetry than in building a room to sleep in it. Later on, we will have a look at his collection of poems where his beloved ones have a better presence and can be seen quite naked.

The Bitter Event of the Father"s Martyrdom

Some stories worth being listened to only once. Some memoirs worth being listened to by the children all the time. The aunt had repeatedly related the bitter story of the father's martyrdom, and yet he used to prick his ears to listen to it once more. Hearing it was sweet and believing in it was bitter. Perhaps when he was three or four years old, and the story which was repeated during the long, cold winter nights, he used to hear it, first sitting, then leaning on a pillow, then when the story reached its end, the pillow was rolled away and he stretched on his back, staring at the beams of the ceiling so that the narrator might not detect his tears. Every time there was a new point, that is, he used to pick up a new point. **Aqa Murtada,** too, had heard it tens of times, and after eighty years he related it like this:

—Our father used to stand in the face of injustice very seriously. In those days the Khans and the princes were very influential. They had rifles and weapons. They were oppressors. They pressed upon the ruler and the ruler pressed upon the people. Whoever had some influence used it. Our father fought against those despots, murderers and transgressors and prevented them from aggression. Once they arrested **Haji Qanbar Ali,** our father's servant, but our father resisted and could, by force, release him, and then he raised a complaint against the criminals. Later, when the complaints increased by the people, **Hishmatuddawlah** arrested **Bahram Khan** and put him in prison, where he died after a while."

We do not know, on hearing these sentences, how did he praise his father's zeal and magnanimity. But we do know that when he heard that **Bahram Khan** died in the prison, his delicate heart regretted the destiny of that man. Probably the aunt observed that, and when she wanted to repeat the said story with the same enthusiasm, she would quickly pass over the death of **Bahram Khan.** This story acquired, each time, a new dimension, and every dimension had a new beginning and end. **Aqa Murtada** had heard it tens of times before **Ruhullah,** and tens of times when it was addressed to **Ruhullah.** In an interview **Aqa Murtada** related his impression of that. Probably if **Ruhullah** himself had related it in details, the story would have been registered differently in history. At any rate, **Ayatullah Pasandideh,** joining together what he had heard, related the continuation of his impression and said: —After that incident the Khans decided to make trouble, and our father continued preventing it. That which encouraged them was their relationship with **Sadr al-ulama.**[81] **Abbas Khan** and the late **Mirza Abdul Husayn) Ruhullah"s** maternal uncle), and **Haji Sayyid Aqa Nazim at-Tujjar** were the sons-in-law of the late **Sadr al-ulama.** So, **Jafar Quli Khan,** the killer of our father, and **Rida Quli Sultan,** father and uncle of **Abbas Khan,** were relatives. **Wakil ar-Raaya** and **Nazim ar-Raaya** were also their relatives. Therefore, those Khans, at whose head were **Bahram Khan, Rida Quli Sultan** and **Jafar Khan,** had only a single claimant, the late **Aqa Mustafa,** our father, whom they wanted to do away with. They knew if they did it we can do nothing, as I and my other brother, **Aqa Nuruddin,** were no more than seven and eight years old, and **Aqa Khomeini (Ruhullah)** was only three or four months old. The women could, of course, do nothing, too. Other *ulama,* such as the late **Akhund Mulla Ahmad,** who, though not their relative, was too cautious and showed no disagreement. Therefore there was nobody to do anything, and by removing **Aqa Mustafa** from the way, they could easily transgress and oppress the people."

No doubt the names mentioned in this story did not go beyond the limits of Khomein's geographical region, and that similar persons in other towns used to appear and disappear. How much did **Ruhullah** like to commit their names to his memory? I think as much as we are not interested to do so, though the names were not so much worthy of remembering, they spoke of incidents deserved to be contemplated. In his childish mind injustice and fighting it, care and carelessness, despotism and fighting it, Khan and Khanism, security and insecurity, were obscure concepts revolving in his indeterminate mind. Later, these concepts were defined from within the religious beliefs. They were the primary materials for the construction of a political thought based on religion.

The part of the story of the father's martyrdom which referred to the way the conflict started, was completely regarded a domestic affair, hence it was quite interesting to the children of the house to hear. If it is to be retold after ninety years it will not be so interesting, because anyone everywhere may have seen, or even heard, thousands of more exciting events. But when **Ruhullah** has his home in the hearts of millions of people, everybody feels him in the treasure of his own heart and likes to hear, or likes, by hearing it, to think he is following destiny of one of his close relatives, and thus he feels excited or tears run down his cheeks.

We do not know the story telling method followed by **Sahibah Khanum** at the snowy nights of winter, but the contents on the tongue of **Aqa Murtada,** with his modifications, were as follow:

Adud as-Sultan was the governor of Sultan Abad, which covered Arak, Khomein, Golpaygan, Khansar and every nearby villages and hamlets. At that time the Shah of Iran was **Muzaffaruddin.** He had a stout figure and a strong stature, yet poor in health and so coward that whenever he remembered the murder of his father at the hands of **Mirza Rida Kirmani,** he was very much terrified. He was so coward that when he came to Tehran to be crowned as a Shah, which he so much desired for many years, he, afraid of being assassinated, neglected the preparations made in Yaftabad of

Tehran, and humbly asked the commander of the cossak's quarter, by the name **Colonel Caskovsky,** who came to give his report about Tehran's security situation[82], to take him to the Royal Palace. Those who were there and heard this realized that the man who had come to manage the country's affairs was an incompetent good-for-nothing person. On the very first days he spent the reserve fund and got a loan from the Russian Bank, admitting the receipt with his own handwriting, but he could not settle it in time, causing the objection of Petersburg Bank and the Russian Embassy in Tehran.[83] He had TB, and the physicians, who were incapable of curing him, prescribed to give him mineral water, so he went camping wherever there was mineral water spring. The most important problem of the government was the mineral water. When no spring of mineral water in the country could cure the king, the flatterers recommended foreign springs so that they may see the West in his company, and he, unaware of what was going on around him, visited Europe three times, and in each time he borrowed a large sum of money from the foreigners. Those who thought that the king is Allah's Shadow on the Earth had no objection and the parasitic flatterers who used to make profit out of the king's extravagances, though they knew that mineral water drinking of the Shah in Europe meant Europe's drinking the blood of the Iranian people, they did not decline this situation. The poor health of the Shah actually pleased the retinue, because they did not have to be questioned by any person. The healthy might of the government turned into an invalid might due to the Shah's invalidity. Consequently, the local retinue became mightier, and the Khans not merely participated, but also interfered in the government's affairs. Those who could afford it employed riflemen and plundered the peasants as much as they could.[84] In such circumstances the responsibility of the men of religion was grave. They were the refuge for the people. But it is much regretted that many of them were so absorbed in their studies and researches that they completely forgot what for they had come to study religion. Nevertheless, on the other side the news of the world's changes and progresses sporadically were arriving, and the Shah's invalidity and incapability caused some sharp-sighted, enlightened and freedom-loving religious authorities to come together and think about changing the government. But before attaining to this aim, the lands of the common people were usurped. The unharnessed retinue imposed taxes, and the Khans threw their hooks into the muddy waters of the situation. Probably the situation of insecurity in Khomein was worse than the other surrounding towns and regions, such that **Aqa Mustafa** had but to decide to have a meeting with

Adud as-Sultan, the governor of Arak so as to find a way out of that state of affairs.

The Martyrdom of Aqa Mustafa

When he decided to go, two persons offered to accompany him. One was **Jafar Quli Khan** who, apparently, intended to get a post from **Adudus-Sultan.** The other one was **Rida Quli Sultan,** who had, too, the desire to become a governmental official. The daughter of **Sadr al-ulama**, the wife of one of them[85], hurridly came to see **Aqa Mustafa** to disclose to him her secret. How could she know that these two intended to kill him? Perhaps the plan had been discussed in her house. Anyhow, when **the Aqa** realized why they offered to accompany him, said: ―There is no need for you to come with me. I will ask for each of you a post." He knew that the roads were not safe, and those two would make it worse. He took with him a number of the riflemen. His sister's son, **Imamquli,** also brought a number of his riflemen. **Karbalai Mirza** and **Karbalai Muhammad Taqi,** who were servants at the house, prepared themselves for the journey. **Sarim Lashkar,** his other sister's son, came, too. He, together with 10 to 15 riflemen and horsemen set out. It was a two-day's journey to Arak. They performed the morning **salah** in Khomein, and till the night they galloped along the dusty road between the two towns. They spent the night in a caravanseray. After midnight they recited *Kumayl dua*, and went to sleep.

What purity one's last supplication has! When death decides to come its smell fills the nostrils, everything speaks of its coming, and worry tells the relatives about it. But when martyrdom opens its wings it diffuses light over the visage, and one's talk plays the tune of departure, in one's eyes truthfulness shines like a pearl, and the desire to stay decreases to such an extent that before parting company with this world, one becomes restless.

The day, Friday, the 12th of Dhul-Qadah of the year 1320, was waiting to register itself in a corner of history in the name of **Aqa Mustafa. The Aqa** resumed the journey. Impatience gave no respite to have the companions get ready. **Karbalai Mirza** and **Karbalai Muhammad Taqi** immediately came in line with him. The sisters' sons and the riflemen were delayed in preparing themselves so that they may not delay the fate. At one *farsakh* from Hasanabad they reached a water reservoir. They went in to pour water on the thirst of galloping. Death, which was galloping behind, arrived riding two horses. **Jafar Quli Khan** and **Rida Quli Sultan,** pulled the reins of their horses before **Aqa Mustafa,** greeted him. **Aqa Mustafa** calmly said: ―Didn't we agree you should not come?" The answer was: ―We could not bear your separation." They brought out bonbons from their bag and offered it to him. Good manner custom required him to have some of it, and martyrdom said, too: —Sweeten your mouth with sweets." Suddenly one of them snatched the rifle off **Karbalai**'s shoulder, so that when they aim at **the Aqa**'s heart no other rifle may aim at them. The whistle of two shots pierced the ears. One shot went through the cloak and pierced the pages of the small *Quran* in **Aqa**'s pocket and settled in the heart. The cries of those two **Karbalai**'s burst out of their windpipes and up the mountain and echoed through the valley. When he fell off the hourse, two men flew away and two men put handkerchiefs on the heart gushing with warm blood. The riflemen came, but, alas! Their coming was to no avail. They had not the face to return to Khomein. They sent somebody to the town with the news. The horse, which an hour before was taking his orders from a man firmly sitting on its back, is now carrying his lifeless body. A messenger hurried to give the news to the people of Sultanabad (Arak). A great number of people came. **Mutamadus-Sadat,** the great religious authority of Arak came in front of them, loosening a turn of his turban and throwing it on his shoulder, as a sign of mourning. When he neared the body, he took off his sandals and with bare feet lifted the body from the horse and let the people carry it on their shoulders. The hands, like waves, took the body to the cemetery of Arak, washed, shrouded, performed the *salah* over it and buried it as a deposit in the private graveyard of **Haji Muhsin,** so that it can later be transfered to Najaf to be finally burried near his **Imam Ali (a)** and next to his father's grave.

The Reaction of Aqa Mustafa"s Martyrdom

The people of Arak announced general suspension of work. In Tehran, Najm al-Waiz in, the famous preacher, in a mourning meeting, spoke of the people's ordeals which the demised had in his heart, but destiny did not want him to relate them to the governor. The orator disclosed those ordeals to the people of Tehran so that they might know what was going on in the small towns. Mourning meetings were held every day for forty days in Isfahan, Golpaygan and Khansar. But Khomein, his birthplace, had a different condition. The youths were hitting on their heads and the old men on their chests. The women, carrying their children, run to the **Aqa**'s house. Business and works stopped. The houses were not a place to stay in. The men wore the black and went to the mosques for mourning. All were tired in the days because of not sleeping at nights. The house of the **Aqa** became a house of sorrow. **Hajar Khanum** had a lump in her throat not yet burst, she used to rest her head against the pillar of the veranda and weep in her inside.

Sometimes large drops of tear would run down her cheeks onto **Ruhullah's** face who was sucking at her breast. **Nuruddin** would hide himself in a corner of the orchard to cry, uninterrupted, over his father's death. The girls ran here and there all day long and did not have any rest till after midnight. The people, enraged and furious, assaulted the houses of the two murderers and with their torches set fire on them. **Murtada** went up the tower's roof to weep in solitude over the father's departure. From there he saw the fires eating the two houses of the murderers, and the smoke which filled the town's air.

As a young boy, when his tender soul used to hear this part of the story, a strange sorrowful veil would cover **Ruhullah's** soul, reflecting its traces on his features. At the beginning natural disposition proved to him the dishonesty of that act. Later on, when he went deep into religion he realized that retaliation was right, as the *Quran* says: **─And there is life for you in retaliation, O men of acumen, that you may practice *taqwa*."**[86] But setting fire on the house of a murderer, was it in religion, too? Were the *ulama* not there to frighten the people of **Allah's** Fire? What happened to the people's religious bringing up? Weren't they hitting on their heads for the town's religious man by way of guarding the religion? So, what happened to them to forget **Allah's** command and let anger overcome them? This question never quitted him. Along the uprising he vigilantly was watchful lest the revolutionary wrath may get the better of the people's reason, and, **Allah** forbid!, the houses of those who had for so many years taken the innocent people to be tortured or caused the blood of so many people to be unlawfully spilt, may be plundered or burnt by the fire of the people's anger. When the Revolution was victorious, he knew by experience that the people's understanding of religion was not on the same level. Perhaps some of them may exceed the limits. So, with the same resolution with which he used to say: ─The Shah must go!" he issued his orders that no one should avenge oneself on anybody, no house should be set on fire and no plunder should take place. Should anybody appear to be criminal, he must be arrested, but no harm should befall his wife and children.

The Fate of the Killers

What about the killers? Escaped? Where to? In Khomein there was no hiding place for them. They took refuge in a village in Aligudarz. They knocked at the door of **Said Khan.** But he refused to let them in. Why there? Questioning was no longer possible. Waiting for the door of the house of **Khan Baba,** another Khan, to open was to no avail. **Iynullah Khan,** too, did not open his door to them. They hurried to Khansar. They thought that the great *mujtahid* of the town, **Haji Mirza Muhammad Mahdi Khansari,** who was not on good terms with the government, and who had many riflemen at his service, would agree to give them refuge, but he refused them. They took the road to Khomein and took refuge in their own fortress in Imamzadeh Bujan, two *farsakhs* away from the town, and stayed there waiting for their fate with bewilderment. At times they were biting the finger of repentance, perplexed at the ugly play of time which splashed them with black color of a shameful murder, such that even their own colleagues would refrain from answering their greetings.

Aminus-Sultan[87], the Premier, in order to preserve the government's prestige, issued his order to **Sardar Hishmat** to immediately arrest the killers. **Shams al-ulama**, who was a relative to **Hajar Khanum,** offered his house to be a base for the riflemen. The distance between the Imamzadeh and the fort is two hundred metres. It is a large fortress whose ruins are still there. It had a gate, a tower and a rampart, overlooking the Imamzadeh. Shots were fired from the fortress, but no one was hurt. They intentionally did not aim at anybody, but they shot at the furniture of the army, maybe trying to tell them that their shots could not miss. They took care not to let anybody get near their place. Many days passed. It was strange that to arrest two persons a regiment could do nothing. **Sardar Hishmat,** which perhaps was a nickname given to **Nusratullah Mirza,** ordered to dig a tunnel from the Imamzadeh to the fortress. When the tunnel was ready, their bullets finished, too. The riflemen entered the fort through the tunnel and up by ladders. **Rida Quli Khan** was dead, but a woman had taken refuge there. **Jafar Quli Khan** and the woman were arrested and their feet were chained and they were transferred to Tehran.[88] There nobody questioned them, or they did not answer questions.

The Minister of Privacy[89] supported the killer. As the crime was proved, he said: "Let bygones be bygone. Do not kill the killer." The leader of the Friday *salah* of Tehran, **Sayyid Abul-Qasim** and his two brothers, **Zahir al-Islam** and **Sayyid Muhammad,** backed by the *ulama* of Arak, insisted on punishing the convict, exerting their pressure over the Prime Minister. The Minister of the Court planned that when the mourning groups from Tabriz come to Tehran, he would assist them to break into the prison and let the killer run away, but the chancellor moved the prisoner to the Big Prison of the city, to prevent his escape.

Adab' [literature] was a literary and political newspaper. The price of each copy—called *numreh*—was three *Abbasis*. It was directed by **Adib al-**

Mamalik. This story was published in that newspaper, briefly, by **Majd al-Islam Kermani,** in a literary style, in the tenth of Rabi al-Awwal, 1323. At that time **Ruhullah** was less than three years old. Later, when he learnt to read, this paper must have been among the first papers, if not the very first, which he read, taking it out of his brother's kept documents.

Stories on the Tongues of the Brothers

The story of how the convict was punished did not worth so much hearing, rather it was shocking, except the part of the story concerning the fall in the prices of bread and meat.[90] But as regards the sightly views in Tehran, particularly the Smoking Engine whose horse was made of iron and which ate, instead of hay and lucerne, coal and fuel oil, and the noisy open and hidden talks in the Capital concerning constitutionalism and tens of other stories, they ran on the tongues of the three: the aunt, **Aqa Murtada** and **Aqa Nuruddin,** and attracted **Ruhullah,** who had seen nowhere except Khomein and its surroundings, as stories deserving hearing. Probably it was the **Aqa Murtada**'s eagerness which prompted him to relate the story to which the aunt and **Nuruddin** added their comments and explanations. When the story reached their coming to Tehran, **Aqa Murtada**'s description of punishing the killer was like this:

In the year 1321 A.H. we travelled to Sultanabad (Arak) to implore for justice concerning our father's murder. Our way passed through the village of Geily. The head of the regiments in Geily was **Badi al-Mulk.** All the people were sitting on the ground and **Badi al-Mulk** was sitting on a chair. We talked to him about our father's murder. Then we went to Arak, where the young prince, **Adud al-Mulk,** was the government's responsible man. We presented our complaint to him.

Then it was decided to follow up the case in Tehran. We were invited to the house of **Muhammad Husayn Khan,** where **Imamquli Khan,** our cousin, was living at that time. **Hishmatuddawlah,** or **Abdullah Mirza,** ordered the purchase of *qabas* and turbans for me and for my brother, **Nuruddin,** who was then seven years old. So, we became turbaned. The *qabas* were of worsted serge, bought at 11 Tumans a yard. After changing our apparels we, in the month of Safar, 1323 A.H., set out to Tehran, accompanied by my younger brother, **Nuruddin,** my elder sister, **Aunt Sahibah Khanum,** our mother **Hajiyah Agha**, our stepmother **Shazdeh Agha**, our mother's uncle, **Shaykh Fadlullah Rajai** and our servant, **Abbasquli Abarqui.**

The women and the young children rode in a coach, and the men rode their horses, mules and jades. It was ten days to Tehran. We stayed one night in Mahallat, one or two nights in Qum.[91]

We hired a house in AbbasAbad, wherefrom we took our complaint to the members of the court, to **Aynuddawlah**[92] and others. One day we even visited the *Imam Jumah,* the late **Haj Mirza Abul-Qasim.**[93] Our servant was with us, and the noted[94] **Dr. Imami,** son of **Haj Mirza Abul-Qasim,** was there, too, as old as myself. A woman was sitting on a chair there, and she seemed to be of the household. We talked a lot there. The late *Imam Jumah* and his brothers helped so much. **Najm al-Waizin,** too, in the mourning meetings (as we were in the months Muharram and Safar) talked about the martyrdom of our father, and the people were on our side. Only a single person, the Minister of the Court of **Muzaffaruddin Shah,** contradicted punishing the killer, and with his Turkish accent used to say: "The bygones are bygone. This is not to be killed." His title was **Amir Bahadur Jang** [The Valiant Prince of War], whose brother, named **Bahaduri,** acted, afterwards, as a communicator between **Muhammad Rida Shah** and the late **Shariatmadari.** At any rate, **Amir Bahadur Jang** could do nothing and was not successful in carrying out his plan and release the killer from prison.[95]

After settling in Tehran, we called on **Aynuddawlah,** the Prime Minister. When we advanced, **Aynuddawlah** ordered his men, who were some ten persons, to retreat. He was wearing a *qaba* and had a thick mustache. I went forth and held his *qaba.* They had strictly told me what to do. I allusively said to him: "If you are equitable, we are not. Hand the killer over to us." He said: "No, I'll kill the killer. But **Muzaffaruddin Shah** has issued his order that even the killer of his father, **Nasiruddin Shah,** may not be killed in the two months of Muharram and Safar. We, too, will not kill in these two months. After that if we did not kill, you can question us." We said: "Before killing the killer we will not leave this building and we will take sanctuary here." He said: "Very well, stay. My feet are aching. If you had accepted my words you would not have kept me standing here." He called **Zahir al-Islam,** and pointed to a building and said: "These sisters stay here until the killer is punished." **Zahir al-Islam** was a man of 40 with a yellow beard. He could convince **Sayyid Fadlullah,** our mother's uncle, and **Sayyid Muhammad Kamarei,** who had come with us, to return to our house which we had rented from a dervish.

In that year **Aynuddawlah** and **Muzaffaruddin Shah** travelled to Europe. **Muhammad Ali Mirza,** the Crown Prince came from Tabriz to Tehran in order to run the country during the Shah's absence. **Mushir as-**

Saltanah undertook the obligations of **Aynuddawlah. Mushir as-Saltanah** was a dervish and a *faqih*. To follow up the case we went to **Mushir as-Saltanah.** In the garden of his house they placed sofas instead of chairs. **Mushir as-Saltanah** took me in his arms and seated me on his knees and showed respect. He said: ─The order to kill the killer has been issued. I'll kill him."

After that, in order to meet **Muhammad Ali Mirza,** we went to Gulestan Building, in Nasir Khosrow St., known as Shamsul Imarah. We entered Shamsul Imarah through the corridor. On our left hand we ascended the stairs to another long corridor upstairs. The rooms on the right were for the ministers and the heads of the departments. At the end of the corridor there was a room to which we went and sat there. After a short time somebody came and said: ─His Highness **Muhammad Ali Mirza** says: Let **Aqa Murtada** and **Aqa Nuruddin** come as I want to see them." He had ordered that we should go to him alone. Both of us, with our religious dressess, entered Gulestan garden. There was a large square pool. We went past it and reached a swimming pool. We passed it to a wide square surrounded by trees. **Muhammad Ali Mirza** was standing there. We proceeded. Seeing us he said: ─You return." We returned once again to the corridor of Shamsul Imarah.

Jafar Quli Khan, chained by the neck, was brought in and seated there. He was an old fat man. He was swearing: ─I did not kill. They are lying let me go!" But he had already been convicted.

On the 4th of Rabial-Awwal, 1323 A.H. he was taken to Baharistan square[96] to be executed. I and my brother were sent home, since we were too young and might be distressed. The others went to the square.

According to the tradition current then, the killer, the Executioner and the Shah (the Crown Prince), present at the square, wore red dresses. **Jafar Quli Khan** was beheaded, and the Executioner took the head to the bazaar to show it to the shopkeepers and get tips from them. The convict's properties were confiscated.

A few days after the execution, our group hired a coach for returning to Khomein. After covering a part of the distance, the coach began rattling and jolting on the unpaved road. It was hurting. We got down. The coachmen were Zoroastrians. They refunded a portion of our money, and we returned to Tehran. Some time later we hired another means and returned to Khomein.[97]"

When the caravan returned to Khomein, there were talks concerning the confiscated properties of the two killers, whether they belong to their heirs or not. If they have right to them, **Ruhullah's** family will have no right to touch them, and if the heirs have no right, still it is more approved by Allah to return them to the heirs, because their children have become both fatherless and disgraced, and if they have to fight poverty, too, they will face humiliation. The religious verdict was that their lawful properties belong to their legal heirs. Therefore, a petition was arranged, signed by the mature members of the family, and also by **Sayyid Muhammad Kamarei** and **Najm al-Waizin,** as witnesses, to transfer all the properties of the killers to their inheritors. Fortunately, it happened as was planned.

The Two Brothers in the Attire of Ruhani

When the two brothers returned from Tehran, **Ruhullah** was passing through the last months of his second year, and was looking at his two brothers with consternation and amazement, because of the black turbans they put on their heads. At the beginning he recoiled from them as strangers, but after one or two days he started to put their turbans on his own head, and in many instances he unfolded them. At last the mother had but to order a turban for him, too. Sometimes he put his turban on his head and imitated the preachers of the town uttering words understandable only to him, then, after finishing his oration he would put his face forward for his mother and aunt to kiss.

The brothers, who had been turbaned by **Hishmatuddawlah,** had now to start taking lessons. Formerly they had learnt oral reciting of the *Quran* and reading and writing at the school of **Mulla Abul-Qasim. Murtada** was ten years old, and **Nuruddin** was eight. **Aqa Mirza Mahmud, Iftikhar al-ulama,** was invited as a private teacher in order to teach them the preliminaries. The teaching sessions were usually held in the room of the tower, and sometimes in the hallways. **Ruhullah** used to climb up the stairs slowly and sit beside his two brothers, disturbing their attention at times, causing **Aqa Mirza** to scold him to calm him down, after which he would magnanimously and sullenly descend the difficult and numerous steps of the tower. Three years later, the teacher-student relation was established among them, and **Aqa Mirza,** in the eyes of **Ruhullah,** was a respectable teacher, and **Ruhullah,** in the eyes of **Aqa Mirza,** was a polite and clever student. As a matter of fact, the title of **Iftikhar al-ulama** [The Pride of the Scholars] was just a title with no evidence in him, as his little literacy was obvious even to the children. On the other side, his mother was a well-learned woman. The two brothers used to call him by **Aqa Mirza,** while they called his mother by _Akhund_, because when **Iftikhar al-ulama** used to go to Isfahan to receive the salary alloted to them by the Court, his mother used to come to teach the children astronomy, astrology and arithmetic.[98] To know these subjects, at that time, even at the level of just being acquainted with them, let alone being able to teach them, was a sign of being a learned man, since they were masculine sciences. Probably **Ruhullah** had learnt something from this learned woman.

On the Saddles of Swift Horses

At those times the children had few playthings, so they busied themselves with anything. Sometimes they climbed the trees, sometimes they rode sticks as horses and asses, galloping into the lanes, themselves neighing like horses. But **Ruhullah** had the chance to ride a living swift horse. **Naneh Khawar,** who had helped his mother in nursing him with her milk, could ride a horse very well. She used to put her feet in the stirrup like as if she was ascending the steps. The reins so artistically moved in her hands that the most restive horse would become tame. She even shot while riding and she hit the target. She had learnt shooting and riding from her husband, **Karbalai Mirza,** the rifleman of the martyr **Aqa Mustafa**. She was even cleverer than her husband who vied her. Now, this woman was **Ruhullah"s** mother by wet-nursing him. She lived near **Ruhullah"s** house. Sometimes she would bring a horse, and hold **Ruhullah** in her arms to teach him the secrets of horsemanship. Later on, when he could alone pull the reins by his small hands, she realized how proudly he uses the stirrup. But when she would deposit the reins in the hands of his playmates, so that they, too, may not be deprived of this exciting amusement, the feeling of pride, which is stirred in the rider, immediately collapses, and **Ruhullah** returns to the child he was an hour before. She had taught him to mount proudly and to dismount humbly.

Butterfly in the Cocoon

Developing silk worm was a good play. A small box and a quantity of silk worm eggs were the primary requirements. Collecting berry leaves, replacing the dried leaves or the half-eaten leaves, with fresh leaves got the children busy. When the worms started spinning the cocoons, to sit hours watching how the spinning was done, was the best way for spending leisure time. From the time the worm enters the cocoon and some time later comes out as a butterfly constituted a complete cycle of the life from egg to egg watched by the children. While the worms were still in the cocoon, the berries ripened. The boys used to climb up the thick branches of the berry trees which cast their shades on many lanes where they were planted for charity. During the World War I[99] there appeared in Khomein an epidemic disease, and it was said that whoever ate berry would die quicker. After that few hands digged a hole to plant a berry tree, and few offered to prune the branches. Consequently, playing with the silk worms became rare.

Well-Pigeons

Information about births and begettings are presented, in our country, in forms motivating chastity. The copulation of the silk butterflies was the first sexual discovery which was not far from chastity and did not seem to be exciting. Keeping a number of chickens, feeding them and collecting their eggs were a good and common play, teaching economy and answering questions about births and begettings quite openly. Knowing about the conditions of time, at the town and at the house in which he was born, helps one to guess that he, too, practised such amusements. But when he was older he had better entertainments. Sometimes he would put some grains of millet, wheat or barley in a small bag and go, either alone or with some of his mates, to the farm where there was a **Kaftar Khan.** [100] It is believed that the farm belonged to his maternal aunt and was situated a little away from his house, near the river. It took its water from the river, and, in the hot sun of July, through the craggy lands, there appeared the snow-white cotton exposed on the stalks. This craggy land of ten hectares was fertilized by the manures from the pigeon-tower. At that time, instead of the immethodical usage of the chemical fertilizers, which turn the soft earth into stones, they used animal dung, which turned the craggy land into a fertile plantation. **Kaftar Khan** was a mechanical fertilizer factory, with a technique as simple as the soul of a peasant, and a product as plentiful as that of a big complicated factory, and meeting a large part of the need for animal fertilizers. A round wall, or four flat walls, made a tower of three to twelve metres, high with an area, according to need, varied from ten to three hundred square metres. They used its earth to make mud and mould bricks, putting brick on brick with hundreds or thousands of holes with some 30 cms in between. After a while each hole became the bridal chamber for a couple of well-pigeons. These well-pigeons preferred these safe nests to the well itself. Out of the yellow wheat stacks and the pine needle leaves they built a nest for their eggs. The grains left over after the harvest were food for these nice and kind birds, and their droppings were gathered in a hole in the middle of the tower, from which the earth for bricks was taken out. Then, every while spadefuls of the dung were thrown near the plants. What a simple technique! How practical and how wholesome in respect of the ecosystem! The excavated earth did not move far away so as to cause disorder in the system of nature. The materials did not come from a distance so as to incur much expenditure. They were given by the farm and taken back again by it.

On his arrival at the pigeon-tower, **Ruhullah** would take a handful of the grains out of his bag and throw it on the ground. The pigeons would leave their nests and fly down to pick up the grains. He would try to catch one or two of them, but they were on alert. At times the heart of one of them might throb in his hand very fast, and he would quickly take it home and place it in a cage made for domestic hens. Mother, who herself had children, would feel worried lest the pigeon captured by her son had chicks which might be waiting for their caretaker. So, she would implore him to set it free. But **Ruhullah** was not a father, and accepting her graceful request was, to him, a kind of wasting his own efforts. The mother had a lucid feeling like poetry. She tried not to give to her request the color of a commanding force. At the same time she could not keep in prison the wild pigeon which cannot be easily tamed. At the first opportunity she would open the door of the cage, away from the eyes of **Ruhullah.** But the play was repeated. One day the mother fabricated a story whose hero was a canary which had four chicks. In this story the chicks witnessed the capture of their mother. The fate of those chicks so much grieved **Ruhullah** that he calmly left the room without showing being sentimental. He stood beside the cage, opened its door and set free the pigeons which he had trapped.

At that time pigeon-fancy was quite familiar in Tehran. The professional pigeon-fanciers used to construct large cages on the roofs of their houses, in which they bred pigeons which could fly from morning till night. The perching of the pigeons on the roofs of the neighbours, and the climbing of the pigeon-fanciers the neighbours' walls without permission, prompted some *mujtahids* to announce pigeon-fancy as *haram,* and, if the pigeon-fancy went to the extent of gambling, its being *haram* would need no *fatwa.* In small towns, like Khomein, keeping pigeons in some houses was common, but no one dared to do as the Tehrani pigeon-fanciers used to do. Nevertheless, a number of professional pigeon-fanciers used to send into the air swift flying pigeons, which, when breathing hard, sat on the tower or the rampart of **Ruhullah'**s house. Some time **Ruhullah** would sit and gaze at the innocent eyes of these harmless pigeons which had become instruments in the hands of the neighbour vexing men. He had put a bowel of water on the roof, and changed its water every day so that the tired pigeons dip their beaks into it. At times he would take to them the leftovers and bread crumbs. One day a young man told him: ─Take your water and food away from the roof, as these would disturb the system of feeding my pigeons, and they would not be able to fly as I desire." He heard the reply: ―Tell your pigeons not to touch my water and grains." The talkative sparrows, the fearless turtledoves and the sweet-singing nightingales had their shares; too, in the food he used to throw for the pigeons.

Pigeon-fancying was one of the ugly hobbies in the country, but fondling pigeons was one of the kindest amusements which even created fables, and, by the support of narratives quoted from the infallible Imams (*a*), it took the scent of a devotional act.[101] That is why almost all the holy shrines, including the shrine of the **Imam Rida (*a*),** have become secured places for the multitude of pigeons, to which people vow to offer millet and wheat to have their patients cured, or their needs fulfilled. In many instances **Ruhullah,** as a grown up person, was noticed to take out from under his _aba' a paper bag of grains and scatter it to the pigeons of a holy place. He was often seen looking with pleasure at the pigeons flying in the sky around the holy tombs.

Is it not that the beloved things are better fixed in one's subconscience, and that even when one consciously talks, the words dancingly spring out of the subconscience? If it is so, then this simile, which he later used in defending the religion and the people against the despotic regime of the Shah, was a memoir of his affection for the pigeons of the holy places:

―We are waiting for imprisonment, torture and execution. Let the tyrannical regime do whatever inhumane act it wants: break the hands and legs of our youths, drive our patients out of hospitals, threaten to kill us and disgrace our honour, destroy our religious schools, dislodge the pigeons of the Islamic holy places from their homes...[102]" In this context the simile of _the cage and thirty million pigeons' in the following statements refers to the far past, to the day on which he opened the door of the cage, with the explanation that this belief in the people had reached its peak, and he so much respected them that his expressions about the people were quite sentimental. When some responsible officials complained of the willful interferences of some people in matters causing disorders, describing them to be _like ants and locusts, wriggling everywhere, preventing the officials from doing their duties' replied in words—instead of using the expression of ants and locusts, which, in gnosticism, glorify **Allah,** but in the conversational culture it bears insult—he used the word _pigeon' so as to completely preserve the dignity of the people:

―For a long time you have been in chains and fetters, we all have been in strangulation. Thirty-five million people of Iran were in prison. Iran was a prison, so all of you were under torture, spiritual tortures, and other brothers were bodily tortured as we heard about. We were spiritually tortured. Thank **Allah,** you rose and you, the youths of the nation, were victorious, and you cut short the hands of the criminals off your country, and expelled the professional thieves. Today as you triumphed, in the day of victory, it is like opening the door of a prison and thirty million prisoners were set free, like opening the door of a cage and set free thirty million captured pigeons. Now it is Revolution. It is different now, it is a change. Yet, with vigilance, firm resolution and strong will, you must also control the situation after the Revolution.[103]"

Peep-Show

Peep-show was a wooden box for showing pictures, and it was regarded as a portable cinema before the common cinema became fashionable. This portable and silent cinema was made in small and big boxes, with a single or several peep-holes. The pictures pass before the lenses and attract the attention of the peeping children. In each quarter of Tehran there were one or two who had such boxes, and from morning till night they used to cry: —*Shahr-e farangeh, az hameh rangeh*" [European town of all kinds]. The children, by paying a small coin, sat behind the lenses for a few minutes and looked at the pictures while the box owner gave explanations as he moved them, which the children thought to be worth hearing. An owner of a peep-show in Khomein was an old, fat and swift man. [104] But instead of the irrelevant pictures which were used in most of the peep-shows of Tehran, and which they used to cut from foreign magazines and stick them together, this man used the pictures of religious and political personalities, and the holy places, such as the *Kabah, Karbala, Masjid an-Nabi, al-Masjid al-Aqsa* and some world spectacles. Whenever **Ruhullah** heard his calls in the street he would run out to him to see the new pictures. Although **Ruhullah** used to patiently peep through the lense, causing the man to become impatient, yet he bore **Ruhullah's** taking his time until he got satisfied with a picture and asked for the next. That was because **Naneh Khawar** used to pay the man generously, including quantities of dried apricot, walnut, figs, almonds and other dried eatables. Sometimes she would give out the old dresses or the too small ones for the boys to the man so as to please his grandchildren. Hence, he once permitted **Ruhullah** to look into the box itself in order to discover the simple secret of a box which seemed to the boys to be magical.

The memory of the old dresses which **Naneh Khawar** gave to the man as the wage for seeing the peep-show had a bitter taste in **Ruhullah's** mind. Some ten years later he blamed **Naneh Khawar:** —When you used to give the old dresses to the man, the sparks of shame covered all my being, but as a child I didn't know what to do." **Naneh Khawar** said: ―If he, too, was ashamed as you, he would not have accepted them." Apparently it was a convincing answer, but **Ruhullah** was never convinced by it, because thirty years later, when he started studying ethics, continuing it till his travel to Paris, whenever there was a hint at spending, he used to recite the noble *ayah* and to tell nice talk about it: ―**You shall not attain piety until you spend out of what you love; and whatever you spend, Allah surely knows it."**[105]

After reciting it, he would tell tens of *hadiths,* and with a gnostic insight he would cleave the strict moral points of spending: ―Spending [for charity] old and used things would bring loss to the moralities of both the giver and the receiver—In the former, it would keep the ethic of generosity undeveloped; and, similarly in the latter, the ethic of dignity".[306]

The Seventh Art

If the seventh art of today is the developed form of the very former ‗peep-show', then he knew its technique before reaching his fourth year of age, and liked to make one for himself, but due to lacking the necessary means he could not make it. When he was around fifty, he used to spend some summer seasons in Tehran, in the resort of Imamzadeh Qasim in Shemiran. One night he accompanied one of his friends, the **Ayatullah Sayyid Husayn Rasuli Mahallati,** the congregational *salah* leader of that quarter, to visit a patient there. The patient had formerly insulted the zealous congregational *salah* leader who had said that buying and selling radio sets were *haram.* This visit, which was with the company of the congregational *salah* leader, could put out the fire of hypocrisy. Before entering the patient's room, his eyes fell on a workshop table placed in a corner of the veranda. He halted for a moment. It was the table of a secondary school student who spent his leisure time in making or repairing instruments such as radios, TVs, gramaphones, film apparatuses and the like. At those days such technical instruments did not appear nice, because, from the very beginning of the importation of these instruments into Iran, the very Western culture, without logical selection, had found its way into Iran, and if there was any selection, it was not for the good ones. Consequently, the buying and selling of these instruments were prohibited by most of the *mujtahid*s, with the exception of the film apparatuses under certain conditions, as well as the recorders. The insult which the patient had directed to the congregational *salah* leader had stemmed from this situation, since his son was a repairer of these instruments, in order to provide his schooling expenses.

111

When he left the patient and came out to the veranda, he asked the young man who was bringing him his shoes: —Whose apparatuses are these?" The boy, perplexed by the situation, said: —Yours!" The **Aqa** smiled, and the boy immediately corrected his mistake and said: —They're mine." The **Aqa** said: —Explain to me some of your work, please." The boy mounted a reel film of Charly Chaplin on the apparatus he had made himself, and gave a thorough explanation. The film included some omissions. The **Aqa** said: —If you increase the speed, these omissions will decrease." The boy thought the cause of the omissions to be something else, but he was astonished to hear him speak of speed. —Have you ever seen such apparatus before?" He asked. —As a child I saw a peep-show," the **Aqa** replied, —but concerning the work of the apparatus, I read about it in a magazine. The basis is the same." The **Aqa**'s other question was: —What is the difference between this apparatus and that of the cinema?" —This is for 8 mm. while that of the cinema is 35 mm," was the boy's answer, —This is silent, while that for the cinema is talking," he added. The **Aqa**'s dress was sufficient for the boy not to ask the **Aqa** if he had ever gone to the cinema, but the boy was too green, and did ask him. The **Aqa** said: —You'd better not go, either. As they say, most of the films are too bad." Then, in order not to discourage the boy in his technical work, he told him things greatly resembled his talks which he delivered in Behesht Zahra'on his returning from exile to Iran. He frankly said: —Our cinemas are centres of obscenity. We are not against the cinema. We are against the centre of obscenity. We are not against the radio. We are against obscenity. We are not against the TV. We are against the things which serve the foreigners to keep our youths backward and cause us to lose our man-power.[107]"

Watching *Shabih Khani*

The vacancy left by the theatre and the cinema in the olden times was filled up by *Shabih Khani*' to some extent. In the early years of Islam, this *Shabih Khani* took the form of dramatizing the glorified tragedy of the Imam al-Husayn (*a*) which lasted for ten days from the first of the month of Muharram till the day of *Ashura,* and sometimes in other occasions. It was played wherever it could be, openly, if possible, in the large squares of the towns and in the villages, every year, and secretly, if not possible, inside the houses, where the play was acted, and mostly in poetry, and the Shiite players used to take the audience to a corner of history in a dramatic, religious show. But they did not let them stay in the past. They brought them round. During the years of despotism, they allusively ascribed evil and wickedness to **Shemr** and **Yazid** of those days, and ascribed purity and injustice-combating to the **Husayns** of those days. But during **Ruhullah"s** childhood this religious and cultural show had become senseless and contentless. Nevertheless, every year it was put on show in all towns, including Khomein. Despite its contentless, it attracted numerous spectators. **Ruhullah,** while still two years old, watched it in the arms of his relatives. Later on he watched it alone.

The Muslims, Shiite or Sunni, all over the world, and almost all the people of Iran, whether Muslims or of the religious minorities, know, more or less, about the tragedy of **Ashura**. Therefore most of the *Shabih Khani* shows tried to react its model, but it could never completely cover the tragedy of Karbala. The spectator must have some prior knowledge of this tragedy so that the show may have its exciting effect on him, and then to cause him to weep. Despite the fact that this show, during the last hundred years, had a common and weak performance, yet when the **Shimr** sat on **al-Husayn"s** chest (in the show) to cut off his head, the women, who were mostly used to sit on the roofs around the square or under the vaults of the second stories, to watch the show, threw stones at him and fainted while crying loudly. Men were commonly more self-controlling. They only wept or slapped their own heads, faces and chests.

Shemr, who was ordered by the two historical wicked men, **Ibn Ziyad** and **Yazid,** to sever **al-Husayn"s** head from his body, is a horrible hero in the tragedy. The **Shimr** in the play usually had a sturdy structure and a harsh voice, but, as a matter of fact, he himself had come to the show to mourn the Master of the Martyrs, and the better he played his role, the better it was accepted by **Allah**. Nevertheless, the **Shimrs** in these plays were not safeguarded against the people's hostile feelings. For the Khomein show they had a good **Shimr**. He recited so good poetry before **al-Husayn,** rode the horse so cleverly and jumped on **al-Husayn"s** chest so briskly, that the cries of curses and abuses rose high from everywhere.

When **Ruhullah** was three, four, or at most, six years old, he accompanied his brothers to attend the mourning of the day of **Ashura** in the village of Bujan where there was an *Imamzadeh.* Every year they used to perform a sensational show near the *Imamzadeh.* In this show **Ruhullah** saw an astonishing scene. When the **Shemr** sat on **al-Husayn"s** chest to press his dagger onto his throat, there jumped a man from among the audience and rushed crying, with perspiration pouring down his forehead, started, with flowing tears, abusing and cursing, and threw unutterable words upon the **Shimr,** and in a minute he seized him by the collar, and angrily said to him:

─Do you want to kill the son of **the Prophet?** I'll fleece you..." Those who had stepped forward to settle the quarrel, instead of taking him out of the place, fell upon the **Shimr** with their fists and legs, boxing, kicking and dragging him out of the scene. From then on he did not play the role of the **Shemr,** though his artistic acting still had its effect in their minds. Perhaps the Imam's expressions highly recommending any role in the society stemmed from this memoir. He said:

─Everybody who does something must do it perfectly. You had seen the *Shabih Khani* show in the past. In these shows the good **Shimr** was the one who played his role well. If that **Shimr** did something becoming only of the **Master of the Martyrs,** he would not be a good **Shimr.** The one who plays **Master of the Martyrs** must also play it well. If he did it well he would be a good actor. Every one of us must carry out as best as he can what is entrusted to him to do. Whatever post one has to manage, one must manage it well. [108]"

Although he loved the arts and his love for them was ever increasing, and although he himself played the role of the leader of an uprising ingeniously, yet, when he was about twenty years old he stopped attending the *Shabih Khani* shows, not because *Shabih Khani* is a bad thing, perhaps because it was not acted well, since no one was able to manifest the positive and beautiful aspect of the astonishing epic of *Ashura* in playing the role of **al-Husayn.** The following expressions resemble the above ones, and they prove that:

─You remember the *Shabih Khani* shows in the past. Many ask [us] now and we, too, say that it is better to recite the *Rawdah.* A good **Shimr** was the one who was good at playing the role of the **Shemr,** and a good duplicate for the **Master of the Martyrs** was the one who could play the role well. [109]"

The Victory of the Constitutionalists

He was about four years old. There were, in the town, talks out of which **Ruhullah** could make nothing. In summer the talks reached their peak. **Ayatullah Behbahani, Ayatullah Tabatabai, Aynuddawlah, Muzaffaruddin Shah,** Adalat-Khaneh, the British Embassy, high living cost, Constitutionalism, the *ulama,* trade unions, the Parliament, the law... all were the words which were used to strike the ear, but they had no clear reflex on the clear mirror of his mind, not just to him, as some of these words had also no clear meaning to the elders. At last, however, one day, when he was exactly four years three months and nine days old, the Town Criers, with trumpet, cymbal and drum, went about. The sounds of the trumpet, the cymbal and the drum brought men, women and children out of their houses into the lane. The drummer would beat his drum with his stick a few strikes, then he would repeat a few sentences which he had learnt by heart, in such a stretched voice: ⌐Do know and tell the others to know that His Most High Imperial Majesty, **Muzaffaruddin,** [victorious in religion and in this world], the king of Iran, has yesterday signed the Constitutional Law consisting of 51 Articles, with his honoured pen..." Nine days later the same public criers came again, but the drummer announced the death of that very Imperial Majesty, on whose burning body with fever the European springs had not sprinkled any water.[110]

Despite the fact that the requirement of age caused the information about Constitutionalism to be mingled with a halo of vagueness, and what he could reap of it were imaginary bunches, yet in his youth, the greatest political event which he admitted to worth thinking about was that very event. He could neither deny that since ‗Constitutionalism‗ was better than ‗Absolutism‗, nor could he completely support it because there was the ‗Canonism‗ which did not take its place. What business was it to the British Ambassador to ⌐set up a tent and take in twelve thousand persons"[111] of different wakes in the Embassy‗s garden?[112] Why did Constitutionalism hang **Shaykh Fadlullah** and put **Rida Khan** on the throne? Constitutionalism was an unripe popular revolution, or an inexpert pseudo-enlightenment reform. [113] Whatever it was, it was, in the new era, the first political experiment tried by the *ulama,* the enlightened, the modernists and the unionists in aiming at the construction of the government. This experience, on the other hand, caused most of the *ulama* to become so disillusioned that they were no longer interested in reading the news and in whatever had the smell of politics as hurting. They even went to the extent of following the West‗s political opinion, which had arrived at the conclusion that the Church must never again come onto the political scene. On this side, they were moulding the other side of the coin by saying that politics must not find its way into religion. The former was more practical, as the Church was no longer the taker of political decisions. At this side politics had plans for the believers in religion, while after the Constitution religiosity had no harmonious program for not being cornered in the mosques. **Ruhullah** for years concentrated his eyes, ears and mind on the *Quran,* narratives, philosophy, history and world news so that he may find out, with sharp-sightedness, where the problem is. Perhaps this was not his first theory about government which was completely mature, but in respect of following up the proceedings of his political thoughts, it is among the first theories which must be considered: To govern without the people is of no consistency. But the rulership is to be absolute, as

115

it cannot bear partnership, it is also not conditional. An origin of this speech is: ―Islamic Republic, neither a word less, nor a word more." ‗Republic' is a sign of the people's participation in governing the country, and the word ‗Islamic', without any suffix, denotes the absolute authority. The basic problem of Constitution was that in its authority it also was constitutional.[114]

Private Teacher

When he was five, it was decided, according to the Aunt's suggestion, that **Mirza Mahmud** should examine **Ruhullah** to see if he had the aptitude to learn reading and writing. This man thought that to use the full weight in education means to come early in the morning and engage **Ruhullah** in reading and writing till noon. But one of the Aunts' husbands realized soon that this pressure might cause him to be disgusted with all learning and studying. So, he suggested that the teaching hours should be reduced, and to be every other day, and to concentrate more on the biographies of the prophets and the Imams, and only at times he may open a book or put a pen into **Ruhullah'**s hand. Mother supported the suggestion, and the teacher accepted.

Pleasurable Wrestlings

In those days the children's drawing on paper was regarded to be lavishment. Color pencils were rare even in the Capital. Yet it seems that drawing is an instinct. **Ruhullah,** with his fine-tipped pen and black ink, and mostly away from his tutor's eyes, used to draw. Sometimes he might draw an old tree with its visible roots out of a brook, and with a number of incomplete circles on it. Should Mother put her finger on a circle and ask him ―What is this?" he would say ―Apple." If she would point to another similar circle and asked: ―What is this?" **Ruhullah** would reply, ―This one is pomegranate." Sometimes **Nuruddin,** in order to stir a childish argument, would object: ―Does an apple tree give pomegranate, too?" **Ruhullah** would, with all his existence, defend the possibility of a single tree bearing apple and pomegranate, because in the garden there was a quince tree on which a pear-scion had been grafted. **Nuruddin,** who loved **Ruhullah'**s hearty defence, would deliberately extend the argument such that at last **Ruhullah** would quarrel with him. **Nuruddin** used to pick up a quarrel with **Ruhullah** through stirring an argument with him. When five, he thought both of them to be almost equals, and that wrestling with him was apparently not so easy, but was really pleasing—so pleasing that the original question concerning a tree bearing both apple and pomegranate, was forgotten. Of cours **Nuruddin** did take into his consideration his age when he wrestled with him, otherwise he could easily knock him down.

The Celebration of the 3rd of Shaban

A day before the 3rd of Shaban, the birthday anniversary of the third Imam of the Shiite, the Imam **al-Husayn (***a***),** the teacher proposed: Out of pieces of unwanted cloths of different colors a number of flags were to be made and to decorate the walls of the house with them. Mother was generous and gave them better pieces of cloth. Then they went looking for poles for the flags. They cut branches from the trees, but they were encountered by **Karbalai**'s objections, as he was responsible for irrigating and trimming the trees. While looking for the poles they saw a brand new reed mat, rolled and kept in a store, waiting for the suitable time to be hanged on a window. They drew out its reeds and used them as poles for their flags. Their unpermitted deed angered their mother. She pulled a reed out of a flag and brandished it in a threatening way and asked **Nuruddin:** ─"Who damaged the mat?" **Ruhullah** immediately said: ─"I did it." **Nuruddin** said: ─"He lies; it was I who damaged it." ─"Then both of you?" Mother asked. Once again **Nuruddin** said: ─"I." **Ruhullah,** in defence of his brother, said: ─"No, I did it." Mother turned to **Nuruddin** and said: ─"You, the elder, why?" **Ruhullah** jumped and stood beside his brother and said: ─"We both are of the same size." Mother was frowning, but her eyes were smiling. **Ruhullah,** who knew that the reed was not suitable for beating and would easily break, felt double encouraged and said: ─"If you want to beat, come on. We are too busy to lose time." Mother did not know what to do. The Aunt intermediated, giving word on behalf of the children that they would not repeat it.

Aqa Murtada's First Speech

Until afternoon the boys could decorate the house with their hand-made flags so nicely that **Murtada** felt so joyful that he prepared for them some sweets, sweetmeats, bonbons, and promised to deliver a speech for them. Boys of four, five years, up to ten, fifteen years from the region were invited. **Aqa Murtada,** who was a young theology student, delivered his first speech in that childish and sincere gathering, and talked on the sensational life of the **Imam al-Husayn (***a***).** The next day on the occasion of the birthday anniversary of **Abul-Fadl (***a***),** whose wonderful love of his brother was almost legendary, the celebrations continued. The good reception of this by the household and the neighbours caused it to continue to the third day, celebrating the birthday anniversary of the fourth Imam of the Shiite, **Ali ibn**

117

al-Husayn (*a*). Aqa Murtada sat on a four-legged seat covered with a bedsheet and a cushion, which fell off at the first leaning. Naturally, his speech on the third day was short.

Aqa Murtada had a good taste and was eloquent. His good memory in learning by heart the events caused him to be practical. He related the historical events, without adding to them any unreal seasoning, as was agreeable to the children. That which the children heard on these three days was worth hearing by them. Except **Nuruddin** and **Ruhullah,** who were serious hosts and had to pair the shoes, bring tea, distribute sweets, the other children sat motionless. These three sweet and memorable days of celebrations went beyond a common childish play and turned to be so serious that the teacher suggested that the 15th of Shaban, the anniversary of the birthday of the last infallible Imam of the Shiite, the Imam **al-Mahdi (*a*),** with only eleven days to it, should see a better celebration. Next morning the boys started their work, and the elders, too, spared no effort to help them, offering to them whatever they needed. The needs of the boys, of course, were not endless, but sometimes they asked for unreal things. It was decided that the whole house should be decorated, but unintentionally it was extended to the lane outside. From the entrance of the lane flowerpots of oleanders were arranged. The district's boys got busy, too. Some brought paper lanterns, which they make for their kites, with lighted candels. **Aqa Murtada** offered little help in hanging the decorations. He was in his father's library taking notes of the subjects he intended to speak about in the gathering so that they may remain fixed in the children's memories.

The Celebration of the Middle of Shaban
The very day on which it was decided to hold the celebration, all the district's boys were invited to take part in the meeting and in helping **Nuruddin** and **Ruhullah** in hanging the decorations. But, unexpectedly, in the afternoon of the 14th or 15th of Shaban, the elders, seeing the decorations in the lane and thinking that it was a public celebration, proceeded to come to the house. The children wondered first what to do. Fortunately **Karbalai** and **Naneh Khawar,** the servants of the house, were clever at such occasions. They spread some rags and carpets in the veranda, and the big samovar began boiling with coal. The others were also helpful in changing the celebration which the boys had arranged for themselves into one in which the elders were the majority.

From some ten days earlier **Murtada** was preparing himself for delivering his speech in the meeting which he thought to be a great one. He

118

had prepared two stools, one higher than the other and put them together to make a *minbar* of two steps. He had also assigned a place from which he would deliver his speech, but when he saw the *minbar* and the audience his throat went dry. He knew that he was unable to manage that gathering. The Aunt encouraged him, but to no avail. He did not confess it, but he sought excuses. He said he had a fever. As a matter of fact, he had. One of the boys, probably by the name of **Murtada,** had promised to recite eulogies. He courageously sat on the *minbar,* closed his eyes and recited poems he had learnt by heart. The audience encouraged him by loudly uttering the *salawat* three times. In those days small boys could not be so much flaunting, but this boy was able to show off his talent by his clear bell-like voice, and to completely capture the attention of the audience. Perhaps it was his success at this occasion that caused him later to become a formal eulogist. Another boy was to recite a birthday poem with other boys clapping their hands. He, too, sat on the *minbar.* But with the first clapping, an old man, who was leaning on a cushion and stretching his legs at the end of the place, called out: ―Is the Imam al-Mahdi a childish play that you clap your hands?" It took him a long time to stand up to his feet objectively and leave the place, beating the ground with his stick. However, in the middle of his way out, he was returned to his place at the intercession of one of the elders. But the birthday recitation stopped short, and the reciter, ashamed, ran away and hid himself behind the trunk of a tree, peeping out at times to have a look at the audience, sorry for himself.

From the beginning, when the door was opened and a number of the elders entered, **Hajar Khanum** understood the situation. Decorating the lane outside the house misguided the elders. As such, she hastily sent for her cousin, **Aqa Shaykh Jafar,** who was a teacher and a preacher at times, so that he might take care of the gathering. **Aqa Shaykh Jafar** was not in good health, but he was coming. **Karbalai** seized the opportunity and started the hospitality so the people might not become aware of the situation. On his arrival **Shaykh Jafar** expressed his approval by loudly saying: ―Bless you! May **Allah** bless you boys! Bravo! It is the End of Time. The old follow the boys..." The people realized that they had come by mistake, and, as they were perplexed at seeing the decorations far from the taste of old people, and more childish, the situation became clear to them. However, the meeting was attractive and it was not easy to leave it. **Aqa Jafar** drank a cup of tea and sat on the first step of the *minbar,* leaning at the second.

The messenger whom **Hajar Khanum** sent to **Aqa Jafar**—most probably **Mirza Mahmud,** the tutor—had told him the whole story on their

119

way back. So, the **Aqa Shaykh** knew, then, the origin of the case. He summoned **Nuruddin** and seated him beside him. He also summoned **Ruhullah,** who was bashful and did not go to him. **Aqa Murtada** took him by the hand and seated him by force beside the **Shaykh.** After a short speech which was usually delivered in Arabic, the **Shaykh** said: ―These two children, our hosts, are the sons of the late **Aqa Mustafa,**" then he informed the audience how the meeting was held, and invoked **Allah** to keep them safe and make them friends of the Imam of the Time [**al-Mahdi**]. The people said Amin' after him in a loud voice. He told them to sit near the *minbar.* **Nuruddin** sat in front of him at a metre's distance. **Ruhullah** came down from the *minbar* but remained half sitting, with one hand leaning on the *minbar,* probing his chin with his other hand, looking at the **Shaykh's** profile. He kept this pose for nearly an hour gazing at him and listening to him with all his being.

Lending Ears to the First Fervent Speech

Aqa Shaykh Jafar was an ordinary preacher handling only topics covering the history of the prophets, ethics or explaining religious precepts. Yet, in his life he handled a few times social and political topics with great fervent. Once, in a meeting on **Aqa Mustafa**'s mourning, he referred to the influence of the British and the Russian Embassies on the Qajar government. In another occasion he talked about The Punishment Committee'. In a third instance he uncovered a secret of great importance in this gathering, but it seems that only few were real hearers of it. The majority had come to obtain the hereafter reward by sitting in a meeting held for the celebration of *Baqiyyatullah* (may **Allah** enhance his appearance). This was the first hot political speech to which **Ruhullah** was the addressee, combining its contexts with stories about his father's martyrdom and the conditions of the time which he had heard. Undoubtedly, it was not expected from him, as a boy, to fully go into the depth of the question, but it was a stone in the mass of his being.

    Aqa Shaykh said: ―There are in these days rumours whose origin no one knows whether true or false. If they are true, then shame upon this country... They say that the British have written something intending to split the country into three sections: one for themselves, one for the Russians and one neutral... If these rumours are true, what is to be done? Men are to wear the *chadur.* May **Allah** make them mere rumours!"

120

Regretably they were true. If that day was the 15th of Shaban, then on that day, or if that was 14th of Shaban, then the next day, the British turned the people's feast into a mourning.

A letter from the British Embassy was sent by **Sir Spring Rice** to **Sadud-dawlah,** the Minister of the Foreign Affairs, which read: ―To the respected Minister. In compliance with the instruction of my government, I have the honour to send inclosed the text of the Agreement of 31st August, 1907, concluded between Great Britain and Russia, for your information.[115]"

Up till that day no newspaper had uncovered that Agreement secretly concluded between the Russian and the British governments. But due to certain causes some persons got information about the said Agreement before its text being officially disclosed. The first cause was that **Muhammad Ali Shah** knew about it some time earlier, as it was not possible for the repulsive Shah to know a secret and, in his disordered court, keep it away from being whispered into the ears and made public.[116]

The second cause can be received from the contents of a powerful Tehranian preacher called **Sayyid Jamaluddin Waiz.** On the same day on which the boys celebrated the birthday anniversary of **Sayyid ash-Shuhada** [the Master of the Martyrs] (*a*), and in which **Aqa Murtada** delivered his first speech, there was delivered in Tehran, in one of the big mosques, a painful speech by **Waiz** for the notables, the elite, merchants and other classes of the people: ―. I swear you by Allah, imagine a little and see if **Allah** has more unfortunate and ignorant servants other than us, the Iranians! It is now more than a year in which all the newspapers of the world report that the British and the Russians want to conclude a treaty concerning Iran, Afghanistan and Tibet. We, the Iranians read all these papers and see this news, and yet, within this long period there appeared no one to raise his voice: O you! What is the matter? Did the Iranians die that you make agreements of affection and friendship to distribute their properties among yourselves? We are dead, and our deputies are like ourselves..."[117]

It is quite possible that the speech of **Waiz** had reached Khomein, chest to chest, such that the speech of **Aqa Shaykh Jafar** was inspired by it. It also seems that it enhanced the **Allamah Qazvini**—who was living in Paris at that time and had good knowledge of the current political events—to write letters to the eminent politicians so that they may find a resolution. But alas! At that time the whole world of Islam was turned into a dead body of a devastating lassitude of negligence. Had **Sayyid Jamaluddin Waiz** delivered his speech in Egypt, he would have said in Arabic: ―Has **Allah** any servants more unfortunate and ignorant than us, the Egyptians?" Had he been born in

Malaysia, he would have said the same words in the Malaysian language. Had he been in Libya, which was then under the Italian colonialism, his words, though different, would have the same content. Similarly in the years when the sperm of the Indian revolution was clotting, **Muhammad Ali Jinnah**, who was known as the Grand Leader of Pakistan, used to speak out words of similar contents to the Indian people. The scholars of al-Azhar University used to blame their coreligionists for the lassitude of the world of Islam. Each nation which at that time had no power, if it looks into its history it will find out what the upper powers had done to its country and what its speakers used to say. A number of countries which were worse than Iran were so unfortunate that they even had no one to proclaim out their distress.

Dividing Iran

What was the reality of the story? Why did they divide Iran? What would they gain from it which they did not gain before? What was the fate of this division? What did the people do?

Profound reply to these questions would consume thousands of pages, and probably **Ruhullah** had spent hundreds of hours thinking about them. As long as he was in Khomein he had asked **Aqa Murtada** more than ten times, and tens of times he had asked everyone whom he thought able to answer those questions. One of the questions which he repeatedly used to ask and to get such answers that he was forced to ask again, was: Were the people, with their long-nozzled rifles, able to drive the British and the Russians out of Iran, but they did not do it? Most of the answers admitted that there were such attempts, but not as they should have been done. Another question would stem from the first one: Why could not they do it? One day a thin shepherd was behind the house-yard wall leaning on his rifle which was taller than **Ruhullah,** who was playing with its sling and chatting with him. The shepherd, jokingly, said: ―This is a foreign rifle. Its bullets are also foreign. Foreign rifles do not kill foreigners." **Ruhullah** remained giddy for a while by this information, and kept asking the Aunt how it was possible that a foreign rifle would not kill a foreigner. For a long time his mind turned from a political question to a completely physiological matter. Later on he realized both the depth and the invalidity of that joke. But before finding the answer to his original question, a deeper matter boiled in his soul: A wrinkled shepherd, fully aware of the ups and downs of the mountains and plains and apparently unaware of the ups and downs of politics, how could he put politics in a brief joke? This, by itself, was a preliminary but a deep receipt of a philosophic sociology, which he could later adapt as a precise theory—the theory which manifested itself in his words in numerous occasions. In short it is this: –One of the important sources of knowledge is the innate and clear receipts of the common people." The theory which had always been with him ,causing him to consult the opinions of his servants, not to have some fun and amusement, but to purify and chastise his own opinions.

At any rate, the division of Iran between Britain and Russia became one of the serious questions occupying his mind, not so much leaving him. Some twenty years later, while living in Qum, one day the question of dividing Iran was brought to discussion. A friend of his, named **Muhammad Sadiq Lawasani,** related a satiric story which might have answered one of his questions. Later on something like that story was put in a book. It can be summarized as follows:

Mirza Hasan Khan, Mushiruddawlah, who had, a little after the division of Iran, gone to Petersburg to inform the Russian government about the coronation of **Muhammad Ali Shah,** in a meeting with **Isolsky,** the Russian Minister of Foreign Affairs, and **Sir Nicholson,** the British Ambassador to the Caesarean Russia, asked them questions about the reasons of dividing Iran. **Isolsky,** in Petersburg, –assured **Mushiruddawlah** that neither of the two governments demand anything from Iran (except Iran itself). Iran can spend all its powers to develop the desert of *Hawd-e Sultan.*"[118]

The Agreement of 1907 had its numerous effects on Iran's political culture, such as the British, who still were not disreputed and their Embassy was the host for some twelve thousand persons who took refuge there for the sake of the Constitutional Revolution, became so disreputed that everyone who frequented the British Embassy was treated as a leprous from whom people ran away. Nevertheless the Embassy remained active and its gates were open to the lepers as before. The more important effect of the division can be traced in the fate of Constitutionalism.

Blood-Colored Paintings
Although **Ruhullah** had no painting teacher, yet he used to engage himself with painting. One of his imaginative paintings which was inspired by reality, went beyond the house and shook hands with the relatives and friends. Two colors were used in this painting—the black ink and the color of mercurochrome. He drew the Parliament building larger than the dimensions of the large hall at his house, placing around it figures with black and white turbans, leather and horn-shaped caps to represent the deputies. On the roof

he drew many circles as cannon-balls, some of which had made holes in the roof and fallen on the heads of the deputies. From under the door of the hall a stream of red blood was flowing out. After that this painting changed hands and after hearing some explanations, he realized that the cannon-balls which were fired at the Parliament were not of the kind of balls which the stone-cutter in Khomein used to hew out of brick-colored, green and white stones for the children's taw games.

In those days one might hear in every meeting exciting, and sometimes painful, news about the fate of the constitutional movement.

Aqa Mirza Abdul Husayn, Ruhullah's maternal uncle, was a sociable personality.[119] He used to call on them every now and then, bringing to his sister, **Hajar Khanum,** political and social news and what was going on in the Parliament and in the country. The boys liked his sweet talking and pricked their ears to hear him telling his report in an exciting story-teller style. **Ruhullah** had heard him say that the Parliament was bombarded. Maybe when he asked him what a cannon-ball was, he pointed to one of those stone-hewed balls.

The Fate of the Majlis

Exactly twenty months and two days had passed on the first session of the Parliament[120] when there happened events which prompted the Russian Embassy to secretly suggest to **Muhammad Ali Shah** to issue his order to the Russian **Liakhov** to order the Cossacks to bombard the newly built *Majlis* whose plaster had not yet been dried up. It was a noteworthy cycle—the imperious suggestion of the Russian Embassy to the Shah of Iran, the order of the Shah of Iran to the Russian Commander, the order of the Russian Commander to the Iranian soldiers to destroy the newly established Parliament.

Nowadays, many persons take the cause of the appearance of every event on that day to be the conspiracy of the British authorities. They say that besides the appearance of those events, the hands of the Britons which came out of the Russian Embassy must be added to the cycle. Others believe that the history must be written anew, because foreigners showed **Muhammad Ali Shah** as a repulsive one, as otherwise he might have been a patriot who spoke of extreme love for his homeland. Some others think that —The advancement of the events was not like that which we see nowadays. The question of bombarding the *Majlis* must be carefully studied according to other analyses taking into consideration the role of the external policies and internal factors. Neither **Muhammad Ali Shah** and his supporting political and social forces were so black, nor were his opposing forces so white as was written in our official history." They believe that ─Concerning the dethronement of **Muhammad Ali Shah** there was no serious contradiction between the policies of the Russians and the British after the Agreement of 1907, as both powers had mutual interests in weakening the central government of Iran and in causing disorder in the country."

There is no space more than a span between the eye and the ear, but between what the eyes had closely seen, and what the ears used to hear from far away, there is such a distance as long as the windings and turns of the roads between the cities. When the calamities are too much disastrous, the lies are also too much big[121], and the truths are so horrible that the kind and clean pens tremble and lag behind in writing, while the rough and unclean pens take their ink from an inkpot of lies so as to show a man of the pen, or an official, innocent. At times the bulk of the calamities, which come successively, fill up the ears of a nation, turning them indifferent to the dreadful events of time. It is this which introverts them and turns the mind elsewhere, in order that one may not be aware of what was happening to one's country and its culture. Such was that period. The present libraries are full of the incorrect memoirs of those days with contradictory and incoherent writings and untrue reports and invalid analyses.

As such, and despite the impressions of some of the contemporary researchers who train the mind to throw light on dark points of history out of the folds, they often fail, or rather make it darker. To those who supported Constitutionalism at that time, those events denoted that **Muhammad Ali Shah** was presented in the mind, heart and the depth of feeling, as the original factor or a quisling playing the role of a champion of despotism. The common chapter surviving of the situation is that the British were the fox, the Russian the bear and **Muhammad Ali Shah** the wolf, and, in that intolerable zoo vultures were numerous.[122]

Muhammad Ali Shah in Ruhullah's Eyes

The day Constitutionalism took its shape till the day on which the *Majlis* was sieged by **Liakhov** forces, and its eastern wall was pulled down by the deputies who went out to the orchard of **Aminuddawlah**[123], where they hid them- selves, there took place more than five hundred incidents, big and small, each one of which, though terrifying, deserved hearing. **Ruhullah** was quite eager to hear them, although some of the servants in the house, the peasants and some of the relatives had lost their interest in hearing them, and continued, like the ordinary day, throwing the laundry in the washing basin, or striking the earth with the spades as before, —as if there was no wolf and it took no sheep!"

We are not quite sure what the exact reports were, and who the reporters were. However, history says: —The 2nd of the month of Tir (23rd June) was the climax of the clashes between **Muhammad Ali Shah** and the Constitutionalists and there was the most heart-rending event. In Tehran, three hundred people died at once, and five hundred were wounded. The deputies were dragged out of their hiding places. **Haji Ibrahim,** the deputy of Tabriz, was killed. Two of the fighting *ulama,* the **Tabatabai** and the **Behbahani**—who were looked at with respect by the majority who kissed their hands—were disrespectfully unturbaned, chained by the neck and dragged till the Bagh Shah Prison, in such a disgraceful manner that even some of the opponents of Constitutionalism felt disgusted.[124] After these frightenings and painful events, Constitutionalism was put in the hands of the police, and the hegemony of the martial law caused the town to be black, lifeless and frozen. This period was given the name of ‿petit-despotism'. When this event finds its way into the paintings of a child, can one, despite the remoteness of time, find one's way into the deep feelings of those who could transmit those feelings into him? If yes, how can one change the scrutinizing mind of this painter within sixty years with tens of explanations? If the argumentation is subtle it can easily be done. But as long as blood was running into his veins, the events which he had directly heard in his childhood, and his following the history minutely, indicated that, with this explanation that the logs of the furnace of the petit-despotism were prepared by the British and the Russians, and the Freemasons' lodges, **Muhammad Ali Shah** cannot be declared innocent. When he undertook the leadership of the uprising, he described **Muhammad Ali Mirza** with the worst possible words which can be uttered by a chaste person: —. They were such tyrants, and that **Muhammad Ali Mirza,** everybody knows what a beast he was!"[125]

Disturbing News

Why did **Muhammad Ali Shah** bombard the *Majlis*? This is a question which has different answers from different points of view. Undoubtedly, the Russians, whose regime was a despotic one, could not bear to have a neighbour with a *Majlis,* trade unions and different classes of people, participating in the government, and, worse still, its people insolently object the dividing of their country. Well, why the British?

The foreign policy of the British government, unlike the Russian policy, which was naked and exposed, was very much complicated in its appearance, though actually it was not so. It based only on a single theory: ―Divide and Conquer!" All the complications which are still causing bewilderment to many historians stemmed from this theory. Of course, this theory, which was the slogan of their foreign policy in the East and in the Middle East, publicized the idea that:

If a mosquito moves on a straw,

That movement is quite obvious to our sight.

Many believed in this and they had their proofs. But they neglected to realize that the whole country was not merely the Court, the *Majlis* or the governmental establishments, and all the people of this country were not mosquitoes, and the Court and the *Majlis* were not completely at the disposal of the foreigners. Yet, the conspiracies of the British before being really big were in appearance big. The documents at hand from those days denote that in the following events, which led to suspending the *Majlis* and to destroying it, the British had a hand in the sleeve so as to weaken the Constitutionalists and have them surrender to their demands.

The Murder of Faridun Gabr

On the 17th of Bahman (6th Feb.) a number of rascals and dissolute men, led by a gang called **Karam Brothers**, broke into the house of a well-known usurer, exchanger and capitalist, plundered his properties and, with the most terrifying method, slew him before the eyes of his household. He was a Zoroastrian by the name of **Faridun.** He was known to be a British subject. Did not the hearing of the news about his twitchings during the flow of his blood stir the emotions of his fellow Zoroastrians? Particularly that a similar accident had already happened to the Zoroastrians in Yazd.

Seventeen days later[126], **Mutadid ad-Diwan**, the chief of the police of Tehran, questioned the killers of **Faridun** and a number of the Court's riflemen confessed of murder and looting.

A month later[127] the announcers called in the city that the killers of **Faridun Gabr** would be slashed publicly. People gathered to see the scene. Nine men were stripped and tied to a mast. The first whips drew lines of blood on the backs of these nine rascals, and the whips continued to rise up and fall down on them for hours. The sentence was that each one of them should get one thousand and five hundred painful strikes. Three of them humiliatingly died, but the whips continued to fall upon their bodies. When it was night, a nocturnal statement was issued to the effect that a group had sworn to avenge the three Muslims on the Zoroastrians of Iran. Afterwards some newspapers appeared full of analyses, lamentation and kindling the fire of disunion.

Unsuccessful Assassination of Muhammad Ali Shah

On the eighth of Isfand,[331] the Shah went to Dushan Tappeh for amusement. Dushan Tappeh was not so trouble-free, but it had a nice weather which attracted the Qajariyan kings. On the said day two hand-made bombs exploded in front of his carriage. There were many casualties, but the Shah survived. All the towns held thanks-giving meetings.

On the 19th of Farwardin (8th April) next year, four men by the names: **Mirza Musa Zargar, Haydar Khan Cheragh Barqi, Mirza Ismail Khan** and **Diya as-Sultan** were arrested and sent to Kakh Gulestan for investigation. A flood of objections flowed onto the Court and popular demonstrations moved along the streets. Eleven days later[129] **Hajibuddawlah,** the governor of Tehran was deposed from his post, and these four men were declared not guilty. Because of this arrest and release, the Russian government demanded compensation from Iran on the pretext that two of these four Khans, **Ismail** and **Haydar,** had acquired the Russian Nationality to protect their own lives.

Killings in Urumiyeh

On the ninth of Ordibehesht (29th April), the rebels of the border attacked the town of Urumiyeh, killing two thousand men and women. Two days later, **Muhammad Ali Mirza** sent to Urumiyeh, as relief funds, the expenditures alloted to celebrating his birthday.[130] Twenty days earlier, **Nayib Husayn Kashi** had stained his hand in Kashan with the blood of many people, plundered their properties, announcing his rebellion against the government. The papers repeated publishing this news on several days, and the courtiers and the Shah just read it.

The Majlis Demands

The *Majlis* demanded from the Shah to dismiss six of the courtiers[131] who were accused either of being spies or of corruption, immorality and ill conduct, disfiguring the reputation of the government. At the same time the Shah wanted from the *Majlis* to hand to him eight of the preachers and journalists so as to shut their mouths and break their pens, or to convince them to back him in the secret war and peace between the Russians and the British.[132] **Taqizadeh** was one of the six persons whose support to the British needed no proof. The Shah did expel six persons from the Court, but among them were only three of the six named by the *Majlis.*[133] One of the expelled took refuge in the Russian Embassy.[134] But, was the *Majlis* able to comply with the Shah's demand? The next day the Shah went to Bagh Shah, a procedure which meant waging war. Yet he wrote to **Mushir as-Saltanah,** his premier: ―As the weather in Tehran is hot and we could not bear it, we moved to Bagh Shah." The deputies in the *Majlis* interpreted the expression ―the weather is hot and we could not bear it" to mean that they must take up arms to defend the *Majlis.* At the same time they elected twelve men to go to Bagh Shah to talk to the Shah. No sooner the elected[135] arrived in Bagh Shah than they were put in chains. The Shah, proudly and impolitely cast a glance at them and triumphantly passed by them. These twelve messengers of peace, together with five other persons[136] who had been arrested a few hours before that, were put into the jail by the officers.

The next day the Shah occupied the post-and-telegraph building, and issued a notice to the effect that: ―The people are to continue their work with complete freedom, and the House of the National Assembly is also to carry out its duties with full power; our object, however, was to arrest some evil-doing persons who cause disorder and revolt between the state and the people."[137] Before cabling this notice to other towns the telegraph cables were cut. The British company, which was running the telegraph, demanded forty thousand *tuman*s per hour for amending the cables—a sum more than the Shah's monthly salary.

A week later the Provincial Council of Fars contacted all the provinces telling them that it demanded from the representative of the *Majlis* to depose the Shah from the Sultanate.[138] On the same day Tabriz prepared to rise against the Shah. Dispatching continual cables against and pro the Shah brought good profit to the telegraph office. For a whole week even the newspapers of the days before passed on from hand to hand, until on the 31st of Khordad (21st June) an order was issued banning all the papers. All the debates of the day before in the *Majlis* went around the self-centred personality of the Shah. Now, no paper was published to inform the people what the deputies had said. The Shah cabled to all the provinces: ―This *Majlis* is contrary to Constitutionalism. If any one from now on disobeys our orders he will be subject to severe policy and punishment."[139] Alas! The word ‗policy', in the common culture still had its former concept of ‗punishment and chastisement', as was its meaning at that time. This was a big shortcoming on the part of Constitutionalism which did not care to redress such concepts.

The next day the *Majlis* was subjected to what the people saw and heard, entailing a wave of rumours. The day after bombarding the *Majlis,* four men were hanged in Bagh Shah. The first of them was **Mirza Jahangir Khan Shirazi** who had named his newspaper by *Sur Israfil* (because at the end of the world, when all die, Israfil, one of the four angels nearest to **Allah,** will blow the *Sur*' (the trumpet) and the dead will rise.) The second man was **Sultan al-ulama Khurasani,** whose paper was also named in the same way by Ruh al-Quds' (the Holy Spirit), that is, the pure and innocent Spirit Who will bring the dead to life. The judge **Ardaqi** and **Malik al-Mutakallimin** were also hanged with them. Although the history of their lives was not free from suspicion, but the way they were hanged was reported so tragic that it moved the feelings of most of the people. At the order of **Muhammad Ali Shah,** the grave of **Abbas Aqa Tabrizi,** the killer of Atabak, was disentombed and his bones were taken out and thrown to the dogs. On this day forty incidents took place which may be registered in the history. However, if the news of a single crow was made as if of forty crows, then woe to the people who had to hear a thousand and six hundred true and untrue news and assume an attitude! One of the true news was that the Shah wrote to **Mushir as-Saltanah:** ‒We separated the *Majlis* for three months."

Complicated News

Complicated news, each one of which weakened the analysis of the other news, engaged the people, and, despite the trench dug between the Shah and the *Majlis,* as wide and as deep as that between this side of the Constitutionalism and the other side of its clash with the Shah, those who were smarter would whisper: There are wheels within wheels, and all these dirty boils cannot be caused by the filthy water of the culture of the rooted Muslim people.

Such being the case, **Ruhullah,** within the flood of the flowing news, which was attacking their house, could not be satisfied with his horse-riding and childish plays. Whenever somebody came to untie his bundle of fresh news, **Ruhullah** would politely sit down and pay full attention to his report, keeping silent and without showing any reaction. But at night he would draw his white bed-sheet on his face, and, closing his eyelashes, he would sink into the depths of ambiguous imaginations, recollecting what he had heard. Sometimes thirst would drag him out of the warm bed to the cool pitcher. In the morning he would get up and go to breakfast with sleepy eyes. His mother's attempts to lessen his hearing of the news were fruitless. That was because at the entrance of every quarter, every market, and in every meeting, the cords of the larynx played the tune of politics, sometimes causing excitement and hope, and sometimes disgrace and displeasure.

Today, the reality of Constitutionalism can be found in the collection of events stated in the incomplete books and documents of history. But on those days, its reality and practical life were mixed together, creating excitement, enthusiasm, love, fear and disgust. Some were dragged out of their palaces to huts, and some were pushed from the studying rooms, and from the small and big commercial offices in the bazaar, towards the field of politics, waging war on three fronts: one in all the corners of the internal and external politics, the other in the structures of the governing thoughts, and the third front, which was terrifying to the religious men, was placing the religious *ulama* to face each other. **Shaykh Fadlullah Nuri**[140], a scholar whose enemies also knew him to be ‗fond of religion', regarded Constitutionalism contrary to religion, while the *ulama* in the holy towns supported Constitutionalism. Some patriots, such as **Baqir Khan** and **Sattar Khan,** who were named national **Sardar** and **Salar,** sacrificed their lives to bring it home. At the same time some traitors backed it with astonishing zeal and heat.

Childish Questions

When the *Majlis* was bombarded and the news reached Khomein, it was circulated in whispers, because whoever was of the supporters of Constitutionalism was afraid of the supporters of the Shah. But whoever came to **Ruhullah‟s** house used to leave his apprehension outside the door and defend his viewpoint inside the house fearlessly.

One day, a verbal discussion about Constitutionalism being right or wrong, among a number of the supporters of these two sides, changed into a serious argument. Many shirts were torn, a man fell into the pool, a young man of the family, with bleeding nose and mouth, plucked a branch from a tree in order to bleed his opponent‗s nose. The children went pale. The mother took **Ruhullah, Nuruddin** and **Mawlud** to the room, so that the elders may make peace among the quarelling young men. She put a little salt in their mouths, then had them to drink sugared water in order to do away with their fear.

It was hard on the Mother because she did not know which was right and which was wrong, and so, she could not give precise answers to the childish questions of the children. On the other hand, she was a free thinking woman and did not like to impose her beliefs on the children. The best method of handling the current disordered conditions was, she thought, to relate to them a course of the Islamic history in a fictitious style. In fact, she

131

could relate the biography of the **Prophet (s), Ali ibn Abitalib (a)** and the story of *Ashura* in such an attractive way that the disturbed Constitutional news appeared colorless before those truthful historical stories. Nevertheless, Constitutionalism, which was a current flow, with new events every now and then, many times knocked at their door hurriedly and excitedly. How many times? Maybe more than a hundred times.

Sattar Khan and Baqir Khan in Ruhullah's Look

One day somebody came and, with a sorrowful and trembling voice said: ─Tabriz became a graveyard. All were beheaded." **Karbalai** inserted his spade into the earth, put his hand on his waist, sat down and lit up his pipe. The women went inside and wore black mourning dresses.

An hour later another person came and said: ─Tabriz is manly resisting and has defeated the forces of the government." The black dresses were taken off. The real story was this: On the 2nd of Tir (23rd June) when the *Majlis* was bombarded, **Mir Hashim** (a turbaned courtier), with the help of the governmental forces in Tabriz, attacked the Constitutionalists and killed many of them. Afterwards no one could restore order in Tabriz, and two unknown common men, named **Sattar Khan** and **Baqir Khan,** took the leadership of the Constitutionalists in Tabriz, and fought against the government's forces that had been besieging Tabriz for months. Those two personalities, later on, received the attention of the poets and the writers, who wrote about them a number of books and more than a hundred articles. When **Ruhullah** came to leadership he spoke well of the two.[141]

Taqizadeh's Escape

Another day there came the news that **Taqizadeh** and **Sayyid Hasan Kashani,** who was publishing the newspaper *Habl al-Matin'*, fled to Europe. His paper was a reliable one, publishing many social and critical articles, though in the European style. The escape of these two was something ordinary to some people who justified it by saying that when there is no security in the country why should one stay back? But others said: ─Is it of the magnanimity norms that, when people are in a difficulty, running away is preferred to staying?" When danger was off, it was even said: ─The question of running away was called an exile so that their lives may not be taken in the street-wars." Few knew the way of their leaving the country. The historians later wrote that few post-carriages, escorted by two riflemen, left the British Embassy taking **Taqizadeh** out of the country. **Mirza Ali Akbar Khan Dehkhuda** and **Said al-Mamalik** were exiled, too.[142] **Dehkhuda,** under the pen-name _**Dekhu**' and the title _*Charandu Parand* _, used to write satirical and humourous articles which the *Sur Israfil* magazine used to publish. _*Charandu Parand*', written in an eloquent and attractive style, was painful to the Courtiers and sometimes to the religious men, too. Some of those articles reached Khomein. Should any of them fall into **Murtada**'s hand, he would read them and relate them to **Ruhullah,** too. Despite his being a child, he had a particular soberness, but whenever he could catch the purport of the _*Charandu Parand* _, his white teeth would show out.

„*Charandu Parand*" and „*Mushu Gurbeh*"

The people of Qazvin used to call **Dehkhuda _Dekhu**". So many stories were told about _**Dekhu**'s' naivety such that the word entered the lexicon with two meanings: One is _**kadkhuda**" [head of a village] and the other _**kawdan** _[stupid]. **Ruhullah** had many times heard the episode of slaying a cow in a jar, then breaking the jar to take out the cow's head, as an evidence of **Dekhu**'s sharp wits, and later he used to use it as a proverb.[143] Therefore, exiling the fictitious **Dekhu** to Europe stirred his feelings. At last **Dehkhuda** returned to Iran through the Ottoman land, and was elected by Tehran and Kerman as a deputy to the *Majlis*. Then he gave up politics and set himself to write an encyclopedia. A good number of the college students prepared slips for him, and within many long years he wrote a very large encyclopedia which could be bound in a hundred volumes. However, it is more a lexical encyclopedia than a general one. Nowadays there is still an establishment named after him, with researchers and officials. The present chairman of this establishment says: ―The cause of the survival of the name of **Dehkhuda** is his loyalty to the household of the **Prophet** (*s*)."[144] Afterwards, besides getting a set of this encyclopedia, **Ruhullah,** one day went to meet the author so as to be closely acquainted with him. **Dehkhuda** received him very well and had a lot to tell him about the Constitutional struggle. He told him that *Charandu Parand* was one of the serious works of his life, as otherwise he would not have been sent to exile. Nevertheless, as **Aqa Ruhullah** himself sometimes had joke-like talk, yet he never tried to imitate the style of *Charandu Parand,* while he much preferred the jokes of **Ubayd Zakani**.[145] Strange enough, he regarded him to be one of Iran's sages[146], and regarded the book _*Mushu Gurbeh*' [Mouse and Cat] by this wiseman, which some *ulama* took to be useless, or even harmful, a valuable and instructive one.[147] It seems that when **Ruhullah** moved to Qum, **Dehkhuda**'s personality became one deserving study, especially that he was named Allamah [great scholar], and **Ruhullah** wanted to know how **Dekhu** of yesterday became the

Allamah Dehkhuda" of today. What has he in his thoughts bag? Can a scholarly title be given out as a gift, or did he really deserve it? Secondly, he had remained loyal to the traditional beliefs, had complete mastery of the Arabic language and literature, and at the same time his name was among those who had seen Europe, become modernists and learnt the language of the foreigners perfectly. Thirdly, he was a graduate of the political school, started his career in journalism, became a parliament representative, then he quitted politics and acquired a cultural title. He composed a collection of poems. On that meeting he offered one of his latest poems as a gift to **Aqa Ruhullah.** There was a talk about the stories of _Mushu Gurbeh'_. **Aqa Ruhullah** said: –As a child I learnt all the stories of *Mushu Gurbeh* by heart. But now I remember only a few lines." Probably during the conversation **Aqa Ruhullah** was gazing at the complexion of **Dehkhuda** and contemplating the tone of his voice in order to find out that when a man becomes weak in the field of politics and retires, does he turn to cultural activities, or that politics require the zeal of youths, but it is quitted in the year of maturity, or that becoming a cultural figure is the last status attained to by some people?

Probably the first time he heard this simple, but meaningful, poem in **Ubayd"s** *Mushu Gurbeh* from somebody who must have been a supporter of Constitutionalism and did not want to be deceived three times by **Muhammad Ali Shah,** who swore two times that he would no longer entangle himself with the supporters of Constitutionalism, but he broke his oaths each time and undid his repentance:

> **Good tidings! The Cat has become pious,**
> **Pious, ascetic and Muslim!**

Tabriz Still in Disorder

Tabriz, where **Muhammad Ali Shah** was born and brought up, was harder upon him than other provinces, and, as it had tried his behaviour during his childhood and adolescence, it could never give up fighting him. But Khomein was half-Constitutional. It was not so active. It could only be excited at hearing the hot news from Tabriz.

Tabriz had several times risen against the forces of the Government, sometimes defeating, sometimes defeated. Sometimes provision did not reach the fighters and they had to go with empty stomach for a week while filling their rifles with gun powder. Once the fighters put down their arms, but no sooner they did so than they realized that they were deceived, and the rifles were oiled once again. The most sorrowful sunset of Tabriz was on the day when **Shahsawan** tribe attacked this town, supporting the Shah, causing many criminal deeds, contrary to tribal magnanimity.

One of the Shah's intrigues was the order which he issued to his Premier, reminding him that the *Majlis* would be opened on the 22nd of Aban (13th Nov.), and only the people of Tabriz would be deprived of taking part in it. On the 22nd of Aban there was held a great meeting in Bagh Shah, the head quarters of the Shah, with the participation of all classes, and there were talks about the wanted type of government. It was in this meeting that **Shaykh Fadlullah Nuri** called out: –Constitutionalism is incompatible with religion," and he read to the audience the cables received from some of the *ulama* in the towns against Constitutionalism.[148] At the end of the meeting a petition was raised to the Shah requesting him to give up Constitutionalism—a request which was for granted, anyhow, as the Shah had already enacted that request. A number of the *ulama* signed the petition. Three of the signatories gave warmth to the Shah: **Shaykh Fadlullah Nuri, Sayyid Abul-Qasim,** the Imam of Friday *salah,* and **Zahir al-Islam.** Five days later another meeting was held in Bagh Shah to follow up the proceedings of the former meeting. The next day the Shah issued a statement to the effect that: –Being an adherent of the sacred religion of Islam, and as the great *ulama* have announced that Constitutionalism is contrary to the Islamic law, therefore, I announce that I have given up Consitutionalism."

Invocation for the Health of Shaykh Fadlullah

The attitude of **Shaykh Fadlullah** in respect of Constitutionalism astounded the family of **Aqa Ruhullah.** They knew him to be truthful and ascetic, and, furthermore, the *ulama* of his level were pro-Constitutionalism and used to dispraise **Muhammad Ali Shah.** One day there came a piece of news that the **Shaykh** was subject to an unsuccessful assassination, resulting in wounding him.[149] After the *maghrib salah* all the members of the house gathered in the veranda and invoked **Allah** to bestow health upon the **Shaykh.** They seated **Ruhullah** in front of all facing the *Qiblah,* telling him that **Allah** responds quicker to the children's invocations.

It was a strange period. There were hailings[150], floods[151], assassinations[152], and local conflicts took casualties, as if the history of Iran assumed, for the first time, a different conduct, opening a new chapter. Street clashes in Kazerun, in Lar, in Minab, between the Constitutionalists and the Shah's soldiers used to create heart-rending incidents at daytime, and at nights, in the mourning meetings the tune of hope, for next morning's conflicts, was played. The body of an American, named **Baskerville,** killed by the government's forces in Tabriz, was so splendidly escorted in its funeral procession that one thought him a self-sacrificing relative who drank from the barrel of martyrdom, and hurried to the other world drunk.[153]

Days Counted in Conflict With Despotism

The flooded Qazvin became a battlefield. The people of Gilan, under the leadership of **Yeprim Khan,** an Armenian, clashed against the government forces. It took days to bury the casualties. A year after the bombardment of the *Majlis,* the country was blazing up with civil war, and from among hundreds of small and big conflicts, only the following wars found their way into the history, and before **Ruhullah** reads history, he heard the events of his period in his own house, his relatives' houses, in the town's mosque, from the mouths of tens of people. Before the details of those events enter into history, he had the details, true or false—which usually developed according to the distances they covered—written on the tableau of his mind, so that he might later sift them.

I believe that the following events had been stamped on the mind of this child:

6th Tir (27th June): War between the forces of the government and the forces of **Sattar Khan** and **Baqir Khan** in Tabriz, and its numerous casualties.

7th Tir: War between the forces of the government and the Constitutionalists in Rasht causing many casualties and wounded.

29th Tir (20th July): Another bloody war in Tabriz. In this war the forces of the government bombarded the town and destroyed many houses.

3rd and 6th of Mordad (25th and 28th July): Other wars with many casualties in Tabriz.

17th Tir: The attack of the trained **Shahsawan** cavalry-men on Tabriz.

28th Tir: Complete siege of Tabriz.

1st Shahrivar (23rd Aug.): Irregular war in Tabriz.

3rd Mordad: The defeat of the forces of the government at the hands of 21000 of the Constitutionalists of Tabriz. In this war it rained bullets on the governmental forces. The day before a cargo of rifles and 12 million cartridges, which had been bought from the Ottomans, were received.

17th Azar (8th Dec.): The occupation of the town of Khuy by the fighters.

1st Isfand (20th Feb.): The murder of **Aqa Bala Khan,** the governor of Rasht, and the arrival of **Muhammad Wali Khan Sepahdar Tunkabuni** the day after, and his joining the revolutionists of Gilan.

17th Isfand: A bloody war between the forces of the government and the Constitutionalists in Kazerun, Lar and Minab.

18th Isfand: A big war in Miyaneh.

15th Farvardin, 1288 (4th April, 1909): Bombarding Tabriz once again. The Constitutionalists of Gilan entering the town of Qazvin under the leadership of **Yeprim Khan,** the Armenian. A severe and bloody war took place causing many losses and many casualties on both sides.

16th Farvardin: The joining of the forces of **Commander Muhyi, Muntasir ad-Dawlah** and **Muhammad Khan Tabrizi** to the forces of the Consti- tutionalists of Gilan in Qazwin.

5th Ordibehesht (25th Apr.): The arrival of the Russian soldiers through Caucasia on the pretext of providing their troops with provisions.

8th Ordibehesht: The massacre of the people by the Russian forces in Tabriz.

29th Khordad: The hasty Movement of **Commander Asad Bakhtiyari,** with a thousand cavalriers and a gun, from Isfahan to Tehran. After six days they arrived in Qum, and, strangely enough, **Commander Asad** had talks with the representatives of the Russians and the British.

9th Tir: Stationing guns at the main streets, **Muhammad Ali Shah** prepared the capital for a big war.

22nd Tir: All the fighters who came from other towns joined together and fought the forces of the government in Badamak. The next day the government forces, bearing a severe defeat at the hands of the fighters, retreated, and the gates of Behjat Abad were opened to the fighters. But the defeat of the government forces did not prevent Tehran from becoming a scene of street clashes, which had casualties on both sides, until at last the Russian **Liakhov**—who had, exactly one year and 21 days before massacred the *Majlis* deputies and triumphantly strolled in the streets—stopped fighting and surrendered, and the next day asked for personal amnesty to return to Russia .Strangely, he did get the amnesty and returned home.

In this period many Premiers resigned or were deposed and the cabinets were successively changed. Most of the members of every new cabinet tried, in their short duration, to collect as much money as they could so as to have a better life after being deposed.

Muhammad Ali Shah in the Orchard of the Russian Embassy

In the morning of 25th Tir, before the sunrise, a tall woman, with a black veil, got in a royal carriage, seating her 13 years old son, **Ahmad,** beside her. Few minutes later **Muhammad Ali Shah** took his place between them, and ordered the driver to move. A caravan of more than twenty royal carriages moved towards the Russian Embassy. The caravan was escorted by five hundred armed Cossacks, riding and on foot, to protect it.

The Russian Embassy owned a large orchard in Zargandeh at Shemiranat, with thickly woven trees, including plane trees. This orchard was situated in a place where the two rivers of Darband and Gulabdarreh joined; always full of water and of rosewater. Besides, a number of canals, formed from the melting snows of Tuchal, run through the Embassy's orchard, causing it to be thrivingly green and cool. Six rooms in this orchard were given to the Shah, three for the household and three as working office. The attendants and Cossacks set up their tents in the gorgeous orchard of the Embassy. The British flag went up, too, the iron gate of the Russian Embassy, so that the Coustitutionalists may know that attacking this Embassy means attacking the British Embassy, too.

Hearing the news of the Shah's asylum, most of the anti-Constitutionalism hurried and sought refuge in other Embassies. The two Russian and British Embassies had no empty room left. So, the flags which they had already provided for such occasions were sent to houses of the pro-despotism to be set at their doors so as to be immune against aggression, and, by this simple way, they tried to convey the message of their governorship from the top of those houses to other citizens. One of them, **Aynuddawlah,** was magnanimous enough not to accept any flag and surrendered, entrusting himself to fate. When things calmed down, those who had taken refuge in the foreign Embassies slowly crept back to their houses, justifying their disgraceful deed by saying: –People follow their kings' religion.[153/1]" When a person is accustomed to meanness, he uses noble *hadiths* according to his mean understanding.

On the other hand, two officials from the two Embassies of Russia and Britain, **Mr. Churchill** of England, and **Mr. Barnovski** from Russia, hurried to Baharistan Building, the headquarters of the fighters. One of them turned to the **Commander Tunkabuni** and the other to the **Commander Asad Bakhtiyari** and reported to them that the Shah had to take refuge in the Russian Embassy. So, they requested that an end should be put to this civil war. What was the reply?

–Yes, with pleasure!"

Had they any alternative other than closing their eyes and say ―Yes"? The diplomats say they didn't, as no one can say ―No" to a call for ending a civil war, and as everybody knew that it had been decided to change the battlefield. If not all, those who had to do with politics very well knew that what the dictators dictate has a beginning and a full stop, though there would be no end to the full stop. The arrowtip of the Constitutionalists was aimed at the heart of the Shah's power. Now that he sought refuge in the Russian Embassy, depriving himself of the ability of looking outside, there would be no worry concerning war. This humanistic recommendation of the two super-powers of the time was the most humiliating abuse directed from two enemies to the heads of the fighters of the Constitutionalism, who, though dear to the Constitutionalists, had not so much intelligence and dignity to give a suitable reply to this debasing humiliation!

Ruhullah is still a boy of seven years, but later on, the shameful answer which the two leaders of the fighters gave to two officials of the Embassy, was decisively and insistingly atoned for by suggesting the slogan of ―Neither Eastward nor Westward.[154]"

The next day, the Constitutionalists chose 28 persons[154/1] from among themselves to take the affairs of the country in their hands. But alas! Those 28 persons were not the best men of Iran at that time, as the files of the secret relations of some of them with the two super-powers of that time were exposed many years later.

The Supreme Council of the Constitutionalists assigned a board of seven members to go to the Russian Embassy to talk to the Shah, the refugee. The board included the two British and Russian officials.[154/2]

Ruhullah's Wooden Pan in the Victory Celebrations
On that day the Constitutionalists announced that for five days there should be celebrations and decorations all over the country. In Khomein, too, there were celebrations, and lanterns were lit at the thoroughfares. Colored flags danced on every district and quarter. Some laid tables with colorful dishes. Strange enough, the tables of those who formerly supported despotism were more colorful. Of course, the celebrations of these days had another meaning for the freedom-seekers and those wounded by despotism. In **Ruhullah's** house, too, the door remained open for a few days, as it was in the days when the master of the house was living, and they received people to the extent they could afford. **Ruhullah** had now reached the age at which he could undertake a task to participate in the celebration of people. He took the large earthenware pot full of yoghurt and started emptying it into a large wooden

pan by a ladle, adding salt and water, and stirred it with skimmer so as to make churned yoghurt. He plucked the leaves of the pennyroyals growing near the brook, putting in each bowel of churned yoghurt one or two leaves. How pleasant to him those days were passing, and how refreshing that scented churned yoghurt was to the guests!

Transferring Sultanate to Ahmad Shah

At the end of the celebration days, which were early in summer **Adud al-Mulk,** an old and proportionally upright man, with two hundred Cossacks set out to the Russian Embassy, not in order to continue arguments, but to talk about taking **Ahmad,** son of the Shah. The Supreme Council of the Constitutionalists had deposed the Shah, with the intention to crown his thirteen years old son as king in his place. The Shah said: ─I am greatly fond of this boy. Throne his younger brother." The respond was: ─If Ahmad is not crowned, the good- omen bird, from the shoulders of the Qajaris will perch on the shoulders of another family." So, he consented. **Ahmad** kissed his mother's face and father's hands. Seven hundred Cossacks saw with their own eyes that even the stone-hearted men were weeping at the time of saying farewell to their dear ones. **Ahmad's** eyes were filled with tears, too, and, sad yet firm, he put his foot in the stirrup. Arriving in Saltanatabad, a cap, as large as a crown, was put on his head. Strange enough, ascending the throne required a speech to be delivered. **Sayyid Abul-Qasim,** *the Imam of the Jumah salah* of Tehran, was a refugee in the Russian Embassy with the deposed Shah. His brother, **Sayyid Muhammad,** the new *Imam of the Jumuah salah,* slowly read the speech of transferring the Sultanate. During the recitation of the speech deposing the father and replacing the son, **Ahmad** had uneasy eyes but a dignified behaviour. He seemed a rather courageous and intelligent boy, but not so much as not to accept the kingship. When he opened his mouth to say something, his small tongue uttered big words. He said: ─I hope that **Allah** will help me to make for the losses caused by my father and to offer my services to my people.[154/3]"

He was too young to be able to offer any service in those misty and complicated political plays. **Adud al-Mulk,** the elder of the Qajar family took the reins in his hands until the Shah grows up and he becomes both a Shah and a governor. The small Shah used to stir up the feelings of the children to feel proud that the Shah of Iran was a child. From then on the childish play _Shah-Wazir', popular with the children, became even more popular, because the experienced, equitable and modernist elders and even the pious people had one day played the Shah-playing game.[155]

Now, **Ruhullah** is six years younger than the Shah. Apparently, he was unconsciously following his behaviour, so that seventy years later he might testify that if that small Shah could offer no service, he at least did not betray. He addressed a few sentences to the last Shah and Shah-players, dispraising **Muhammad Rida,** and somewhat praising **Ahmad Shah.** Those sentences were as follows: ─You who came and sat here and said: ‗I am the Shah, all things must be done by me.' You received the lists and acted according to the orders of the foreigners. Was not it betrayal? Have you any excuse for that? Quit! Say: ‗I'll not commit such a betrayal, and I'll quit.' **Ahmad Shah,** in this last thing, was put aside, as it was planned that when he left for abroad, they would have him, at the table, I mean, at the party, they gave him the agree- ment to sign. He did not sign it. Thereupon it was planned to drive him out and bring **Rida Shah** in, as it did not avail them not to sign their agreement. You, too, could not sign this agreement. Was it other than you had to quit?[156]"

The pleasant memories of the celebrations were still palatable when some souls drank from the cask of the events the bitter cup of poison. ─Shaykh Fadlullah was hanged, and his son clapped his hands at the gallows." The fact was that on the day of the victory the Shaykh's house was sieged and a court was set up to look into the crime of the pro-despotists. The members of the court were eight, headed by **Shaykh Ibrahim Zanjani,** a turbaned man, who was to try **Shaykh Fadlullah.** In the tumultuous political condition of those days **Shaykh Ibrahim** was (said to be) an enlightened *mujtahid,* but **Shaykh Fadlullah** an old-fashioned *mujtahid!* (It was said that) **Shaykh Ibrahim** supported freedom, but **Shaykh Fadlullah** supported despotism! How hard it was to the pro- *ulama!* A *Ruhani* to try a *Ruhani,* and how simply the sentence was issued! That was because the *ulama* of the holy thresholds [*atabat*] had already said: ─Shaykh Fadlullah disturbs tranquility." Even if they had not said it, the rumour went so, and even if the rumours were untrue, documents were shown to make them appear true. When the knot of the rope marked its trace on the Shaykh's neck, he said: ─Neither I was a despot, nor **Sayyid Abdullah** was a Constitutionalist.[157]" **Adud al-Mulk,** Naib as-Saltanah [the regent], was full of pains for hanging the Shaykh and objected to **Commander Asad** and to the **Sepahdar** (the leader of the army). He ordered the body to be respectfully buried and held a mourning meeting. Even if it was not an order, still two black flags would have been set up on the door of the house of **Ruhullah,** and in the afternoon of Friday two big samovars would be filled with coal, and the town's inhabitants would fill the yard of the house. In the glorious mourning meeting for **Shaykh Fadlullah, Shaykh Jafar** ascended the *menbar* and said what he should have said. He said: ―Woe to the people who kill their notables! How bad is the day when a Constitutionalist becomes a despot. The Shaykh had something to say and we and you have something else. The Shaykh killed nobody that you should kill him. He had forgiven his striker. The hand of **Commander Muhtasham Bakhtiyari** is smeared with the blood of thousands of freedom-lovers. When he was defeated, he joined you and with great welcome you went to receive him, but you prevented the martyr Shaykh even from telling the people what proofs he had for seeking a lawful regime... The people must know that the Shaykh of Zanjan is not less than the **Judge Shurayh**. He is not a Constitutionalist. His hand is in the hand of the foreigner.[158]"

It took tens of years to become known that **Shaykh Ibrahim Zanjani,** the *Ruhani* apparently freedom-loving and enlightened, was an official member of the fearful secret Freemasonry organization. Seventy-one years later **Ruhullah** mentioned the name of this Shaykh in shocking expressions, which few could dare to repeat, hadn't he uttered them first. He said: ―If there was no refinement, even the knowledge of monotheism would be of no avail. Knowledge is the greatest barrier. The more the knowledge accumulated, even the more monotheism—which is the greatest of knowledge—accumulates in man's mind and in his heart, the more it drives him away from **Allah** if he is not refined... You do know the man who tried the late **Shaykh Fadlullah Nuri.** A turbaned Zanjani, a *Mulla* from Zanjan, tried him and sentenced him to death. If a turbaned *Mulla* is not refined, his corruption will be greater than others. In some narratives it is said that in Hell some of its people are tortured by rotten smell of some *Ruhanis*. This world, too, is tortured by their rottenness.[159]"

When **Shaykh Fadlullah** was arrested and nobody objected, it seemed that it was time for the British to define the limits for their old friends, the Russians. Therefore, **Sepahdar** sent a letter to the Russian Embassy, reminding them that sending five hundred armed Cossacks to escort **Muhammad Ali Shah** was apt to stir disorder, so, they must be disarmed. **Sepahdar** was then the Minister of War, and his letter was important. On the same day, however, **Sattar Khan** and **Baqir Khan** sent a cable to **Sepahdar** asking him what to do: ―The Russians want to send both of us to Ottoman in exile. What are we to do?" **Sepahdar** answered: ―The Russians are bastards! Come to Tehran." This decisive reply made the Russians to believe that **Sepahdar** depends on some support.[160]

On the day the Shaykh was arrested it was announced that the elections in Tehran would be in two stages, and each district would have its deputy, and from among 45 persons who would get more votes 15 would be elected anew .This was the first violation of the election law. It did not appear important ,but it opened the way to other violations.

Six days after the martyrdom of the Shaykh, **Sayyid Hasan Taqizadeh** returned to Tehran from his exile—what a return! A few days before he was in Tabriz. The date of his arrival in Tabriz is not known yet [36] .However, on the 31th of Mordad (6th Aug.) he was in Tehran. A good number of the people were gathered to receive him from Karaj. Many tents were set in Karaj, and Taqizadeh's arrival was concealed behind branches of flowers. A generous dinner was served, and he was accompanied to Tehran with music. Were they making him big for a big task?

A month later [162], the Supreme Council of the Constitutionalists held a comprehensive talk with the deposed Shah. It was decided that he and his household go to Europe and receive a yearly allowance of one hundred thousand *tumans*. When he set off, one hundred and twenty Iranian Cossacks, under the leadership of a Russian officer, three Indian and three Russian horsemen and the representatives of the two Russian and British Embassies escorted him to Anzali harbour. Strange enough that illiterate and despot, whom the people hated, and who had committed numerous crimes, and who had, not merely theoretical, but practical clashes with the Constitutionalists, should be seen off in such a way, while **Shaykh Fadlullah** should be seen up the gallows in that way! Does it mean that the Shah was holier than the *ulama*? History tells us that during the past two centuries it was not so, and that was the first humiliation of the *ulama* with complicated arrangement. Yet, it was not the whole thing. It was decided that the Shah should be put in salt water [i.e. preserved] so that if the Constitutionalists stretched their legs farther than their rag, he would return again. Astonishing enough he remained from 18th Shahrivar (9th Sep.) till 7th Mehr (29th Sep.) in Anzali. In the mornings he used to go hunting and in the afternoon to go swimming in the sea.

Constitutionalism in those days was like the two millstones, the lower one fixed, based on the religious, logic and intellectual instructions, and the upper stone was, limpingly and carelessly, moved by the foreigners. That which was ground down was the culture of this nation.

How hard this feverish period of contradictions was on a child, though still unschooled, yet researcher and sensitive, unwantedly got caught between those two stones. The weak ones were crushed by the stones, and their thoughts have now got rotten. But **Ruhullah's** pains between these stones changed into a grace causing him to revolve and to experience so as to know the society, religion, sociology and politics as well as to understand the contradictions pretty well. In 51 speeches and interviews he directly referred to Constitutionalism 113 times. Although from these alone one cannot easily follow up the progress of his opinion concerning the bases of a constitutional government, yet one can find a way through them to discover his point of view. In his younger years he regarded a constitutional government as _wanted'; in his youth, it was _accepted', and some time later, it was _acceptable'. Then it was –bearable if properly applied.[163]" Lastly, he said: –The constitutional kingdom can never be acceptable to us and to the nation.[164]"

The Old-Fashioned School of Mulla Abul-Qasim

In those days the types of the schools were not the same as they are now. _Maktab' they were called, and they undertook the primary teaching of the children. The late **Mulla Abul-Qasim** was the second[165] official teacher of **Ruhullah,** who had already learnt reading and writing to some extent from **Mirza Mahmud** as a private teacher.

Mostly those schools were coeducational, boys and girls sat together. It, however, depended on the teacher's wish to take the pupils together or to separate the girls from the boys. Whatever the case, we do not know whether the school of **Mulla Abul-Qasim** was coeducational or not. Even if it was coeducationally directed, it caused no serious problem, because the families, before sending their children to the _maktab', they used to immunize them with chastity vaccination. In their houses they learnt such continence that any shameless stare of a dirty eye would be like a nail piercing the eyes of the others. Of course, the teachers used to intimidate the children by the long sticks stretched beside them, and occasionally they were brandished in the air and brought down on the head of a wretched child. We do not know who told them, and why, that: –The teacher's stick is a flower, he who does not taste it is an idiot," despite the fact that directing a class with rod and stick is quite contrary to the prophets' teaching method. But the coeducation and the children not being coeval made it difficult to manage the class, and if the teacher had no sternness and no attraction, the stick would be a good help— the same thing which appears in the arena of politics, though of more complicated type. However, the fear of the stick made it easier for the teacher to control the class, and woe to the boy who would stare at a girl, the stick and the bastinado would cause his feet to be so blistered that for many years

144

the district would be safe of such cases. Of course, this was not the only excuse for the teacher to use his stick, as he could every now and then find an excuse to keep the picture of the stick and the bastinado stamped in the memories. Naturally, this was the worst way of teaching and educating, yet, when the new schools were established everywhere, the stick and the astinado were more or less applied. Anyhow, it was very much improbable that any stick had ever touched **Ruhullah**'s hands and feet, since his was a respectable family, and the teacher would not break that respect. He so carefully observed the regulations that there could be no pretext for the teacher. He had learnt the lesson of chastity at home so strictly that there could be, in this respect, no reason to worry. All along his life chastity waved in his looks. Never looked into an eye except of a lawful woman. Even when he used to watch the local or foreign film to see how art dealt with the religious precepts, so that he might not open his mouth admonishingly before personally watching the film, if he noticed a woman with incomplete *hijab,* he would complete it with his eyelids before suggesting an example, and the next day he would remind it to the authorities. This in itself was one of his most wonderful and sharp-sighted *fiqh,* which was not merely a personal matter, but it was a general judgement which took its place in the society.[166]

It is unknown what his age was when he attended the school of **Mulla Abul-Qasim** and what he learnt there, and when he could no longer find the answers of his questions in the school. But we do know that when he was seven years old, one day this teacher and the other pupils, who most probably were boys, were invited to this house for dinner by way of thanksgiving for having completed the recitation of the whole *Quran* without any mistake. Maybe it was his last day in the *maktab',* though it seems unfair to give a dinner party just because one was good at a subject. But if it was the last meeting with the teacher of the *maktab',* it would be the most symbolic lesson which could be learnt from a *maktab':* The best reward for a good deed is to be fortunate to do another good deed!

The old-fashioned *maktabs* taught reading and writing to the children to the extent of enabling them to manage their affairs. **Sadi**'s *Gulistan* or simpler texts were taught, but the basic text was the *Quran.* In case the head of the *maktab'* had a good voice, or he thought he had, he would resort to *tajwid*[167] in reciting the *Quran.* If he could learn by heart, he would enhance the children to learn the *Quran* by heart. The *surahs* at the end of the *Quran* were learnt by the children by heart, as they are short and melodious. Sometimes a few *hadiths,* quoted from the **Prophet (s)** or from the purified Imams (a), were the relish for the lessons. One of the *hadiths* which the children used to learn was attributed to the Imam **Ali** (*a*): ―Whoever teaches me a letter makes me (his) slave.[168]" Encouraging or compelling to learn this speech, though more agreeable to the teachers than to the children, yet, it was a speech, which, like a seed, grew in the souls of the children resulting in continual politeness and respect for the teachers. No doubt that **Ruhullah,** before going to the school and read this *hadith* in his text books, had grown it in himself to the extent that till the end of his life no one had ever seen him, when one of his teachers entered a meeting unless he stood for him in solemn respect. When ill and somebody came to visit him, he would immediately stand up respectfully, if the visitor had taught him even for a single day, and it was unbecoming to see him stretching his leg in his presence. Later he realized that whatever the teacher said might not be the very truth. One who has not learnt this, he can never present new suggestions, because the requisites for perfection, development and fruitfulness are pithy doubts and heartfelt criticisms of the sayings of the ancient. In respect of criticism one should begin with what he has learnt. This means direct criticism of one's own teacher. The intellectual and scientific environment of **Ruhullah** was brimful of such criticisms, as the atmosphere of the time and the tricks of the age could attract many of his teachers to think what religion has to do with politics. But the more **Ruhullah** listened to the talks and lessons of his great teachers the better he realized that religion without politics has nothing to do with believing in religion. Under the spectre of believing in religion he stood quite opposite to some of the teachers, and manly insisted upon it. Surely he was certain that that idea was truer, and that the clouds would not cover the sun forever. Therefore, in order to prove this idea and disprove the other one, he did not rest for a moment, but he, as a critic, mentioned no name of any one of the teachers so that they may not be disrespected even to that extent.

A Gift to the Teacher of the Maktab

It was a custom on the day of graduation that mothers put bundles under the arms of their children to hand them over to the teachers of the *maktabs* as presents and tokens of gratitude. The children felt shy of doing so, but, at any rate, they had no option. The manners and the norms of politeness in the house of **Ruhullah** make one imagine the moment when he untied the bundle to give the present to his teacher. It might be a length of cloth, an _aba' left over from the father, a long shirt, a pair of hand-woven woolen stockings, or one or two sugarcane. Now **Ruhullah** is a polite and courageous boy capable of performing the regulations of greetings and formal courtesies with the elders, but in this matter he is not so courageous. He is shy—a state which

146

never parted him, at certain occasions, till the end of his life. When he was undoing the knot of the bundle to bring out the present, large drops of sweat appeared on his forehead. When the teacher was thanking, he, too, had on his tongue childish sentences of thanks, though still keeping his head lowered. I have this picture of him from his old age. One day, when one of his students became frenzied of his lesson on ethics, followed him to his house. When he was opening door, he noticed the student behind him. "Any thing I can do for you?" he asked. The student shyly answered: "I want your _aba' for tabarruk." He invited him into the house, entered a room and brought out a bundle, undid its knot and took out a brand new _aba', and, while offering it with both his hands respectfully, sweat of shyness covered his forehead. It seems that on presenting a gift to somebody he always thought it unworthy— a feeling caused him to perspire, and to lower his head while hearing the other side's words of thank and praise, and sometimes he would say: "It is less than what you deserve."

Ruhullah at School

After saying farewell to the *maktab,* the teacher and the mates, he directly went to school, but what school? This we do not know well. Once he said: "I remember the two World Wars. I do not think anyone of you remembers the World War I... I was a child, but I used to go to school...[169]" Maybe by _school' he meant the *hawzah* for teaching religious subjects. The book *Tehran's History*, in its chapter about schools in the thirteenth century, there are information if coincided with reality, it would seem unlikely that at that time Khomein should have schools of the same present schools.[170] So, probably he meant the *hawzah* for teaching religious subjects. Yet, it is also probable that as Khomein had more wealthy Khans, the new schools were established there earlier. **Ruhullah's** cousin, whose name was **Hasan Mustawfi,** and who was only a few months older, yet was his school-and play- mate, said: "We went to a school which, like the French schools, had chairs and benches." How many schools were there in Khomein? Which one of them answered his morning greetings? How many classes did he pass at this school? We have no definite answers for these questions. [171] But we do know that **Aqa Shaykh Jafar, Hajar Khanum's** cousin, the very preacher at the celebration of the middle of Shaban, was the dean or a teacher of the school to which **Ruhullah** directly went, after leaving the *maktab* or the new school, to start learning religious lessons.

Entering the Theological School

Procuring book, notebook and pen was not easy at that time. But the monetary status of **Ruhullah**'s family, however, was not so bad, though not as it was when the father or the grandfather was living. **Aqa Murtada** procured them. The books he found in his father's library. They were old books with leather covers and yellowish papers. **Aqa Murtada** knew with what sentences the lessons would commence. He taught **Ruhullah** those sentences. Mother saw him to the lane and her invocations for him resounded in his ears till the school. Perhaps **Aqa Murtada** had escorted him to the school, or somebody else, as at that time **Aqa Murtada** was on a journey, preparing to continue his studies in Isfahan.

In these days, on the first day of the school, the father or the mother or both of them take the small hands of their children in their hands and escort them to the school, and, while still en route, thousands of thoughts assault their minds: After twenty years what profession would their children have? But almost nobody would be able to rightly guess this secret. Though his father was not there to press his son's hands, yet when his mother saw him to the turn of the lane and followed him with her eyes, she was almost certain what his future profession would be.

Persian Literature and Arabic Grammar

The sweet Persian literature and the complicated Arabic grammar were the first lessons which a newly coming student had to study. Unfortunately, age was not considered. If a forty years old man got the desire to enter the theology centre, together with the boy of seven or eight years, both had to start from the same point, though the teacher's taste was decisive in selecting the text books, yet, the availability of the books had something to do with that selection.

In teaching the Arabic grammar all the teachers were taskmasters. But in respect to the Persian literature they were not equally severe. The Persian literature usually began with **Sadi**'s *Gulistan,* and what a difficult start! Discounting the prophets and the pure Imams, **Sadi** was the sole contending eloquent writer in the history, although there is no comparison between him and **Mawlana** in love-sickness. As regards spirit exhilarating, **Hafiz, _Lisan al-Ghayb**" [The tongue of the invisible], was the vanguard, but as regards eloquence **Sadi**'s language was sweet, wise, melodious, concise and most beautiful. Nevertheless, understanding its expressions seem too difficult for the young boys. After a few sentences there come some lines of poetry, but those very sentences are also poetry in the form of prose. After the *basmalah,* it starts with the following phrase: ―Praise be to God, the Mighty, the Glorious, obeying Him causes His proximity, and gratitude to Him increases His grace." But in the next page, most of the students of the Persian literature feel lost: What a sentence construction this is! ―He told the chamberlain of morning breeze to spread out the emerald carpet, and ordered the nurse of the vernal clouds to cherish the daughters of plants in the cradle of the earth. He clothed the trees with the garment of green foliage as the New Year's robe, and crowned the offspring of the branches with blossoms at the coming of the season of roses. The juice of the cane changed, by His power, into excellent nectar, and the stone of a date, through His upbringing, became a high date palm." **Ruhullah** had to learn these sentences, even by heart. So, from then on, this young boy had to sleep less and to read more.

If he had started his study of the Arabic literature with the book *Sharh al-Amthilah,* then he must have learnt by heart the hadith of **the Prophet (s)** with which the book starts, after the *bismillah.* It is an astonishing *hadith:* **―The beginning of knowledge is to know the Omnipotent, and the end of knowledge is to entrust things to Him.**[172]" No doubt the first time he learnt this *hadith,* he got something out of it in proportion to his childish understanding, but the nature of knowledge is such that everyday thousands of people think about it, and tomorrow and other tomorrows they would think about it. But anyone who cannot understand this deep expression about the nature of knowledge—which also explains the doctrine of Fatalism and Volition—he wastes knowledge and life. One can positively say that till the end of his life he concentrated his heart and mind on this wonderful *hadith* and carefully scrutinized it. Let us keep this saying from him in mind, to which we shall refer in more details later: ―Commit your will to **Allah,** so that the Sacred Essence may make you the manifestation of His will, and assign you to exercise functions in His affairs... and this is other than the impossible and invalid absolute volition.[173]"

At Dawn on the Salah Carpet

It is true that **Ruhullah** has not yet reached the religiously legal adolescence, but besides the Islamic education which says: ―Teach your children the *salah* before adolescence," the theological lessons are another motive for getting up every morning before sunrise. He gets up with the first call from his mother, greets her warmly, hears a warmer reply, goes to the yard, dips his hands into the water of that heart-shaped pool, washes them three times, with his right hand pours a handful water on his forehead and receives it at his chin. Although his feet are always clean, yet after wiping his feet he washes his hands the second time, and, on his way back to the room, he pulls down his sleeves, greets once again. The first greeting was at getting up. The second greeting is more formal. This was the tradition when the lavatory was in the yard, and the pool was the place of washing and performing the *wudu.* Sometimes the mother watches him from behind the window glass, and a smile appears on her lips denoting her content of his daily bodily cleanliness which adds to his spiritual purification. If the brothers had not by then collected the *salah* carpet, he would use it for his *salah.* Otherwise he himself would unfold and spread it towards the *Qiblah.* The mother never interferes in this act, as she knows that the deep love for her child is to let him perform his own affairs by himself.

Having Breakfast in the Yard

By the arrival of the sun, the breakfast is ready. In summer the *sufreh* is laid in the yard or on the veranda. In the atsmosphere of the garden, when the sun is still pink and the singing of the nightingales at times gently caresses the ears, it doubles one's appetite for eating. Sitting at the brimful pool, under the long shade of the trees, besides one's brothers and sisters, facing mother and drinking tea, renders it a joyful breakfast. Mother took care that her children were eating enough. Sometimes she would prepare with hot, or wetted, bread, cream, scalded cream, butter or cheese. From a flask laddels of hot milk would be poured into the children's bowels. The fruits which every year were picked from the trees in the garden, washed and put in a pot to be cooked into the morning marmalade, were also adding to the colors of the *sufreh.* Mother took it to be her duty, which she very carefully observed, not to let her children, in the years of growing up, suffer from malnutrition and then grow up lean, weak, good-for-nothing and ever-invalid. But when she remembered that in the town there were hundreds of children who spent the night with an empty stomach, while her children left the *sufreh* filled up, the food tasted like poison in her mouth. So, she used to busy herself with an engagement so that the others may not find out she left the *sufreh* still hungry. Probably she thought that it was time to exert her best in implementing two objectives by well feeding her children, that is, first to bodily strengthen them so that illness may not get the better of them, and second, to satisfy them to satiety so as to be safe from the disease of slipping in stomach's desires, then when they grow old they can choose the kind of *sufreh* at which they like to sit.

150

Brushing the Teeth as a Tradition of the Prophet

In this house brushing the teeth three times after meals is a necessity. Before being a sanitary care for the teeth, their brushing was practised after breakfast, lunch and dinner more as a religiously supererogatory act. The noble **Prophet (s)** advised the people to brush their teeth so ardently that one thought it to be obligatory. He himself, at the moment of leaving this world, pointed with his hands to his *miswak* to be brought. He could hardly speak, nevertheless he brushed his teeth to let his *ummah* know that it was thanksgiving for the favour of being able to hand over to the angel of death one's organs as sound as possible, as a token of being grateful to **Allah** for His graces. At that time the toothbrush was the *miswak,* a piece of a stick taken from the (Arak) tree, and the toothpaste was salt. Some travellers used to bring this toothbrush as souvenir to their relatives. Those who did not know the wisdom of this supererogatory act put the *miswak* in their *salah*-rugs, and after each *salah* they polluted their mouth with it. **Ruhullah** was so disgusted with such sticking to narrativism that one day he took the *miswak* of someone's *salah*-rug, broke it into pieces and threw the pieces away, and then he washed his hands several times, and said: ─You have taken a definite *mustahab* act down to the border of a *haram.*" However, he himself practised much exertion in brushing his teeth. We do not know in which school he had heard a narrative quoted from the Imam **as-Sadiq (a)** who advised to brush the teeth crosswise, not lengthwise.[174] So, he used to brush his teeth crosswise three times every day, except in the month of Ramadan, during which he brushed them only twice a day. Even when he fell sick he did not forget it. In his youth he used to throw away the old stick brush every few days, and in his old age he used to throw away his modern toothbrush after a while. After washing his mouth perhaps he used to go for a stroll in the garden, going over his lesson of the day before.

Finishing Learning Grammar

We do not know whether the father's pocket-watch with its chain was in his pocket or in his brother's. At any rate, either by instinct or by a watch, **Ruhullah** was so punctual that during his schooling period he never delayed the class or the teacher even for a moment. Likewise, when he himself became a teacher, the students knew that he would never be late. The kind care of mother, the encouragements of the two brothers, the pleasant air in the garden, punctuality, purity of the conscience, politeness, aptitude and effort, all backed each other so that he may learn the hard and complicated lessons of the grammar of the Arabic language as quickly as possible. Thus, he could very well conjugate a sentence, but alas! The meanings hidden behind the words were difficult for him to understand, but it was not his fault, it was the fault of the method of teaching the Arabic language in the schools of theology. The grammar was very well learnt but what was taught was not teaching the language.

Aqa Shaykh Jafar, his mother's cousin, announced that he had completed his job, and entrusted **Ruhullah** to **Mirza Mahmud, Iftikhar al-ulama,** who had studied few years more. He began with the preliminary subjects. After a short time these were finished, too.

With the Logic

Haj Mirza Muhammad Mahdi was **Ruhullah's** maternal uncle. Studying under one's uncle is a little difficult, because an uncle in relation to his sister's son, who lost his father, feels to be a sort of the boy's guardian, or to be a father before being a tutor. The positive side of this situation was that when it is a question of kinship, the tutor would come to the house of the student, and if there was no particular topic for conversation, the house would be filled with loud discussions and discourses, and mother would be watching her son's question-and-answer way of discussion with his teacher, and, seeing that this student has no shortcoming, the lightning of joy and contentment would flash from the mother's eyes. **Ruhullah** paid back a part of his mother's caretakings in this way.

Sisters instinctively love their brothers. **Allah** has arranged the scene in such a way that, to return the hidden kindnesses of the sister, the brother tries to carefully absorb the lessons given to him by his sister's husband as best as he could. He started the sweet lessons of logic under the tutorship of one of his sisters' husbands, **Haj Mirza Najafi.** This subject was very much agreeable to **Ruhullah.** He would attentively lend his ears and heartily indulge in discussion. He used to go to his sister's house, on the pretext of learning, to renew the sight of the tall stature of a brother, the sound of whose coming brings the smell of the father. The rules of logic had been settled by the _first teacher', **Aristotle,** but now he was learning it as a solemn Islamic subject.

When Islam illuminated Iraq, Iran, Egypt and other countries, all the corners of the people's lives were aglow with this upright religion. Even the traditional customs of the nations got the Islamic color. For the purpose of guarding this divine gift, every Muslim scholar put on paper whatever he had in his mind and the scientific _jihad_ started. The great Prophet of the upright religion said: —**Get knowledge even if it is in China.**[175]" Every Muslim, who regarded Islam to go beyond nationality and racism, travelled to wherever he heard of a book worthy of reading. At times he even endured the torture of nostalgia at the cost of his life just to copy a book. Philosophy and logic, which had been established in Greece, were translated by the Muslims into the Arabic, which is the common language of the Muslims. As the *Quran*, in the sweetest language, says: ‒**So give thou good tidings to My servants who listen to the word, then follow the best of it.**[176]" The logic, too, was translated from Greek into Arabic by **Hunayn ibn Ishaq,** who mastered both languages. It cleaved its way within the Islamic world as if it were an Islamic book. Every Muslim researcher who wanted to learn Islamic theology, *fiqh* and philosophy, had to take the logic from **Aristotle,** feeling that by learning the logic he was studying the religion. As a matter of fact, the Muslims added many chapters, annotations and criticisms. But when **Francis Bacon** and **Descartes** attacked that, the Islamic world gave no heed to that and continued to add details and annotations to it, and regarded it a respectable science. Thus, **Ruhullah** is learing it from his sister's husband as a lesson of religion, that is, whatever falls within the frame of knowledge is religious. There is no doubt in this, but is this logic the only method of thinking rightly? We do not know whether **Ruhullah** suspected that science at that time or at a later time when he relearnt it.

The *Mathnawi* of **Mawlana Jalaluddin Balkhi** was the ornament of the father's library. At times **Ruhullah** had something to do with it, especially the following line of poetry:

The legs of the rationalists are wooden

And wooden legs are quite unstable.

At the beginning of learning logic, a strong doubt in respect of the truth of logic, stirs images in the mind of a young person, because apparently it was up to the responsibility of the rules of logic to prove the realities of philosophy; so, what if the legs of logic were made of wood? The last time in which he showed that he believed in that line of poetry was when he not only had learnt philosophy perfectly well, but also he was teaching it perfectly well and had philosopher students. Rather he had gone beyond that and was ascending the last steps of the status of the theoretical gnosticism to practical gnosticism. In his exegesis of the *surah* of *al-Fatihah*, which was his last lesson on exegesis, he used the first hemistage of that poetry twice: **"All praise is for Allah.** If only these few words are believed in, all kinds of polytheism will be dismissed from man's heart. He, who says that he would never associate anyone with **Allah** till the end of his life, says it because it is his conscience, he found it in his disposition, and he found how to invent.

Proofs cannot have so much originality and art. Proof is good. I do not say that it is not good, it must be, but the proof is a means. Of course, the proof is a means so that you may understand a question according to your intellect, and to try to believe in it. _The legs of the rationalists are wooden.‘ Philosophy is a means; it is not wanted for itself... The proof for _the legs of the rationalists are wooden‘ is that it is the wooden legs which help man to walk and actually man is able to walk with them. It is about the legs which show man as a manifestation of **Allah,** the belief which enters the heart, and the conscience is the enthusiasm which creates faith in man. This is a stage, and there is a higher one, too.[177]”

The Brother on the Chair of a Teacher

Aqa Murtada said: ╋taught him the three subjects of *logic, al-Mutawwal* and *as-Suyuti.*” Undoubtedly, he discussed these three subjects with his brother during his visits to his family on his leaves from the *hawzah* in Isfahan, especially the logic, which, if not discussed, would not become a mental habit. It needed much discussion until it was completely stamped on his mind. **Aqa Murtada** was a good arguer.

Learning at home had a priority over learning at school. In case of a problem at home, the teacher was at hand. Another advantage: At school it was only the teacher who sat on a pelt, while the young students had to squat on a thin carpet which caused pain to their legs and sent them asleep. But at home it was not like that. When it was fine he used to stroll in the yard, as the Peripatetics used to do, or, at times, he sat under a tree, sipping from a lean-waisted *istikan* of hot tea, handed to him by the hands of the affectionate mother, which doubled the sweetness of learning and made it so pleasing that nothing could sever its continuation except the *adhan* from the *minaret,* which would stop it for a short while. The school, however, had a priority over the house. The schools were so simple that they taught simple living—a living which did not force man to sell his life in advance to continue it. In those schools there was nothing of tables, chairs or teaching aids. So, no memoir could remain in the mind of these schools except the teacher and the school-mates.

Penmanship Exercise

Calligraphy was both a necessity and an art. It was necessary because at that time there were no typewriters and no computers. Most of the manuscripts were printed thus. Readers were encouraged to read by the books‘ nice penmanship, correctness and beauty. It was also an art because there were no radios and no TVs to fill one's leisure time. One likes to be alone for some time, to think, to day-dream, to be in privacy with nature, to look at the waves ceaselessly attacking the shore, to gaze at the fire with its beautifully dancing flames, to stare at the crystal fall where water falls upon water, while in the heart everything remains intact, and not to think of anything in these moments, as if ecstasized. Sometimes art takes the place of nature and, without disturbing the seclusion, becomes closely intimate with man and opens a window on another world. Calligraphy is one of those arts. Sometimes it engages the heart deeper than painting, music or handicrafts. Sometimes a beautiful poetry penned in a beautiful penmanship acquires multiplied beauty and is recited ten times. In his youth, **Ruhullah** liked penmanship very much. Whenever he got tired of learning, reading and discussion, he used to pick up a pen and a piece of paper aiming at diversity. **Aqa Murtada** taught him the ABC of calligraphy, how to sharpen the pen, the use of flakes of cotton or silk in the inkpot, and how to solve the dry ink in water. But in penning he went farther than his brother, maybe because **Aqa Hamzah Mahallati**, who was an expert calligrapher, used to write models for him to copy. One day **Aqa Murtada** wrote half a page in the Persian cursive style, and **Ruhullah** imitated him on the other half of the page. Afterwards nobody could tell it was written by two hands. Although this art took, in boyhood, a part of his time, yet in his youth and old age he compensated for the lost time. Because of his good handwriting, the type-setters did not find difficulty and had not to say: ─What is this writing of yours? It is unreadable.[178]" The paper, on which he used to write an order assigning someone to a post, or its copy, was neatly framed.[179] Although this art was mingled with his other talents making his living more artistic, yet both the draft and the fair copy were fair copies. If he wanted to send a statement to the printing house, he was keen not to use good paper. He would open a folder, in which he kept scrap papers with one face white, and choose the size of the piece enough for his purpose. Quite often it was a used envelope which he had already cut off its borders, making a square piece. One day he told the servant not to throw away the packet of the tea which he buys and to give it to him. The servant thought he intended to call him to account. But he later realized that the packet was opened and its other blank side, on which one can write, he kept for draft writing. In fact, one of his most revolutionary declarations in Najaf was written on a fruit packet and cabled to Tehran. Despite the fact that it was written on the cheapest kind of paper, yet it was no reason for not writing it beautifully. Didn't he know that those handwritings would one day be of great value? He should have bought expensive papers. If he knew, or if he cared for such things, probably those writings would not have been valuable.

Praising a Beautiful Handwriting Is Praising Allah

The society, too, got its color from his penmanship. The Calligraphers Society was about to lie hidden in a corner, but came back to activity for two reasons: One was when some of the *Basij* members were informed that their Imam wrote beautifully.[180] At times when the enemy's attacks were slight, they used to stay inside their trenches to write their wills or letters. Many of them used to ask their mates, who were known to have good handwriting, to teach them how to improve their writing by way of imitating their leader in writing legibly, to please the reader and the Lord of the reader. It further encouraged the receivers of the letters, the wives or the fiancjes, to improve their own handwriting. The worst handwritings are those of the physicians. A physician took a sentence from his commentary on the *surah* of Opening and started practising writing it until he became an expert at that, and he could then write so beautifully that his prescriptions before curing the body cured the soul. He used to say: ―It suffices me just to have this single sentence: „**Praising a beautiful handwriting is praising Allah.**' If from someone a different thing is expected by the people, when they see a beautiful handwriting, they will involuntarily praise it, and praising it is praising **Allah,** for which I was the means." The Imam's sentences are: ―You think you are praising a good handwriting. It is praising **Allah,** not a handwriting. You think you praise the light. You think you praise a scholar, it is not praising a scholar, it is praising **Allah.**[181]"

Breakages of Head, Brows and Hands

At the beginning of his exercise he could write more beautiful. Then, due to the breakage of his hands, he could not write as beautiful as before. He was energetic and active. Instead of calmly ascending and descending the stairs of the veranda, he used to leap from the yard to the veranda. Whenever his mother called him he would respond on the spot, then in a moment he would be at her side. As a result, the ground had many times kissed his head. [182] But he had a healing flesh. When a handkerchief was tied round his head, in few hours he would untie it and wash off the dried blood. But he twice, and each time for a month, had to hung his elbows to his neck due to breakage. Hence the deterioration of his penmanship.

Jumping From High and Breaking the Leg

Once they had to bond his leg with three splints. In a contest of high jumping with his playmates, he climbed a sharp roof and jumped from about three and a half metres high down to the yard. When he fell on the ground one of his playmates hurried down the steps and stealthily ran away and hid himself in the store of his house for two days so that he may not be accused of killing **Ruhullah**. Another playmate came down slowly and put his ear on **Ruhullah**'s chest. Assured of his being alive, called the other boys and all gathered around him, not knowing what to do. Mother was informed only when he had come to his senses. **Naneh Khawar** fetched a cup of Egyptian willow water, and **Haj Muhammad Hasan**, the bonesetter, using the yoke of an egg, the leaves of plane tree and two splints wrapped his leg in a white cloth to remain so for a month. Despite the fact that it did not stop him leaping and jumping, yet it made him to be more cautious in jumping.

Avicenna: I am Afraid of Cows

In those days when his leg was broken, using a stick to help him walk, there were (in the world) thousands upon thousands of children, youths and old men and women who had their legs broken, their hands fractured, their eyes plucked out of their sockets, their intestines spilled out of their bellies, their brains crashed in their skulls, their houses burnt, their skin and flesh got the smell of grilled meat. After a month **Ruhullah** could walk again as before, but from among the thousands, whose numbers reached, after four years, millions, numerous of them had their legs severed from the thigh or the knee. Bodies of others decayed and others became prey to the beasts and vultures. That was because the madness of politics had roused the wild monster of the World War I. Each day thousands of people were burnt in the flames of the war. Other thousands cried blood tears because they had lost their dear ones, and many other thousands lived in an atmosphere of violence, pain and smoke, dizzy with an ambiguous expectation. When the drummers of the war started gasping for breath and the flames of evil subsided, there were the West and a heap of ashes.[183] The modern civilization was shamefully crouching in a corner, and the social constructors and the philosophers hugging their knees with painful thoughts. During two decades, hundreds, thousands, and even hundreds of thousands, of photos, essays, novels, poetry and paintings portrayed the brutality of the West, but none of them could clearly manifest the cause of the madness which had become common in the West.[184] **Ruhullah,** who had witnessed a tiny part of the crimes of the war, which he followed up later in the history, concluded that when the weapon is

157

in the hands of a bad person the situation becomes like this. In a speech on the occasion of 19th Deymah[185], he said: ‑heard that the late **Mudarris** had said to **Rida Khan**: ‑I heard that **Avicenna** said: I am afraid of cows, because they have weapons, but no reason.' Even if Avicenna did not say it, it is a wise saying, i.e. if weapons are put in the hands of bad and undeserving people, evil things will happen. The World War I, the Word War II, the war in Vietnam which happened later, those massacres of the people, all were because the weapons were in the hands of unsuitable persons. Improper ones had the weapons in their hands.[186]"

Iran in Penumbra of War I

The war started in the West, and in the West, behind grey clouds, the trouble set down so that the madness happened once again in the World War II, but its smoke darkened the whole world, and its splinters fell everywhere all over the world. The most noiseless of these splinters was the heavy expenditures which were mostly weighing upon the countries which took no part in the war. Meanwhile the Ottoman Empire was cut into pieces. Iran was passing through a strange destiny. Even after the war it found no calmness. On one hand, in the world of Islam, apart from Iran, only the dying Ottoman Empire was independent, as other countries were under the ancient French, British and Belgian colonialism. On the other hand, the independent Iran became, as from 1907, under the semi-official occupation of Russia and Britain. The governments were apparently assigned by the Shah and the parliament. But secretly the agreement of the Russian and the British Embassies, or the upper one of them, was the basic condition for appointing the prime minister. The government resembled a thin-bearded man. The seeming independence would show him thick-bearded and it could boast of not being colonized by any power, while he was a thin-bearded man whose beard was plucked by those two. Hence, in the World War I it was neither able to independently take a decision nor inclined to completely obey the two powers, which with France formed a triangle against Germany, Austria and the Ottoman Empire. More important was that the Iranian and the Ottoman States were hostile neighbours as from the days of the Safavid Dynasty[187]—A hostility whose aim ,like most of the historical hostilities of the states, stemmed from desiring power, with the pretext that Iran's government was Shiite and the sect of the Ottoman government was Sunni.

After the arrival of Islam in Iran, for the first time there was a Shiite kingdom and a strong and harmonious government.[188] The Ottoman Sunni kings, from the very beginning, under the name of Caliphate spread their

Sultanate over many Islamic countries. It goes without saying that when there are two monarchist Sultans with sectarian differences, war, blood-shedding and hostility show their claws and teeth. But despite this permanent hostility between those two states, which had its shadow over a part of the social conduct of both nations, the religious *ulama,* the scholars and the people of this country and that Empire had a past of complicated sociable scientific, religious, economic and friendly contest, and in the crucial moments, when Islam and the Islamic lands were threatened by serious danger, they used to haste to help one another. But when there was no danger from outside, Shiism and Sunnism were good excuse for fleecing one another's head. In this instant a stranger was threatening both nations. Therefore, in this war the majority of the Iranian people were inclined in helping the Ottomans, but one of the signs of the Ottoman's last gasps was to become blind and deaf towards understanding this tendency, and, instead of using a polite language, they resorted to violent words and threatened that if Iran did not stand beside them, measures would be taken against it. Naturally, the language of force, whether on the part of the northern non-Muslim neighbour or on the part of the neighbour which claims to be Muslim, could not be amicablly answered, whereas at the beginning of the war the Ottoman Sunni religious authority issued a *fatwa* of *jihad* against Britain, France and Russia. This *fatwa* was supported by the Shiite *ulama* of Najaf and Karbala.[189] Had the Ottoman rulers curbed their language of force, probably the Sunni and Shiite *fatwa*s could mix and maybe the Ottoman Empire could have survived. When after the war the Ottoman Empire was cut to pieces, the Muslims were giddy, irresolute and did not know what to do. Anyhow, after that, in large parts of the world of Islam, politics and religion got divorced.

The Parliament*'*s Division over the War
In the Iranian National Assembly there was a division in opinion for a while. A group, who had established a party named democrat, believed that Iran, like the Ottomans, must support Germany and the other members of the Axis and fight on their side, and, in this way, it would release itself from the chains of the Russians and the British. The more religious ones believed that the Ottomans should be supported to protect the world of Islam so as not to taste the bitter savour of military defeat. But those with milder temperament took neutrality to be nearer to the country's interest. They justified that by saying that Iran's forces were only eight thousand Cossacks who were under the management of the Russian Command. Other seven thousand gendarmes were under the control of the Swedish officers.[190] So, with such a force,

which is not under the command of the Capital, and even if it was, it would have been a single meal for war, how can one not be neutral in such a war?

Perhaps they were right, particularly that the government did not recognize the original power of the nation, but how could one practically be neutral? When there is no war, the politicians respect the legal rules of neutrality, but when war exposes its teeth; its technical rules are more respected by the commanders.

Iran's Neutrality in the World War I

At last, **Mustawfi al-Mamalik,** the Prime Minister of the young **Ahmad Shah**[191], declared Iran's neutrality in the First World War. Despite the fact that this was the best way to escape from a disaster, and that emotional policy kept Iran within the pre-war geography, yet it did not protect it against attacks, killings and plunder, because the Russians regarded Iran to be the back support of the front. Their troops were flaunting in the roads, setting up their tents in the mountains, valleys and woods, forcing out the provision of their troops from the poor stores of the peasants. The crying of the old women over losing their yearly supply, the hope-sickness of the farmers and the gardeners for untimely harvesting their farms and picking the fruits of their trees, the groaning of the shepherds over robbing their sheep and the crying of the terrorized children at seeing the fierceful Russian soldiers, no one could cause any mercy to be shown by the army that was stirred by the war drum and trumpet. Even the life of the wild was horrified by the barbarism of the foreign troops. The pregnant deer of the valleys, the fast rams of the mountains, the well-doves and the partridges were not safe from the bullets which were shot out of the rifles so as to prepare for the troops soup and *kabab*. Even if they were not hungry, they set the traps just for fun in order to watch the dancing of the wild cat in the pitfall, or they would go hunting in order to uproot the race of the lions. Not only the human and animal lives were endangered, as the forests apprehensive at nights, and the individual trees visionary at dawns, were cut at the roots to provide logs for the troops' fires. In this war not only the roars of artilleries and the war drums and trumpets in the days hurt the ears, but the flutes of the night banquets played the tune of destruction, too.

The Worries of the Ottoman Government

At the beginning, the stationing of the six thousand Russian troops in Iran worried the Ottoman government, and it continually sent objective notes, asking the Iranian government to immediately oust the Russian and the

British forces from the country, but the Iranian government was unable to do that. Therefore, it could only dip its pen in the inkpot and to convey the Ottoman objections to the two countries in respectful letters. Each time a messenger was sent to the Russian and British Embassies, new armies would come over from India (representing Britain) and from Russia. At last, after the Ottoman's last memorandum of Nov., 1914, the threat was put to practise and, on 14th Jan. 1915, they occupied Azarbayjan, and, consequently, all the northern and the south-west provinces of Iran became the scene of clashes of the Russians and the British with the Ottoman forces. One day the war was in favour of the Russians and a village would burn in fire, and on another day the Ottoman forces would be victorious, and other villages would be pulled down to the earth. At times the Ottomans would explode the oil pipes in the south in order to paralyse the British war machinery for want of fuel. At other times, the British troops would attack the Ottomans and along the road they would plunder whatever they happen to see. In a single attack, in which the Russians ousted the Ottomans from Urumiyeh, only the Ottoman's casualties were seventy thousand. If supposedly in this war no harm was directed to Urumiyeh, it sufficed the nearby villages and the people to suffer, for many years, from the stench of the decaying bodies of those Ottomans who were killed. During those years thousands of children and old people innocently lost their lives because of the prevalence of cholera in many towns. On the other hand, contrary to the government's desire, thousands of the Iranian youths, under the leadership of some religious authorities obeyed the *fatwa* of *jihad* against Britian and Russia and fought them, but as they had not been militarily trained well enough, and due to lacking an intelligent guide, it was nearer to defeat than to victory. Once, a group of the religious men from Tehran went to Qum and formed a National Defence Committee. But the Russians attacked them on the road from Qum to Saveh and defeated them in no time. Strangely, it was the British who got the reward of the attack, that is, afterwards, the neutral zone stated in the agreement of 1907 was annexed to the British domain, while the Russians got permission to annex to their own domain whatever they can capture of the Ottoman territory. The defeated Committee flew to KermanShah and established a government under the name of _The State of the Emigrants' so as to fight against the Allies. They recruited some four thousand men from the nomads and the citizens. They were trained by German officers and several times attacked the British forces. But, at last, as the British forces could defeat the Ottomans back to Baghdad, the Ottomans gave up manlihood and laid their hands on all the weapons in the possession of the State of the Emigrants, first by means of deceit and then they took everything, including their provision, money and all.[192] Some of them returned home disillusioned with hanging lips by two defeats[193], and some others took refuge in Germany and many other countries. On the other hand, the British, whose military and administrative control over India and Afghanistan was weakening, and a large part of whose forces was defeated by the Ottomans in *Kut al-Imarah* such that they lost their prestige and were mocked at and were afraid that the Indians and the Afghans would celebrate their defeat, and a revolt would take place and the Ottomans could cross the Iranian borders and find their way to Afghanistan, this victory caused them to go into such an ecstacy that they pushed aside all usual civility and acted as they could.

On those days they used to buy more than 60 percent of the agricultural and animal products of the central and dry southern and eastern provinces as provisions for their troops. If someone refused to sell they would still buy! As an example out of thousands: The chief of a village of Birjand, who had said: ─Do not sell the supplies of the village to the British," was so afflicted that a month later he sold out all that he had for ten *tumans*, and signed an agreement according to which he was to receive one *rial* in cash and the balance was divided into 99 instalments of a single *rial* each, to be paid to him over 99 years!

It is said that in wars disunion between the government and the nation gets pale and national union gets into shape. But in those years there appeared a deep gap between the government and the people, and, to some extent, among some classes of the people. The government had announced impartiality, whereas inside the government some were siding with the Russians and some others with the British. Some others made use of every opportuniy to strengthen the Ottomans and the Germans confidentially and secretly, while others had their luggage packed ready so that if there was a serious danger threatening their safety they would ─prefer fleeing to staying." But what was common to the majority of the people, both the enlightened and the men in the street, was that they were disgusted with both Russians and the British. Only a few number, perhaps no more than five thousand, preferred being servants of the British than to bear the hunger and the famine of those years. When the British formed the police in the south in order to straiten the heroes of Tangistan and to control Bahrain, the hungry Iranians formed the greater part of that army. They, beside the hungrier Indians, ate soup and rice and aimed their weapons at their zealous countrymen. On the other hand, a greater number who regarded defending the Ottomans as defending the Islamic lands, provided weapons in their defence, but there was no experienced leader who knew all the corners of politics and could guide that dutifulness in such a way that a logical and reasonable result could be obtained. So, when the Ottomans were occupying the Iranian towns, with a little less rough behaviour than that of the British and the Russians, they were astonished and felt giddy. Another group had not read history to become aware that a foreigner is a foreigner. They thought that by helping the Germans they could get rid of the Russians and the British. They never thought that if Germany triumphed it would take the place of both of them.

The Germans and the Heroes of Tangistan

As a matter of course the Germans had a special position in Iran. They did not interfere in the internal policies of Iran, and their engineers and workers were engineers and workers. They did not assume superiority, and despite their rough culture which is obvious even in their language, they were not complicated. For this reason, although the Germans, in their bloody history, were known as trouble instigators, which is not in harmony with the temperament of the Iranians who do not think of instigating troubles, but are able to digest them, yet, because of some causes which they did not know, later, in explaining some collaborations, or encouraging collaborations, they said that the Iranians and the Germans were of the same race, and they themselves believed it, and, with the help of their own and the Austrian plenipotentiary ministers[194], and a number of officers, they armed the tribes of the south, and the courageous men of Tangistan, who knew the central and southern plains as they knew the palms of their hands. They incessantly attacked the British with German weapons and finance, not, however, with the intention of taking part in the war on the German side, as they had realized that if a German was polite in his country, he was more polite in a foreign country out of weakness, but if he felt a little strength, he would use, in his German dialect, the same mean abuses of a vulgar. When he draws his weapon and kills somebody, he looks at it as if he has killed a fly.

At any rate, this collaboration, which was at the beginning accompanied with kindness, was more to have the Tangistani teach his manliness in fighting against the British to his children, and to show that if the government was unable to oust the enemy out, the Tangistani tribes were capable of defending their family prestige, and they would put their lives at it, so as to prevent the foreign commanders from touching, with their capricious claws, a Tangistani girl from whose skillful fingers drop artistic crafts. They are clever enough to know wherefrom to get weaponry they need. Despite the courage of the zealous southerners and the brave

Tangistanis and the supports of the Germans could prevent the British from occupying the provinces of Kirman, Shiraz, Isfahan and Sistan; yet the British could very well understand that the official annexation of Iran to their colonies was not possible with the existence of those zealous tribes[195]—the tribes whose even aged men, with eyelashes whitened by the snows of time, used to daringly attack the enemy, and, when running away they either descend to the gorges, or ascend up to take the color of the mountains, as if they were pieces of ice that melted under the sun of July. Probably it was because of these brave and courageous acts afterwards in the last fifty years and the results of their fruitful efforts that when **Ruhullah** became leader and when he used to praise the forces defending the country, the name of the tribes was frequently mentioned by him despite the fact that they constituted no more than 3% of the population.

The name of **Rais Ali Delwari,** the hero of the hard days of occupation, is the name of an epic hero of a real story which could escape the scissors of the censorship of the pre-Revolution years, and appeared on the white curtain under the title _The Heroes of Tangistan', and it was worthy of being put on the show once again after the Revolution, to stir enthusiasm and to invite the Leader of the Revolution to watch it.

Ruhullah in the Trenches

When **Ruhullah** freed his legs from what was tying them, it seemed that this freeing himself was just to be quick in offering his help to those who were trenched around the city in order to block the way to the city in the face of the foreign enemy. Of course, in the daytime he used to go to school, and at nights, after having his supper, or wrapping it in a handkerchief, he would head for the trench to have it with his mates. Some nights he would stay at school to defend it, with the other boys: On holidays he could be on the watch all day. When, for the first time, he stayed from dawn to the afternoon in a trench, and when he came home hungry and thirsty, and when his mother, his older brother or somebody else, said to him: ─May **Allah** help you!", he felt very much proud as if it was said to a victorious commander who has just come back from the front. From then on he got accustomed to hear: ─May **Allah** help you!"

Ruhullah's House Had Towers, Ramparts and Gun-Holes

The extent of the war was not so much aflame in Khomein; therefore, the trenches were not always full. Whenever the Russians wanted to get supplies for a battalion, or when they were afraid lest the youths might take to arms to help the Ottomans, they used to come to the town, where there would arise clamour, and whoever had a gun, hurried into a trench, and whoever had no gun would arm himself with a dagger, a spear, a club or a stick to keep his watch. **Ruhullah's** house, which had towers, ramparts and gun-holes, was one of the good fortresses of the town, and whenever there was a more serious possibility of an attack, a number of the citizens would ascend to the towers of the house and keep watch, and their wives and children would be the guests of the house. But **Ruhullah,** as a youth with certain desires, evaded watching in the house. He liked to go to other trenches on the other side of the town. Mother was always worried about him and much as she used allusions by saying: ―Many people come to our house to guard, while our sons go elsewhere to guard!" Yet he acted as if he did not hear it. At last one day she had to give up allusion and resort to open talk. She said: ―Is watching in the house *haram*?" Or: ―Is it that you don't like us, that you don't want to guard us?" and things like that. But the answer she heard was something like: ―If all men cared to defend only their houses, what should those who have no men do? You have two other sons older than me, and **Naneh Khawar** alone is capable of defending this house. My aunt is here, too, as well as others. Were I a bit worried about you, my legs would not have moved away from you." Tears of joy welled in the eyes of the mother and the aunt, as they realized that maturity was budding in him. Yet, maturity of the son could not subdue the storm of anxiety in the ocean of Mother's heart. One rainy morning, after his leaving the house, the mother traced his footsteps on the muddy road. But at the other side of the road the footsteps vanished, and Mother had to return home with increased worry. When sometimes later this incident was disclosed ,he fell at his mother's feet with his kisses, bitterly crying in such a way that those present cried, too, and uttering expressions such as: ―O mother, hearts are connected to each other. I asked my heart how much you love me.[396] But the officer who gives us military training told: ‿No one other than the Commander and the fellow fighter is to know where your trench is.‘ Forgive me, mother, for having to wipe off my footprints." On the excuse of having the duty of providing food and crackers for the trench-mates of her son, she got his promise to inform her, from then on, where he was to be on duty .Afterwards he used sometimes to parade on the roof of the house, rifle on shoulder, so as to let his mother watch him in the uniform of a guard[394] .

Khomein Besieged by the Russians

A number of decrepit old men and women in Khomein still remember the World War I, but, due to old age and weak memory, their observations do not coincide with each other. One believes that the Germans attacked Khomein. Another says that the British besieged the town. But **Ruhullah** mentions the Russian soldiers: ―I saw the Russian soldiers in the same centre which we had in Khomein. I saw them there and we were attacked by them in the First World War.[198]"

There is no strict information about the attack of the Russians on this town, but it seems that the presence of the Russian forces around the town caused trouble for the Khans and the wicked ones. **Zallaqi** and **Rajab Ali**[199] were two wicked plunderers who, if not collaborators with the enemy, were like them in looting the town under those confused conditions of famine and blockade. They, thus, uncovered their mean nature. He mentioned them as specimens to show the state of other towns: ―We were attacked by men like **Zallaqi** and **Rajab Ali.** We ourselves had rifles, and although I was still young, nearly mature, I used to call at the trenches which were in our locality. They wanted to assault and plunder. We used to go there for inspection.[200]

Glorious Moments of Overwhelming Emotion

There is no exact information concerning how long the siege and the plunderings lasted. The conclusions of a number of sayings denote that from the beginning till end of the war Khomein was in its half-shadow. **Ruhullah,** at least within four years, in that confused condition, got acquainted with ugly deeds of his country-mates and foreigners, and also with fine and delicate deeds unexpected from persons except in particular glorious moments of overwhelming emotions. One of the finenesses was done by two foreigners. The episode goes like this: Two Russian soldiers were ordered to usurp a donkey's load belonging to a villager boy. The load seemed to be some large water-melons. The boy resisted them. They beat him on the head with their gunstock. Blood gushed out and reddened his head and shoulders, then he fell to the ground and fainted. Two other soldiers were watching the incident at a distance. They could not stand it and quarrelled with them. When the quarrel got hotter, the plunderers shot at the two, so that they may keep them motionless until they bring help. A bullet settled in the thigh of one of them. Now there were two wounded bodies on the ground. The other did not stay idle. With his bayonet he cut a water-melon in two, emptied a half from its contents and placed it on the head of the boy so as to stop the bleeding and to make a shade on the head of the wounded. Then he mounted his wounded fellow on the donkey, and carried the boy on his hand and, seaked in sweat, took them to town, but the boy died at the first moments on the hands of the soldier. The guards in the town, thinking that they were drunkard quarrelling with one another, and that the boy was their victim, arrested them. The two helpless men, knowing no Persian, could not make them understand that they were not only innocent and chaste, but it was their mercy which brought them to that situation. First they were disarmed, one of them was imprisoned in the stable, and the other, handcuffed, was entrusted to the physician to be treated. The Russians instead of sending a messenger to receive the two soldiers, they sent a company, and the district spent few days in war with the Russians. The two soldiers, through a broken Persian language of an interpreter, they could tell their sacrifice, and said: ―The Russians did not attack you to release us, but they came here to punish us. If you hand us to them they will leave you." Somebody said: ―What a trickery! An army came, but we did not give you up, now do you want us to so easily hand you over to the enemy so that you may lead them to our trenches?" The two said: ―If you think that our suggestion is to save our lives, send to the Russians our dead bodies." This time the people believed their truthfulness, but it was far from manliness to hand them over. They were at a crossroad. They neither could face their own army nor support the people of an Iranian town in a war against the army of their own country, which they took to be treacherous, nor could they watch the army's merciless and unmanly plunderings. Therefore, suicide seemed to be the only way to put an end to the disturbance. And, in order that the suicide may not add to the complication of the case, before hanging themselves or cutting with the knife the viens of their hands, they wrote the whole story in a letter to their commander.[201]

Two coffins were prepared, wrapped in a shawl, and a small group of white-beard men of the town escorted them with respect till the back of the Russian's tents. The commander of the Russian army opened the letter, after a moment he closed his eyes, and the earth, the size of a coin, turned into mud. The bodies were burried according to Christian rites. An old man demanded that the killer of the boy should be punished. The commander said that he was to be excused, but he promised to punish and send him back to Russia, and offered a sum as blood money, which the boy's family rejected. The same afternoon a group of people came to the cemetery, in which there were only two graves, and a Russian company of soldiers respectfully saluted the dead. The people invoked mercy on the souls of the two dead. Somebody said: ―These are martyrs, send blessings on their souls." Another one shouted: ―They are not Muslims. It is not allowed to send blessings on them." There was a little fuss, and then it subdued at the words of an old man.[202]

Perhaps **Ruhullah's** statement that: ―Once they occupied a quarter in Khomein, and the people resisted them with their rifles, and I was with those people,[203]" is a hint at this episode. It was expected that from then on the Russians would not attack Khomein, but it was not so, because the army and the commander did not stay in the vicinity of a town, but that which was proved and constant to **Ruhullah** was that whoever is standing in opposite rank and regarded as an enemy, is, in reality, on the other side and is in fact an enemy, but not all the military and political enemies are enemies of human dignity, as it is possible that many noble-natured heroes of good disposition are on either side, and whose honour drives them up to the border of martyrdom. These are the real heroes, because every victorious bellicose hero is, to the other side, a bloodthirsty and murderous devil, but such heroisms go beyond the limit of friendship, stirring praise in the hearts and minds of both sides.

Anyhow, **Ruhullah** did defend his town as best as he could, but he neither killed nor wounded anybody, since he mostly was on the guard duty, and used to call on the trenches to provide them with their needs. We tried to find out whether an enemy had been strangled by his hand or not. All our researches had negative replies. This is not because his friends want the religious leader, who preaches moralities and refined soul and rejecting mundane desires, should not have killed anybody, and that they want to evade relating the facts, so as not to injure his ethical dignity, since such a thing is no rouse for pride for him or for anybody. In fact, the prophets, too, treated social diseases ‗surgically'. Even **Moses, Allah**'s co-conversor (*a*), killed a Coptic with his fist, and the Prophet **David** with his melodious tunes and charming voice which enchanted even the birds, killed with a stone the stonehearted **Goliath** and sent him to Hell, and, as a result of the invocation of the Prophet **Noah** (*a*), thousands were drowned in the flood, while he closed the ship's entrance and stood watching the suffocation of the people, feeling sorrow but not regret. And the greatest teacher of moralities [the Prophet **Muhammad** (*s*)], who said: ―I have come to complete the noble characters,[204]" heroically used his sword; and **Ali** (*a*), who, after **the Prophet** (*s*), continued enhancing morals and humanity, and who set forth on the road of humanity so vehemently that his such humanistic conduct became legendary, used, in each one of his attacks in the war of Siffin, to reap the head of tens of the enemies like the reaping of grass, and at nights, when militarism was absent, he used to go out to dates plantations, where he wept so bitterly as if all his relatives were beheaded before his eyes. Then the next day it would be the same as before. **The Prophet** of upright religion portrayed the men of his *ummah* as to be: **devout men at night and lions in daytime.**[205] So, not killing is not an honour, nor a moral characteristic. It is, at times, immoral. Whenever one must kill, one must kill, but **―Whoever kills a man, not for a man, nor for corruption done in the land, it is as if he killed all the people.**[206]**"** The noble Prophet (*s*) said: **―Monasticism in my religion is the *jihad*.**" In *jihad* they do not tell their beads, and if they do, their beads are bullets. The glorious *Quran* promised those who kill, or are killed, in the way of **Allah,** the lofty Paradise, attesting it by proofs from the Gospel and the Torah.[207] Defending one's town, honour and religion is a duty in the religious lexicon. Getting wounded in the defence is pleasant like drinking a cool beverage in a hot summer noon, though thinking of killing is, like the coldness of a wind of an autumn sunset, sorrowful and burning. No conscious Muslim, who is acquainted with the spirit of religion, is pleased with killing even the meanest of enemies. Even without religion, sentiment would testify to hating killing, as it is enough to imagine for a short moment the family and the children of the murdered, one's heart would be so shaken that the weapon may slip off one's hands. Nevertheless, evading killing does not please a Muslim, because this, too, is an open disobedience to God and a big unforgiveable sin. As long as the society exists, as long as the relief is awaited, there are also the insanity caused by greed, meanness, envy and opportunism, and the good, the bad and the worse are always filed up against each other, and even if you are not the beginner, still the danger is there, such as the neutrality of Iran in respect of the international craziness of the World War I. It was good only for being registered in the history, and, had it not been for the self-ardour and manly enthusiasm of the people in defending their honour, the boys at the schools would read in history that a geographical country was named Iran and its people spoke a language called Persian, and were followers of a religion called Islam.

I Was in the War
During the early years after the victory of the Revolution, he referred to the First World War seven times. In three of them he insisted on stating that **―I was in the First War. I had a rifle and I used to go to the trenches.**" Although in those years he was in the highest *fiqhi*, scholarly and philosophic position in the scientific *hawzah*s, and the realm of such (war) questions, compared with the scientific and *fiqhi*, were, in *hawzah*s, in the sixteenth or seventeenth

degree, often some of the scholars, such as the ironed analysts, took it as a point of weakness in him. Nevertheless, despite his deep knowledge of both sides, he did not evade retelling these memoirs, not just to relate a memoir, but to break the ugliness of raising a rifle in hand, compared with teaching, supplication, pen and telling beads, and uplifted it to the limit of a religious value: ―We, in the place where we were, i.e. Khomein, made trenches. I, too, had a rifle, but I was a child, a child of sixteen, seventeen. I had a rifle at hand and I was training how to use it... I used to go to the trenches. We faced the wicked ones who were attacking to occupy and do such-and-such. There was chaos, and the central government had no power.[208]‚‚

The People Had Power

Going through the history of the Islamic lands of those days, one can clearly realize that, if there was no powerful government to defend the Islamic lands against the covetous desires of the foreigners, there were, more or less, brave and zealous men who, driven by their feeling of responsibility or by instinct, could stop the attackers and drive the drunkness of pride out of their heads. The people of Khomein had, by nature, chosen a number of these brave young men as their worthy leaders. One of them, by the name of **Mirza**[209], was a good-looking, sturdy and alert man, who had learnt horsemanship and shooting from the highway bandits. But he had sincerely repented and was atoning for his past sin by sacrificing for the people. He was the commander of a group of guards of which **Ruhullah** was a member. Whenever everything was quiet in the town he used to send **Ruhullah** to guard. When there was the danger of an attack, he used to take **Ruhullah**'s rifle, on the pretext that it was new, clean and handy and that a commander must have such a rifle in hand, and found another job for **Ruhullah** to do. **Ruhullah** disliked this very much, but he deemed it necessary to obey orders, though the commander laughed secretly at his frowning, but he kept silent lest the commander might frown at him. After the fight, when the people were preparing a gift for their worthy commander, the commander, in returning the people's kindness, said: ―My gifts to you are these young men who were mere children and now have grown up. Their mouths smelled of milk, but now their flesh smells of gunpowder. Each one of them can be a commander for a rainy day." Then he added: ―This **Ruhullah,** I received him from his brother sound and safe, and now I return him sound and safe, too. He is so fearless that, hadn't I sent him after blackpeas [to get rid of him], he would have assaulted the heart of the enemy, and he would not have been among us now. When I die he will be a good commander." That was why **Ruhullah** had not wounded nor killed anybody with his direct bullet. However, maybe it was at the beginning of the fight that by a ricochet of the bullet of an enemy or a friend his side was scratched, which he concealed from his mother and sisters, though his brothers knew it.

In the Context of Realities

The First World War had not been kindled so as to make **Ruhullah** acquainted with the bitter realities of war. That war was a note on the theory of the balance of forces, which put its annotation on tens of other theories, and at the end caused the appearance of a new system in the international relations. But fate, which has so many wonders, started his youth with the start of the war and sent him to a trench so as to show him the ugliness of the empty attacks, famine, homelessness, pain, suffering, poverty, orphanage, and, on the other side, the greatness of self-denial in the uproar of defence, and to make him sensitive to such realities. Probably, if this young boy had not closely been in touch with those realities, the inclinations of some isolationist teachers who were attached to mentalism in the environment, culture and the contents of the subjects, could have made out of him an imaginary person evading reality—a result which they achieved in respect of tens of *faqih*s, ascetics and philosophers, who used to weave nice ideas in long threads, and to present drolleries which, mentally, belonged to the shrub of possibility, but ,in practise, they were counted with the possibilities which were never possible. Later, when he became a gnostic, raising his head high in the sky, staying, in the prayer of devotion, at a distance from himself, the world and its pleasures ,putting his wings in the wings of the angels so as to watch the beauty of the beloved, and interpreting religion in such a way as if the mundane world had no external existence, there suddenly appeared a line extending from the sky to the earth and brought him down to the earth, rolling his tongue with the words: —The religion in which there is no war is incomplete one[330] ."

Maybe the First War was deeper than the Second in affecting his political thoughts, because the world powers of those days, on whose conduct depended the international system, dragged it to the wheat field behind his town, and once parts of his town was hurt by the occupation of the foreigners. This—despite the hindrances in communications as far as following up the current events of the world and the conduct of its powers— caused him to be so sensitive that he regarded, afterwards, his continual following the news a duty.

Ruhullah's Features in His 15th

Two and a half years had passed over the war when **Ruhullah** reached his 31th year of age. On his upper lip grew thin hair, and the hair on his face gradually grew like black velvet on the chin. The ringing of his voice, though not yet manly, but it did not have the veins of childhood. He recited the *Quran* faultlessly. He was acquainted with the Persian literature and knew the Arabic grammar. He wrestled with the formal logic, and he habituated his fingers to beautiful penmanship. He had finished the preliminary studies and read parts of the seminary text books, and followed the news of Khomein, being sensitive to the events happening in the country. On the nights of his turn he took post as a guard in the town. On his guardings he cleaned his rifle which he had bought, or had been bought for him, for sixty *tumans*, then he would hide it in a suitable place. Sometimes he would ride a horse so as not to forget horsemanship. On Fridays he would go to the exercise grounds so as to perfect himself in the techniques of defence. He was never worried of having a hand or a leg broken, or an eyebrow or face injury. He would jump over any height or a channel in his way. At times he would throw himself into the river which had a stone dam, running behind his house. On Fridays he would go to the public bath in the town to have his body rubbed with a coarse glove and massaged by a rubber, and, at the same time, perform the Friday *ghusl*.[211] The house, in which his mother, sisters, brothers and his eldest aunt were living, was his own share of his father's legacy. The others had chosen theirs from other properties. So, he was a man who had a house, too. It was probably for this reason that his mother cherished in her mind the necessity to start looking for a girl suitable for such a man, so that, at the first chance after his brothers, she may attend to him, as he was the last son, and the mother had to live with the wife of this son in this house. But alas! The dead bodies of the war casualties had done their job, and, if defending the town by the youths had been carried out, yet the town was defenceless against the cholera.

The Cholera in the Town and the Departure of the Aunt and Mother

The druggists business flourished, but the traditional doctors could not do much. Yoghurt was not a bad medicine, but the Russian army had taken it more than the people, and thus it became scanty. The suckling infants, in the hands of mothers and before their tearful eyes, flickered away, and the old men and women pounded the ground with their legs for thirst, and with their last vomiting they gave out their lives. **Ruhullah,** following his mother's advice, used to take a bucketful of yoghurt to the poor families. The neighbouring children were eager to vigilantly help him in his job. It had never occurred to him that, that merciless plague could possibly knock at their own door, too. **Sahibah Khanum,** the courageous and kind aunt, was the first to give out her last breath and close her eyes. Just before the agony choking the throats of the family burst out, the mother's guts were polluted. The doctor told them not to get near the mother. Reason also said so. But the feelings had a different judgement. They had to use chamber pots so as not to have the mattress, the covers and the pillow polluted. Yet, mother would run to the yard so that the others may not become subject to states of vomiting. At midnight she was too exhausted to be able to move. She signed to them to go outside so that they may not get polluted, but who can prevent oneself from staying near mother and from pouring water into her throat? When they realized that she would never leave her bed, they sat beside her and started reciting in the *Quran* the *surahs* of *Yasin* and *as-Saffat*. Lumps burst into the throats, and the girls began wailing and crying. **Ruhullah** kissed his mother's coldish forehead, went out to the yard and, filled with deep sorrow and grief; he sat in solitude with his God. A few days later, **Akhund Mulla Jawad,** the second husband of the second aunt, was the third member of the family to travel to the Eternal Abode, in 1336 A.H. May their souls be flooded with mercy, as they lived well and brought up **Ruhullah** well.

Two Years in the Sorrows for the Departed

Thenceforward, for two years, when **Ruhullah** used to directly go back home from school, affliction doubled the gloom of the sunset. **Naneh Khawar,** his foster-mother, used to answer his greeting. But the position of a real mother can be filled only by a real mother. He would perform the *wudu* and go to *masjid* to join the congregational *salah.* At times he would go to the trench. He preferred to be alone when on guard. On his coming home he would find a lantern hung by **Naneh Khawar** at the door of the house. She used to do so every night at the order of **Aqa Mustafa** so that the passersby might not tumble down in the dark. But now she hang it only for love of the young **Ruhullah.** Probably mother's grave was near the aunt's.[212] If so, on Friday nights a single lantern would light both graves. Visiting a graveyard at night is disapproved. So, at the sunset of every Thursday **Ruhullah** would start by sending his greetings to the sleepers in the graves, reciting the *fatihah* quietly and without meaning, and then, with a white handkerchief he would wipe off the moisture of a tear which had run down from his eyes and lost inside his still young beard. But if mother's grave was in Qum, there is no information about how it came to be there, nor about whether **Ruhullah** had accompanied the coffin to Qum.[213]

Frightful News

During these years when he was approaching his sixteenth year of age, two events inside the country and one outside it took place. The interior ones which engaged attention seemed important, but the one which happened beyond the frontiers was much more important. The first internal event started by the assassination of the Head of the Silo in Tehran, **Mirza Ismail Khan**. He held, for a while, the post of the financial agent in Sistan and Baluchestan. He had benefited by misusing his post. At those times when the poor, in the famine of bread, put their heads on the bedside and, due to intense hunger, never raised them again, he sold a large quantity of wheat to the British army for an insignificant sum with which he built a house in Kushk street in Tehran—a house not below a palace. He never came to terms with the Financial Office. Despite such a background he was appointed as the Head of the Silo in Tehran, and was openly smuggling for the British Embassy. Consequently, he got a bad reputation, rather he was quite detestable. It was a cold Saturday afternoon, the 28th of Bahman, 1295 [1916] when he left his office in the silo and climbed into his two-horsed carriage ,heading towards his house. Suddenly two men appeared and the horses stopped. A pistol was fired at his chest, and the two men ran away. He was dying with difficulty. The carriageman drove very fast in order to take his half-dead body and deliver it to the police, as probably he knew him to be dying, and that he had no chance in the hospital.

The newspapers of the next day published about his assassination. No group undertook the responsibility of his murder. It was said, however, that he was killed because of his connection with the British and for betraying the people. There was a strong rumour to the effect that all the traitors and the spies would soon be punished.

Comiteh-ye Mujazat (Punishment Committee)

The name of the _Comiteh-ye **Mujazat**' [the Committee of Punishment] was soon on all tongues, because the Head of the Silo had, a few days before, received a letter in which his crimes were counted, and at the bottom a rubber stamp with the name of **Comiteh-ye Mujazat,** sealed it. In the sketch of the stamp the outline of a bullet was shown with inscription _punishment' and that of a cartridge with the word _**Comiteh**' which gave the indication that:

This bullet is the punishment aimed at the heart of the traitor, whereas the cartridge which shoots the bullet remains bearing the name _Comiteh'.

The second assassination, whose responsibility was undertaken by **Comiteh-ye Mujazat,** was the murder of the man who had carried out the first assassination. It was later known that the person who shot the Head of the Silo was **Karim Dawatgar.** He had years earlier attempted the life of **Shaykh Fadlullah Nuri** and aimed at him many shots wounding a number of people and he himself was arrested and jailed. But the Shaykh forgave him. Years after his release, he joined the **Comiteh-ye Mujazat.** Now, this **Comiteh-ye Mujazat** issued its order to punish him. The reason was not known, though it was said that he had betrayed the **Comiteh.** It seems that his crimes were two: having a loose tongue which, when drunk, disclosed the secrets of his friends to the enemies. The other was that he kept demanding more money, as along two months' respite for killing **Ismail Khan,** he used to come every other day and demand more money from his friends. Within this period he had received 650 *tumans,* which, at that time could buy a house. However, the sentence of the **Comiteh** against him was carried out on 13 Ordibehesht, 1296 [1917] near the Armenian Church, by a person named **Rashidus-Sultan**. By this assassina- tion a pessimistic shadow hovered over Tehran, not because of his death, but because the nature of the **Comiteh** became more obscure and that in matters of punishment it was hasty and rash.

Successive Assassinations
On the first or eighth of Shaban of the same year, the third assassination caught the skirt of **Matinus-Saltanah Thaqafi** behind his desk. He was the director of the *Asr-e Jadid* newspaper. A few days before he had praised the British policy in order to please the government of **Wuthuquddawlah.** It appears that when the attackers were running away, there appeared an Armenian boy crying: ─What is the matter?" A bullet put an end to his life. After his murder statement was issued, saying: ─We have got rid of three of the heads of the chain of the unprincipled and disgraceful to humanity, so that the followers of such dishonoured path may change their conduct... **Comiteyeh Mujazat,** with complete surety, says that the safety of everybody depends on his leaving betrayal and changing his shameful deeds...[214]"

The attempts of **Wuthuquddawlah** government to arrest the members of **Comiteyeh Mujazat** were useless. But the result of the assassinations was the fall of the government, giving way to the government of **Alaus-Saltanah.**

When the new government was introduced to the *Majlis,* the **Comiteh-ye Mujazat** undertook the responsibility for the fourth assassination.

Assassination of Mirza Muhsin Mujtahid

Sayyid Abdullah Behbahani, one of the top class *ulama* on the side of Constitutionalism, had a son-in-law named **Mirza Muhsin,** known as the **Mujtahid,** who enjoyed close relations with the high class elite of the country. Before Constitutionalism takes shape, a number of the *ulama* went to the town of Ray where they sought sanctuary. Thence they wrote a letter to the Chancellor demanding the reformation of the judicature, and the establishment of a House of Justice. The Chancellor showed the letter to the Shah, who, addressing the *ulama,* stated the name of four of them, including the name of **Mirza Muhsin Mujtahid.** The Shah's answer was as below:

―The letter of His High Excellency the Shah to the distinguished *ulama,* may **Allah** the Exalted keep them safe:

Your message, which was sent by the gentlemen **Mirza Mustafa, Mirza Abul-Qasim, Mirza Muhsin and Itimad al-Islam** to His Excellency the Chancellor, was shown to us. It may not be hidden from the distinguished *ulama* that our favours have been covering all the subjects, especially the *ulama,* who pray for the government and wish well for His Imperial Majesty. We have always paid particular attention to their right demands... You shall have enough security to come to the city and you will have the honour, with the Chancellor, to meet us so as to orally assure you of our well intention, and that you may, with calmness and quietude, be able to pray for our government.

Dhul-Qadah, 1323 A.H., His High Excellency the Shah.[215]"

As from the issue of the above letter, **Mirza Muhsin's** participation in politics increased. He stood as a candidate of *hawzah* students in Tehran for the first term of the *Majlis* and was elected. When it was decided that the *Majlis* should have a newspaper, **Muzaffaruddin Shah** issued his decree as below:

―Honourable Chancellor. As the newspaper named *Majlis,* which was permitted to be issued, will be the first newspaper to publish useful articles concerning public welfare, the interests of the kingdom and nation, and the preserving loyalty to the government, it will need a particular and excellent freedom of pen, it should be under the supervision and approbation of a person possessing the requisites for scholar, religious and political information, and his honesty and piety must be perfectly known and visible. Therefore, according to this noble writing, this important matter, partly and wholely, including the selection of the members, the appointment of the reporters, the printing and publishing matters and the like, are granted, by our grace and favour, to **Aqa Mirza Muhsin,** may **Allah** keep him safe, since, in addition to his possessing the said levels, he is from a great and respectful family, accepted by the nation and completely trusted by the government, and as known for his loyalty and patriotism, and acquainted with, and well-informed of, the information of this new era. We entrust this great privilege to his guardianship and honesty, so that he may form the *Majlis* of the impartial, pious, loyal and insighted ones, and supervise over this important matter, with ultimate strictness and watchfulness, implementing it the soonest possible and as best as possible.

Shaban, 1324, the Shah.[216]"

Anyhow, **Mirza Muhsin Khan** was entrusted by the government. Of course he was also on good terms with the people. Some people thought him to be intelligent and clever, with the resolution to guide the government. Others thought that his piety was more mundane than religious.

It was 10:20 on the morning of 17th Shaban, that is, 16 or 8 days after the third assassination, when he left **Qawam as-Saltanah**'s house and near his own house at the cross-road of **Masjid Shah,** two unknown men came and shot at him from behind and the side. He fell dead on the spot. His servants were with him. One of them was injured. His white ass or mule was also wounded. The people were stupefied. They did see the faces of the two killers, but they did not recognize them. At the beginning they quietly went away, then they ran away and, climbing into a carriage, flew off.

On the same day a statement was published by **Comiteh-ye Mujazat,** written in a poetic style, though flat and meaningless:

-It is night. The disk of the moon, like a coquettish bride, is manifest in the horizon of Iran, spreading its slight light on an ancient land which has witnessed thousands of diverse events... At this time an invisible messenger angel whispered into the ear of this Board) **Comiteh-ye Mujazat)** and said: Gentlemen! In addition to the past betrayals, the documents of servitude and bondage, which are prepared for the sons (of Iran) in different associations of the city, are gathered into the pseudo-Islamic archives of **Mirza Muhsin,** and, after indorsement and registration, they are sent to the relevant authorities. The said Board, including the active members of the **Comiteh-ye Mujazat** saw that their beliefs were confirmed by all the heavenly signs, as if all particles of the beings demanded the punishment of this irreligious being. Thus, the **Comiteh-ye Mujazat** unanimously ratified the sentence against

Mirza Muhsin, this homeland-seller, and notified it to the liaison of the Executive Chief.[217]"

Thence onward such a horrible situation surrounded the politician authorities that they were frightened by their own shadows. A personality of those days and said: —One day in autumn I was with **Wuthuquddawlah** in his house in Tajrish... At times, the sound of the leaves of the plane-trees falling down frightened him, imagining that somebody was hiding behind the thick trees of the garden.[218]" But the people had a dual feeling of the **Comiteh-ye Mujazat:** They did not feel displeased with the murder of the Head of the Silo, but they were displeased with killing of **Mirza Muhsin**. Nevertheless they did not so much attend, due to their fear, the mourning meeting held for him. **Sadr al-Ashraf,** the chameleonic politician, who had been threatened by the **Comiteh-ye Mujazat,** dared to attend, with a number of guards, that meeting in *Masjid Shah,* said: —Those who were there did not exceed a hundred persons, whereas formerly the whole bazaar used to close down and tens of thousand people would gather at a sign from him.[219]" The enlightened also divided into two groups: Those who were displeased with the ever increasing intrusions of **Mirza Muhsin** in different affairs, approved his assassination. Others condemned the very acts of assassination, but, for fear of the Committee, they used words of double meaning.

Assassinating Muntakhabuddawlah

At that time it seemed that the government, out of the one hundred and fifty thousand Tehranian citizens, could not find someone capable of managing the police department. A Swedish, by the name of **Westedahill,** was in charge of that. He issued an AD offering a reward of 150 *tumans* to the one who could identify any member of the **Comiteyeh Mujazat.** But before being keen on the subject, he was keener on the bottles of whisky lest they might arrive late.

Twenty days passed. It was the 9th of Tir. No one was identified. Suddenly it was said in the city that the **Comiteh-ye Mujazat** had assassinated **Muntakhabuddawlah** in Amiriyyah Street in Tehran. **Muntakhabuddawlah** was the Director-General of the Accounts Office and brother of the son-in-law of **Wuthuquddawlah** whose cabinet had recently fallen due to the former assassinations. The new government engaged itself in thinking for a week, and, after much anxiety and consultations, it published a statement in the papers. Some expressions in that statement denoted that the government was afraid of the power of the **Comiteh-ye**

Mujazat. The statement did not conceal the belief that a great number of people had joined it:

―The present council of ministers, while deciding on serving this land, was not unaware of the extraordinary difficulties of the affairs and of the shortcomings of the means of the job, nor was it thinking that the obstacles were absent and the exigencies present, nor the situation was easy... But, regretfully, it is derived from recent events that the government was probably mistaken. It seems that some people have not yet been awakened by the past events, and have not recognized the means for reformation, because the regretful realities and the horrible crimes, which took place within the past few months, were repeated. If those who commit these crimes imagine that by such acts they can provide the means for redressing the affairs, they must know that they are on the wrong path, and they will be the origin of acts from whose effects they cannot be benefited. Since the government is quite aware of the bitter results of this situation, and knows to where the result of these acts and evil thoughts will drag the country, now it takes it to be its duty to draw the attention of the people to the grave consequences of such a situation. It only leads to chaos, ruining the country in the interests of the purposeful elements. The government seriously and particularly notes that as long as the question of reforming the affairs has not been remembered by the public, and well-wishers of the country from every side recommend that the government must prepare the means for the happiness and the future of the homeland, reason, responsibility and patriotism necessitate that they should give up their personal interests and shallow and baseless fancies, which mean putting weapons in the hands of the evil-wishers. So they are to let the government alone to carry out the reforms which it had from the beginning intended to do, but were delayed by the recent events. The situation should not be dragged to where the government would be compelled to take a decision which might be contrary to what is expected.[220]‖

Comiteh-ye Mujazat, answering the government's statement, issued a statement four times longer in details, referring to the regretable history of Iran within recent centuries, starting from the last Safavid Shah. At the end it threatened an enlightened, free thinker, well-disposed and reputed man. The threat was cautious, but had the smell of terrorism: ―At the end of the statement, with a degradation and sharp tone we blame the director of *Nowbahar,* for the purposeful matter printed therein, and tell him: The very aim and intention, which caused you to present these objections, will not let you understand the realities of things through the eyes of truth. **Comiteh-ye Mujazat,** with its clean intention and special love towards all its fellow-

179

citizens, sees, for the time being, that this rebuke is sufficient for a fellow-citizen who has recently tied up the tongue of truth, and, regretfully, wore a different dress. It is hoped that from now on he could deduce the truths of the situations better than this.[221]"

Malik ash-Shuara **Bahar,** who was then the director of the newspaper *Nowbahar,* was the first who severely criticized the conduct of the **Comiteh-ye Mujazat.** After that fear collapsed and there appeared signs denoting that the people had approved the **Comiteh-ye Mujazat** only for the murder of the Head of the Silo, but afterwards they were only afraid.

The Serial of Hezardastan
Nearly sixty-five years later, that is, in the early years of the victory of the Islamic Revolution, an attractive serial film, under the title of *Hezardastan,* about the **Comiteh-ye Mujazat,** was photographed. The story went even beyond what the historians had recorded, rebuilding it with the theory of conspiracy. The sixteen-years-old **Ruhullah,** who was sensitive to the rumour-like news concerning the **Comiteyeh Mujazat,** has become now an old man stricken by years, and used to sit, after supper, to carefully watch the serial over the TV. After watching, he used to give to those present in the room some explanations. In fact, he confirmed parts of it and refused others. He once said: ―When I was a child, there was in Khomein a man, a raffian, who wanted to join the **Comiteh-ye Mujazat.** The boys used to ask him: ‚Well, if you could join it, whom would you kill?‘ His answer was: ‚At any rate, I will find somebody.‘ They asked: ‚What would you do if the **Comiteh-ye Mujazat** did not admit you?‘ He said: ‚I would kill all its members.‘ I said to myself: This man is just a man-killer. At last, however, he did kill somebody, though not for the **Comiteh-ye Mujazat.** Although we were very young and the news of the **Comiteh-ye Mujazat** did not reach Khomein the same as in Tehran, yet, we did not like it. One night we went out to the desert near the town and prayed that **Allah** rid us from those killers, not for killing good people, but because they even killed the bad ones without permission."

Another night he said: ―Despite being young, we knew that there were wheels within wheels and those foreign hands were behind it. Our proof, however, was only rational."

In another night he said: ―When we heard that the members of the **Comiteh-ye Mujazat** had been arrested, and that they were only few persons, we and our friends held a meeting and discussed how a few persons—some of them were said to be careless [of piety] and drank wine—

could be so much daring! We came to the conclusion that one must have a support to have one's daring increased. **Mirza Kuchak Khan,** by depending on **Allah,** felt brave (In those days **Mirza Kuchak Khan** was seriously standing in the face of the Russians). **Comiteh-ye Mujazat,** too, by depending on the protection of the Satanic Powers, was assured. But at last all of them were misfortunate. It was said that they wept in the Court. **Rida Khan,** too, as long as he was backed by Satan, he was very much daring, but when they stopped supporting him, it became known how cowardly he was."

In another night he said: –From the beginning we disliked this **Comiteh,** because its deeds were far away from natural disposition. It is related that the **Imam Ali (***a***)** was vanguard in all wars, but his use of his sword was in conformity with natural disposition. That is why so many poets composed poems in praise of his heroism, but no one can write even a single line of poetry to justify the man-killing of **Hasan as-Sabbah.** This **Comiteh** acted like **Hasan as-Sabbah.** Yet even if among them was somebody with an air of patriotism he must have been fooled."

The late **Haj Ahmad Aqa** had said: –One cannot dislike a personality like **Abulfathzadeh."** The answer was: –Probably he was not bad inwardly. He was said to be a patriot, but his thought was corrupt. Once he visited a personality to get a job, with the intention to be serviceable. When he was rejected, he said: _So-and-so must be removed from the way.' This thought was so bad and corrupt that even his collaborators objected him."

The last talk worth hearing in this respect was: –The kingdom's authorities thought that the **Comiteh-ye Mujazat** was enjoying the support of many people. Therefore they treated the people tactfully for few months, but we guessed that the members of the **Comiteh** must not be numerous, because such acts can never be approved by the public...[222]"

Arresting the Members of the *Comiteh-ye Mujazat*
The members of the **Comiteh** were arrested on the 22nd of Tir, 1296 [1917], and stayed in prison for 9 months. At this time, **Ahmad Khan Safa,** who was their investigator, was killed, and after a while they were set free. When **Wuthuquddawlah** became premier once again ordered them to be arrested. After the first assassination, **Wuthuquddawlah** used to give money to them through **Bahadurus-Saltanah,** in order not to be killed. At the beginning he paid 700 *tumans*; the second time, 300 *tumans* and the third time he paid 500 *tumans*. It was agreed, however, to pay, at least, 20000 *tumans* more.[223] It is not yet quite known if **Wuthuquddawlah** had paid these sums to really secure his own life, or there was a different trick in that.

Husayn Laleh among the Arrested

Among the arrested there was someone called **Husayn Laleh,** who was one of the important members of the **Comiteh-ye Mujazat.** Formerly he was a shopboy working for the butler of **Sardar Afkham,** head of the police of Tehran. Seeing that the Constitutionalists were about to be victorious, **Sardar Afkham** put his Jewellery into an iron box so as to take it with him to Russia and then get asylum in Austria, but by **Husayn Laleh's** plot he was killed in Rasht with 18 bullets and the Jewels went to the Russian Embassy as a deposit, and when they were given back they fell into the hands of **Husayn Laleh,** who sold them at law prices to a number of Jewish Russians to provide for his drinks. His mouth was always emitting the bad smell of cheap spirit. Also due to the bad smell of his feet all were avoiding him. Strange enough he was counted with the fighters and the fanatic supporters of the Constitutionalists. Stranger still was that the wife of **Sardar Afkham, Muftakharus-Saltanah,** who was on the side of despotism, invited the murderer of her husband and the thief who stole her jewellery and was, moreover, her stern political opponent, to her semi-palace in Estakhr St., in order to protect her life. In the *biruni,* a large room was decorated for him; a mattress of duck- feather was laid for **Husayn Aqa** to lay on when coming home. Every night a servant used to take the boots off his legs and wash his feet. Nevertheless, even after washing his feet they still smelled like the corpse of a rotten body. After supper they brought him wine to drink. After drinking he became cheerful and proudly retold the stories of his crimes. One night he told the boys, bombastically, about the martyrdom of **Sayyid Abdullah Behbahani,** one of the *ulama* of Constitutionalism. The son of **Muftakharuddawlah's** sister, who was present that night and heard the real, but ugly, stories of **Husayn Laleh,** retold it as below:

The Meanness of Husayn Laleh Related by Him

—We rode our four horses and galloped to Sarpulak. I and one of the friends dismounted and asked our other two friends to take care of our horses. Two and half an hour had passed of the night. We entered the lane of **Sayyid Abdullah.** It was pitch dark, and not even a bird could be seen in the lane. The door of the Sayyid's house was wide open. We two, without hindrance and blockade, quite easily stepped into the yard of the *biruni.* The yard was darker than the lane, only a kerosene lantern was hung flickering on the wall. A weak light was visible from under the door of the butlery of the Sayyid. No sooner had we entered the yard than we drew our Mausers out of our pockets, and on our toes, Mausers in hand, we entered the butlery. Three of his servants were busy preparing the hookahs and brewing tea, as the **Aqa** had guests. We threatened the three of them with our Mausers and drove them into a cellar in the same yard and locked them in. Then, Mausers in hand, we slowly ascended the stairs to the upper story. I first stepped on the threshold of the room of the Sayyid. I saw him among a number of businessmen from the bazaar with their henna-dyed beards, dressed as himself with black and white turbans, engaged in conversation, leaning on a cushion. His chest was bare. Without losing time, I aimed and fired a shot at his head and two shots at his chest. The smell of the gunpowder smoke and the gushing of blood from the Sayyid's chest gave me a sort of ecstasy and vividness. Then my friend also fired two shots at the Sayyid's head, or face, or chest. Horrified, the seven, eight or ten guests of the Sayyid fell to the floor face down and motionless. We, with complete coldbloodedness, and after finishing our task, left by the same stairs which we had ascended on coming. We descended slowly, and, without unlocking the cellar, left the house, and, running, we reached our horses, and, galloping, we left the place.[224]"

It is said that **Sayyid Abdullah Behbahani** was killed at the instigation of **Taqizadeh,** a man of religion who had quitted the religious dress and completely dressed like a European. His expression: ―We must become Europeans from top to toe to be humans," caused him to be detestable to the religious men. When **Ayatullah Behbahani** was killed by **Husayn Laleh,** the following line appeared on the tongues:

Taqizadeh ordered and *shaqizadeh* (son of a wretch) killed
The one who was a supporter of Islam.[225]

The Footprints of the Masons

If actually **Taqizadeh** had ordered and **Husayn Laleh** had obeyed, then one may guess that the sperm of the **Comiteyeh Mujazat** had been clotted before that, and the Masons had their hands in it, too. On the same night **Husayn Laleh** had told the boys about the assassination of **Mirza Muhsin Mujtahid,** too. **Muhammad Rida Ashtiyanizadeh,** the son of **Muftakharus-Saltanah**'s sister, a supporter of despotism, was also **Mirza Hasan Ashtiyani**'s grandson[226], a scholar supporting Constitutionalism, had heard the story at his aunt's house from the thick lips of **Husayn Laleh** who, when talking, saliva spat out of his mouth and he intentionally talked like a rogue. This was what he heard:

―Ihanullah Khan, Rashidus-Sultan and I were ordered by the **Comiteh** to kill **Mirza Muhsin.** Whenever the killing of the *Akhund*s was referred to us, we almost jumped out of our skins for joy, because for me and my friends killing an *Akhund* or a *sayyid* was the greatest service to the freedom and the homeland. It was three before noon when **Ihanullah Khan, Rashidus-Sultan** and I went to the bookbinding bazaar. **Ihanullah Khan** said: ‚I know that **Aqa Mirza Muhsin** would not leave his house before 3:30 or 4 o'clock in the afternoon. At that time he would certainly go to a mourning gathering.' For almost an hour we strolled in the bookbinding bazaar, the blacksmiths bazaar up to the Chaharsuq Buzurg. **Ihanullah Khan** turned to **Rashidus-Sultan** and to me and said: ‚I have been invited to a dinner at a friend's house, and I can take you both with me.' **Rashidus-Sultan** refused to go to the banquet. I, together with **Ihanullah Khan** went to his friend's house, had our dinner, and at two o'clock in the afternoon we returned to the bookbinding bazaar. Once again we paced the place for about an hour. **Rashidus-Sultan** did not move away from the blind alley where the house of **Mirza Muhsin** was, and with his two eyes he was watching the door of the house. At 3:30 in the afternoon [334] ,the white mule of the Sayyid was brought, and the Sayyid came out of the house and mounted his mule, followed by five of his servants. The first shot was fired by **Ihanullah Khan** at his forehead. Two other shots were fired by **Rashidus-Sultan** at his face and chest, and my shot, too, while bleeding. The *Sayyid* fell over from the mule to the ground and died. Hearing the noise of our Mausers, the shopkeepers in the bookbinding bazaar closed down their shops and, together with the passers-by, ran away. We, running too, left the yard of *Masjid Shah* behind us...[228]"

Husayn Laleh had also related the story of murdering his colleague, **Karim Dawatgar,** to the boys. He told them that he fired five shots from behind at him. The narrator showed surprise at the fact that although **Husayn Laleh,** fearlessly, revealed the names of his colleagues in the **Comiteh,** yet he never mentioned **Imad al-Kuttab** and **Kamal al-Wizarah.** Likewise he did not mention the name of his Indian partner in killing **Sayyid Abdullah.** 45 years later, when the narrator was having dinner with **Wuthuquddawlah** at Focus Restaurant in Paris, the latter talked about his hanging **Husayn Laleh** and **Rashidus-Sultan.** ‚I asked him," the narrator said: ‚Concerning **Kamal al-Wizarah,** who, during the activities of the **Comiteh-ye Mujazat,** was one of the high rank authorities in the Ministry of Finance, and **Imad al-Kuttab** and the British, had they any connection with the **Comiteh?**" Smiling, he said: ‚Those man-killers, pushed by their own feelings and personal ideologies, used to kill people. **Kamal al-Wizarah** and **Imad al-Kuttab** both were agents of the British Embassy. They undertook the leadership of that group. During my cabinet, governing and leadership, afterwords, no severe action was taken against **Kamal al-Wizarah** and **Imad al-Kuttab. Ihanullah** fled to **Mirza Kuchak Khan** and joined him in the jungle wars in which he had direct interference.[229]"

Now, eighty years have passed since the **Comiteh-ye Mujazat** was organized and disorganized, nevertheless, the real nature of the **Comiteh** is still ambiguous. Tens of questions are still without answers. It is even unknown on whose fingers the **Comiteh** revolved. What was it looking for? Who were on the list of assassination? Before practically carrying out its intentions, the **Comiteh-ye Mujazat** used to send a letter with the same drawings of a bullet and a cartridge. **Mudarris**—who was known to the friend and the foe as a patriot, a freedom-lover, a truthful and pious man— also received a letter, but before killing him the **Comiteh** was betrayed. Some writers regarded them to be pure freedom-lovers. Others took them to be mean and hypocrites who, by the orders of the foreigners, resorted to weapon .Was their original purpose not to cause disorder in the country such that all classes would hope for a saviour?

The Fate of the Members of the *Comiteh-ye Mujazat*

Some of the members of the **Comiteh** were tried. **Husayn Laleh** and **Rashidus-Sultan** were sentenced to death. For **Abulfathzadeh,** a principal member of the **Comiteh,** and who had a beautiful wife, and maybe somebody was looking at her with covetious eyes, his sentence was, together with **Munshizadeh,** anothor one of the members, 15 years of imprisonment in exile. But, on the way to the exile, between Simnan and Mashhad, they were shot dead on the pretext that they tried to escape, so as to keep the secrets of the **Comiteh** hidden. One of the accused connected to this organization related a long story. He said: ─"When it was decided that I must be interrogated in the afternoon, the Chief of the Police, **Westedahill,** went home and slept. A cat jumped on his chest and waked him up and..." Strange stories! Then he continued: ─ thanked [**Allah**] for living in a country in which even a cat interferes in politics.[230]"

At those days not all the news of **Comiteh-ye Mujazat** reached Khomein, and that which did reach it was mostly void of truth. But the young man, **Ruhullah,** was seriously used to follow up the oral news of **Comiteh-ye Mujazat,** and after each news his disgust with them got deeper. At last, one night, probably Thursday night, he, with some of his friends, went to the desert to pray, in solitude, for their destruction. He had, by obvious evidences, found out that behind that clamour there was a foreign hand. A

185

nice story of the preliminaries of the event of Karbala had effaced the term assassination from his lexicon.[231] Probably the activities of the **Comiteh** caused him to be sensitive to all armed activities of the underground groups, and to see the soundest of them subject to the danger of continual deviation. After that, he, by a particular way, entered into politics. If he had known the members of an armed group and individually supported them, he never put the stamp of endorsement on the group organization of any armed underground group, except when a group of thought had become so popular that it could be given the name of a nation or people, such as the struggle of the peoples of Algeria and Palestine, or the bravery of the people of Tangistan, or the fervent Jungle Uprising.

The Jungle Uprising
Unlike the **Comiteh-ye Mujazat,** he used to praise the **Jungle Uprising,** which was very active in those years. He spoke well of **Mirza Kuchak Khan** and prayed for his safety. What was the Jungle Uprising? How did it get mature? What objective did it announce? Whence did it start and to where did it expand? What happened at last? How was it recorded in the history of Iran ?... These are our today's questions. But when the heart of the uprising was throbbing, the **Jungle Uprising,** to **Ruhullah**—the young man who was experiencing the World War I on the margin—had only a single question, i.e. how can one join it?

One day his brother, **Murtada,** who was studying in Isfahan, came to Khomein on a leave with a satchel full of the news of the **Jungle Uprising** which he had heard in Isfahan. **Ruhullah** hugged him, and, after hearing his news about the situation, held with him and **Nuruddin** a consultation meeting about whether it was not a *wajib* to join the **Jungle Uprising. Aqa Murtada** went pale, and commandingly said: ―If the elder brother has a right to be obeyed by the younger, I say it is not recommendable. Stay here and go on studying. If it was necessary we would go together." **Ruhullah,** by way of respecting **Aqa Murtada,** kept silent in this respect, but he did not keep inactive. He asked permission to send provisions to the fighters of the Jungle. The two brothers agreed and three *kharwars* of wheat from the three brothers were loaded on the mules.

After the victory of the Revolution another TV serial artistically depicted the **Jungle Uprising.** There are evidences that he had carefully seen this serial, too.[232] In case he had seen this serial, probably, like the **Hezardastan** serial, he must have annotated it by criticizing, for example, why the cameras did not see the public's provisions which were sent from all over Iran, including the provisions decided to be sent by the three brothers, and even the widows of Khomein, who despite the famine of those days, offered part of their scanty food, to be sent to the Jungle, in a long train of mules which formed a great train appearing like a commercial caravan, whereas, actually it was an aid to the brothers in the Jungle. If Khomein, as a small town, far from the **Jungle Uprising,** could be of such a service to the brothers in the Jungle, then it would be certain that the other nearer towns were in a better position to act similarly, as otherwise the **Jungle Uprising**, which was fighting on several fronts, could not have lasted for more than a single week.

The **Jungle Uprising** became for him a model for an Islamic revolution, though afterwards he knew it had big weaknesses. For example, the Jungle fighters resorted to arms before a fundamental and deep change takes place in the public thought and culture. Or, in other stricter words, the Uprising, from the beginning, by taking up arms, proclaimed its existence. However, this reservation on his part occurred when the flames of the Uprising had subdued, and when he had already witnessed forty stormy springs and autumns, and got acquainted with philosophy and the philosophy of history. The history of Islam, particularly its first 23 years, before being a lesson, was a source of which 13 years were the core of his attention. Despite all the pressures and tortures, **the Prophet (s)** undertook the mission of wakening, but he did not take up arms except when it could serve as a guard protecting faith. Now, every uprising which announced its existence by taking up arms, the conditions for preparing the military equipments must have had direct effect in the destination of that uprising. Anyhow, on these days when the **Jungle Uprising** was ablaze and its flames reached beyond the jungles, giving warmth even to Khomein, he could say nothing but to praise the Jungle fighters.

An Epic Inspired by a Dream

One day **Aqa Murtada** found a poem between the leaves of a notebook in which mother used to write down the daily expenditures. He knew it to be **Ruhullah's**. Asking him: ─To whom is it?" The young **Ruhullah** said: ─To **Mirza Kuchak Khan** who was some time ago our guest." Surprised, he asked: ─Mirza, himself?" **Ruhullah** answered: ─Yes." The question was repeated, and the answer was repeated, too. **Naneh Khawar** interfered and said: ─A month ago I noticed Ruhullah very cheerful. I said to him: ‗Eversince the death of your mother you have been sad, how is it that you are so joyful today?' He related to me the dream he had seen the night before: ‗It was night, but the sun was still up in the sky. This house was a jungle. The Jungle fighters came in here on their horses. **Mirza** was among them. I brought him tea. He smiled, then without a word, he said good-bye." Usually he did not relate his dreams to anybody, but this one he did relate to **Naneh Khawar,** as if he wished, by exposing his love for **Mirza Kuchak Khan,** to make the light of hope shine in his own heart. As long as **Mirza** was not yet martyred, he was keen on hunting for the news of the Jungle. He talked with his classmates about the heroic deeds of **Mirza,** praying for his safety.

On those days, how much did he know about the **Jungle Uprising,** famous under this name, whereas its actual name was _The Union of Islam'? We do know that he was not so much acquainted with its minute and strict particularities, except what was orally transmitted from one to another. Of that part of it which the Embassies of Russia, Britian, Ottomans, Germany and the central government had full information, he knew nothing at all, because their information, which was rather complete—and parts of which years later were gradually published—was neither in Persian nor in Arabic. But, contrary to the Embassies which registered, rather strictly, the news about the **Union of Islam,** they were alien to the spirit of uprising. **Ruhullah** was cohabitant with the spirit of the Uprising.

The Jungle Uprising had arranged for a newspaper which was published whenever the possibility for publishing was provided. This newspaper did not publish many copies, but every leaf of it used to pass, from hand to hand, to the farthest spot in the country. In its edition No. 28, which reached Khomein, the objectives of the Uprising were stated without any ambiguity: —Before everything, we want the independence of the kingdom of Iran—a complete independence, that is, without the least interference by any foreign country ;fundamental reformation of the kingdom, removing corruption from the official organizations, as whatever has afflicted Iran was due to the corruption of the organizations. We support the unity of all Muslims. These are our opinions and we invite the people to be consonant with us and we demand their help[311] ."

Although the above statement resembled, in some aspects, the statements of the **Comiteh-ye Mujazat,** yet their reactions were different. The **Comiteh-ye Mujazat** was sowing the seeds of horror in the hearts, while from the **Jungle Uprising** the buds of hope were blossoming. This Uprising gradually got powerful. Strange enough, contrary to most movements, the more it got powerful, the more it got popular. In most of the towns in the north it established branches, as well as in Azarbayjan and in

Tehran, run actively by six of reputable men.[234] In Tehran, however, the conditions necessitated that the activities should go underground.

The **Jungle Uprising** realized that it was time to uphold the government so that, under the difficult conditions of the aftermath of the World War I, it may not fall into the arms of the foreigners more and more, and, furthermore the Uprising itself may be secured against a possible attack from the capital. The Tehran Branch was ordered to make use of whatever it had in mind and heart to attract four personalities of good repute among the people to help. This was not because the Uprising was just in need of a two-sided cooperation, but it extended its hand for help in order that the independence of the country may not lose color in the independence of the Jungle. It even gave complete permission to start conversation like this: ―In order to protect the interests of the kingdom, the members of the Jungle are prepared to grant their votes in the affairs to them, and only to execute their opinions.[235]"

The first one to respond was **Mustawfi al-Mamalik,** who said: ―Refraining from hostility is a kind of assistance, and it must be regarded as sufficient." He had, however, a complaint: At this year of famine in which people die every day of hunger, why did the **Board of the Union of Islam** prohibit the export of rice from the province of Gilan? **The Union of Islam** manly replied his disappointing reproach, by allowing the export of rice from Gilan to the people of Tehran, in addition to a quantity of it as a gift to the pious people in order to be cooked and to invite the poor in Tehran to it. **Allah,** by way of rewarding their generosity, ordered the sky to pour down, and the soil to grow well! The next year the loaded ears of rice were waving under the wind.

Mutaminulmulk did not admit the Board.

Mukhbiruddawlah, whose back shivered whenever he heard the name of the Russians, asked: ―If I did not cooperate, what would you do to me?" The answer was: ―We would leave you to your God."

The fourth person, **Mushiruddawlah,** had a statement which coincided with reality. But if he had helped, the reality would have been different. He said: ―This society has only a historical advantage, it has no other advantage." Asked what he meant by historical advantage, he said: ―Later it would be written in the history that when the people of Iran found a window of hope open to them, they tried hard to break their chain of captivity. This, by itself, is a sign of a nation being alive, otherwise, this society, and societies like it can do nothing against the foreigners, and they would not be able to prevent any kind of their operations.[236]"

The First Visit to the North

When **Ruhullah** first travelled to the north to visit the **Imam Rida (a),** the eighth Imam of the Shiite in the sacred city of Mashhad, he was more than 20 years old. He had accompanied a caravan by the old road between Tehran and Mashhad. He sought the help of the head of the caravan to introduce him, on the return, to a caravan which would pass through the northern road. He wanted to see as much as possible of his country, but probably he liked more to trace back the footprints of the fighters of the Jungle. When he reached at some *farsakhs* from Gunbad-e Kawus he saw the Jungle for the first time. Formerly he had seen millions of hectares of roasted desert, but never a thick jungle. On arriving at Bandar-e Turkman, he undressed, hanged his clothes on the pole of the tent, wrapped his _aba‘_ round his body, and, despite the rough sea, committed himself to the waves. He put a handful of water in his mouth, and, like vomiting, he spat it out. He did not think the water of the largest lake in the world to be bitter and salty. When the members of the caravan went to the bazaar to buy the rice and the tea of north, he returned from the bazaar empty-handed. After few days the caravan parted into two groups. A group chose to take the quadruped road, putting Damawand, the most unruly peak of Iran, behind them, heading to Tehran. The other group headed for Gilan. He joined the latter in order to see Masuleh. Masuleh is a sightly village, built on the green and flourishing heights of the slope. The roofs of the houses were the yards of the higher houses. This village one day stood upright in the face of the Russian army. **Ruhullah,** who had a disciplined personality, in this journey, was careless and restless such that the head of the caravan reproached him for leaving the caravan every now and then. Sometimes he went into the heart of the jungle. The head of the caravan did not know that **Ruhullah's** heart was stormier than the sea, and that he rushed into the jungle so that from the trunks of the old trees, which had seen the **Mirza,** he could make a boat. **Kuchak of the Jungle** had marched throughout the jungle for more than two thousand days and nights, and had leaned against some of the olden tree-trunks to relieve him from his fatigued back. The bereaved trees, which used to protect the **Mirza** against the enemy's bullets, were still wounded. There was a correlation between the depth of the wounds of the trees and the depth and intensity of the fights.

At the end of the trip, **Aqa Ruhullah** returned to Qum through Rasht-Qazvin route. During the nights of several weeks he would open his souvenir- box, in which he kept nothing of value except his diary in which he used to write in his leisure time, and read out of it to his room-mates, and at the end, he would recite the **Fatihah** for the **Mirza** and his companions.

While he was in Khomein, the exciting **Jungle Uprising** had already been started, and when he came to Qum, that Uprising had turned into ashes behind the hillocks of plots.

We are now in Khomein where the firewoods of the **Jungle Uprising** are still kindling. On returning to Qum, we shall then lament the fall and the nippy winter of the Jungle.

News about the Formation of the Russian Revolution

It is worth mentioning that the news about the formation of the Russian Socialist Revolution, along with the news of the Jungle, were reaching Khomein, yet, about its particularities we have little information, except that we know that because of Khomein's remoteness from the provinces bordering the USSR, which was in the process of formation, the Bolshevik propaganda was dim and of little effect (in Khomein). Of course, sixty years later, in a tarpaulin tent of 50 m.,[236] set up in the yard of his house in Neauphle-le-Chpteau in order that the autumn rain may not soak the visitors, he, a man who had seen much rain and was witnessing the decline of the USSR's Revolution, delivered, for the listeners who had come from different quarters and stood on their feet so as to drink a cup of his words, a speech which, if expertly scrutinized, appears that its leaven had been kneaded in Khomein's cask, and that this was an inexact footprint of his concern about the formation of a Communist Regime at that time. He, standing in that meeting, said:

–Those who supposedly speak of human rights are, actually transgressing humanity even more. All the killing machinery which they produced and all the wars which they brought forth in the world are made by those who had signed the Universal Declaration of the Human Rights. This very France had signed that Declaration, but what did it do to Algeria? Even now, if they can, they will do the same. America is busy, the USSR is busy, they are busy plundering the peoples, swallowing them. Do the people believe that the USSR, for example, is a state which wants to serve the people, a Communist state which wants to work for the masses? If you note carefully, you will realize that the answer will be: –No." They are more brutal than the others. They, more than the others, humiliate the people. One of their leaders[237] once said: They must come with an abacus to see how much the people of this country work, how much they eat. If they eat more

191

than their work, they must be thrown into the sea. It is the humanists who utter such remarks![238]"

An old man with good memory, who lived in Arak and was younger than **Ruhullah**, by way of explaining why the Communist Revolution could not seriously creep into Iran, said something which is more like **Ruhullah**'s statement. This likeness was, probably, due to the general culture of those days, which was a portrait of the Communist Revolution of the USSR in most towns of central Iran. He had said: ―When we were children the Russians made a revolution. There appeared a lunatic who ordered that the old persons should be thrown into the sea because they had mouths for eating, but no strength for work. In those days famine prevailed over all the towns of Iran. Many died of hunger. Some women used to grind the date-stones with hand- mills into flour and baked bread for the poor. When that little man (Lenin), ignorant of **Allah**, said: Kill the old so as to decrease the number of the eaters of bread, not only the poor, but even the women, whose hands blistered because of the hand-mills, were disgusted with the cruelty and unawareness of the Communist Revolution of **Allah**. My mother used a chamber pot for ten years for her father-in-law who had fallen from a ladder and had his back broken. She ate little so that he would not sleep hungry...[239]"

Temporary Good-Bye to Khomein

Although Khomein was his birthplace, and he was fond of its lanes, and whatever was therein had the color of a memory for him, yet it was time to move to another town because this town had offered him everything it had in its knowledge bag. If he had to be a preacher it would have been sufficient for him to have some free studies and to learn the art of oration, and to stroll in the yard of the house, as if sitting on a *minbar,* and to practise reciting two or three mourning, feasting and *tarhim* sessions, and then to start with a village around Khomein, and ascend a *minbar.* Then, acquiring boldness, he would return to Khomein, and, after delivering hundreds of such sessions, he would become the famous preacher of the town.

But [the town of] Arak had opened its arms waiting for him so as to pour in the cup of his heart continual drinks. **Aqa Murtada** put yellow and black coins, of the Nasirite era, in a purse, to cover the expenses of a year's stay in Arak (away from home). He, without asking how much they were, inserted the purse, with difficulty, into a suit-case already full of his dresses and books. He kissed the cheeks of his brothers, friends and relatives, and, probably with moistured eyes, he said farewell to the town and the house.

192

IN ARAK

The city of Arak is now the capital of the Central Province. It is proportionally an industrial city with factories which provide a part of Iran's heavy industries. When **Ruhullah** was born only 80 years had passed over the reconstruction of this city. Then it had two names: Sultanabad and Iraq. In Shahrivar of 1314 [1935] the Council of Ministers changed its name to Arak. Probably because Sultanabad was more associated with a village, and also its second name could be mistaken with the name of the neighbouring country of Iraq.[240]

Iraq is an Arabic name which has many meanings: a river- or a sea-shore; root, vein or nerve; juice, sweat or moisture; tribalism, and a bare bone. Arak is also Arabic. It is the plural of arikeh, i.e. the seat of a king, or the tree from which toothbrushes are made. As a term it means, as is stated in a lexicon: a very large place in which many buildings and houses are built, also a bathroom is built in it, and in its space numerous trees are planted such that it can be called an orchard. This Arak is where the *harim* of the rulers live.[241]"

After Islam 'Iraq' referred to a spacious region with some five big cities and more than 300 villages. Sometimes one of those cities was named Iraq due to certain conditions such as the influence of local governors. And, in order that it may not be mistaken with the two Iraqs, i.e. Kufah and Basrah, the two important cities of the country of Iraq, it was named Iraq-e Ajam'. The year in which **Aqa Ruhullah** moved to Arak, this newly built city, which was regarded as the centre for the surrounding towns, was mostly called Sultanabad, and sometimes, Iraq.[242] Most of the Iranians whose family name is Iraqi are originally from Arak.

Now, the young **Aqa Ruhullah** is stepping into a town which, historically seems ancient, but actually it was only 98 years old ever since it was built and continually expanding, particularly that the World War I caused more serious losses to this town than to Khomein. The Committee, to compensate for the losses, alloted a sum of 30 *kurur tuman*s to be spent on this town and the nearby villages.[243] So, in the efforts for the rebuilding, large drops of sweat were still visible on the foreheads of its men. No help came from the Capital, but the people themselves rolled up their sleeves and the walls started to raise up out of the ruins. Witnessing the efforts of the people in reconstructing their town strengthens self-reliance in one's mind. Then, the endeavours of the people in rebuilding their town could bring about a situation which, in later decades, when all the possibilities were assembled in the Capital, helped this town in attracting a good number of Iran's mother industries to be established in it.

This town seated a number of great scholars on the throne of science. The most famous of them was **Shaykh Abdul Karim Hairi Yazdi.** He was a scholar of steadfast thinking, and had brought soft temperance and good conduct from the culture of his birthplace, Yazd, to Arak. Yazd is the name of an old town as well as the name of a Province. It is brackish and waterless. It is so dry that to get to a quantity of water sufficient enough for turning mill-stone, tens of kilometres of subterranean canals must be dug. The Yazdian well-diggers sometimes spent their whole lives in digging a canal under the earth, and how patiently! **Ayatullah Ha"iri,** had worked, as a boy, in one of these canals. Probably it was then when he learnt how to be forbearing, as he was really patient and talked little. He became the top-ranked scholar in Arak, though **Aqa Nurullah Iraqi** was more known to the people, because he was born somewhere near Arak. **Ruhullah** was not so advanced yet in his theologian studies to be admitted to the classes of those two great men.

A Room in the Sepahdar School

He was given a room on the ground floor in Sepahdar School. Its floor was damp and the carpet spread on it got humid. He asked the head of the school permission to build a suspended floor with brick, plaster and soil. Fortunately, the architects of those days used to build the ceilings as high as their ambitions so as not to depress the hearts. So, even if a suspended floor was built 50 cm. higher than the platform in front of the room, the ceiling would have remained higher than today's ceilings. **Mirza Muhammad Husayn,** a young boy of 16 years old, who got a warm friendship with **Aqa Ruhullah** on his second day of arrival, undertook to arrange the matter with the architect and the worker, and to prepare the needed building materials. He was a fervent, brisk, smiling, gay, practical and friendly young man. The workers used to receive their wages on the same working day. **Mirza Muhammad Husayn**—whom **Aqa Ruhullah** started to call afterwards **A Mirza**—gave them their wages at everyday sunset, but when it was time for him to settle the account with **Aqa Ruhullah** he did it ill-humouredly.

Financially, he was not well-off, but he was a flaunter [*dash-mashti*], and liked to financially help **Ruhullah** to prove his friendship better. But this friendly kindness irritated his friend who was not in need, and also because he was keen on settling his debts the soonest possible. However, after building the room as desired, their friendship got deeper. Although **A Mirza** had been in the school four years earlier than **Ruhullah** and was not his room-mate, yet he was most of the time found in **Ruhullah**'s room.[244]

Two New Teachers for Rereading Logic

When the room was ready, he inquired here and there and found out that two Shaykhs, one, **Muhammad Golpaygani,** and the other, **Muhammad Ali Burujerdi** who was the father of **Mirza Mahdi Burujerdi,** were teaching logic better than others. At first he attended the first one's lessons, then he began attending them both by turns, one day in between. He used to sit politely and humbly and listen once again to logic. [245] It seemed to him that whatever he had learnt of logic in Khomein was not all that this art had. He thought about that and discussed with his teacher many times whether logic is a science or an art. Does it guard the thought or the reason against making mistakes? Is revelation the logic of existence or does it go beyond that? Are the prophets logical? Those who know the coquettish elegance of logic, do they never make mistakes of thought? Is it that these are wise and the others not? He got more knowledge of logic, but none of those questions was answered in any of the discussions. However, the more he knew of logic, the stricter the Aristotelian logic appeared to him. This belief accompanied him for, at least, 25 years. In his *Kashful Asrar* [Discovering the Secrets] he referred to Aristotle and his rules of logic, saying: —Aristotle son of Nicomachus of Stagire was one of the great philosophers of the world. The logical regulations and the rules of the Science of Balance', which is the foundation of all sciences, is indebted to the valuable efforts of this great man. Since he founded logical teachings, he was known as the First Teacher. **Ash-Shaykh ar-Rais [Avicenna],** the wonder of the time, bowed before the teachings of this great man and kissed the ground out of respect for him. As he said, so far nobody could criticize the rules of the logic presented by **Aristotle,** nor were his subtle ideas subject to revoca- tion or ratification. It seems that the French **Descartes,** and some of our respectful writers, thought that they had done a revolution in logic, but those who enter this field on the basis of knowledge and insight know that **Descartes,** in this respect and in respect of theology, how weak and childish he was![246]"

Acquaintance with Grammar

He had learnt the rudiments of the Arabic literature in Khomein and had acquainted himself with conjugation and syntax. He could conjugate some Arabic words into 1008 cases. Once he wrote in a notebook of 40 sheets 14 forms of the word *_nasara'*, in active voice, passive voice, unaugmented verb, augmented verb, past tense, present tense and some in the form of imperative. In each page he wrote 14 active voices, and in front of them 14 passive voices for those which had passive voices. In the notebook there were a few white pages left. According to the calculation of **Aqa Murtada,** if he filled up the pages left white, he would have completed learning conjugation. Two more notebooks were prepared, one for the defective and the weak verbs, and the other for the sections of 4- and 5-letter words and joined and separate pronouns. As to the grammar, he did not know it completely. The **Kumayl dua** excited him, particularly the first sentence of it which reads: ─O **Allah,** I ask you by your mercy which encompasses everything," and the third sentence ─and everything submitted to it," and the ninth ─and by your everlasting Face after the annihilation of everything." Whenever he wanted to submit himself to the waves of the *dua* and to plunge into its boundless depth, three cases dragged him out of the depth of meanings to the surface of the form, making him busy with the rules of grammar: _everything' in the accusative, nominative and genitive cases.

Aqa Abbas Araki used to give, early every morning, lessons on conjugation to the newcomers of the students, and in the evening he gave lessons on grammar to the students who had completed their conjugation lessons. One afternoon **Aqa Ruhullah** went to him and put forth his question. In that meeting, which was held after the *maghrib* and *isha salahs* and lasted for a part of the night, many of his grammar questions got their answers. At the time of saying good-bye, **Ruhullah** held the lantern of a student so as to see the teacher to his house. Two other students accompanied him. The teacher felt that he had found a new serious student. On the way he continued his lesson, not on grammar, but about his teaching method. When he pushed his body into the yard, saying good-bye to the students, **Ruhullah** put the lantern on the ground so as to take the teacher's hand to his lips, but the teacher drew back his hand and took a step backward, then he came forward and kissed **Ruhullah** on the forehead. The next day the teacher started his class late, expecting **Ruhullah** to attend, but he did not. A week later he saw him in the yard near his room. He said: ─I was expecting you to come but you did not come." The answer was: ─A letter came from Khomein telling that someone from the Ministry of War was ordered to recruit, with the help of **Sardar Hishmat,** a thousand soldiers and dispatch them to Tehran. The name of my brother, **Nuruddin** was among the thousand names. I went to Khomein, but **Salar Muhtasham** crossed out the names of a hundred persons, including my brother's. I hurried back here, and as from today I will be present at your class."

In the Presence of Aqa Abbas Araki

Aqa Abbas Araki had taught Arab literature for several courses, and he had good control over the class. He used to explain and analyze some of the pre-Islamic Arabic poetry, stupefying the young students with his teachings. One day **Aqa Ruhullah** asked him: ─Which Arabic poetry do you like more?" He said: ─To me the most beautiful Arabic poetry is that which is recited by the master of oration, **Sadi Shirazi,** in praise of the merits of the **Prophet (s)**:

He attained exaltedness by his perfections,

Removed darkness by his beauty,

Good are all his characters,

Send you blessings to him and his offspring.

In those days **Ruhullah** regarded **Aqa Abbas Araki** to be the best expert in the Arab literature. Later he was acquainted with more tasteful teachers. **Imra al-Qays**, the pre-Islamic Arab poet, describes his imaginary lover, recited poems, whose beauty was praised even by **Amir al-Muminin, Ali (a),** the most eloquent of the eloquent orators in history. **Aqa Ruhullah,** in one of his pilgrimages to Mecca had a discussion about the poetic compositions of **Imra al-Qays** with an Egyptian scholar.[247] He said: ─Although you have no complete command on Arabic conversation, yet you have good knowledge of the Arab poetry." In reply **Aqa Ruhullah** said: ─We, Iranians, are weak in speaking Arabic, but not in understanding the meanings and writing." The Egyptian said: ─Your ancients were foremost in writing, but not now. In order to have a better scientific relations with the Arab world, you should pay attention to writing and speaking, too." **Aqa Ruhullah** named his teacher, **Aqa Abbas Araki,** and said that he, too, had the same opinion. **Aqa Abbas Araki** had advised all his students not to utter even a single Persian sentence in his class so that they may improve their dialogue talent. Some students practised this even in the street and bazaar, such that the grocers and the bakers learnt a number of Arabic words, like bread, cheese and butter. So, whenever a student of theology entered a shop of these, the shopkeeper, smiling or sneering, used to pronounce from his gullet the non- guttural letters. **Aqa Ruhullah** had repeatedly reminded that speaking Arabic is to be in the room, not in the streets or the bazaar, as the baker and the grocer would mock at it.

Inquiring About the Day's Events by Writing an Arabic Letter
Once **Aqa Ruhullah** wrote a letter in Arabic to his brothers asking for information about the recruiting of soldiers by **Sardar Hishmat** who was then the government's representative in Khomein. The reply came in Persian, from which he realized that his brothers could not understand the contents of his letter. He thought that it was too early for him to write anything in Arabic, and that in a Persian speaking country it is meaningless to write about common matters in Arabic language. The second letter he wrote in Persian, seriously asking his brothers to investigate this soldier recruitment, what was it for? Did they expect a war? The exchange of letters lasted for months, but the reason was never known. The rumours were so much that each one negated the other, while the origin of the affair remained ambiguous. One day he received letter whose answer had to be given immediately. The letter said that the Ministry of Finance had increased the taxes many folds, and that the small landlords who could not pay the taxes were putting their properties on sale. So, he was asked either to personally go to Khomein or to appoint an agent to do as interest requires. **Aqa Nuruddin** was appointed as the agent. From the next letter he got information about the disorder in the financial situation, but concerning the large amount which had been paid he showed no concern. He asked **Nuruddin** to help the family of **Naneh Khawar** so that they may not feel the burden of the back-breaking taxes.

One day **Aqa Abbas Araki** asked him in Arabic: ─How are you?" He replied: ─Not so good" and both laughed. The teacher again asked in Arabic: ─What happened?" He said: ─Ever since I came to Arak every now and then I receive letters, each one worse than the other. The last one said that **Hishmatuddawlah,** with the help of **Rajab Ali,** had started plundering and killing the people. So far he had killed more than 40 persons." **Aqa Abbas Araki** said: ─Ask the people to write a letter to the Prime Minister. Probably they would sack him out and there might be a relief." Thus, the pen was dipped into the inkpot and his first political letter was set on the paper. In that letter, addressing his uncle, he wrote: ─I was informed by my brothers about the difficulties in Khomein. If I can do anything tell me to come. But my opinion is that you should write a letter about these matters to the Prime Minister, and send it with a trusted one to personally hand it to him, and to stay there until he receives the reply and come back." When **Aqa Ruhullah's** letter reached Khomein, a penman had written a nice complaint requesting that **Hishmatuddawlah** and **Rajab Ali** should be sued. Some sixty persons of **Khomein"s ulama,** the elite and the landlords signed the complaint, and had to be handed to **Sepahdar Rashti,** who, on the 4th of the month of Aban of that year, had replaced **Mirza Hasan Khan Mushiruddawlah,** the Prime Minister. It was disclosed that the people of Khomein had already written to the former Premier. But before receiving any response, the problems of the foreign policies forced **Mirza Hasan Khan**—who was appointed as prime minister as from the 7th of Tir, 1299 [1920] up to the 3rd of Aban of the same year—to resign. The Central Government was too disordered to attend to the problems of other towns. On the 15th of Aban the British Minister, together with **General Ironside,** who had replaced **General Champion,** the Commander of the British forces in Iran ten days earlier, had a meeting with **Mushiruddawlah,** and officially ordered that **Astarvosleski,** the Russian Commander of the Cossacks' Quarters, should be deposed, because seven days before the local Communists, led by **Khalu Qurban** and **Ihanullah Khan,** had attacked Rasht with their artillery, and **Astarvosleski** had drawn his forces back to *Manjil.* **Mushiruddawlah,** before being afraid of deposing **Astarvosleski,** he was disgusted with the bare orders of the British officers. Hence he had to resign two days later, as the next day those two British men; who spoke arrogantly, went to FarahAbad Palace, and, while stressing their demand, they notified that if it was not granted, the British cash aids for managing the army's affairs would be stopped. It was not the first time in which **Ahmad Shah** gave negative reply to the British demands, though he used polite expressions: ―If **Astarvosleski** was deposed, possibly the Cossacks would revolt and with the Bulsheviks they would attack Tehran."

The letters which were sent to **Aqa Ruhullah** by his relatives, friends and brothers were all including insecure news, yet none of them offered a strict analysis of the affairs, and nobody could connect the insecurity in Khomein and other towns to what was going on in the Capital. Arak was insecure too. Recruiting soldiers and increasing the taxes several folds were the topics on the tongues. Without knowing what was going on behind the curtain, it was very difficult to follow up the causes of insecurity, recruitment and multiplied taxes, nor could the analysts and the journalists easily find out the causes of these, probably feigned, insecurities, since they had merely news.

The Analysis of the Insecurity by Documents

Most of the politicians, who had some information from behind the curtain, know things which, if spelt out, would take off their heads. For this reason some important official documents were kept inside the houses and hidden in a closet. Fortunately, most of the heirs of those men regarded them to be valuable antiquities and were serious in preserving them. When the possibility of the victory of the Islamic Revolution strengthened, some of those who had black dossiers smuggled the documents in their possession out of the country. Others, who were busy accumulating money and wealth, forgot to take the documents with them. After the victory of the Revolution a good portion of those documents fell into the hands of the revolutionary establishments. Now there are many documentary centres, and by referring to them one can analyze the insecurities and other obscure affairs of those days in Iran. One can also get a better understanding of some of the events of the world of those days.

Among the heaps of the available documents, some 500 papers[248] concerned the questions of **Aqa Ruhullah** on those days about the confused situation in Khomein, as he had written letters after letters to his friends and brothers, asking them to investigate and write him about the results. Although his hand did not reach those documents, but they are an answer to us in respect of his questions of those days. One of the documents, a cable from the Premier's Office, which, after 75 years of silence, says: ―The non-official task of **Sardar Hishmat** is the recruitment of 400 soldiers and 200 horsemen, not one thousand." The number thousand was spread in order to attain to the 400. But even the 400 soldiers could not be recruited, because people were not so idle to send 400 soldiers and 200 horsemen from a small town to the Capital without knowing the reason. The text of the cable sent from the Premier's Office to **Sardar Hishmat** was as below:

―Your High Excellency, **Aqa Sardar Hishmat**.

As is cabled by the Ministry of War, you are to recruit 400 private soldiers and 200 horsemen with horse and excellent weapon, and to bring them, together with yourself, and immediately move to the Capital. The efficiency and merit of your High Excellence have always been expected, and now I am still expecting within this period to manifest your efficiency so as to be more favoured by the government.[249]"

An official from the Ministry of War named **Abbas Mirza Yawar** was appointed to follow up this task. On the 17th Mizan, 1299 A.H., without referring to the disorder and the killings of **Sardar Hishmat** and **Rajab Ali**, he, in three lines, reported to the lofty Premier Office: ―A regiment was despatched, the rest and the horsemen within few days will follow together with His Excellency.[250]"

News from the Capital

As from late in Aban till early Esfand a seeming calmness prevailed in Arak and Khomein. It was a chance for him to finish, within two and a half months, his studies of the Arabic literature, with complete diligence. He could then read the *ayah*s, *hadith*s and the Arabic texts fluently, and understand their apparent meanings without having to translate them first in his mind into Persian. Of course, during that period the Capital was still expecting bitter events, while he followed them only casually.

On the 8th of Aban, the Prime Minister issued a statement addressing the people and discussing some difficulties of the country with the citizens. This familiar conduct could, in itself, lessen his problems. On the same day, however, **Astarvosleski,** at the order of **Narman,** was sent out of Iran by the Premier and his popular conversation sank into ambiguity.

At that time a letter came from Khomein with the concept that: ―The government prohibited the selling of the crops from Khomein to other towns, except Tehran. Will you sell the crops or will you store them?" The reply was perplexing: ―Hoarding is *haram.* Whoever needs it sell it to him, but do not give tribute to anybody."

On the 25th of Aban, the Ministry of Foreign Affairs received a letter from the British Embassy demanding the enforcement of the 1919 Agreement. Seventeen days later[251] the British Embassy, in a memorandum sterner than the former one, said: ―The Cossacks‘ Quarters must be under the British Commanders." On the same day, **Ahmad Shah** held a meeting with the 67 deputies of the 4th *Majlis,* the Ministers, the elite and the notable politicians, consulting them about arranging a reply to the British Embassy. The details of this session were fully reported to the British Embassy. It reached all the towns, including Arak, in a distorted form.

Death of the Late Tabatabai, a Constitutionalist Scholar

On the 18th of Dey a general mourning was announced all over the country, because **Sayyid Muhammad Tabatabai,** the very *Alim* who was active in upholding Constitutionalism, died. **Aqa Ruhullah** had somewhat good knowledge of the life of this man. As a child of four years, he had heard his name along with the name of **Sayyid Abdullah Behbahani,** as the revolutionary Constitutionalists, on the tongues. **Ruhullah** had preserved the names of those two struggling scholars in his mind.

One day, when he was putting on his clothes to say good-bye to his mother and go to school, his mother told him that the school was closed that day. Asking her about the reason, she said: ─A few days ago a number of men entered the house of the Sayyid." There was no need to say any more, as the addressee could comprehend the general matter, asking for details. But mother did not know the details. In the afternoon of that day all the members of the family went to town's General Mosque to take part in the mourning ceremony for the late Behbahani, the news of whose martyrdom had reached Khomein a few days late. The preacher of the town talked about the political and scientific personality of the deseased. He said: ─At the instigation of a deputy of the *Majlis* four persons of the so-called fighters for Constitutionalism entered his house and murdered him. The name of that deputy was **Taqizadeh,** an *akhund* who went to Europe, discarding the apparel of the theologian students and became a so-called enlightened. After the incident five of the *ulama* of Najaf, including **Akhund Mulla Muhammad Kazim Khurasani** and **Shaykh Abdullah Mazandarani,** pronounced him as *fasiq.* Consequently, the *Majlis* gave him a three-month compulsory leave to depart to Europe.[252]

The names of **Behbahani** and **Tabatabai,** the two Constitutionalist scholars, come together in Iran's contemporary history. One of them, when **Ruhullah** was eight years old, quitted the practical political field to the area of theoretical discussions.[253] The other, on the occasion of his natural death, caused the country to wear black.

Aqa Ruhullah helped his elder school-mates in dressing the walls of the school in black. In the first mourning gathering in the general mosque, **Ayatullah Hairi** delivered a speech. It was the first time in which he lent his ear to the unaffected speech of this old man, and it was in that session that he felt himself very much attached to that great man. Formerly he used to see him only in the yard of the school and greet him, or at times he used to join the congregational *salah* and perform his *salah* in the rear line after him.

Getting Prepared for a Big Work

After 75 years of the age's tumult, it is not easy to find out on which day of this month or early in the second month of winter, in early morning or at sunset, he left his room in order to prepare himself for his most exciting day of his life. Holding a tinned copper ewer with undulate mouth, he came out to the yard. He used to fill up the ewer with water by a large wooden ladle from a reservoir which they wrapped up with gunnies, in winter, so that it may not freeze like the water of the pool. He also used to wash its bottom and take it to his room and put it on a tray in a corner to get a little warm, and may not cause him to shiver when washing his face for *wudu*. He sat at the edge of the garden, took a handful of its water, put it in his mouth, and swallowed a gulp of it. This procedure he did as an imitation of the tradition of the **Prophet (s)** who said: ―It is supererogatory to drink from the water with which one wants to make *ghusl* or *wudu*." The wise reason behind it is that the water intended for purification must be as pure as that intended for drinking. But some people, when performing *wudu* or *ghusl* by the water of open pools or bathing-reservoirs, whose water was stagnant for weeks, still put it in their mouths, committing a *makruh*, thinking they were doing a recommended act. **Aqa Ruhullah** used always to fill his ewer for *wudu*, and the other one, from the closed reservoir of drinking water, and, in order not to be subject to the objections of **Mashhadi Ramadan**, who was in charge of the water reservoir, he used to give him 10 *Shahis* per week.

On that day he performed the *wudu* with its recommended procedures[254], returned to his room and put on his newest shirt which contemptuously boasted over the leaves of jasmine, and which had been passed under a coal-iron to smooth its wrinkles, and took his *qaba* from a nail driven into the wall, its head wrapped with a piece of cloth so that it may not tear what is hung on it. He took his turban, which was hung on another hook, unfolded it and refolded it anew. He had three *aba*'s, one in the color of fresh hazelnut, which was presented to him by his brother **Nuruddin** when he changed his official apparel. The color of the other two _*aba*'s was like the African curled hair. One of them was thin, used in summer time, thrown on his shoulder by **Aqa Nuruddin Iraqi** when he entered his room. The third one, for winter, he had bought for five *tumans* from the bazaar in Arak. This latter one he took from the hook spread it on his shoulders and stood facing a small square mirror placed on a shelf such that he could see down to his waist in it. He sized up himself. Today tens of fancies and questions parade in his mind. It is good to ask the mirror: ―Am I a man now?" If the answer was in affirmative, he would go to do something else, then he would return to it. It is recommended to look oneself in the mirror three times before leaving the house, though a single is confirmed, which, as a child, he used to practise, while, as a mature young man he did not neglect to practise the other two times, too. Probably, later on, he came to know that to look in the mirror three times was a tradition of **the Messenger of Allah.** But the situation on that very day moved his feet towards the mirror once again, and in each time a question occurred in his mind, this time probably: ―Is it man who puts on the dress, or is it the dress which puts on man?" The image in the mirror did not yet know the answer of that question. But his third question in his third conversation was replied by Sadi's poetry:

The body of man is honoured by the soul of humanity

Not this beautiful dress is the sign of humanity!

In those throbbing and sensational moments when he was preparing himself for the appointment, was it right that Sadi should come out from behind the mirror and taunt him who had put on his best dress to appear handsome in the appointment? Yes, let him taunt, since a great event is anticipated. If at such sensitive moments taunting remarks are not used, what would be the use of wise men?

Was it right for him to take off the new dress and put on the dress of the day before so as to appear truer at the meeting? He took the _aba' off his shoulders, intending to take off the *qaba*, but he changed his mind and put on his _aba' once again, and, with his small wooden comb, he arranged, with more exactness than the days before, the young thin hairs of his beard next to each other. A few teeth (of the comb) entered his thick course eyebrows. The mirror gave permission to leave. It does not seem that the mirror could be so sensitive to smell the scent of the heaps of roses that had gone into a boiler and poured out their essence into small vials. His room-mates, however, must have felt it that every day when a vial was uncorked so that a drop of it could scent the air, they, involuntarily cried sending blessings on **Muhammad (s)** and his progeny. Now two of the room-mates sent blessing on the **Prophet (s),** and this was the last thing to be done in the room.

When he pushed his feet into his shoes, he appeared better dressed than ever. Two school-mates stood side by side with him and sized him up, as if that day he suddenly became older than the day before.

The flower-leaves of _Bismillah' bud sprayed perfume on his lips. The smelling ears of the two mates smelled it and two buds grew on their lips, too. He was encouraged and descended the steps and passed the turn of the lane, and continued through the back alleys of the town. He neither hurried, as this had never been his custom, nor was he very slow, which he disliked, too.

The alleys were cold, snow-clad and empty. On the way the talks were brief. In the last alley more men were seen going to the same direction of these three friends. The younger ones drew aside to make way for the three turbaned young men, and the elders only answered greetings, and, without stopping they went along the narrow alley. When they arrived at the meeting-place they took off their shoes and arranged them in pairs near the door. A young man took them to the tea service room. A turbaned Sayyid at the door answered their greetings, and, to know which one of them was **Aqa Ruhullah,** he loudly said: ―Welcome, **Aqa Ruhullah!**" From the thanking reply he knew who **Ruhullah** was. He took his hand and seated him beside him, and pointed to the other two to sit a little farther, because the place was crowded and the elders were too many to give space for the two mates to sit beside **Ruhullah.**

Sensational Moments

Who had chosen **Aqa Ruhullah,** from among tens of young men of the *hawzah* of Arak, to be invited to deliver a speech in that meeting? **Aqa „Abbas Araki** was the first name to spark in the mind. Had **Aqa Ruhullah** reached such a stage of maturity to preserve the prestige of **Aqa „Abbas Araki**? Surely he had confidence, but he could not stop his anxiety. So, he thought it better not to attend the meeting in person, since those two room-mates would report what he had said and how it ended.

Performing *wudu* with all its supererogatory acts, wearing the best of his clothes, using perfume and looking into the mirror several times, were not for the purpose of going for wooing. To most theology students ascending a *minbar* to deliver a speech for the first time is more exciting than going to a proposal rendezvous. Some of them would vow in case they could manage the situation agreeably. Some others would count the steps of the *minbar* on which they expect to sit, and think about how to sit on it.

Nowadays some *minbars* are unnecessarily high. But when there were no loudspeakers yet, the steps of the *minbars* in large mosques sometimes exceeded ten steps that the speaker may sit so high as to have his voice reach all the audience. How many steps had the *minbar* of this very mosque? It was one of the small or medium mosques of a quarter in the town, so it should not have more than four steps.

Sitting on a certain step of the *minbar* in a certain period in certain mosques was a sign denoting the level of the speaker's knowledge. To sit at a height of 1.5 m to 4 m. seemed horrifying, especially if the audience were crowded. Speaking for the first time in a meeting in which the addressees were common people, though not so easy, yet it was easier than to speak before an audience including even a single *Alim*. If there was a famous orator or an *Alim* in the meeting, the first oration would seem very difficult and tiresome, causing perspiration on the speaker's forehead.

Aqa Murtada soon learnt that his brother had ascended the *minbar,* and inquired to know whether he had managed it well or not. He inquired: ―On which step did he sit?" They said: ―On the last step." The second question was: —Who of the well-known *ulama* of Arak were there to hear him?" They named some persons, but they were not so famous for **Aqa Murtada** to know them. The last question was whether he talked without tumblings or with stammering? The answer was: —Thank God! He did much better than what was expected."

Later on he related to some of his friends how he was chosen to deliver his first speech and its topic. However, none of them is living to tell his exact words in this respect. So, what comes next may not be strictly in conformity with reality: —When it was decided that I should ascend the *minbar,* I accepted. I slept little that night, not because of being afraid of facing the people, but it came to me that the next day I will have to ascend the *minbar* which belonged to the Messenger of Allah. I prayed to **Allah** to help me, in my ascending the *minbar,* now and ever, that I should never say any sentence in which I do not believe. This want was a covenant I concluded with my Lord. My first speech turned lengthy, but no one seemed to get tired. I think it was good, as a number [of the audience] shouted approval. By returning to my heart I noted that I was pleased with those approvals. That was why I rejected the second and third invitations, and for four years I never stepped up any *minbar.*[255]"

The Subject of the First Official Speech

What was the subject of his first speech, ethics or politics? I should say: ‗Political ethics'. But as this term is polluted, I redress it to ‗ethical politics', because he never talked, in his life, on politics unless he also talked on ethics, too. Even in the mourning meeting on the late **Tabatabai,** a political theologian, can one neglect talking politics? Even if he wanted to take a different course, the conditions of the day necessitated that, and he responded.

On the other hand, the late **Tabatabai** was a theologian, but his name was seen among the politicians. To believe that in those days dividing the theologians into political and non-political was not current, is an unlikely belief, but it was an actuality. So, if **Aqa Ruhullah** has spoken of this personality, it cannot be said that he had spoken politics, nor can one say he didn't.

How did he start? What did he say? What is obvious is that his analyses of the life of that man did go beyond praising. He believed in that personality, washing clean his skirt from any rumour. In those days there were rumours that the late **Tabatabai** and **Behbahani,** in order to bring Constitutionalism home, gave permission to the people to take refuge in the

British Embassy's garden. Probably the British themselves had spread that rumour and forged evidences. Despite the fact that this subject can still be analyzed and discussed anew, but **Aqa Ruhullah,** after every analysis, arrived at the belief that the late **Behbahani** and **Tabatabai** were quite above such rumours as to give such a permission. Perhaps the reason for choosing, from among all the orators of Arak, a young inexperienced theology student to deliver a speech in a mourning meeting for **Tabatabai** was that in the friendly sessions of 1299 he spoke in defence of that personality in such a way that after 63 years: ─It is a cause of wonder and regret that the educational system of the Islamic Republic of Iran should accuse the late **Behbahani** (may **Allah** have mercy upon him) of something which even **Kasrawi,** with his anti-Islamic past, had not ascribed to him. **Kasrawi,** the anti-religion, after paying homage to **Behbahani** and **Tabatabai,** rejected accusing them of allowing the people to take refuge in a foreign Embassy.[256]"

Nobody Accepted to Be Premier
As from the day on which the late **Tabatabai** died, up to a week later[257], tens of reports were registered in the history of Iran's external and internal relations. The most important piece of news which the people showed sensitivity in repeating and following up, was the news concerning the resignation of the Prime Minister **Sepahdar Rashti,** titled as **Sepahdar Azam.** A few days later it was rumoured that no one was ready to accept the post of premier. Of course the rumour was not incorrect, because **Ahmad Shah** ordered **Mirza Hasan Khan, Mustawfi al-Mamalik,** to become Prime Minister, but he evaded it. Three days later another **Mirza Hasan,** with the title **Mushiruddawlah,** wanted from him to accept the post, but he, too, did not accept. **Sultan Abdul Majid Mirza,** with the title **Ainuddawlah,** also refused the post which he had so much tried to get to it. Why? What was the matter?

At the first night of Bahman a heavy snow started down and the next day Tehran was half-paralysed. Five days had, however, passed over the country without having a Prime Minister. Delay was not allowable. Once again **Ahmad Shah** summoned the deputies to have a consultation with them. Young and inexperience as he was, he was intellectual enough, in a difficult situation, to involve all the politicians and to submit to the opinion of the majority. Even the lazy deputies who were not prepared to leave their houses on that snowy day, discontentedly grumbling and abusing, arrived at the palace, and, after several hours of discussion and argument they decided that **Ahmad Shah** may not make fuss about the resignation of **Sepahdar**

Rashti, and once again dip the pen into the inkpot and issue the decree in his name appointing him Prime Minister.

A Tour in the Village of Arak

The *Majlis* waited 28 days for the cabinet to be introduced. During this period the country was apparently calm. **Aqa Ruhullah** used to visit, with other preachers, the nearby villages to set up gatherings to mourn the late **Tabatabai.** On holydays he used to visit some villages which he had not seen before. He was so serious about it that he caused difficulties for his room-mates, as when winter snow and rain turned the earthy lanes of Arak and the nearby villages into such muddy water roads that in every visit his *_aba‘, qaba* and *charuq* shoes got muddy and soaked, and when, at sunset, or even after that, he came back to the school with cold-swollen feet, he used to take off his *charuq* and stockings, wash them and push them under the *kursi* near the stove. His room-mates, because of his kindness to them, used to help him in washing and drying his *aba* and *charuq*. One day one of the students siezed him by the hand and took him to the market and bought for the room-mates covershoes called *galush,* which were newly offered to the market, and few people knew that those covershoes were waterproof. He friendly asked **Ruhullah** to pay for all those *galushes.* Now he could, instead of his *charuq* shoes—which were somewhat aristocratic with their long laces causing delays for his companions—use his *giweh*, cotton shoes, and, on rainy days, he could protect them by the rubber *galush.* At that night there was a discussion concerning Arabicizing the three words: *charuq, galush* and *giweh.* Having declined them, these young men of letters wondered whether those words were concrete 4-lettered or conjugatable 3-lettered verbs. The discussion went beyond literary questions to logic, at first, then to physics and then to other realms. The Arabicized *_giweh‘* became *_jiweh‘*, and *_jiweh‘* [mercury] was a simple liquid metal, while *_giweh‘* was a compound of an outer layer and a sole, and it never was a liquid. So, there is no doubt that the Arabicized *_jiweh‘*, which is worn on the feet, has only a literal similarity with the metal *_jiweh‘* which is used on the glass to make mirrors. Such amusing discussions were like sparks which put aflame the stock of his mind in quest of philosophic knowledge.

Catching Cold and Knowing Medicine

It must have been on those cold days when he once visited Farahan village, the birthplace of Amir Kabir, or some months ago. But on these very days, he, together with five, six, others, set out, on foot, to one of the nearby villages, and, on the way back they were caught by a snow-storm. The howlings of wolves and jackals were resounded by the wailing of the wind. The sun set but that group did not come back. **Aqa Ruhullah** had not said he would not come back. Friends, lanterns in hand, hurried hither and thither until they could find their footprints. When the eyes of these five, six, persons fell on the searching friends, they did not waist their leftover energies to keep standing and they all fell down. The friends shouldered them to the room and made them lie down under the *kursi*. Cold had deeply penetrated to their bones. Hot tea was quite lovable but it did not warm the bones. Into the pot of porridge boiling on a stove they threw a number of turnips, because in the traditional medicine it is said that turnips had a healing element for chestache and flu. In the middle of the night one of the room-mates was awakened by **Ruhullah"s** moaning. He noted that a severe fever had thrown red rose on his cheeks. He washed his feet. The next day the doctor came and approved the foot-washing and prescribed some medicine. Nevertheless the fever did not quit him for a week. His other friends experienced a similar situation in their rooms. **Ayatullah Hairi** called upon them all, and in **Ruhullah"s** room he took out two bags from under his _aba' and put them near the *kursi,* and, by way of presenting a gift of tranquillizing terms, he, jokingly or seriously, said: –You have turned the school into a hospital!" When **Ayatullah Hairi** was taking the hand of the lying patient into his wrinkled hand, invoking for his health, **Ruhullah** attempted to sit up out of the lying position. But **Ayatullah Hairi,** with his left hand, pressed him back on the bed. The natural and sincere behaviour of the *hawzah's* old professor took its light from affection, showing his visage in **Ruhullah"s** eyes like moon. On his leaving he took one of the bags. **Ruhullah** knew that he was neither the first nor the last whom **Ayatullah Hairi** visited. It was known what was in the bag. It was dried figs of which some bags were sent every year from Yazd. The room-mates ate it all in a single day on the pretext that sweet things are not good for **Ruhullah** to eat.

Along the week during which he was tortured by the cold and chestache he became attracted to traditional medical books. They brought him some books from the school library. Probably *Tibbur-Rida (a)* was among them. Whenever fever and coughing gave him a respite, he would read a few pages and take notes. By reading a number of medical books and acquiring knowledge about the characteristics of foods and medical herbs, for years he felt himself in no need of consulting physicians. At times he would prescribe some herbs for his friends. However, after becoming versed in philosophy and *fiqh,* the situation changed, as he believed that medication was completely a matter of specialization, as well as a sacred profession. One day he was going from Qum to Tehran by bus, with one of his close friends, **Ahmad Lawasani.** In the bus a young man, pressing his forehead with his hand, paced the passage between the seats up and down. After a while he stopped before their seats and, as if addressing them both, asked: ―*Haj Aqa,* have you got a headache tablet?" **Haj Ahmad** pushed his hand into his chest-pocket and, from a 10-folded bundle; he picked out a tablet and gave it to him. While the young man was tearing the paper off the tablet, **Haj Aqa Ruhullah** said: ―Were I in your place I would have tolerated the headache." ―Why?" the young man asked. ―Because this friend of mine," pointing to **Haj Ahmad,** ―is not a doctor," he replied. This attitude he applied to his own family, too. He used to say: ―Wise people do not prescribe for others what the physicians prescribe for them." In his further years of maturity he had commitment towards many specialties; at their head were the medical specialties. At his last years his doctors used to say that few patients were so obedient as he. He obeyed their instructions unquestionably, like a complete follower. His brief knowledge of some medical books in his youth gave him courage to use it, at least, on his own self. This courage was taken when he was forced—in order to get a better understanding of the connection between spirit and body and the difference between soul and spirit—to get a bit acquainted with the complicated world of biology and anatomy.

When he became an expert *faqih,* in the case No. 2 of his *Religious Instructions,* he wrote: ―According to a *wajib* precaution, one must follow a *mujtahid* who is not keen on worldly matters, and who must have more knowledge of all other mujtahids, that is, he must be more expert in under-standing **Allah's** judgments than the *mujtahids* of the time." Concerning medication he had a similar opinion. He always tried to consult, for himself or for his friends, such doctors who were not tradesmen nor greedy, and whom he believed to be the best in their profession, in which case he would be a *muqallid.* In case he asked a question, it was not by way of interference, but just to consult or to obtain some information.[258]

At any rate, in these days when he is in bed and looks into the medical books, he feels that to learn medication is not more difficult than learning Arabic literature. So, when he got better, he called on the doctor who had attended him, and requested to borrow from him a few medical books, or recommend to him suitable books to purchase them. The doctor said: ―The time in which Avicenna could, simultaneously, be a philosopher, a *faqih* and a physician, has passed away. You keep to your studies and let us do our job."

But **Ruhullah** could finally lay his hand on a 2-volume French book on anatomy, from whose pictures he got information about the location of the intestines, the bowels, the bones, the nervous system, to some extent. The book stirred his eagerness to learn the French language, but for persons like him the cultural conditions were not available to learn a European language.

A Comment on the Hadith: Science Is of Two Kinds

The first *faqih* who explained the precepts concerning artificial pollination, blood donation and transplantation of kidneys, hearts, eyes and other organs, was he. To explain such precepts he needed to know strict details of anatomy and physiology. So he referred to the specialists. But to understand the answer to each question he had to know generalities of the science of medication. So, when he recovered from the flu and bone-ache, and not being sure of going to be a *faqih* in the future, he gave himself to free medical studies just to satisfy his research instinct. Apparently he could not know that being acquainted with those medical generalities would cause a change in the *fiqh*.

Later on, supported by a Prophetic *hadith,* he further justified his inclination to that knowledge. **The Prophet** had said: ‑Science is of two kinds: the science of bodies and the science of religions.[259]" This *hadith* was worthy of deep contemplation. Theologically, in the words of the infallibles no shirking is admissible. So, if the science of the bodies has literal priority to the science of religions, and if that priority is not removed from it, then it will remain constant. On the other hand, another *hadith* says: ‑Science is Allah's light.[260]" The science of the bodies is one of the two pillars of science. So, the science of the bodies has intrinsic honour. A wise saying said by the wise men of the centuries proved the belief that ‑The healthy mind is in a healthy body." Therefore, to him, medical knowledge got a doubled objectivity and, in his consciousness or subconsciousness, he acknowledged a kind of nobility in this branch of knowledge. Due to this, both before and after the Revolution, he referred more than forty times and on different occasions to the scarcity of physicians and medicine and the regrettable condition of sanitation and treatment, and offered his advices to the committed physicians. Yet, more important was to know whether **the Prophet (s)** regarded only these two branches of knowledge to be science: the empirical medical sciences and the rational and traditional sciences extending into *fiqh*. What about geography? Is it not a science? History, has it a place in the *hadith?* Astronomy, is it not a science? What about mathematics? Chemistry, physics, road and construction engineering, geology, are they all out of the science circle? Is psychology the science of religion, or is it not a science at all? Consequently, philosophy has divorced science, with its wide concept, and management is nonsense knowl- edge, and weather forecast is a non-scientific prophecy.

Hundreds and thousands of scholars had washed their hearts' eyes in the fountain of that noble *hadith* and with tens of expressions let it flow with current of the thought river. This *hadith,* at the beginning, with a determination, like that of a youth, inspired the heart and mind of **Ruhullah,** the young man, with the science of medicine and the knowledge of theology in their primary and apparent concepts, prompting him to be attached to medication as much as his attachment to acquire religious knowledge. As a matter of course, he took into consideration his teachers of religious knowledge. No one knew of this strong attachment except his close friends and brothers.

His little acquiantance of this branch of knowledge went beyond the state of that in his youth he should medically treat his friends, while in his maturity he should know that he must never have the slightest interference in it, because he had raised this scientific knowledge from the sphere of empirical knowledge up to the rational knowledge and knotted it with gnosticism, growing out of them another knowledge—a knowledge which, essentially, is gnosticism, but it does not fit into the current theoretical gnostics divisions. It is philosophy, but a philosophy to which some godly hilosophers are also alien. It is science, but a science which the epistemologians should find a new name for it. It is an easy but impossible matter whose depth is easily comprehended by common people of nowadays as they drink a cup of warm tea, while a traditional mind is incapable of understanding it .People of today, who have to do with the computers and know about softwares and hardwares, can very well understand his concept of soul and body .His expression says: —Science is of two kinds: the science of the bodies and the science of religions. The soul and the body are united. The body is the shadow of the soul. The soul is the interior of the body. The body is the external appearance of the soul. Both of them are one. They do not separate, and just as a man's body and soul are united, the doctor of the body and the doctor of the soul must be united, too. They must be a single one, but, alas! They separated us from one another[363] ."

These surprising expressions were first heard by the physicians who called on him after the Revolution. That very night millions of the eager people listened to those words from the Radio and the TV. Yet, they are words which to some people remain unheard. Should these be considered deeper, one would realize why **Mulla Sadra** was ousted out of the town.

Anyhow, it seems that the severe flu in those days and the reading a number of medical books were the original cause for his inclination towards _the science of the bodies‘, which later on was united with _the science of religions‘. After recovering he tried to make up for the lessons which had been left behind. He once again attended the lessons of the late **Araki,** spending two weeks in hard work to overcome the difficulties in his studies of the Arab literature. From then on he could read the *Quran, hadiths* and Arabic texts, and to understand their apparent meanings without having to translate them first into Persian in his mind. Before finishing parts of these lessons there came the news that a military Coup d‘état had paralyzed Tehran.[262]

The Black Coup d‘état in a Cold Dawn

Arak, before Khomein, enjoyed a telegraph office; hence, the Capital‘s news reached it earlier than Khomein. By means of this telegraph office the name of **Sayyid Diyauddin Tabatabai,** a mysterious man who was the manager of *Rad* newspaper, was circulated among the people. He was a man who, with the forces of a Cossack called **Rida Khan,** in a cold dawn, started from Qazvin and attacked Tehran, and, without any serious resistance, all the offices fell into the hands of the Cossacks.[263] This piece of news was both important and ambiguous. No one knew well what the nature of the Coup d‘état was. Many thought that the Russian Bolsheviks had to do something with it, and that Communism was showing its teeth. It took more than a month for the township people to know that it was the hand of the British which appeared from the sleeves of a journalist. The Tehrani citizens, as well as the foreign diplomats, could not very well understand what the objective of the Coup d‘état was. Those whose heads were worthy of their bodies were arrested and thrown into prison. Within two days, poets, orators, writers, resistant pros and cons of Constitutionalism, wealthy businessmen and famous politicians, amounting to more than two hundred people [264] were jailed. The first one who was arrested had come by himself. The early hours of the morning of the Coup d‘état were still tied to the night when the most cunning Qajarian prince, i.e. **Abdul Husayn Mirza,** known as **Farmanfarma,** in his carriage, found his way into the headquarters of the Coup d‘état people in order to obtain information, so that if he knew that the power was powerful and the control of Coup d‘état people was inevitable, he would congratulate them and get a post. But this time he had hit at the barn and was arrested. In the prison he knew that **Rida Khan,** a Sawadkuhi, was the commander of the Coup d'état forces. It was painful to know that it was at the order of **Rida Khan** that he was arrested, because a few months before, in KirmanShah, it was this very **Rida Khan** who was to protect his life, and sometimes **Farmanfarma,** whom power and the high position of being a prince made impolite and insolent, used to hurl vulgar and ugly and unspeakable abuses at this cossack, and now and then he did not refrain from having this helpless cossack flogged. However, after an hour he would atone for his abuses and floggings by throwing an *ashrafi* at him.[265] Now, at this cold dawn, he is caught in the rough claws of the very person whom he had treated so brutally. If **Farmanfarma** was not **Rida Khan's** first teacher of morality, he, then, was one of the best, because, at this sensitive time, **Rida Khan** recited his lesson very well. Later on he also imitated him in reviling and flogging, and then he used to give an *ashrafi* or more to the one who could bear him best.

The offices, shops, business closed down completely for many days. Martial law was announced in Tehran and the Governor, **Rida Khan,** issued the first announcement by the coup-government in nine Articles:

--|command!

Art. No. 1. All the people of Tehran must keep quiet and obey the orders of the martial law.

Art. No. 7. All the governmental establishments and offices remain closed, except the Provision Office, until the formation of the government. The Post, the Telephone and the Telegraph will also obey this order...

> 14 Jumadi ath-Thani
> Commander of Cossack Division
> His Blessed Sovereign Majesty and the
> Commander-in-Chief
> Rida.[266]"

Secret Information

Up to ten days afterwards no information was received about the Coup d'état, except the governmental announcements, and some travellers' reports. Some people wondered what a calamity was that inflicted upon the country. After the 12th of Isfand, though apparently the communications, telegraph and post were free, the letters were still inspected by the officials of the martial law. Of course it was ridiculous, since most of the Cossacks were illiterate and at times they took the letters upside-down to read them.

The coward people's frequent calls on the foreign embassies, especially those of Britian, Russia and France, to obtain asylum, somewhat uncovered the nature of the Coup d'état. It was known that the British had decided to enact the Agreement of 1919. That Agreement had been signed a year and a half before, on 17th Mordad 1298 (solar year), by **Nusratuddawlah Firuz,** son of **Farmanfarma**, the Foreign Minister, and **Sarimuddawlah,** the Financial Minister of **Wuthuquddawlah,** the Premier, and **Cox,** representing the British Foreign Minister. Most of the freedom-lovers so opposed it that it remained suspended. This 6-Art. Agreement, its first Art. was a repetition of political compliments, such as: _With respect to Iran's independence and integrity'. Its other articles concerned granting the British concessions to establish an army unified in appearance under the supervision of the British consultants, to revise the customs tariff, commerce, the railway concession etc., which were incredible, not only to the Iranians, but even to the foreigners, too. The French newspaper *Temps* wrote: —This Agreement deprives Iran from political independence." **Albert Thomas,** the French Minister of War, said in the French Parliament: —By this Agreement, the British can extend its Empire." In the American Senate it was said: —By signing this Agreement the British state put Iran under its protectorate." The USSR issued a statement saying: —By signing this Agreement Iran had entrusted its fate into the hands of Britain." The opposition against the Agreement was so much that a martial law was imposed. **Wuthuquddawlah,** the Prime Minister, called the opposers negationists, and on the 17th of Shahrivar 15 of the opposers were arrested and 5 were banished to Kashan.[267]

Because of fear of the public opinion no politician was prepared to accept the disgrace of carrying it out. The British found a Cossack who was thirsty for power. He was, sometimes before, recognized by **Ardashir G. Reporter,** the head of the British spies in Iran, and was trained under the supervision of **General Ironside,** how to carry out a successful Coup d'état. He was regarded as fit for the job, but he was illiterate and undistinguished, while **Sayyid Diya** was somewhat literate with good style and conduct, though not with good reputation, since he was known as a British agent. Thus, he was chosen as officially in charge of the Coup d'état.

Rida Khan was so thirsty for power that when he was told, though at the bottom of undistinguishedness, to say: —command!" he said it without hesitation. This ambitiousness spoke of the fact that **Sayyid Diya** had to leave the political arena, presently.

The Coup d'état, whose identity had not yet been known, deranged the studies in the scientific *hawzah* of Arak. At that time **Aqa Ruhullah** was following political news, but, alas! He had neither a radio nor a newspaper. By means of the logic which he had learnt he had to pick out, from among hundreds of rumours and weak talks, the reality of the event. This became one of his merits which helped him later to analyze the hidden realities of the political events, out of countless rumours, without having trustworthy news sources. At that time he knew, however, that he was still a young man and his political analyses, were immature and inconsistent. He, thus, was not to disclose the results of his analyses of this event.

The Feelings of any Young Patriot
As long as he was in Arak, probably he obtained desultory and stale pieces of news, although we do not know what his feelings were on hearing them. But as one can guess the feelings of any young patriot on hearing confused news of those days, one can also guess what effects such news can have on the spirit of the young **Aqa Ruhullah.**

Sepahdar Rashti, the Premier, had sought sanctuary in the British Embassy before the Coup d'état. Didn't he know that it was the British who caused the Coup d'état? If he did, then what a mean he was to seek asylum with his enemy! If he didn't, then what a fool he was!

All the ex-premiers who were still living, whether of good or bad reputation, and everybody of the official or non-official rank, were arrested. Likewise, all the members of **Sepahdar Rashti's** cabinet were imprisoned. Doesn't this mean that high rank, cabinet, glory and power in Iran are quite disloyal! Later on, when he encountered saying by **the Imam Ali (*a*)** to the effect that disloyalty encloses the entire history and all lands, he seriously believed that although the tendency towards power and position is endless, yet whenever a status is somewhat taken to be a position, it will one day come to an end: –Any status obtained by man, whether spiritual or material, will one day be taken from him.[268]"

Sayyid Hasan Mudarris among the Arrested
Some of the *Majlis* deputies, including **Sayyid Hasan Mudarris,** were arrested so that no breathing creature may stand against the Coup d'état. It was the second time in which he committed this name to his memory. Later, he many times admired this great man's knowledge of politics. This man's courage, derived from his reliance on **Allah,** sometimes shook the hearts of his friends. Few days before releasing him, **Sayyid Diya** sent a rough and merciless man to levy money from the prisoners, saying that the prison would remain for a suitable time, but the one who would not like to be shot

must pay a prescribed sum of money. The helpless prisoners wrote to their families, on slips of paper: ―Our lives are endangered! Please send the demanded sum immediately." When it was the turn of this turbaned Sayyid, he, with a loud voice which all could hear, told the messenger: ―Tell this cousin (**Sayyid Diya**) on my behalf that you could do it on the very day on which you arrested us. Now that you did not, it cannot be done. So, you must go away![269]" **Farmanfarma,** known as the Fox of Qajar, was afraid of the words of his cell-mate, but he could not understand the concept of this analysis until **Sayyid Diya** had to leave Iran. Then the Fox congratulated **Mudarris** for his prophecy.

Ahmad Shah Recognizes the Coup d"état

It was said that **Ahmad Shah,** a young lad as he was, had run away to somewhere for fear of imprisonment, but on the second day of the Coup d'état it became known that the somewhat free Shah, in order to protect his throne, had submitted, in a way, to the Coup d'état, and that he wrote, by his hand, a cable and ordered it to be spread all over the country:

―To the governors of the provinces and towns: Owing to the negligence and carelessness of the former rulers, causing general abeyance and insecurity in the country, and as we and the people were distressed lacking a firm government, we decided to appoint a strict serviceman to provide for the happiness of the kingdom, so as to put an end to continual crisis. Consequently, due to the talents and abilities we see in His Excellency **Mirza Sayyid Diyauddin,** our complete intention is directed to him, and we chose him for the post of the Prime Minister, granting him all the authorities needed to carry out the duties of premiership.

> The month of Jumadi al-Akhar, 1339 AH
> Ahmad Shah.[270]"

On the same day he issued another decree in favour of **Rida Khan Mirpanj,** giving him the rank of **Sardar Sepah** [Army Commander]. The rank of Mirpanj has no equivalent today, maybe it is regarded a rank higher than colonel. In those days, it was regarded as the commander of five thousand soldiers, and the rank of Sardar Sepah was the last rank of Timsar, a high military rank. The Sardar Sepah, who, the previous day, with the rank of Mirpanj, said: ―I command!" wrote out his slavish gratitude as below, and which had to be cabled to all the provinces:

―On the part of His Majesty, the owner of honour, the ShahanShah, I have been granted the rank of Sardar and honoured with the title of Sardar

Sepah. My slavish thanks I offer to the attention of his Imperial Majesty, imploring **Allah,** the One, to bestow upon me success and assistance so that with all my might I can perform any service and sacrifice, in gratitude for his favours. **Rida**.[271]"

As a result of **Rida Khan's** promotion, the next day all the Cossack revolters were promoted to a higher rank.

The Attitude of Dr. Musaddiq, Governor of Fars

Three days after the Coup d'état he heard the name of a man who, after 23 years, played the role of a national hero. He had studied law up to doctorate. He was acquainted with the current political events of the world as he could. He knew what strategy meant, and he was, then, governor of Fars. This man, at that misty suffocating situation, dared enough to send a cable answering that of **Ahmad Shah**. It read: —Tehran. Handwritten telegraph was received through the Central Telegraph Office. Being loyal to the government I will put what I know at the feet of the blessed [one]. If this telegraph is spread in Fars, there will be many Coup d'états and disorders, which will be very difficult to redress. [Your] servant did not want in [my] loyalty, such Coup d'états should place. So far I kept it concealed. Should the said telegraph, according to his Majesty's order, be spread, he may issue his blessed command to the telegraph office to circulate it.

Muhammad Musaddiq"

No doubt the Cossacks in the telegraph office, whose salaries were, then, paid by **Rida Khan,** would send **Musaddiq's** telegraph to their boss, not to the Shah. **Musaddiq,** whose popularity was well known and was loved by the Shirazians, showed that although he was an expert politician and knew the nature of the Coup d'état, yet, in selecting the method of practical action, he was weak. In another instance, in another Coup d'état, which **Rida Khan's** son raised against him, he showed this weakness even clearer, and was ousted out of the political arena.[272] **Musaddiq** is a good example for confirming the theory that the strategists are poor in understanding the tactics. The strategists look at things as a whole, and the tacticians look at things in details. Probably **Aqa Ruhullah** had learnt lessons from **Musaddiq's** tactical weaknesses [273], because, later on, he showed himself a wonder at knowing the tactics of struggling. However, **Musaddiq's** cable reached **Sayyid Diya,** and two days later he sent an answer which deserves reading. It seems, however, that **Aqa Ruhullah** had never seen that reply, or, at least, he only knew a gist of it, since its text was later published. The answer denotes that whatever clever the revolters may be at politics, they are unable to make use of the compound words of alluring and threatening, rather they used the alluring and threatening terms in an unskilled and mixed way.

Sayyid Diya"s Answer to Musaddiq

─The telegraph of **Aqa Sayyid Diyauddin to Aqa Dr. Musaddiqus-Saltanah,** the Governor of Fars: The Great Province of Fars: I was informed, in a roundabout way that you did not spread the telegraph concerning my appointment as prime minister, telling of some difficulties. This report informed me that your Highness did not know about the situation, and took the horizon of Tehran to be the same as you had formerly seen and eye-witnessed. No, it is not like that. Being far away and lacking information deprived you from useful information. This newly formed government, with the weapons and fire of the only Commander and representative of the power of an army, will not treat those who create obstacles in its way except with fist... In a single moment, the life, the wealth and the family of the problem-maker will be under the threat, as a hostage, to prove his truthful- ness. This rude and rough conduct is not for personal interests, but for the national interests which make lawful any procedure... I hope, for the sake of the homeland and for the sake of reforms, that you, despite the far distance, open your bosom and brotherly hug me and grant me your assistance and support by way of respecting the national interests...[274]"

Probably it was the first time in which the political terminology of the Iranian statesmen used the expression ‗national interests‘, and how untimely and meaninglessly! A week later **Musaddiq** delivered his resignation to the Shah so that he might not recognize the government of the Coup d'état. Despite the fact that it was regarded to be the most honourable procedure that a statesman, in those entangled conditions, could do, yet by going through the collection of the **Imam Khomeini's** political theories and ideas within the half century which followed, it seems that he took this procedure, on the part of great politicians, to be a respectful cleverness. He firmly believes that the sound, pure-natured and philanthropic nationalists would sacrifice only up to the limit of their good reputation, while the suppressed and backward people, before needing a national hero, they are in need of sacrificers who can give up even their reputation. The constructions of the patriotic ideas can be excitable up to this limit, or even to the higher limit of martyrdom for the sake of a good reputation[275], but not more than that! This is a point if not taken into consideration, the Imam's dispraises of the conducts of some great politicians, may be looked at as political rivalry blames, whereas gnosticism had made him so high-flying and heavenly that rivalry, this primary principle necessary for advancement in worldly matters, he had left down. At the same time, he was too great a man to regard the great men of this soil, or of any other soil, mean, and disregard their services.[276]

Three Glad Tidings

When he was following up the news about the Coup d'état, which were mixed with exaggerated rumours, some news complicated the conduct of the government. It appeared so entangled that some of the enlightened persons, *ulama* and local personalities began to gradually forget the origin of the Coup d'état. Those news filled up their eyes and ears. Some people, hesitatingly and some others decisively, praised the Coup d'état. The three tidings, which were spread some fifty hours before the New Year, were a good present for the majority of the people[277], and strongly engaged the minds. One was the cancellation of the Capitulation in respect of the USSR's Azarbayjan, Caucasus, Gurjestan, Armenia, Ottoman, Mesopotamia and Shamat. The cancelling of the Capitulation, without analyzing which countries were bound to it and which were not, and what the political power of those countries was at that time, was pleasing by itself, and it was an old desire of the majority of the people. It took time for the majority to understand that they fell out of the frying pan into the fire! The other was the modification of the salaries of the Shah and the Princes. Before the Coup d'état **Ahmad Shah"s** salary was forty thousand *tumans* which he received from the treasury. From then on he had to put up with thirty thousand *tumans*. The pleasure-seeking princes used to get three thousand *tumans* more than the Shah. Now the salary of each one was reduced to twenty thousand *tumans*. That news would run the princes' ships aground, causing pleasure for the people, because the more the princes received from the treasury the more powerful they became in levying from the people. The third news was: —According to the resolution of the cabinet, the importation of alcoholic beverages from abroad to Iran is banned. According to the order of the Prime Minister drinking alcoholic beverages is prohibited for all classes. In the parties, instead of alcoholic beverages, *dugh* or *sharbat* may be served."

All the three tidings were cabled on 27th Isfand to the centres of all provinces. But this third one was more pleasing to the *ulama* and the majority of the people, and it was more in conformity with the time and the era than the other two tidings. That was because the New Year was arriving and careless people, in nice weather of spring, used to stroll, dead drunk, through the lanes. The people were much bothered by the hands and tongues of careless gangs. The authorities had no instructions for fighting this evil. If the result of forbidding the evil was quarelling, sometimes the forbidder would have to pay indemnity.

O Young Man, May You Live Long

Probably it was some time before this Resolution when two stalwart drunkards took the sack of a salt-seller old man and emptied it on the snows of the road so that in their drunkard staggerings they may not slip over. On trying to empty the second sack, the young **Ruhullah** arrived and, seizing one of them by the wrist, twisted it so hard that he began crying out: –I made a mistake, forgive me!", while the other, hearing his friend's cries, ran away. The old man, mourning, was cursing the drunkards loudly: –May **Allah** kill them!" He invoked **Allah** in favour of **Ruhullah** to grant him long life. After some fifty years, the following line of poetry, written on the back of a truck drew his attention:

You said: –O young man, may you reach old age." I did. Come,
See the curse you uttered in the dress of a pray![277/1]

The driver of the truck, who was having his lunch in a coffee house on the way between Tehran and Mashhad, was relating, with full details, the reason for writing that line of poetry on the back of his truck, to one of his mates so loudly that those at two farther table could hear. He had heard the story of the emptying of the salt-sacks from his father who had heard it from his father. The old man was the driver's grandfather who lived in the same alley through which **Aqa Ruhullah** frequently used to pass. Explaining why he had that line of poetry written on his truck, he said: –When **Ayatullah Taliqani** passed away, and **Imam Khomeini,** in elegizing that great man, said: ‿Living long has the shortcoming of every day losing a dear friend and sitting bemoaning a personality and absorbing in sorrow for a brother...[278], I remembered this line of poetry." He assuredly and confidently was saying: –At least one day of the **Imam**'s life was because of my grandfather's pray for him, and his other days were because of the prays of thousands of others. A proof of that is that the two young drunkards, in another fit of intoxication knifed one another and after a few days they both died."

The Coup d"état"s Statement on Domestic and Foreign Policies

At any rate, perhaps the Resolution prohibiting alcoholic beverages and cancelling the Capitulation which was losing its color was the sweetmeat which overshadowed another Resolution ratified by the cabinet ten days before. According to this Resolution military, disciplinary, monetary, judiciary and agricultural consultants were to be invited from four countries to interfere into all the country's affairs. In this Resolution, which was ratified by the cabinet on the 16th Isfand, 1299, it was decided to invite 25 persons from Sweden for the gendarmerie, 11 persons from Britain for the monetary and economic affairs, 11 persons from America for agricultural affairs, and 5 persons from France for the judicial affairs. The Resolution banning alcoholic beverages did not last long. After that the simple-minded and the naive people became optimistic about the government of the Coup d'état, the bars were once again opened and prospered, because in addition to the careless and some of those who had visited Europe, many of the enlightened, disappointed in religion and politics, took to drinking, too. But as to the first Resolution, it was multiplied by 1000 and put all the country's political and administrative affairs into the hands of the foreigners.

Five days after the Coup d'état, **Sayyid Diya** issued an announcement which was to explain his internal and foreign policies. It was written in a rather charming style admirable to the people. Four days later it was published in *Iran* newspaper which was directed by **Zayn al-Abidin Tajaddud.** It was the only newspaper allowed to be published 11 days after the Coup d'état. An expression was quite exciting, especially to the younger people. It said: –Θ citizens, after fifteen years of Constitutionalism, for which we paid a high price of the blood of Iran's youths, after fifteen years of experiments and trials, and enduring diverse calamities and hardships, after fifteen years of contentions, the unimaginable internal and external problems threw our homeland into such a situation that not only all the politicians of the time did not want to undertake the heavy burden of the responsibility of ruling, but even the deputies, the representatives of the people dared not to perform their duties and to accept the burden. Who were the cause and responsible for this situation and abeyance?

Those who deceived the people with promises of Constitutionalism, freedom and the establishment of law and justice, tried to use these promises as a veil to set up behind it the vision of disorder, the basis of personal advantage and unrestraint—the principles of feudality of the medieval ages, the principles surrounded with the darkness of disasters and crimes.

A few hundred persons of the nobility and elite, who had the reins of the kingdom's affairs in their hands by inheritance, were sucking the blood of the nation, like a leech, causing its uproar, corrupting the political and social life of our homeland to the extent of annihilation... Then the time became suitable to put an end to the situation. It was time for the life of the government of this class to be terminated... At last it is the day for overturning it and taking revenge... O compatriots! It is necessary that a shaking building, in which the parasites had built their nests, should be pulled down... It is necessary that the value and the toil of the workers and the farmers should be estimated, and the term of their poverty must be ended.

In order to attain to this objective, the first step to be taken is to distribute the crown lands and the lands of the government among the peasants, and to enact new laws to increase the benefit of the farmers from the landlords' properties, and to change the landlords' behaviour towards the farmers... Only our brave soldiers are able to secure the kingdom's life and existence, and arrange for its advancement, happiness and power.

Before everything and above everything is the army. Everything is first for the army, and once again: the army.

As to our foreign policy:

... Our relations with each of the foreign countries must not prevent our good relations and friendship with the others.

Because of this very friendship I will cancel the Capitulation which is against the independence of the nation... No nation, however strong and powerful, may limit our freedom. We are free, and free we shall remain. According to these very principles I announce the cancellation of the agreement of August, 1919 between Iran and Britain...[279]"

Rida Khan's Announcement

Now **Rida Khan** issued an announcement, too, the same in style as that of **Sayyid Diya.** Since he was illiterate and incapable of writing such an announcement, the educated class very well understood that the director was behind the scene. Excerpts of it are as below:

—We did not occupy the Capital, as we could not raise our weapons in a place where our sacred crowned King was present. We came to Tehran just to give to it the real meaning of the kingdom's guardianship and the centrality of the government.

A government which is concerned about Iran; a government which may not be just a watcher of its people's misfortune and poverty; a government which regards respecting and endearing to army the first happiness of the Kingdom, taking its power and comfort to be the only way for saving the Kingdom; a government which would not make the Muslim's treasury a means for the voluptuousness of the lazy, self-indulgent and indifferent hangers-on; a government which would not make the large cities of the Muslims centres of wickedness, injustice and cruelty; a government in whose vast lands thousands of the kingdom's children may not say goodbye to their lives because of hunger and misfortune; a government which admits no difference between the honour and the chastity of the Gilani, Tabrizi, Kermani girls and its sisters; a government which would not allow a Kingdom to be afflicted just to afford for the luxury and opulence of a few individuals; a government which would not be a plaything in the hands of the foreign politicians and a government which would not disgrace Iran everyday for a few hundred thousands of foreign currency, nor would it cause its own Kingdom to bear the burden of humiliation...[280]"

Ayatullah Hairi in Qum

We do not know whether **Aqa Ruhullah** had seen the announcement of **Sayyid Diya** in the newspaper or not. **Ayatullah Hairi,** however, had seen it. Despite the fact that the statements of the announcement terrorized the big landlords and the ex-statesmen, and found their place in the hearts and the minds of the patriots and most of the people, but in the two announcements there were three points which deserve thinking. First: This promise of freedom and acting according to law by the people of the Coup d'état, is it trustworthy? A Coup d'état in itself is a breaker of the law and a usurper of freedom, otherwise it could obtain power by law, not by force. Furthermore, a Coup d'état is successful only when it establishes martial law and starts with depriving the people from all freedom. So, how ridiculous it is to hear from these people promises of giving freedom and enacting the law. Then, in both of the announcements the power of the army is confirmed.

Probably **Ayatullah Hairi** had smelled what was behind the curtain, and that the power of the army, which was going to crush the culture under the boots of the Coup d'état, cannot be encountered except by strengthening religious knowledge. Consulting some farsighted persons, he decided to pack up his furniture and move to Qum to set the foundation of a larger school in a town nearer to the centre of power. **Ruhullah** returned to his town to renew his visits with relatives on the New Year's ceremonies.

Once Again in Khomein

It was in the morning of the 26th or 27th of Isfand when he went to the market to buy presents for **Aqa Murtada, Aqa Nuruddin,** the sisters and **Naneh Khawar.** He had learnt to be somewhat thrifty in the daily expenditure, not to the extent of meanness and not getting the advantage of his money, nor spending it in spillage to the verge of poverty. Out of the leftover of his yearly expense which **Aqa Murtada** had wrapped in a handkerchief and put in his pocket as he was about to leave, he bought presents for his relatives, expending, of course, more than that **Aqa Murtada** would expect, because one of the results of the Coup d'état was a sharp inflation, which lasted for few months. He hired a carriage to Khomein. His luggage was much. A Yazdian striped bed sheet with white background and blue stripes was put in the rear. It had two small firm knots, which could not easily be undone in Khomein. For each of his brothers he bought a suit. We do not know what he bought for the sisters and for **Naneh Khawar.** For four of his close friends he bought *giwehs* or *galushes.* All these were well arranged in the bed sheet. He also bought an _*aba'* for **Haj Aqa Abbas Araki** and presented it to him in Arak. He had two quilts, one of them he had brought from Khomein and placed it in the bundle. The other quilt with the trumpery of a single man—with the exception of a cotton handkerchief he used as a towel ,and a glass he had bought in Arak for drinking water—he gave to a room -mate. A Russian bronze samovar, coal boiled, which he had bought very cheap on his moving to Arak though with no chance of a vacancy to artistically use it, he had placed in the middle of the bundle so that it may not be deformed. Nevertheless, a spot on its plump belly gave way. **Aqa Murtada** smoothed it with a hammer, but it did not return to its original form.

By the way of hugging and kissing his friends it was clear that he had no intention to return to Arak again. Many of his friends were preparing to leave Arak to Qum. One of those friends who, together with him, reached the stage of becoming religious authority, was **Muhammad Rida Golpaygani.** His second-day friend was **A Mirza Muhammad Husayn,** who had come to this school four years earlier. His father, **Haj Mirza Mahdi,** due to his conflict with **Amneh,** a Khan of Burujerd, had to leave his home and move to Arak and became a teacher at the same Sepahdar School. It was he who first suggested the migration of **Ayatullah Hairi** to Qum, and which was accepted by **Ayatullah Hairi** without hesitation. He himself moved to Qum earlier in order to prepare for the movement of the theological *hawzah* from

Arak to Qum. For this reason he had a polite conflict with **Haj Mahdi Yathribi,** the manager of Qum's small theological *hawzah.*

Muhammad Husayn, who had become a bosom friend of **Aqa Ruhullah** and whose son, **Aqa Mahmud,** became **Aqa Ruhullah's** son-in-law later, did not go with his father to Qum. Probably he wanted to hire with **Aqa Ruhullah** two horses for riding and two mules for the luggage so as to prove his friendship. But **Ruhullah** had posted a letter saying that he wanted to spend the night of the feast near his family.

The New Year of 1300

An hour before arriving in Khomein his letter had arrived, despite the fact that it had been posted 18 days before. The family was waiting for him, since only few moments remained to the beginning of the New Year, and even if the letter had not arrived they would have kept waiting for him. The weather was still cold, but, despite the Coup d'état, the people, away from the noise of the Capital, received the New Year with new clothes. The alleys were broomed and sprinkled with water, and with drizzling rain they got cleaner. The tall Tabrizi trees and the trembling poplars blossomed and the buds appeared on the branches and greenery stemmed out of the earth, and the cedars, which usually bow under storms, stood errect. The last moments of Isfand were passing away fast, and the throbs of the beginning of the New Year were resounding. A coal stove with kindled embers was put in the veranda, so that they may, as a reception rite, sprinkle wild rue on the fire and have it smoked.

When the door was opened for him to step in, *Nowruz,* mounting the wing of the breeze, was calmly overstepping the wall to put its foot inside the house. After huggings and kissings and inquiring after the health of those present in the yard, he sat at the pond, performed the *wudu* and went to the room to perform the *salah* at the time of moving to the next year, and to tell the *qunut* at the moment of the change. Surely he had hummed: *Ya muhawwil al-hawli wal-ahwal* in his *qunut.* **Aqa Murtada** and **Aqa Nuruddin** were also performing the *salah* in another corner of the room. The sisters returned to their houses to be near their husbands while receiving the New Year Feast.

Nearly a month before *Nowruz,* most of the women in the houses start general house-cleaning. That is, they wash the window-glasses, the curtains, the carpets, the clothes and every washable thing, carefully. The useless things are thrown away and the shortages are provided. All men, except the selfish ones, help their wives, in these days, in house-cleaning and purchases for the feast. When the moments get nearer to the New Year everything, new and old, acquires fresh color and smell. Excitement, fear and hope are flutter over the house. Everybody tries to prepare a new suit. Particularly for the children, great pains are endured to provide for them new shoes, socks, clothes and caps. All these things had been well provided for in his absence. **Aqa Murtada** had provided the servants with new dresses. During the feast's house-cleaning, **Aqa Nuruddin** hid the rifles which had been prepared to defend the town, and which got dusty in the storehouse. However, afterwards, no news was heard of them, as on the ninth day of the Coup d'état, i.e. the twelve of Isfand, the Martial Law issued a strict and stern announcement that: ―Within six days everybody must hand his weapons over." The articles 4 and 5 of the announce -ment read: ―If after ten days from the date of publishing this announcement ,the owners of weapons did not comply with its commands and disregarded it ,besides confiscating the weapons, the infringer would be subject to severe punishments, even up to sentencing him to death. The policemen and the gendarmerie are given the right to enter and investigate, in any time, any suspected place or house313 ."

Naturally, some of the notables in Tehran, who were worried for their lives, handed over a number of their weapons, but in the towns of the provinces only countable rifles were handed over. Those who had seen and tasted the division of Iran and the World War I and its calamities, and they themselves had rolled up their sleeves and bent not their backs in defending their own town, took this announcement to be a disarmament caused either by ignorance or by a wicked conspiracy. So, they buried the rifles into the earth just in case needs be. Probably **Aqa Nuruddin** had seen this *ayah:* **Those who disbelieve would like you to be inattentive of your weapons and luggage so that they may (all) turn upon you in one attack** [282], and so, he did not hand the rifles over to the government of the Coup d'état. A few moments after passing to the New Year **Aqa Ruhullah** asked **Aqa Murtada:** ―Where are the rifles?" **Aqa Murtada** beckoned that it is **Aqa Nuruddin** who should answer. When he asked **Aqa Nuruddin** where he had hidden the rifles, his answer was: ―They are safe, they are safe![283]"

Nowruz a National Feast
More than a thousand years before the arrival of Islam in Iran, the Iranians used to celebrate *Nowruz* in the best possible innovations still carried on. Some of these innovations have become old traditional rituals. When Islam threw its light on this territory some of these traditions not only retained their colors, they even acquired brilliance, because they were in natural

compliance with three ethical regulations of the Islamic Law. One concerns observing kinship relations, which is serious religious instruction and seriously observed in this Feast [*Nowruz*]. Sulkiness changes to reconciliation. Aversion and rancour are swept out with the trash. At least once a year all the relatives, far and near, visit one another and the very close ones kiss each other. The other is that cleanliness, neatness and tastefulness are other instructions of religion. Besides the personal affair they extend to the streets, lanes and markets. As to the third, which has the smell of philosophy, denotes that man's conduct in respect of *Nowruz* coincides with nature. If these are good, how cannot they be of Islam's assertions? But the first one who judged this rational assertion to be religiously permissible might have said: –If the **Messenger (s)** had heard that the Iranians wear new dresses in *Nowruz* and throw away all rancour, he would approve *Nowruz*. But those who are not much trustworthy in quoting have quoted it like this: The Prophet (*s*) had heard how the Iranians celebrate the *Nowruz Feast* and approved it. Two trusted *hadiths* are quoted from **the Imam Ali (*a*)** and from **the Imam as-Sadiq (*a*)** to the effect that both these Imams had approved the *Nowruz Feast* of the Iranians. Anyhow, the Iranian believers in religion were not satisfied with Islam's rational assertion, but they, strengthened it by Islamic invocations, even in the Arabic language, the language of the *Quran*. The Islamic enlightened men, who believe in Islam's comprehensiveness such that they find in it no vacancy to be filled up with their own national traditions, have also honoured this Feast.[284] Concerning honouring the *Nowruz Feast,* **Aqa Ruhullah** had played a small role. In the years of 57 to 67, every year, a moment after passing to the New Year, the Iranian TV used to show his picture, as he had a message for his people and to send them his blessing, causing them to be pleased with hearing it from their leader. His collection of poems begins with this ode about *Nowruz:*

> The wind of *Nowruz* blows on the mountains and desert,
> > The dress of the Feast all wear, whether king or beggar.

> In the Feast all go to the desert and to gardens,
> > Intoxicated, I proceed from the tavern towards **Allah.**

> Blessed be *Nowruz* to the rich and the dervish,
> > O beloved love, open a door in the idol-temple.

> For years I was in line of the turbaned ones

Till I reached the beloved, would I make no mistake again!

Chahar-Shanbah-Suri and a Heart-Rending Event

The night of the last Tuesday of the year is called _Chahar-Shanbah-Suri'.
It is a part of *Nowruz* traditions and, for the children, it is an exciting sunset.
Some people go to the hills to pick certain thorny bushes to kindle fire in the
sunset twilight, and jump over it, saying: **"Let my yellowness be yours and
your redness be mine."** By the invention of the firecrackers and play-
rockets new means for the fireworks of these rituals accompanied by
terrifying noises and, at times, causing fires incurring great losses. After the
fireworks, spoon- ringing starts. Some frivolous men wear *chadurs* and, with
a cup or a bowel in hand, go to the houses and, with a spoon and the bowels,
they play dancing tunes. Commonly, somebody comes out of the visited
house and throws some coins or some eatables in the bowel. These coins or
eatables are called the _sur'_ of the Wednesday. Despite the fact that the
Islamic Revolution had almost abolished the _spoon-ringing', but it only
weakened the color of the fireworks. The days on which **Aqa Ruhullah** was
still a schoolboy, one day the boys of the quarter gathered a large quantity of
the bushes for *Chahar-Shanbah-Suri* rituals and set fire to them at sunset.
They were so engaged in the fireplay that they did not see the bulk of a
woman passing through that narrow lane and, while running and jumping,
they so collided with her that she fell into the fire. Her *chadur* caught fire,
and from the *chadur* the fire reached her skirt. The boys were afraid and ran
away. Somebody carried her to the nearest house, which was **Ruhullah"s.
Sahibah Khanum, Aqa Ruhullah"s** aunt, started applying first aids. Due to
the deep burns the woman was heart-rendingly screaming. **Ruhullah,** who
smelled the smell of the burnt flesh of the woman, was so yelling and
running round the yard that mother, could not easily calm him down. The
next day the woman died of severe burning. **Ruhullah** remained in such an
intense fever for a week that the soaked towel put on his feet quickly dried
up. Undoubtedly, **Aqa Ruhullah,** at witnessing that heart-rending scene
could not have an indifferent feeling towards the *Chahar-Shanbah-Suri.* Yet,
no disapproving expressions were seen in any of his speeches. One reason
was that this tradition, to the Zoroastrian minority in Iran, which is of good
reputation, has a deeper meaning than celebrating a national tradition.

Sufreye Haftsin

One of the traditions of *Nowruz* is the **sufreye haftsin,** which is still
observed by some of traditionalists, particularly by such women. In the

middle of the room the most valuable *sufreh* is laid, and no less than seven [haft] things whose names start with the letter _S‘ [sin], are arranged on it. Each one of these _eses‘ is a symbol. An ear of wheat [sunbul] is a symbol of spring, the *sabzeh* [greenery] of wheat or lentil is a symbol of growing and flourish, *samanu* is a symbol of patience for the consistency of a sweet eatable, a cup of *serkeh* [vinegar], a small plate of sumac, a larger plate of *senjed* [sorb], and seven red *sibs* [apples], each as a symbol of something. On the *sufreh* they place a glass pitcher with one or two red fish in it, a *Quran*[285], candles and cookies in addition to the S-things.

In **Aqa Ruhullah‘s** house, similar to some 60% of other houses, there were no signs of **sufreyeh haftsin** and the legend of **Uncle Nowruz**.[286] These were looked at as merely superstitions, but as these legends had no serious conflicts with the religious beliefs, they, too, did not oppose them, or, at least, they took them to be ineffective ancient traditions. They did not mock at those who lay the *haftsin* tables, but it was quite ridiculous to lay themselves such a table with *haftsin* arranged on it. **Naneh Khawar** used to irrigate some wheat grains in one, two or three plates to grow green. They got pleasure from their growth and freshness in the cold season, and they, too, irrigated them so as not to get dry, but they did not believe these greeneries should be taken, on the 13th day of the year, to the desert and to knot them. They might have preferred to throw them before the domestic hens, or the neighbour‘s goat, to eat them with enjoyment.

Memories of Childhood in the Moments of Passing to New Year

The artillery man, in every city having an artillery, used to fire a training and noisy cannon to announce the arrival of the New Year. If Khomein had an artillery, the noise of the cannonade must have informed him of the moment of passing to a new year. If not, the clock would inform him. As a younger child, he had heard from his friends that at the moment of passing to the New Year the earth jerks, because each year it is the turn of a huge animal to receive the earth from the former animal which had carried it for the past year. Probably the term _the change of the year‘ was originally a Chinese riddle which found its way into the Iranian legends, and afterwards **Khayyam** and **Khwajah Nasir** used it in a scientific way. Anyhow, the boys had heard from the elders—who did not know that _the change of the year‘ was merely a conventional matter—that if they gaze into a bowel full of water in the moment of _the change of the year‘, the bowel will jerk and the water will have waves. If there was a fish in the water it would swiftly swim around.

Hearing this, **Ruhullah,** one year, caught a red fish out of the pool of the house with a sieve and put it in a large basin which mother had filled with water. He wanted to try the experiment himself. He spent hours gazing at the basin and the fish, and whenever the fish moved he would excitedly shout to his mother to come and see his son's discovery. The mother would come each time, but she would say: ―It is still too early." It seems that in that year the year changed around the middle of the night, when the boy had dreamt of seven kings and seven angels. In the morning when he woke up, before washing his face and hands, he hurried to the basin, but the fish had been taken by a cat or a crow. The fish-thief had made bitter the first day of the New Year for the fish-eater. But perhaps the first sweet philosophic discussion about the eater and the eaten must have sparked in his mind on the same day, and later, when it was blended with gnosticism the following composition became pleasing to his heart:

As an inanimate I died and became a growing (plant),
And as a growing (plant) I died and came out as an animal,

As an animal I died and became a human,
So, why should I be afraid? The more I die the better I become!

Now that he has become half an *Alim* and has some knowledge of the conventionality of this change of the year, he thinks about the other aspects of this traditional feast, although later he made it clear that he regarded the religious feasts, such as the feasts of *Fitr, Qurban, Ghadir, Bithat* and the birthdays of **the Prophet (s),** other prophets (*a*) and the Imams of guidance (*a*), as to be original feasts. Regarding the national feasts he also values them. Concerning celebrating the anniversary of the victory of the Islamic Revolution he said: ―Greetings to the 22nd of Bahman, the Day of **Allah,** and to its creators.[287]"

An Amazing Event in a Nowruz Meeting
It is a tradition observed almost all over the world that the youngers should first call upon the elders. But in *Nowruz* feast all families could exchange visits, though they still observe the said tradition to some extent. But if it could not be followed, nobody would take it to heart. **Aqa Ruhullah,** the youngest member of the family, dressed himself with the intention of visiting his neighbours, relatives and friends. **Aqa Murtada** and **Aqa Nuruddin** did not let him go alone. When they crossed the yard to the gate, the door was

knocked at. It was his teacher at the school. Few moments later the second, then the third and the fourth... guests came in. On the first day they could not leave the house. The second and the third days went like the first day. As for the fourth day they decided that two of them should remain at home and the third would go to visit the relatives. **Aqa Ruhullah** and **Aqa Nuruddin** remained at home. No one came that day. The next day **Aqa Ruhullah** and **Aqa Murtada** remained at home. No one came, too. On the third day **Aqa Murtada** and **Aqa Nuruddin** stayed at home, but still no one came. On the fourth day all the three remained at home. On that day the guests were so numerous that the three of them could not attend on them well enough. At the supper table the three brothers discussed this rather astonishing incident and its causes, until the cock flapped its wings and started its dawn song. It was too late for *salahullayl.* The morning *salah* was performed led by **Aqa Murtada.** The *salat al-layl* was later individually performed as a defaulted *salah.* And, without reaching any conclusions in their discussions, they took off their outer dresses and, side by side, fell asleep.

When the sun peeped inside through the window, **Aqa Ruhullah** got up later than his two brothers and his eyes were still heavy. Probably he, in his heart, was asking forgiveness for last night's disorder. Actually, ever since he came of age, particularly when in Arak, he officially wore the usual dresses for the theological students, he vowed, or made an unuttered pledge, to practise systematic order in performing the *salah*s, sleeping and getting up, and to assign a time for every act. But last night's unnecessary discussions put things out of order. The brothers were busy doing something in the yard. He, too, went to the yard, greeted them, washed his face in order to wash sleep off his eyes, or he, undoubtedly, performed *wudu* in order to wake up his heart, too. Then he threw a few lumps of coal in the fire-whirler, kindled them and whirled it round several times to get it aglow. He took the embers with a pair of coal-tongs and threw them into the brazier of the samovar— which he had bought from Arak—intending to prepare tea for the breakfast of his brothers.

Fire-Whirler and Tautological Answers
He got pleasure from making fire in the fire-whirler. Hence, **Aqa Murtada** waited for him to boil water in the samovar. When he was younger, there used to visit them some friends who asked for hookah. **Naneh Khawar** would put some coal on a dust-pan, set fire to it, then she would put it in a wiry fire- whirler and whirl it, because the wind caused by whirling would kindle the fire. The chain of the fire-whirler is commonly 1.5 M. So, on

whirling, it makes a fiery circle of 3 M diameter. Whenever **Naneh Khawar** wanted to whirl the fire-whirler, she would call **Ruhullah** to come and watch. The first time **Ruhullah** saw it it was in a moonless night. The darkness of the night caused the fire-work delightful, particularly when some sparks flashed out of it. Once he asked her: ―When the fire-whirler goes up and turns up-side down, why do the coals not fall down?" **Naneh Khawar** answered: ―Because when the fire-whirler is whirled, coals do not fall down." **Ruhullah,** child as he was, this senseless repetition[288] made him laugh. **Aqa Murtada** came to the rescue of **Naneh Khawar.** The following answer came to his mind: ―When the coals go up, the wind caused by their whirling keeps them up-side down." In those days few persons in Khomein could scientifically explain the law of centrifugal force. **Ruhullah,** who doubted the truthfulness of his brother's answer, too, one day tried, with some coal remnants and strong puffs at an up-side down fire-whirler, to carry out a dangerous experiment. Mother, however, was quick in hurrying to him, but the skin of his great toe of his right foot blistered. When **Naneh Khawar** was preparing the hookah by puffing at it, the gurgling of the hookah, to his ear, was like an animating tune, but it seemed very bad, and it was very bad for the children to touch the nozzle of the hookah, a pipe or a cigarette, with their lips and puff at it. Now that **Aqa Ruhullah** has grown up to a man, he could, if he wanted, use the coal, with which he had prepared for the samovar, to prepare a hookah and, after the breakfast, sit in the veranda and listen to its gurgling. Actually, he might have done it. Perhaps when he was acquainted with the ancient belief of matter, as they thought water, fire, wind and earth, to be the original elements, it reminded him of the hookah, because a hookah has water in its belly, and fire, ash and tobacco on its head, and, when they puff at it, the air passes through the fire, the ashes and the tobacco into the water, and the result of these four elements will be smoke, sound and headache or hilarity. Later he showed that by paying attention to such matters, which are apparently amusing and negligible, he could compose, powerfully and delicately, speaking examples explaining the most obscure and complicated philosophic concepts.

The Last Day in Khomein

On the 13th day, which is the end of *Nowruz* feast, when people go to the valleys or to Mount Bujeh Sultan[289], so as to throw away the ominousness of No. 13 in green meadows, he was preparing himself for a greater emigration. He had many times gone to the flat part of Bujeh Sultan Mountain, which was suitable for hockey, with his friends to play. So, he knew the cultural position of this place on the days of diversion. In his mind's register of memories he remembered the rude behaviour of a number of the youths who, away from the eyes of their families in the *sizdah bedar,* uttered indecent jokes, and some rogues even touched wine, and, more than drinking, acted as dead drunk, and other heart-tormenting deeds.

When the bell of the caravan of **Ayatullah Hairi** played the tune of Qum, **Aqa Ruhullah** had consulted the *Quran* whether to take the road of Qum, or to go back to Arak. The *Quran* read: ―**From it We have created you and We shall return you to it, and from it shall We bring you forth a second time.**[290]" So, he was preparing provision for the journey, stamping farewell kisses on the hands of his teachers, kissing the cheeks of his friends and play-mates. At the same time he was watching the people who, disregarding the Coup d'état, were pleasingly heading for the fields, joyfully, like sparrows. Perhaps he asked himself: Is 13th really ominous that people leave their houses to the deserts and mountains so as to throw the ominousness in the mountains and the plains? If not, why the months of the year do not go beyond twelve? Why the Prophet **Jacob (a)** in the vacancy of the 12th son, he did not have the 13th to lessen the pain of the vacancy? When **Moses, Allah's** interlocutor (a), struck the rock with his stick, twelve springs gushed out, and when he was crossing the Nile, twelve springs gushed out, and when he was crossing the Nile, twelve paths dried up in it for his people to pass. The *Quran,* in many instances counts from the number one to twelve, but apparently the number thirteen is never seen therein. Why the immaculate Imams are only twelve, as the 13th is a liar? Doubtless, legends have their roots in some mysteries. But *Nowruz* and its traditions have appeared in Iran before the arrival of Islam at this land. In the law of existence, are mysteries beyond time and place, and are manifested in every culture in different ways? Later he found answers for these naive questions. But which science could give the suitable answer? Migration from one's mental habits is the first step, which he had to take. Migration from Khomein and Arak was the first step to migration from habits.

The day after, a carriage with two horses—lest the rough road of Qum may not exhaust a single horse—was waiting at the door. The heavy luggage was loaded. He passed through the smoke caused by the explosion of the grains of wild rue which danced out of two braziers into the spring mist of the alley. He hugged those who had come to see him off, and they entrusted him to **Allah.** Two old men raised their hands like an ark so that he may pass through under the *Quran.* After the third passing under the *Quran* he turned and kissed it, and, relying on **Allah,** he got on. Many eyes in this side and two eyes in the carriage, filled with water. The wooden wheels of the carriage slowly drew a line on the flat of the alley.

EN ROUTE TO QUM

Is anyone accompanying him on this perilous journey? The roads were not safe. His father had lost his life en route. It is thought that his family and friends, worried as they were, did not find it advisable to let him travel alone, without a caravan, but who were accompanying him? No one remembers now.[292] However; the carriage driver is a fellow-traveller who sits in front on the saddle, taking the reins in his hand. He gave his word to drive in such a way and to have stops along the road so that they may not feel fatigued and to arrive in Qum before the month of Ramadan.

If the horses gallop, the gates of Qum will show themselves in three days. But if they rub their hooves slower against the earth, there will be a chance of six to eight days to have a look at the valley, the mountain and the plain. Now that the horses have no intention to gallop, there appear, from the valley, the mountain, the green plains, the ruined and prosperous villages, and the Shah-Abbasiyan caravanserays, thousands of images in ambush raise their heads in order to invade the mind of this emigrant.

Nowadays the roads are somewhat safe, since the robbers have also hid the rifles, but no political or religious personality, and no poet, writer or artist felt secured, because it was possible that anybody, who had a head moving among other heads, to be arrested. The day before the journey, that is the day of *sizdah bedar,* when people were returning home from outdoors, some 1400 km away, in the sacred city of Mashhad, the powerful governor of Khurasan, **Ahmad Qawam as-Saltanah,** an ingenious political man, had spent *sizdah bedar* in Malikabad village, at 3 km from the city and was returning home when, arriving at the gate, the commander of the gendarmerie, **Colonel Muhammad Taqi Khan Pesyan**—one of the old friends of **Qawam as-Saltanah,** with whom he had concluded union pledge—ordered him to be arrested and sent to the prison. **Qawam** could not believe that his old friend, whom he himself had put in that post, should break his pledge and on such a day. Seven other persons who were common friends of both **Qawam** and **Pesyan,** were also arrested because of being **Qawam**'s friends. Worse even, on the same day all the furniture of **Qawam**'s house, all his jewellery, money and documents were transferred to the gendarmerie, and, for fan, one of the gendarmes swept clean all the rooms. At the order of **Sayyid Diya**, **Pesyan** replaced **Qawam,** who, due to intense grief, fell ill on pileless seemingly cotton carpet. If he did not ask himself whether he had not thrown away ominousness of the 13th in the plain 3 km away from the city, what was, then, this ominousness with which he was now afflicted? He was certainly pledging never to trust any friend and never to keep any promise, should he live. On the same 13th of Farwardin the governors of Quchan and Turbat-e Hiydariyyah were also arrested, and, on the day after **Qawam** was no longer alone in his prison. **Ruhullah** heard this story few days after his arrival in Qum and followed it seriously.

The Russian and the British Forces Leave Iran

When **Aqa Ruhullah** was nearing the gate of Qum, the British were taking their forces out of the gates of Zanjan and Qazvin to support the government of the Coup d'état, and to prompt the Russian forces to leave the northern cities. On the same day the Russians started withdrawing their forces from Iran. **Sayyid Diya** knew that the withdrawal of these occupation forces was intended to strengthen his government. Nevertheless it took him a week to issue a statement congratulating the people for his own efficiency and skill. After a week, by changing the order of the words, the phrases were arranged in double meaning so that the British may not become vexed. The final sentences denoted that he thought the people of the Capital would feel insecure after the departure of the occupation forces: –Θ citizens! The British forces, whom the conditions of the International War brought to northern provinces of our kingdom, have now left Iran, returning to their country. The services of those forces cannot be denied. But... the movement of the great British Army once again proved that our great neighbour, the USSR had no intention of transgressing Iran's rights... But you, people of Tehran, may rest assured and be comfortable under the light of the sacrifices of the state and the army of the Capital of Iran and their protection.[293]"

After the said announcement some flags were hung on the doors of the shops, and the people, with illuminating the city and distributing sweets set up a celebration. Despite the fact that they concealed their shame of being incapable of dismissing occupation with disgraceful silence, they instinctively knew that the foreigners would never give up their avidity very easily. Nevertheless, it was a good chance to condemn occupation by means of displaying merriment. When **Aqa Ruhullah** was en route to Qum he did not know what had really happened, though he heard in the stations of the road about the movements of the Russian and British armies. Perhaps, along with the people who ambiguously talked about it, he, too, ambiguously thought it over. This was because **Sayyid Diya**'s statement had not yet been prepared. So, if he got an information, it was certainly from Qum, not en route.

A Review of Memoirs

It is now exactly 18 years, six months and 14 days since he began seeing the world. Maybe he cannot very well remember the first three years, but his strong memory preserved every moment of the other 15 years in their original colors. Undoubtedly, of the news and events, which, along those years, passed over the whole country and the world, and did not reach Khomein, he had, more or less, some knowledge. So, that which attacked his mind during the journey was but a small portion of the historical events of the world and Iran. Yet, how can one know what were his mental engagements on those days of emigration? The simplest way is to look into his works, and whenever we found a trace of the events of those days we take it as one of his engagements of those days, unless we find an analogy definitely denoting that he knew it or thought about it later.[294]

Did the carriage-driver know who was this taciturn emigrant who was leaning against the pillow, in a privacy with mountains and plains, and only at times he asked or replied? In general, he realized that this young man of some 19 years of age knew more of the rules of decorum than his coeval ones and behaved magnanimously. His magnanimity is manifest in his mature humbleness, not like the princes, the nobility or the elites, nor even like the sons of the notable ʻulama, in pride and vanity. The carriage-driver had transferred hundreds of great and small people from one village to another and from one city to another, and by means of continuous compulsory travels he had become an experimental psychologist, estimating and assaying his passengers. On his eager return with a letter of the safe arrival of **Aqa Ruhullah** to be handed over to his family, it seems that he was expecting to be invited into the yard, and, with the excuse of bringing the letter, to have a cup of tea and smoke a hookah, so as to be more familiar with this family. In his final sentences which he uttered aloud on his leaving the house, he expressed his impression of his fellow traveller. He said: —My **Allah** send mercy upon **Aqa Ruhullah**'s father who gave him *halal* bread! May **Allah** send mercy on his mother who nursed him with pure milk!"

Did **Aqa Ruhullah** himself know that he was gradually acquiring an attraction which passed his utterances and behaviour over to his silence? Surely not yet, because if he knew, his conduct would become spurious.

Auguries and Legends

Yet, did he know that by this migration a new chapter in the history of religious reflection would begin? Naturally no. But some fabulous stories say: yes! This is because when he was still fed through his umbilical cord, a gipsy palmist, by examining the lines of the mother's palm, told her that she would give birth to a son who would do such and such. Nobody remembers what she exactly said. So, everybody related it according to what he liked. Hence, this discrepancy in reporting is sufficient to make us neglect this story. Some people like to regard the great ones great from childhood (though he is so), but when they cannot trace the footprints of greatness back to childhood, they resort to fancy. It is quite possible that this story of fortune-telling is imaginary, or perhaps it is real. That which is more important is that he himself never believed in fortunetelling. Not that he denied the possibility of its being true, nor regarding it to be interfering in the will of the Creator who is ever in producing another creation, not because Islam does not allow this method of getting information about the future. Once in Qum, too, a fortuneteller, by looking at the lines of a palm, as if he was looking into a mirror displaying picture of tomorrow, attracted the curiosity of some students so much that they placed their hands in his hand, and heard obscure things which they took to tell about their future. Perhaps it was to satisfy his curiosity instinct, or to know the tricks and secrets of this foretelling, or to respond to his friends' insistence, at last the palmist looked at the lines of his palm, too. Probably the insistence of his friends helped the fortuneteller to guess his great personality. Whether affected or actual, he spent a long time gazing at the lines of his palm, then, describing his greatness, he said things, which embarrassed **Aqa Ruhullah** and made him say: —**Allah** alone is Knower of the secret and the hidden." One of the prophecies of this fortuneteller was: —You will change the world." This was very easily credible to a number of the students, although he, by way of idol-breaking, said: —Changing the world is by **Allah**'s will." Nevertheless, he had in mind the noble *ayah*: **"Allah does not change what is in a people until they change what is in themselves."**[295] Anyhow, it does not seem that he, on this way, was thinking of an emigration which, after fifty-seven years, became —The Burst of Light". Later, he knew that civilization starts with migration and that behind every great revolution there is a migration. But now he just knows that migration is an Islamic principle and a companion of *jihad*. Perhaps he is in search of an answer for the question: Why did the Muslims not take the birthday of **the Prophet (s)** to be the beginning of their calendar, as the Christians did, or his *bithah*, which is the beginning of

Revelation? There must be a hidden secret in emigration, not found in those two great days. On those two days the Muslims, celebrate the manifestation of Light. Yet, the birthday and the *bithah* of **the Prophet** happened only once, whereas emigration is repeatable and can be imitated.

A Load of Books on History

Now that he is in the carriage, on his way from Khomein to Qum, it is natural for him to revise the lessons which he learnt of religion and piety, but the history of the world and Iran of those days was too hot to let one be careless and attend only to one's lessons.

Although history was not regarded as an official lesson in the theological *hawzahs,* but his grandfather was very much attached to the history of the orient and of the Islamic world. Thus, he used to buy any book on the history of the East. His father, too, was interested in history, but he preferred hearing it to reading. However, he, too, had bought a few books. *Tarikh Tabari, Tarikh Yaqubi, Sireye ibn Hisham* were of the books which most of the theologians had in their personal libraries. As to the history books on India, Rome, ancient Iran, Islamic Iran, Egypt, Iraq, north Africa, and some booklets on the history of France, Britain, America, Russia... were in the father's library, in which **Aqa Murtada** was so attached as if they were his own, and **Aqa Ruhullah** used to handle them with caution. **Aqa Murtada,** of course, had this right, to some extent, since the personal properties of the father were given to his older son. Furthermore, **Aqa Murtada** was very much interested in the historical events, and was benefited by his father's books more than his two brothers. He remembered the events better than **Ruhullah**. But **Ruhullah**, without himself knowing it or others know it, cared more for the philosophy of history. For this reason, **Aqa Murtada,** in old age, though older than **Aqa Ruhullah** by seven years, could very well remember the strict dates of most of the events, while **Aqa Ruhullah** could only remember the general trends of the events. He did not press his memory for events which were unlikely to be repeated. However, **Aqa Murtada** put a few books on the history of early Islam and few books on the contemporary history of Iran, in **Aqa Ruhullah**'s suitcase, as he had formerly ran his eyes through parts of them, and now he liked to be more acquainted with their contents. Later on he read them all with care and took notes. But it was clear that he trusted only parts of the contemporary history, because everybody knew that most of the registerers of the events had wives and children, and it was in the interest of themselves and their families not to disregard the interests of the kings and their retinue. Then, there was nothing of any law

241

concerning protecting the legal rights of the writers. So, he felt that the historians only rarely looked out of the Palace. Of course, in early Islam, all, including the slaves, were present in history, but that was exceptional. Likewise, that part of the historical topics, which had no direct connection with politics, was more dependable. Therefore, in order to get stricter understanding of the contemporary history, he had to lend his ears to stories more like legends.

Realities of the Legends of Shahnameh

Probably, in one of the caravansarais en route, he listened to the narration of a recounter who narrated the *Shahnameh.* Through his narrating he used to allusively mock the justice of the past kings, as well as to allude to the tyranny of the contemporary kings. In his father's library there was a precious copy of the *Shahnameh* presented to the martyr **Aqa Mustafa** by somebody. Now he had read parts, or all, of that precious book and learnt by heart some of its nice poetry. What has he got from the legendary realities of this valuable work? Once he said: —I know no more modest poet than the sage **Ferdowsi**. In the entire *Shahnameh* there is no word of discourteousness."

The sage **Abul Qasim Ferdowsi** is one of the most famous epic poets, yet, despite his fame, his religious and political ideas have not yet been understood. He was a Muslim scholar and a deep thinker who deserved the epithet of a sage. *Shahnameh*, the wondrous masterpiece of this Shiite poet, is one of the books of deep political thoughts. This sage could wipe off racialism, tribalism and nationalism of the despotic Abbassides and the Ghaznavi dynasty from the delicate spirit of the teachings of Islam, and take the Sokai legends, which had penetrated the Irani culture, into the sack of his deep religious thoughts and reconstruct them. Out of the positive heroes of his stories he creates such divine men as if they were the true followers of the prophets. He could send the Arab tribalism to war with the Iranian nationalism, and show that in this test of power nationalism would knock tribalism down. He states that if the Irani had surrendered, bodily, spiritually, cordially and mentally, to Islam, it was not because the sword of the Arabs was sharp, rather because the names of **Muhammad (s)** and 'Ali (a) occupy the heart of every pure-hearted person. He humiliated the tribalism of the Arabs and the Turks by presenting legendary heroes. And, in order not to afflict the Iranians with pride, deceit and the spell of anti-religious nationalism, he did not select the heroes of his stories in such a way to believe that whoever is on this side of the border is absolutely good, and whoever is on the other side is absolutely bad. He confined the good and bad to neither the national limits nor to regional limits.

Ruhullah is now acquainted with the general features of thought and the far-sightedness of this modestly speaking epic poet. Later his knowledge of him became deeper. When he obtained better knowledge about the social and temporal conditions in which the *Shahnameh* was written down, he realized that, despite the simple poetry of this simple epic poet, the personality of the poet was extremely complicated. So, if he is to be estimated, the estimation must be like his personality, simple and complicated. How can this unimitable simple style be possible? On the anniversary of the birthday of two ‚lights‘, addressing a group of the authorities, he said: —Onthe birthday of **the Messenger (s)** certain events took place, rare events, as stated in the narratives related by the Shiite and the Sunnis. These events should be studied to know them. Among these events were the cracking of the *Taq Kasra* and the falling down of fourteen crenations of that palace, the extinction of the firetemples of Fars and the collapse of the idols. The question of the cracking of *Taq Kasra* may be a sign that at the time of this great prophet, the *Taq* (arch) of injustice, the archs of injustice, will break, especially that the arch of *Kasra* did break, because that arch of *Kasra* was the centre of **Anushirwan**‘s injustice, contrary to the things forged by the poets, the courtiers of that time, the Zoroastrian priests and the *mullas* of the court. He was one of the Sassanide despots for whom a *hadith* was fabricated alleging that **the Prophet** had said: —Iwas born in the time of a just king..." (The people) are to fight; they are to do the jobs, while others only eat. They did not allow the low classes to study. It was prohibited. The *Shahnameh* refers to the story that it was complained to him, **Budharjumehr** complained to him that there was a deficit in the budget and that the army needed help, and that there were persons among the low classes who had wealth. They searched and found someone who is now said to have been a shoemaker. He said: ‘I am ready to pay‘, as the *Shahnameh* relates, ‘but on the condition that my son should be allowed to study‘. They went and told him, but he refused and said: ‗We neither want his money nor shall we agree, because if we allow a man from below to study, he will then want to interfere in the affair, and this cannot be‘, This was the justice of **Anushirwan**.[296]

Children Create Legends
For sometimes now **Ruhullah** takes the legends seriously and sends his mind to dig for the facts of the secrets which mysteriously ooze from legends.

Following these lines of **Mawlana** he gropes in the ruins of the legends so that he may find a treasure:

> Children create legends,
>> In their legends are much secrets and advice,

> In the legends jokes they say,
>> Look for treasure in all the ruins.

Anushirwan the Just!

In those days the majority believed that **Anushirwan** was a just king. They used to say: He had a bell tied to a chain running from his sitting room down to the back of his palace, so that whoever wanted something or had a complaint he could pull at the chain. One day a lion rubbed his body against the chain. **Anushirwan** followed it. The lion came to a thicket and made him understand that his female mate was suffering from giving birth. **Anushirwan** ordered a doctor to help. The lion gave some seeds to the king. The seeds were sowed, and there grew a shrub with large fruits. The *khar* (ass) ate of it and he was pleased. It was given to a *buz* (goat), he said: —Excellent!" So the fruit was named *kharbuzeh*" (melon).[297]

The story was incredible even to the children, but this legend they meant to show **Anushirwan** as a king spreading justice, and even the animals knew about his justice, and a *hadith* was forged saying that **the Prophet (s)** had proudly said: —Iwas born in the time of the just King.[298]" **Ruhullah** had heard this *hadith*. Later, when he studied under **Shaykh Abbas Qumi** and was acquainted with the science of traditions, he doubted it. Afterwards, when he was more acquainted with the dark depth of history, he uttered the afore-mentioned expression. He had the courage—disregarding the beliefs of some of the elders to announce his beliefs publicly, but not with the intention of showing merits, nor of explaining an historical point, but he learnt that history should be read for its lessons, and should be retold for its lessons. So, the historical events are to be connected to the present. Isn't this satiric connection a promotive lesson?

—**Anushirwan**'s spreading of justice is like the peace-loving of the American President, and like the USSR's communism. At the present time we see these things. If the writers of history, and, I don't know, those who are poets and those who are orators and those who are courtiers, if they convey the propaganda which is going on nowadays in the world, if such propaganda reach the ears of those who are not informed of the events, they, too will believe that as **Anushirwan the Just** was just, the American President is also peace-lover, equitable and the like, whereas you are informed and know how the case is.[299]"

Isfahan is Half of the World

The searching mind of an emigrant cannot be but an emigrant. His body takes a single road for six days until he arrives in Qum, but his mind, without a permission calls, in every step, on hundred of ruins. Now, at ten *farsakhs* from Qum, he dismounted, beside his body, in a caravansarai from **Shah Abbas** era. This caravansarai, which is now about to fall down, is a memorial of the powerful era of the Safavid rule. Now, the Safavid Kings, to him, were religious men, under the shade of whose power the Shiite could create wonderful works. Isfahan, their Capital, was the example of the required city, which **Ruhullah** had not yet seen, but he had heard about it hundreds of stories worthy of being heard. When he was a boy of eight years, **Aqa Murtada** left for Isfahan to continue his studies but used to frequent Khomein at short intervals, bringing Isfahan with him. This city was really worth seeing, and its sightly places were really laudable. Description of its wonders always worth hearing. It had a *minaret* which rocked. It had a bathroom which was always warm without fuel. It had a dome under which the echo was clearly heard several times. It had a bridge over the river not for crossing, but for sight seeing. Its mosques were large, but more than being great, they were delicate. Their colorful tiles were magnetic and the eyes could not turn away from them. The main street of the city was by itself Chaharbagh [The Four Gardens]. Its handicrafts—which are now marking time for three hundred years—are still three centuries ahead of the present handicrafts of the whole world. When this city became the Capital it was rightly said: —sfahan is half of the world." **Murtada,** every time he came home, he told stories of the sights of Isfahan. He was interested in history and geography. He received from the mouths of the Isfahanis how the buildings of the city were built, and jokingly imitating the witty accent of the Isfahanis, he related them to **Ruhullah**. He had promised **Rahullah** and **Nuruddin** to take them one day with him to Isfahan. But **Ruhullah** had to go to school, so he had not the chance to go to Isfahan with his brother, until he settled in Qum and, with his friends, travelled to that wonderful city. This city, the half of the world, beautiful, fresh, lively and sightly was built by the Shiite Safavid Kings. In the style of some of its guest houses hundreds of caravansarais were built on the roadways between the towns. On a wooden divan in one of these caravansarais he is stretching and looking at its imaginative walls and doors. As soon as he entered it he descended the high stone steps to the water reservoir, which was still full of the rain water and muddy. He also saw the pen with horses and mules in a raw with their heads in the manger. He also watched the stoves and the log places. Probably he was thinking to himself: What an aptitude this nation could have if the government was formed according to its desire! What effective and artistic works it could do! In the time of this dynasty, theology together with architecture galloped ahead.

Mulla Sadra took philosophy to the peak. A big encyclopedia of a hundred volumes on the Shiite *hadiths* was compiled. Numerous schools of theology were established in every town. So, what has happened now to that dynasty which is no longer there? Why did those aptitudes wither and that dynasty die? Is the saying: **The rule lasts with disbelief, but not with injustice**[300]", a *hadith* from the **Prophet**? If not, still it deserves contemplation.

Shah Ismail and Shah Tahmasib the Safavids

Were the Safavids unjust kings and for this reason their rule did not last? He knows that **Shah Ismail** the Safavid[301], the founder of new Iran, was a zealous, courageous and of sufi conduct. It was surprising that a sufi had forsaken the axe and picked up the sword.

As a boy of ten or twelve years, **Ruhullah** had prepared a number of large notebooks, in one of which he decided to write down historical points and delicacies. Had this notebook not been lost we could have now known his opinion about **Shah Tahmasib**, the second king of the Safavid dynasty. But, undoubtedly, he knew that **Shah Tahmasib** had killed his two brothers, and, in his days, two persons took refuge in his court: One, **Humayun**, son of **Babur**, the Emperor of Delhi, who was received with respect. He returned to Delhi and joined India once again to Iran. The other, **Bayazid**, son of **Sultan Sulayman**. He had quitted the Ottoman Darul Khilafa, because of his father's tyranny, and took refuge in **Shah Tahmasib**'s court, but the latter handed him, with his four sons, to **Sultan Sulayman,** so as to be relieved from his attacks for a while for this good service. Some politicians may say: —This is politics." But we know that the spiritual bringing up of **Ruhullah** did not allow him to support Machiavellism.

Shah Abbas the Great, the Other Side of the Coin

If we had at hand the notebook he allocated to history, we would have copied it to show how he described the Safavid kings. Now that we do not have it, we refer to *Sahifeh-ye Imam* so as to see what his opinion was concerning the most famous king of this dynasty. **Shah Abbas the Great** defeated Iran's enemies, reconstructed Iran's ruins, ousted the Portugese out of Gumbrun Port which was named after his name: Bandar Abbas. Once he travelled on foot from Isfahan to the sacred city of Mashhad in order to express his attachment to the eighth Imam of the Shiite and show it to the Imam's followers. He got such a high position in the eyes of some religious authorities that they gave him the epithet of ―Jannat Makan". Nevertheless, this was one side of the coin. The other side of the coin is when the required government acquires other characteristics, and that is clear in his saying:

―The matter is not a joke. It is the matter of a nation who has been along the history under the hegemony of the tyrannical kings. Along 2500 years it was under the rule of Sultans of injustice, even the just one of them was wicked. Even **Anushirwan** the Just was wicked. Even that **Shah Abbas**, Jannat Makan, his place was among the unsuitable. He blinded his son. Along the history this nation was under the rule and the boots of these wicked kings.[302]"

Is the government which is wanted by the religious men other than the Safavid government? Can the Shiite who had historically experienced the governments of **the Prophet (s)** and of **Ali (a)**, the guardian of the believers, be contented with a different government?

These were his later questions. Now, there is no place for such questions, because the governments of **the Prophet (s)** and of Ali **(a)** are regarded by many researchers to be historical examples which can seriously be used in theological arguments, and the future government of the world, which, with the advent of the Occult Imam (may **Allah** hasten his advent), will have its own characteristics, cannot be compared with any government.

But how can mind fill up the gap between the government of early Islam and the government of the Living Imam of the Prophet's progeny (*a*)? If the period of the occultation lasts for other thousands of years, must we then remain asleep in the darkness of this gap? Or must we endure the governments, be sulky with the worst of them and come to terms with their bad ones, and, in agreeable matters, partly cooperate with some of them, as many of the **ruhaniyyun** did with the Safavid government?

Strange enough that this principal question, basically, had only a faint mark on some minds. Stranger even was that the popular justice-demanding uprising, which led to the constitutional system, the theoretical principles of this discussion were not seriously put on the analytic table of any theoretician. **Shaykh Fadlullah**, who was hanged, had enough intellect to take into the principles of this discussion, but he neither got the chance to well present it, nor was he so much multilateral thinker to be completely cautious so as not to mix between the principles of legitimacy and the tyranny of **Muhammad Ali Shah**.

During the time of Constitutionalism, **Ayatullah Naini**, a relatively well-known *faqih*, spread the notes about this discussion on his desk, but **Ruhullah** did not know what he was breeding. When he arrived in Qum, he became familiar with his ideas.

What he has seen during the journey leading him to this deep subject is still unripe and unsuitable to be presented. When he arrived in Qum, he cleverly used to present his topic in question form, questions such as: Has **Ayatullah Hairi** come to Qum to cooperate with the government of the coup d'état? Has he come to Qum to quarrel with this government? Or to quit the comfortable *hawzah* of Arak and migrate to be nearer to the center of power and to complete what **Shaykh Fadlullah** started and remained incomplete? Has the coup d'état come to overthrow the Qajar dynasty? If this is its intention, what must be done? Are we to cooperate with them?

The Qajars: Inefficient and Bloodthirsty

As his mental debates have not yet become sufficiently consistent, he regards the Safavid government acceptable because of the cooperation of the **ruhaniyyun** with it, at least, more acceptable than the Qajar dynasty, because whenever the aggressions of Qajar princes became unbearable, people related stories about the discretion, the magnanimity and the intelligence of the Safavid dynasty. So, he was acquainted with the Safavid by the margin of history which he used to hear from the lips, while the weakness and cowardice of the Qajar dynasty he himself had experienced within his own life, and how bitter they were!

Agha Muhammad Khan

The Qajar dynasty was not only undesirable, but it was both inefficient and bloodthirsty. The head of the dynasty was **Agha Muhammad Khan**.[303] **Aqa Ruhullah** detested this man very much. Afterwards he dispraised him four times. The last time was in Paris. He said: ─We must be afraid of these dictators. At their last days they become insane. **Agha Muhammad Khan** Qajar went mad, too, at his last days. **Nadir Shah**, too... **Rida Shah** was mad from the beginning.[304]

By madness he means here bloodshedding, because **Agha Muhammad Khan,** one hundred and eleven years before the birth of **Aqa Ruhullah,** by mercilessly massacring the government of the Zandians—which had, somewhat, a good name, and the head of which called himself **Wakilur-Ruaya** [the guardian of the subjects], instead of Shah—demolished them. When he chased **LutfAli Khan** and attacked Kirman, he plucked out 35000 eyes on the pretext that they might have seen **LutfAli** and did not report him. He further captured 30000 Kirmani women and children. He ordered the bodies of the massacred to be taken to Bam in order to make a *minaret* of their heads with the intention of terrorizing the people.[305] When he laid his hand on **Lutf'ali**, he, with his own hands, plucked out his beautiful eyes. Strange enough, with his still polluted hands he used to perform the *wudu,* This very cruelty was the factor for becoming successful in continuing his rule. The same as **Nadir** who acted likewise, as he believed that might is in prevalence, suppression, eradication and bloodshedding. If the head of the dynasty is like this, how will be the others? Of course, the Persian proverb: —Ahandful is the sample of a kharwar" [300 kg] was not applicable to this instance and the bloodshedding was not inherited by all the heirs. If he had dispraised the first of them, he, concerning the last, the youngest of them, as the coup d'état of **Sayyid Diya** and **Rida Khan** was actually against him, addressing the son of **Rida Khan,** praised the young **Ahmad Shah** who did not betray the nation, and that was why **Rida Khan** came.[306] Of course, at that time when he praised **Ahmad Shah**, the kingship system was, to him, the most rotten form of ruling, and this praise, before honouring **Ahmad Shah** it was a dispraise of **Muhammad Rida**'s anti-patriotism. Once, when he made a comparison between the rule of the Qajars and the Pahlavis, he exonerated **Agha Muhammad Khan** on an aspect.[307] The aim of this comparison is not exoneration, rather, it is to show the depth of **Rida Shah**'s treachery.

Inefficiency and Bloodshedding: The Two Sides of a Coin
Anyhow when he in these days looks at the stature of this chain of kings whose warp can be pulled out of its woof, he feels duality: Some of them were bloodshedders, some incapable and some were both. Probably at that time it was strengthened in his mind that the inefficiency and bloodshedding were the two sides of a coin. Some religious men cooperated with this government; others did not talk against it. Another group used to express their displeasure with this government openly, as in the constitutional uprising, the *ulama*, who were not careless in respect of the social affairs, their talks to the people denoted that before disbelieving in the absolutism of kingship system, they detested the Qajar government. Of course, most of the

kings of this dynasty guarded Shiism, respected the *ulama*, visited the holy places, performed the *salat,* did not drink wine publicly, but their piety, in the eyes of some pious people, was detestable, even worse than irreligiousness.

The head of their dynasty practised rudeness for twenty years, and this rudeness still lives in the mind of everybody who had read history. Yet, some extremist nationalists forgave his rudeness for his conquests. But **Ruhullah** could not be so. One day, with discomfort, said: —Allknow the Qajar dynasty... They came, seized, killed and caused chaos.[308]" No doubt if he did not reach killing, he endeavoured to have others killed. Fortunately he was sterile and had no children, otherwise he would have, like **Shah Abbas** and **Nadir Shah,** killed or blinded his own children, so that they may not covet his crown.

Fath'ali Shah

Agha Muhammad Khan treated his brothers as **Cain** treated his brother. He deprived his brothers from being Crown Princes, so, his brother's son, **Baba Khan**, **Fath'ali**, became king. After few months of ascending the throne his beard drooped down to the edge of the throne. **Aqa Ruhullah** was also disgusted with this rootless long beard, because, for one thing, long beard was a sign of the nobility of pre-Islamic time, and the **Prophet (s)** fought it by saying: —fIthe hair of the face is longer than a fist, it is in the Fire." The other thing is that the owner of this thicket beard had gathered a *harem* of girls, widows and maids so large that no historian knew their number, and they just said _hundreds'.[309]

Nasikhut Tawarikh is the title of a book which **Ruhullah** read in Qum and said something like this: —This book lacks content, contrary to its pompous title." The book listed the names of 158 of **Fath'ali Shah**'s temporary wives, who gave him 60 sons and 48 daughters. Within the next two generations his grandchildren amounted to more than two thousands in number. Most of those princes found provinces in which they ruled and looked at them as pastures. On that day when **Ruhullah** was playing in his room, and a sturdy ruffian man came in and, addressing him, asked: —Wat did **Sarim Lashkar** do to be punished?" and he himself replied: —Because he had taken a morsel bigger than his mouth," that man was the grandson of **Abbas Mirza** the son of this Shah. Naturally the system of creation is astonishing. It gave **Abbas Mirza** to this evil-charactered and wicked Shah. Although, by imitating his father, he had a long beard and numerous wives, but his ambitions were longer. By his self-sacrificing in defending the country against the enemy, and by his effort, he made up for his father's inefficiency. He was well behaved and was tactful, intelligent and reasonable. The father, contrary to the head of his dynasty who was very much interested in conquering, was a little annoyed for the country being invaded by the foreigners, but it was not good for his temper to think about its consequences, **Abbas Mirza,** generously and without casting it in the teeth of his father, did not put down his arm for ten years, and without being cruel like the head of the dynasty, he practised bravery in the battle-field.

In the days of **Fath'ali** the Russians attacked Iran several times, and in each attack they occupied parts of the fertile soil of Iran and concluded disgraceful treaties whose scars are still felt by the people.[310] In order to prevent the conclusion of such disgraceful treaties, **Abbas Mirza** spared nothing, but the trench of hypocrisy and stratagem was too wide for him to be able to do anything. One of the treaties, named Gulistan, was concluded with the intermediation of the British Embassy in Tehran. In fact, by intermediating in the conclusion of this treaty, the British aimed at two objectives by supporting the Russian side and offering the treaty to them as a present: The first was that Russia had defeated Napoleon and was demanding its reward from the European rivals. The second was that the French military counsellors were training the Iranian Army with new military equipments, and, had it not been for the defeat of Gulistan the British possession in India would have been threatened by Napoleon through Iran.

The Gulistan and Turkmanchay treaties not only resulted in Iran's military defeat, but they gave free hand to the Russians to interfere, seriously, in Iran's internal affairs, and, at the same time, sewed boots for the feet of the British. If **Fath'ali Shah**, instead of running after women, had thought a little about the fate of the country, probably the situation would have been different.

A Portrait of Fath'ali Shah"s Conduct

The portrait of **Fath'ali Shah** showed him more like the manager of *haram* than the ruler of a country. When the picture of this Shah's conduct reflected in the minds of the people, the simplest reaction was discouragement and slackness in respect of work and effort, evading paying taxes when possible. It is natural for the people to ask themselves why they should toil and sweat, and a good part of the product of their labour be paid for the wine drinkings, intoxications and the lust of the court.

Before **Fath'ali Shah**, Iran's industrial products were still exported to the neighbouring countries. When he came to power the state of work, employment and economy became so weak that production diminished and the concept of commerce, in the dictionary of the businessmen, meant import rather than export.

Witnessing the conduct of the court had more immediate effect on the local governors. On those who were weaker they inflicted more injustice, and they levied more from whoever they could, and they evaded, as much as they could, paying tribute to the central government. Consequently, the Shah was forced to travel to the provinces to collect the unpaid taxes. The first city he went to was Isfahan to collect the delayed taxes and to weaken, through the might of kingship, the reputation of the religious judge, **Sayyid Muhammad Baqir Shafti**, an efficient *mujtahid*. But before being successful in this matter, he fell ill and died.

Creed-Forming

During the rule of this Shah, the British, who were experienced in the application of the policy: _Divide and Conquer', tried hard to cause disunion among the religious and political personalities. But, due to the cleverness of **Sayyid Shafti**, they were unsuccessful. So, this time they resorted to the formation of creeds. They knew very well that, in Iran and in other Islamic countries, religion was not merely a part of life, but it decides the type of life, too. Therefore, their orientalists, instead of ousting out religion, they gave permission more to creed-forming. Of course, not that they employed some planners to sit down and put sketches for new religions, since this matter is not as easy as extending the rails of a train. They looked for persons who, in their religiousness, have strange and bizarre understanding of religion, and which one of such Islamic impressions has the ability to fan the fire of a religious conflict. Whenever they located such persons they would support them through complicated political ways and rear followers for them.

In the days of this long-bearded, short-minded Shah there were founded in Karbala teaching classes by a fame-seeking Shaykh named **Ahmad Ihsai**. Concerning the question of waiting for the advent of the last immaculate Imam (*a*) he said things which had no proofs, but some people found them novelties, as, instead of a strong logic, he strengthened in himself the art of argument. In his discussion with the *ulama* of his time he, by resorting to the tricks of altercation, could knock his adversary down in the eyes of the common people. Some lazy students very much approved the teaching lessons of this Shaykh, because relying on narratives caused a kind of mental comfort.[311] The talks of **Shaykh Ahmad**, though precedented, seemed, in those days, new, as he could mix *Akhbarism* with the Greek philosophy.[312] He had a fascinated disciple from Iran called **Sayyid Kazim Rashti** who was more than his teacher fame-seeker. After the death of the teacher he stepped farther than him. He talked and wrote as if he was the agent of the rightful Imam of the Time (the 12th Imam) and had a connection with him. **Sayyid Kazim**'s love for fame was much more than that of **Shaykh Ahmad**. For this reason **Shaykh Ahmad** had more followers, and some of his followers became rearers of followers, and there appeared several **Shaykhiyyah** groups with followers all over the Islamic countries. As to **Sayyid Kazim**, he had a disciple from Shiraz by the name of **Muhammad Ali,** who started from calling himself the deputy of the Imam of the Time. After the death of **FathAli Shah**, he even regarded prophethood to be less than what he deserved. Two of his followers, who were brothers, formed two strange and peculiar groups known as Bahai and Azali. The Russians preceded the British in supporting these two groups, but later the fate of the two groups was knotted to the British political policy, and now they are backed by the Americans, the British and the Israelis.

The Shiite have always detested the beliefs of those two groups, yet despite manifesting their detestation, because they were begotten in the Shiite Iran, some writers looked at them as two Islamic Shiite sects. Before them, another person, right in the opposite side, was **Muhammad ibn Abdul Wahhab**, who studied in Basrah and Isfahan. He was supported to kindle religious wars. He was successful in shaping his beliefs in an ideological system, and, by means of several bloody wars led by the Sa‹udi family, he could impose it on Arabia. This belief is still advocated by the official system of the present government of Sa‹udi Arabia.

'**Abdul Wahhab** did not claim prophethood. He claimed to be a reformer trying to wash away the dust of superstitions from religion. For this reason his beliefs were explained clearly. So, there was no reason for the Muslims to think them out of religion. Yet, from the very beginning, most of the Muslims showed aversion or regret and sometimes they even criticized **Abdul Wahhab**'s superficial, stiff and brainless beliefs which got the name of Wahhabism.

In these days **Ruhullah** was around nineteen years old, and he had some knowledge about the beliefs of the **Babis** and the **Bahais**, as well as the beliefs of the **Wahhabis** which are so plain and superficial that anyone who has some knowledge of the Islamic sects, especially the ancestral Hanbali sect, can, in one or two sessions of discussion and argument, understand all what they have to say. After twenty years from the days of migration, **Aqa Ruhullah** wrote a book under the title *Kashful Asrar* [Disclosing the Secrets], in which some beliefs of the **Wahhabbis** criticized. Yet, in those years **Aqa Ruhullah** was completing his studies on these three sects. Then he followed up the news about the conducts of the **Babi** and the **Bahai** sects, particularly their influence on the organizations of the last Shah of Iran. But in the later years he showed little interest in reading or hearing about the principles of their ideology, as philosophically and theoretically they had no interesting thing to say.

In a stage on the road he witnessed a dispute and argument of a **Babi** and a **Bahai** who wanted to spend the night in the caravansarai, but the caravansarai keeper was refusing to give them a place.

Muhammad Shah

After the death of **Fath'ali Shah**,[313] dispute among all those princes over the throne was inevitable. **Muhammad Mirza,** the son of **'Abbas Mirza,** was one of the princes living in Tabriz. After the father's death he became the crown-prince, though there were other sons. The Russian and the British Embassies for the first time interfered in Shah-selecting, and they supported **Muhammad** against his uncles who claimed the throne. In 1250 A.H., he, together with an army under the command of **Sir Henry**, came to Tehran and went to the palace of his grandfather. Why was his army under the command of **Sir Henry**?

When a young man reaches this section of history gets fervently angry, and, before finding faults with the British and the Russians, feels astonished at his ancestors. How could they be so deeply asleep? What is certain is that **Aqa Ruhullah** did not very well know that the foreigners had interfered in choosing **Muhammad Shah**, too, as the history of the Qajar was still being written down by the Qajari historians. But he knew that **Muhammad Shah** was both dissolute and superstitious, besides being more inefficient than **Fath'ali Shah**.

Qaimmaqam and Mirza Aqasi

He had two chancellors: one by the name of **Mirza 'Abdul Qasim**, known as **Qaimmaqam**, and the other was **Haj Mirza Aqasi**.[314] The first had a serious complexion and a powerful pen. He was a scholar and a man of resolution. He was a thousand times more suitable than **Muhammad Shah** for the kingdom, though conceited. He used to stamp the ground with his feet such that it seemed that pride pours down from the folds of his *qaba*, drawing a circle with radius of three metres within which no one could keep pace with him. Concerning this man **Aqa Ruhullah** had a twofold feeling. On one hand he praised his knowledge, resolution and gravity, especially when he knew that **Taqi**, the small son of the cook of **Qaimmaqam**, had his learnings from him, and later he became the greatest chancellor for the Qajaris and one of the notable personalities of the country. On the other hand, his proud steps showed a man who, in the Badr War, challenged fighters, whereas the **Prophet (s)** had said: —Ecept in war-field, such strutting is detested by **Allah.**"

The face of the second chancellor was triangular, with an angle from his chin. Stupidity was obvious on his face more than anything else. Despite his sick mind and having insufficient intellect for a chancellor, he pretended to be a pole of religion and an expert in sufism. He liked more to be referred to, before the Shah and the people, as an expert in sufism and a man of miracles, than to be called chancellor, and, at the same time, to be benefited by being a chancellor. This clever pride and selfishness, which were not below the pride of Qaimmaqam, if were hidden from the eyes of a superficial observer, they could not be hidden from the sharp eyes of **Aqa Ruhullah**—if in those days, no, at least when a man of nearly forty, because in those years, when he taught ethics, he used to be vexed at such immoral cleverness.

The Big Mistakes of Muhammad Shah
Muhammad Shah committed many small and big mistakes, but two of them were historical. The first was killing **Qaimmaqam** and appointing **Aqasi** in his place. The other was attacking Hirat, at the instigation of the British, and, by the instigation of the British themselves, he retreated, knowing no cause for being instigated to attack Hirat, and, when he did, the very British supported the government of Hirat against him. Some good deeds of him found their way into history. One was the event concerning **Ali Rida Pasha**, the Ottoman Minister of Interior in Baghdad, who, seizing the opportunity of **Muhammad Shah**'s absence during his attack on Hirat, launched such an attack on Muhammareh (Khurramshahr) that it acquitted **Agha Muhammad Khan**.[315] Six years later, **Najib Pasha**, who was the Ottoman governor of Baghdad, felt the pre-Islamic fanaticism for massacring the Shiite boiling in his veins. He attacked Karbala to exterminate the Shiite. It is narrated that he killed even the cats. Asked: —Wy these innocent creatures?" He said: —They eat the flesh of the Shiite sacrifices!" Many persons incited **Muhammad Shah** to attack the Ottomans in retaliation for **Najib Pasha**'s massacre of the

255

Shiite, by massacring the Sunnis. Instead of that, **Muhammad Shah** sent **Mirza Ja'far Khan**, **Mushiruddawlah**, with the intermediation of the Russian and the British Embassies, to put an end to the disturbance. **Mushiruddawlah** was preparing for the negotiations when he died. The second selection was preferred to the first, as **Mirza Taqi Khan** was chosen for the negotiations. He had nothing less than his teacher, **Qaimmaqam**, and while preserving his gravity, his conduct was quite modest and popular. **Mirza Taqi Khan**, who was to conduct such negotiations with foreigners for the first time, manifested such insight that even the foreigners praised him.

—Arznatur-Rum" has no place in today's geography of Iran, but, in the history of Iran, it is the name of a sweet pact which **Mirza Taqi Khan**—who had not as yet become **Amir Nizam**—put his signature at its end. The Arzanatur-Rum was worthy of writing many books explaining it. One of those books was written by **Robert Curzon**. About **Mirza Taqi Khan** he said: —Among the representatives of Turkey (the Ottomans), Iran, Russia and Britain, who were present at Arzanatur-Rum meeting, the one who drew more attention, and whose personality could not be compared with the others, was **Mirza Taqi Khan**." [316]

Amir Kabir in the Eyes of Aqa Ruhullah

As a child **Aqa Ruhullah** had heard the name of **Amir Kabir** many times. Deep in his heart he looked at **Amir** as a hero, a hero whose mental portrait showed him as a real Muslim. At night he went into a privacy with his **Allah** and poured the griefs of a century of inefficiency in tears onto his prayer-mat, and in daytime he manly stood to do something for his people. Reason was strong in him, and he sacrificed feelings at the feet of reason. But feelings in him were in conformity with the logical mind, and overcame domestic economy.

Aqa Ruhullah mentioned this champion of the political field many times, suitably or pretentiously. Forty years after those days, in the first day after the elapse of forty days from (the massacre of) the martyrs of Faydiyyeh School, starting giving lessons on *fiqh*, he began advising the Shah, saying things which, looked at from different aspects, spoke of different matters. The most obvious aspect is that in the entire history of Iran, he only remembers **Amir Kabir** from among all the chancellors. He absolutely regards him to be the pride of the nation. Searching for a second example he has to dive deep into history and bring out **Ali ibn Yaqtiin**, who was **Harunar-Rashid**'s chancellor, guiding the system of the Caliphate towards equity. The third example is general, as the pure Imams are mentioned as counselors of the Caliphs. A part of the paragraph in which the name of **Amir Kabir** is stated, reads as follows: —‗Iwas a bad year, because the ruling government, the tyrannic system, was disgraced. We did not want, and we do not want, that our kingdom should be known outside the country to have such wicked elements at the head of the state. We did not want this. We want our country, from its first point to its last, to act, to behave, in such a way as to be the pride of a kingdom, to say: ‗We have **Amir Kabir**"...‖[317]

In another instance he said: —‗Ever since **Amir Kabir** established the university up till now it is some seventy years… many years have passed, but they did not allow our youths to become all right." [318]

In 1313 solar year, a university like today‗s type was established in Tehran under the name of Tehran University. Then, 80 years had passed since **Mirza Taqi Khan Amir Kabir** was martyred. So, was there a mistake? Or he wanted by this expression to say two things: One was that the Polytechnic Institute whose foundation stone was laid by **Amir**, and thirteen days after his martyrdom it was inaugurated, was the foundation stone of the present day universities, which still have the same nature laid by **Amir Kabir**. The other thing was to say: Change the universities to other than what they are.

Although it is possible that these impressions appear very much intimately, and, according to the indication of the seventy years which he stated, it shows nothing but a literal mistake which took place. Anyhow, both those impressions declare that **Amir Nizam** was always present in his mind to put the big works. Nevertheless, the first impression cannot be left unnoticed, because it contains words which are evidences of other things, as he said: —‗The progress of the kingdom does not depend on the 17th of Dey. The progress of the kingdom depends on the university, which you turned such. ‗It is a hundred years now we have, in a way, universities,‗ but still when they want to operate on the king‗s tonsils, they have to bring a physician from a foreign country319, the Karaj Dam is to be built by foreigners, and a line and a road are to be planned by foreigners."[320]

Sultan-e Sahib Qiran

‗Sultan-e Sahib Qiran‗ is the name of a TV serial. It portrayed the lives of **Nasiruddin Shah** and **Amir Kabir**. After the Revolution, when the TV of the Islamic Republic of Iran showed it, **Aqa Ruhullah** used to watch it. When the executioner cut the wrists of **Amir Kabir** to put an end to his grand life, together with the warm drops of blood dripping from his powerful hands on the cobblestones of the bath, drops of hot tears ran from the eyes of

Aqa Ruhullah down his cheeks. But before becoming under the effect of the serial, he had read *Amir Kabir or the Hero of Fighting Imperialism*, by Ali **Akbar Hashimi Rafsanjani**, and praised it. Perhaps, if he had time to write about some corners of the contemporary history of Iran, he would have started with Amir Kabir, because this great political personality of Iran was the greatest personality in the contemporary history of Iran. Without declaring that religion was not separated from politics, his politics was mixed with his religion. The impressions of **Amir** of religion were somewhat in conformity with those of **Aqa Ruhullah**, up to his age of thirty. In a more correct expression, **Amir** was a prominent evidence of the belief that at the present time, too, it is possible to keep one's religion and enter into politics at the same time, and not to step back even a single pace from religion on behalf of politics. Later on his impressions of religion and politics became much deeper than those of **Amir**, and brought them both to complete unity.

Who was **Amir Kabir**? What did he do? What had he to engage the mind of the young **Aqa Ruhullah**?

The Hazaweh Village

Hazaweh is a somewhat prosperous village at a 12 km from Arak. When **Aqa Ruhullah** was studying in Arak, he visited this village, with a number of his classmates, to see how the birthplace of **Mirza Taqi Khan** was. 138 years before that, that is, in the year 1222 A.H. he was born in this village. There is no doubt that **Aqa Ruhullah** had only seen the village, as the snow and squall had washed out the house of **Karbalai Muhammad Qurban**, Taqis father, which was a modest house made of clay bricks and mud. **Karbalai Muhammad Qurban**, with his family, migrated to the village of Farahan to work as a servant to **Mirza 'Isa**, to overcome poverty.

The father at the beginning was a simple servant, then he became cook-in-chief for two Deputy-Governors: One **Mirza Isa**, and the other **Mirza Abdul Qasim**, who was the elder son of **Mirza Isa**. The son became servant for the children. But he served in such a noble manner that the children became his playmates. The second Deputy-Governor employed a private teacher. One day he examined the teacher by asking the children successive questions. The children's backs bent under the weight of the father's difficult questions. Suddenly the mouths fell open. The mouth of **Mirza Taqi** in uttering correct answers, and the mouths of the Deputy-Governor and others to chew the finger of astonishment.

Stunned, the Deputy-Governor asked: —You lad, who taught you these things?"

Taqi said: —Wenever there is a chance, I stand behind the door of the room and listen to the lesson. Even when I bring the lunch for the children I stay behind the door to hear more."

Perhaps the Deputy-Governor was thinking that if the *haram* act of overhearing could be *halal* in any instances, this is one of them. Trying to encourage the boy with a present, he asked him: —Wat do you like me to give you?" **Mirza Taqi** expressed his magnificent desire and, sobbing, said: —Tdlthe teacher to accept me as a pupil."

The teacher was pleased to teach this sane young servant.

Days passed in learning knowledge, and at nights, by force of natural need, he had to close his eyes. Months went by in this way, and then years, till he became a sturdy and able man. One day he wrote deep and artistic letter to the Deputy-Governor, who, reading it, said: —Rightly, _its oil almost glows' [*ayah* 35, *surah* 24] is true to his faculty of understanding. _Allah is the best as a protector, and more merciful than those who have mercy...' [*ayah* 64, *surah* 12]. This boy will have many promotions and will give great laws to the time. Wait till the morning of his state rises." [321]

During the days of **Muhammad Shah** he put his signature at the bottom of the Arzanatur-Rum pact, lessening the humiliation of the defeats of the British and Turkmanchay, and, when **Muhammad Shah** died, it was the dawn of his rule. He fetched **Nasiruddin**, the crown prince, from Tabriz to Tehran, crowned him, and on the way he thought him lessons of the wisdom he knew, as much as the Shah's capacity could contain. [322]

From the State of Servitude to the Highway of Chancellorship

This man had a number of good characteristics which were in harmony with the soul of every living, including the young **Aqa Ruhullah**. One was that from the state of servitude to the highway of Great Chancellorship he galloped on the horse of high-mindedness, and in the state of Great Chancellorship he did not lose himself. He did not forget serving the people, and did not serve the foreigner. Another one was that he gave priority to discipline over relationship. To him no one was exceptional before the law. He tested courage in the field of overcoming feelings, in defeating the enemy and in having no fear of doing great deeds. One of his big acts was the building of the Polytechnic Institute after the style of the Western institutes, but with the Irani architecture. The establishment of this institute—to which **Aqa Ruhullah** referred as university—was of exceptional importance, as the experimental arts and sciences, which, at the early years of the arrival of Islam in Iran, were studied side by side, or at times in complete harmony,

259

with the religious sciences, in the universities in Iran, gradually remained without a guardian, and were transferred from chest to chest, from teacher to student. So, they kept moving away from the progress of the time, and thus, the establishment of such an institute, with the intention of catching up with the sciences and arts of the time, was a necessity. Nevertheless, it did not do as it had to. The words of **Aqa Ruhullah** were not exaggerating when he said: —Stl when they want to operate on a king's tonsils, the physician must come from outside!"[323]

Waqayi-e Ittifaqiyyah

Among the other useful deeds of **Amir** was the establishment of the paper _Waqayi-e Ittifaqiyyah'. During the days of **Shah Abbas**, foreign merchants used to bring with them to Iran some of the newly appeared newspapers. Some translators, who knew European languages, used to translate them for the Shah and the courtiers. Yet, it never occurred to anyone of the powerful Safavid kings to establish a newspaper.[324] In the days of **Fath'ali Shah**, **Abbas Mirza** sent a number of men to Europe to learn the art of printing. One of those five persons, by the name of **Mirza Salih Shirazi Kazeruni**, who was sent for translation, was clever enough to learn journalism, too. In 1233 A.H. the first printing press, with Farsi characters, was established in Iran. It mostly published advertisements.

In the last days of **Muhammad Shah** the first paper, under the name _Kaghadheh Akhbar'_, being the literal translation of —News Paper", under the directorship of **Mirza Salih**, was published on the 25th of Muharram, 1253 A.H., with some political news. **Amir** published that *Kaghadheh Akhbar*, as a regular weekly publication sold at a price of ten *shahis*. At first it was published on Fridays, and then, on Thursdays. The price of this paper was quite expensive, because each copy of eight—and rarely of twelve—pages, was sold at an equal price of half a *man* of lamb meat [1 *man*=3 kgs]. But there was no possibility to publish it at a lower price especially that **Amir** believed that the prices should be real, and it never occurred to him to pay subsidy. So, this newspaper could not have many buyers. Of course, the Embassies did need to know its contents, as well as the local governors who had to buy it at the order of the government, so as to be acquainted with the situations in the country and in the world. Nevertheless, despite its expensive price, the information obtained by those who had it within their reach helped, to some extent, to uplift the people's political knowledge. This publication continued for ten successive years go under the printing press every week, prompting begetting other newspapers. The year in which *Waqayi-e*

Ittifaqiyyah was published, 382 years had passed over the manufacture of the first printing press in the world[325], and hundreds of newspapers in thousands of copies in the West bound life with politics. Apparently this long temporal separation only means that Iran, as far as the generalization of the communicating news with the West is concerned was nearly four centuries away from the West, and had it not been for **Amir**'s ambitions, the distance could have been longer. However, the actual reality was not so, because the mosques, the coffee-shops and the bazar filled up the void of the newspapers to some extent, and the important political news were galloping with the speed of an imaginary horse even in the alleys of the villages. But each news changed color in the imagination of each narrator, and sometimes one crow became forty'. In its first issue, this was cited as the most important reason for publishing *Waqayi-e Ittifaqiyyah*: ‒The false news and rumours, which are sometimes contrary to the commands of the government and the actual situations, in some towns and frontiers, used to mislead the common people of this country. From now on this will be stopped by the *Ruznamcheh*.[326]" So, the existence of a newspaper was a grace, which, however, due to the misusers, sometimes turned to be a rancor.

Amir issued his order that no news should be censored, and to be written in a simple and easy style. He stressed that his name should not be mentioned in the newspaper, except when necessary, and still without stating his title. But **Amir**'s deputy, by the name of **Mirza Aqa Khan Nuri**, ordered that his name should appear in each issue, and with title. In one of the issues it was said: ‒*Janab-e Jalalat Maab-e Kifalat wa Kefayat Entesab, Muqarrabul Khaqan, Itimaduddawlatil Alliyyatil Aliyah.*[327]" [His Excellency the Dignified Deputy, Merited Relative to the Monarch, the Trust of the High and Lofty State].

Waqayi-e Ittifaqiyyah among Ruhullah"s Furniture

The **Allamah Sayyid Ahmad Hindi**, the grandfather of **Aqa Ruhullah**, subscribed to the issues Nos. 4 and 5 of this newspaper up to the last issue No. 471. After ten years he asked a bookbinder to bind them in two large volumes of 1500 pages. Later, friends of the martyr **Aqa Mustafa** could collect the few early issues of the newspaper. **Aqa Mustafa** sticked them to the beginning of the first volume, and, of course, they were a little projected out of the cover. **Ruhullah** was about ten years old when he stood on the tips of his feet to bring down the two volumes of the newspapers from the shelf so as to artfully page them. He did not know that each volume weighed seven kgs. So, when he pulled it out he lost his balance and the volume dropped on the ground and its binding broke up. The aunt came to help in mending it before the arrival of **Aqa Murtada**. But **Aqa Murtada** arrived and angrily said: —Æ these books a child's play?" **Aqa Ruhullah**, after three or four months, by reading all its pages proved that in this respect he was not a child. Now that he was covering the road from Khomein to Qum, although he had read both volumes very carefully, yet he put them in his luggage, so that he may read them again with a more mature look. Probably he had in mind some subjects about which he wanted to write, supported by those newspapers. However, no one of his writings had any references to them. But by scrutinizing some of his sayings one can imagine that the source of some of his information about the events of the years in which *Waqayi-e Ittifaqiyyah* was published has been the trusted news of that newspaper, although its worth decreased after **Amir**.

Hakim and Mahkameh, Physician and Clinic

Medicine has always been a science present at all times, starting from witchcraft to experimental knowledge, from chest to chest, and from book to book all over the world. The Chinese used their strange interpretation of creation as the basis for medicine which wonderfully progressed. The Egyptians, too, created independent schools. The Greek upheld surgery. The Indians explained the four temperaments on the basis of the four elements: water, soil, fire and wind. The Zoroastrians attached great importance to body health, and so they nourished the medical science. Islam regards body health as obligatory, and for this reason many of the jurisprudents and philosophers were physicians, too. Strange enough, in the Islamic culture, by _hakim' they referred to the scholar, philosopher, the time's sage as well as the doctor. _Mahkamih', the court of a judge, also meant the doctor's clinic. Consequently, large hospitals were established in most of the Islamic countries, and there appeared great *hakims*, such as **Avicenna, ar-Razi** and **Sayyid Ismail Jurjani**, who, besides treating patients, educated the medicine students, a number of whom can be regarded as the founders of the new medicine. Therefore, the establishment of hospitals in the towns was always regarded to be *kifai* duty in the religious culture. But when the religious culture mixed with the pre-Islamic superstitions, and knowledge declined, medicine was handled by novice physicians, instead of expert doctors. Geomancy and sorcery flourished once again, as was 4000 years before, and the busy hospitals turned desolate, though expert doctors kept, more or less, their clinics firm. Yet, during the Qajarian era the important question of medicine was endangered by extreme vulgarity.

Medicine of a Bulky Old Woman

During the years in which plague attacked most of the towns of Iran, and in its successive assaults it took three members of **Aqa Ruhullah**'s family. A bent bulky old woman used to come to the houses, demand a bowel of water, murmur some incantations, puff at the water, spit in the bowel, filling the boys with nausea at that. Nevertheless, some families endeared the coming of that woman. One day, supported by her stick, she called upon **Ruhullah**'s aunt. The aunt preferred to die rather than to pollute her mouth with her dirty spit. Due to the insistence of the old woman that all the children must drink from that bowel so as to dismiss the jinn carrying the plague, all the three brothers ran away from the room to prevent vomiting.

Such being the case, in order to rid this science of the scienceless ones and the magicians, **Amir Kabir** tightened his belt to establish a big governmental hospital. In 1266 A.H. he laid its cornerstone, and while its walls were going up brick by brick, he decided that whoever claims to be a doctor must obtain a certificate from skillful *hakims*, including **Dr. Kazulani**. Two years later four hundred patients were stretching on its hygienic beds under the care of **Mirza Muhammad Wali,** the *hakim*, as president of the hospital, and Dr. Kazulani, who had come from Italy. Within less than a year two thousand two hundred and thirty-eight patients were cured in that hospital free of charge.[328] The hospital which **Amir** established, and the other modern hospitals which were established in most of the large towns within a hundred years after that to undertake the medical matters, caused medicine to get, on one hand, the color of modernity, and get rid of the disordered personal experiences of the unlearned *hakim*s, and, on the other hand, to be separated from philosophy, and the Iranian physicians of today, like most of the physicians all over the world, no longer act as sages.

Traditional or New Medicine

After the victory of the Revolution, some physicians, thinking it was time to revive the traditional medicine under the name of Islamic Medicine, called upon the Leader of the Revolution in order to get his support. But, contrary to their expectation, he said: ―We have at hand basic questions which attract our attention. In such a situation when these questions are at hand, to present other matters is a mistake. I have repeatedly said that when an earthquake takes place and destroys the houses and people are under the ruins, do you give permission to yourselves to sit down and talk about the questions of medicine, mathematics or other questions, or you must all hurry to rescue those stricken by the earthquake? We have now a kingdom which has fundamental corruptions. We now have questions which are the basis of our Kingdom. We must now set forth our basic questions and all of us must follow up these basic questions. When we set these basic questions right and established the foundation of our Kingdom, at that time you may go for the traditional medicine, and they may go for the imported medicine. Today it is not the time for you to spend your forces to see whether the Islamic medicine as you call it, or the traditional medicine of Avicenna and ar-Razi should be practised or other medicines. This must not be set forth now. You are now in a situation between the existence and non-existence of your country, between the existence and non-existence of your religion and Islam. You are now at a cross-road. Do not think that as you have dismissed the former regime, all other questions have finished.[329]"

Amir's Achievements

Amir, like most of the political heroes, had his weaknesses, too, to which, undoubtedly, **Aqa Ruhullah**, at those years, did not seriously pay attention, but later paid serious attention to the causes of these weaknesses. One was that the political heroes of Iran did not give heed to consolidating their objectives and programs, and when they are not on the saddle, whatever they had built will fall to pieces, and so, what remains behind them will be the stories about their thrilling heroisms and the relics they leave behind, not the outcomes of their achievements. **Amir**, too, was not exceptional. When the sharp edge of the razor fell on his veins, a sharp axe fell, too, on the roots of his reforms, because he did not think of finding a way to protect his practical aims against the pests which were recognizable. **Wish Gortsev,** a Russian chief merchant, had presented to **Amir** a nice samovar and a set of teacups. **Amir**, ingenious as he was, realized that if he orders coal to be put into the samovar, place it on a seat near a brook, lean on a pillow and fill a slim-waist teacup with hot tea poured from the spout of a tea-pot and the elegant cock of the samovar and sip at it, the money of the nation will be spent on purchasing hundreds of samovars from **Wish Gortsev**. So, he ordered the governor of Isfahan to send to him the best craftsman of Isfahan. The governor found him and sent him to Tehran. **Amir** gave him the samovar to make a copy of it. When he saw the copy faultless, he gave him a capital of 200 *tumans* in order to help him in mass production and offer each one at 15 *riyals*. After deposing **Amir** from chancellorship, the officials of the governor of Isfahan went to the maker of the samovar and asked him to pay back the sum which he had received. They estimated his tools at 170 *tumans*, and in order to receive the balance of 30 *tumans*, they took him around the bazar and beat him on his head with wooden sticks to stir the sympathy of the onlookers and have them pay his debt. Afterwards the craftsman became blind and turned into a beggar. If Amir, instead of giving capital to a single craftsman, had given capitals to all the craftsmen, **Aqa Ruhullah** could have bought a samovar made by an Irani craftsman from Arak bazar when he wanted to purchase what he needed in his room. But what was regretted very much was that the governor of Isfahan himself had chosen that craftsman, but when he was brought before him to receive back the capital from him, he said to him: ―**Mirza Taqi Khan Amir Kabir** is deposed and he has no authority any more. So, you have to pay back the 200 *tumans* the soonest possible to the State's Treasury. It is unknown why **Amir** distinguished you so much?"[330] How could this be, and how low is this morality! Probably this was because the reforms of the **Amir** were merely imperative—orders which caused temporal reforms on one hand, and created blind psychological knots, on the other hand.

Amir Kabir and Qaani
Amir was disgusted with pompous and empty titles. So, he prohibited the titles causing pride. But after him the market of dealing in the titles flourished as before. **Amir** liked the sincere poetry of great poets like **Mawlana, Hafiz** and **Sa'di**. He was pleased with the poetry praising the prophets, Imams and saints. But he abhorred the hateful and meaningless flattery and blandishment of the eulogist poets who befouled the words to win a prize. One of those prize-seeker poets was Qaani—a talented, semi-educated and flattering poet. He was such a flatterer that one day when **Mirza Aqasi**, the despicable chancellor of **Muhammad Shah**, had cold, the poet, describing his successive sneezings, wrote:

From the disposition of **Ahmad the Messenger**, was there a breeze
    That wherever I go there are Tibet and Tatar?

The Khajah's catching cold testifies to this, as if
    This breeze is from the disposition of the **Chosen Messenger**!

Far above this nonsense be the name of **the Messenger** of **Allah** (*s*)! Then other poems he recited in praise of **Amir**. In the eleventh he said:

The breeze of Paradise blows from the brooks,
    As the scent of musk smells the air of the meadows.

265

Pleasant is tonight, O **Sanam**, to drink to **Jamshid**'s memory,
As the state of Iran became strong like mountains.

By the efforts of the famous Chancellor, the great righteous **Amir**, who opened wide the doors of the forts and blockades,
The Shah's prince, the Shah's trustee, the Shah's left, the Shah's right who, at the Shah's applause, repeatedly rubbed his head against the empyrean.

In the seven lines and four limits, in every region and every country,
Beyond restriction, count and limitation, self-sacrifices are yours,

By the bigwigs, the princes, the experts, the insighted,
By the ministers, the commanders, the counsellors, the consulted.

When **Qaani** reached this line in his recitation he raised his voice and pointed to **Amir** with his hands, and said:
In lieu of an unjust and wicked, is seated a just and pious one
In whom the pious believers have many prides.

Amir could bear it no more. The history narrates two reactions: One is that he raised his hand and asked: —Whom do you mean by 'wicked'? Do you mean **Haj Mirza Aqasi**? The same person about whose catching cold you composed poetry? Tomorrow, in another poetry, you will call me a traitor, and call him as a servant." He ordered him to be flogged and his stipend to be cut. By the intermediation of **Itidadus-Saltaneh**, it was decided that he must from then on say no poetry, and, instead, he was to translate an agricultural book from French into Persian. After **Amir** he resumed composing eulogies, and was a clear evidence of: **"And as to the poets, they are followed by those who go astray. Do you not see that they wonder in every valley?"**[331]
The less famous narration is that **Amir** said: —Your reward for the poem in my praise is this line:
Say whatever I am, do not say what I am not."
When in Najaf, **Aqa Ruhullah**, once at a lesson on ethics, referred to this less famous narrative and, in the continuation of the discussion, said: —If four, five other persons, like **Amir Kabir**, had ousted such courtier eulogists, the position of poetry and poets would not have become like the pre-Islamic era of Ignorance."

I Seek Refuge From Vanity

In the first parliamentary elections the majority of the people of Tehran voted in favour of a celebrated writer and preacher by the name **Fakhruddin Hijazi**. He, with his fiery speeches, along the uprising period, stirred enthusiasm in the hearts of his addressees. The lively effects of his synonymizations could be compared with poetry. The deputies, to start the work of the *Majlis*, came to the Husayniyyeh of Jamaran to hear from the lips of the leader of the Revolution his words. The said orator, representing the other deputies, stood up to say something, to thank and probably to offer a report about the elections.

The TV of the Islamic Republic used to broadcast all his general meetings, and millions watched them with great interest. That night the watchers saw and heard the beautiful expressions of that able orator, which revolved out of his mouth like an illustrious poem in praise of the leader of the Revolution. The leader's head was drooping on his chest, with frowningly knotted eyebrows. When the camera focused on the leader's complexion, waiting for him to speak, he, still drooping his head, started his speech as below:

—Ì am afraid of believing in what **Mr. Hijazi** said about me. I am afraid that his remarks and those of others like him create a sort of pride and degradation in me. I take refuge in **Allah**, the Exalted and Most High, from pride. If I recognize for myself a status in respect to the common men, it will be a mental degradation, a spiritual degradation. While appreciating **Mr. Hijazi** as a fruitful and a committed speaker, I complain that in my presence he said things which may make me believe in them." [332]

One cannot positively say that **Amir Kabir**'s behaviour with **Qaani** was the origin for this speech, since both were intoxicated by the Islamic teachings, though it cannot be definitely said that that behaviour had no trace in this speech. Yet, it is still higher in rank, because **Amir**'s reasoning was in his saying: —Tomorrow you will call me a traitor and call another one as a servant," while the reasoning of the leader of the Revolution was in saying: —İmay possibly believe in them and become proud and degraded."

Amir Went and the Shah Remained

Amir was martyred, leaving behind him a good reputation. But the Shah remained for nearly fifty years, acquiring the title of *Sultan-e Sahib Qiran*, sometimes, of course, with good reputation and sometimes with bad reputation. Whenever he became weak, he got bad reputation, and whenever he became powerful, raving courtier poets would recite poems in praise of his religiosity and governing. The preachers of the Court praised his merits to the extent of upsetting the people. As a matter of fact they were not only the courtier preachers who praised him. Some preachers from outside the Court did pray for him, to which the people said: Amin! Most of the journalists and some of the Europe-educated graduates, who were not on good terms with kingship system, did not, sometimes, fall behind the exaggerations of the courtier poets. When after nearly fifty years of ruling, he was assassinated, he was called _The Martyred Shah', and those who used to criticize him stopped their criticism. Nowadays some historians and political analysts refer to him as the man of politics and understanding. But the following words criticize their point of view:

—Durig the Qajari (era) they so much praised **Nasiruddin Shah** (calling him) The Martyred Shah and the like, whereas he was a treacherous despot, probably the worst of them." [333]

Of course, in those days he had not yet reached a decisive view about him. Perhaps he was trying to solve the contradictions which he had created. On one hand he was hearing that **Nasiruddin Shah** used to hold sessions commemorating the martyrs of Karbala, and to weep hard at the sessions mourning the Master of the Martyrs [**the Imam al-Husayn (a)**], and to respect the *ulama* and to observe religious rites. On the other hand, the tactics he used to satisfy his sexual desires, sometimes they tresspassed the religious norms to disgusting limits.

Although **Nasiruddin Shah** was a king, with kingly conducts, he was a disciple of **Amir**, and, despite the fact that he had killed **Amir**, yet he repented that and continued to remember him with respect, and to follow **Amir**'s instructions concerning defeating the followers of **Bab**, and issued his order to kill **Qurratul Ayn**, the daughter of **Haj Mulla Salih Qazvini**. [334] This woman was very beautiful, and yet shameless, and further than that she was daring. She became the propagandist for the Babist group. For this purpose she used her naked figure. [335] After the murder of this woman, a man, by the name of **Mulla Shaykh Ali**, intended a riot in the capital, aiming at assassinating the king through a conspiracy, but he failed. Owing to his extraordinary sensitiveness to the being of Islam, **Aqa Ruhullah** followed up, to some extent, the history, the current news and the propaganda of this group. When the descendants of the **Bahai** group penetrated, with the help of the Israili State, into the court of **Muhammad Rida**, the last Shah of Iran, he, addressing the Shah, said: —Wœrever you put your finger you will find an Israili agent in an important post, a dangerous post. By **Allah** these are dangerous to the crown of this **Aqa.** They [the Shah's retinue] are inattentive. These were the ones who planned, in Shemiran of Tehran, to assassinate **Nasiruddin Shah** and have Iran in their control. Look into the history. You do know history. They conspired in Niyawaran. A number of people went to Niyawaran to kill **Nasiruddin Shah**. Others were in Tehran to seize the government. These people take the government to be theirs. In their books, in their articles, they write that: _The government is ours. We must set up a new sultanate. We are to create a new government, a government of justice.' Those who have such ill intentions, ill views, they are found everywhere. In the Court down to the farthest spot in the kingdom these people can be found. Fear them! What beasts they are!"[336]

Shah, Dissolute and Vagrant

Nasiruddin Shah was whimsical, dissolute and vagrant. The best description of his capricious heart was said by himself. By way of obtaining permission from one of his favourite wives to wed another girl, he said: —Dœing **Anis...** but you do know that each woman has her kind of distinction, and you are superior to them all. But what can I do, as my dissolute and beauty-adoring heart sometimes is entrapped by the curly hairs of beautiful faces!"[337]

When he was uttering these words to sooth **Anis**, his *harem* was full of women the names of some of them he had forgotten. He in a royal hunt had entrapped **Anisuddawlah** in the village of Amamah. Her name was **Fatimah**. After **Jeiran** she became the most favourite wife in the *harem,* and was titled **Anisuddawlah**. But the vagrant Shah, unlike his usual custom, remained in love with **Jeiran** till the end of his life. When he was shot in the shrine of Abdul Azim, he dragged himself up to **Jeiran**'s grave, and, hugging it, he passed away.[338] However, this love, too, could not bridle the heart of the dissolute Shah, nor could it stop his restive heart from giving itself out to other moonfaced beautiful ones.

Kamalul Mulk, the Famous Painter in the Court

This sensual Shah, as he himself said, adored beauty, but, alas, his eyes did not go into the depth of beauty. He was acquainted with the art of painting to some extent, but his painting was spiritless. **Kamalul Mulk**[339] was one of the celebrated painters of Iran and a contemporary of the Shah. He could make the Shah's hand familiar with the brush, but he could not make him see the spring of art.

Poetry Ascribed to the Shah

The Shah liked love poetry and composed it, but his weak composings were revised by the Court's poets for him, such that the words and the concepts were changed, in which case he believed that he himself had composed them and hailed himself. Of course, those who did not know that the poetry ascribed to him was not his praised his graceful temperament. However, many learned people understood that. **Aqa Ruhullah**, concerning this matter, said: —Fomerly poetry was composed for **Nasiruddin Shah** and was ascribed to him." [340]

A Journey to the Holy Shrines at the Peak of Despotism

Truth should not be neglected. His prose was simple, eloquent, clear and proportionally novel, but autocracy was quite obvious in his writings. He left several travel books. One of them, which was written down in a nice handwriting, belonged to his trip to the holy shrines of **Imam Ali (a),** and **Imam Husayn (a),** the Master of the Freemen. In this journey he had the chance to see the golden domes and silver shrines and the colonnades of these two holy places, which the Muslims of the world, especially the Iranians, bedecked with their artistic craftsmanship and their valuable gifts. What he saw was only these decorations which he beautifully described. But those decorations which he saw prevented him from seeing the wonders of those two great souls[341], because he had gone to visit things which those great men stood away from them in their lives. In his travel book the Shah showed that he was getting nearer to the decorations, and getting away from the conducts of those great Imams. **Imam Ali (a)** governed a vast land of which Iran was just a province, at a time when somebody, by way of forbidding evil, took off an anklet from a Jewess, scratching her leg. When the Imam heard about that, he got angry and slapped his face on the *minbar*, crying out: —fl one died of the disgrace that in an Islamic government a non-Muslim woman should be wronged, one should not be blamed." Now **Nasiruddin Shah** steps into the shrine of this Imam of justice and finishes his travel book, and in this very travel book we read: —.. Then we got into the carriage and drove. On the road a group of common people of the town stood shouting. It appeared that they were repeating their complaints from **Imaduddawlah**. Despite the fact that I had spent few days in setting right the matters in Kirmanshahan and in settling the points which caused the complaints of the common people and had born difficulties, I regarded this repetition of the complaints a kind of commotion causing much ado, and got a bad temper. I ordered them all to be sent to jail. I was quite right in my bad temper, as I had given no cause for those people to complaint, such as appointing a reliable agent, removing many innovations, carrying out some arrangements and sending to exile persons causing injustice and aggression. So, the subjects are not allowed to impose their demand from the government to depose a governor and cause so much trouble. I ordered them to be kept in prison for two days to be punished and give up their mischief making." [342]

The Qualities of the Martyred Shah
Despite his despotism, this Shah could rule for some fifty years and spend it with full free-living at the side of his *harem*, come to terms with his time's rival powers, make three trips to Europe, become a modernist and yet visit the holy shrines and be on good terms with the *ruhaniyyun*, and when drunk put his signature at the bottom of the death sentence against one of the best personalities of the country, caress the singers, paint, compose ugly poetry, write readable travel-books, appear with pride, splendour and glory among the people and ascribe to them his own bad behaviour, empty the treasury and borrow from the foreigners, lose a part of the country, and get the epithets of _the martyred Shah' and _Sultan-e Sahib Qiran'.

Was the Shah Complicated?
The one who can rule for some fifty years under such conditions must be a complicated one. But, strange enough, originally he was not so. Even his temporarily wed wives knew his particular whims. It was the culture of the country which was complicated and could solve the contradictions within itself. On one hand, among the treacherous kings who governed this country was **Nasiruddin Shah**, and, on the other hand, the Shiite-wanted rule was the very government of the first ten years of Islam and the nearly five years of the governing of **Ali ibn Abi Talib (*a*)**, and the few months of the government of the second Imam of the Shiite. So, how was that, with such high hopes, persons with such behaviour should govern the land of Shiism?

Aqa Ruhullah had for tens of years been in argument and combat with such contradictions. But now, as he is on his way to Qum, he thinks of an incident which was small in appearance, but actually was so big that some historians thought it to be a good start for commencing the writing down of the contemporary history of Iran.

From the heart of this small big incident a theory can be derived to the effect that governing in Iran and in many Islamic lands was not completely in the hands of the ruler, as to him belonged a part of governing. Had it all been in his hands, he would have lost it all to the foreigners in the political gamblings. This theory, in a nutshell, is: **Governing in Iran belonged more to religion, than to the governor.**

Regie Agreement, Europe Souvenir

This big event had a short story.[343] In his third trip to Europe[344], **Nasiruddin Shah** enjoyed a very pleasant time, and, for receiving a sum of money as a bribe, he signed the draft agreement which got the title of **Regi.e.** It granted the full concession of monopolizing the purchase and export of the tobacco to a British company.[345] A man, by the name of **Einstein** came to Iran, bought an orchard and established a big company for the purpose of carrying out the contents of the said agreement. Everyone who had to do with cultivating, buying, selling and trading in this profitless product, and had lost, was displeased[346], because, before that, everybody was free to sell his product to anybody he liked, while, after that, there was only a single purchaser who bought at any price he liked to pay. The cause of their displeasure was not only the question of profit and loss. The nation had been very much humiliated by that agreement. More than that humiliation was that most of Iran's merchants used to study the _Makasib‘[347], in one of whose lessons they read: —Haing option is one of the compulsory conditions of any transaction, as imposd transactions are *batil*." Fourth, if the people kept silent in respect of this agreement, the next agreements would enslave their children to put brick upon brick in building British pyramids.

The Russians, who were worried about the influence of their rivals, and in order not to lag behind, tried to take side with the people's discontent in order to compel the Shah to cancel it, or to have him, at least, grant them a matching concession.[348] When the discontent was aggravated the commotion increased and the *ulama* of the country effectively interfered. The nation could not keep silent, and conflicts started with the officials of the British company and the agents of the government. Strange enough that in a riot in Tabriz the Russians interfered on the side of the governmental forces.

Matches Under Thousands of Bags of Tobacco

A torrent of protests and petitions flooded the Court, but the Shah was so dare to become the executor of the Company's orders. The people were nervous, unaware that in nervousness desire imposes the lighting up of the hookas and the pipes. The Shah and the countries, who had been bribed to let this *haram* semen clot[349], were nervously filling up the heads of their hookas with tobacco soaked in rosewater. Thus, the consumption of tobacco products increased. It occurred to nobody that to encounter such a humiliation required giving up the cultivation of a crop which was nearer to the culture of the Europeans than to the culture of the Muslim nations. A patriotic merchant from Shiraz refused to sell his tobacco to the British Company. The company threatened to confiscate his wealth, but he stroke a match under twelve thousand bags of tobacco. [350]

Sayyid Jamal's Letter to Mirza Shirazi

The *ulama* of the country sent letters to the *ulama* in the holy cities so that one of the religious authorities may issue *jihad* decree. In those days **Sayyid Jamaluddin Asadabadi**, the enlightened and experienced theologian (*ruhani*) of the world of Islam, was spending a period of exilement, at the order of the Shah, in the Ottoman country. He wrote many analytic letters to the Shiite authorities, explaining to them the consequences of that agreement. **Sayyid Jamal**'s style was always vehement and sharp, with a prose causing one to shiver. As far as bidding the good and forbidding the bad was concerned, his pen was like a sword. When in Basreh, he wrote a letter to a man who was the greatest authority of the time, living in Samerra'. That letter was not less sharp, though he wrote it very politely, bestowing the most respectful titles on that authority. He wrote: —This letter is the humble request of the Islamic nation offered before the presence of their great authorities, the pure souls in whose hands are the reins of the nation. O leader of religion! O the bright rays of the Imam's lights! O the foundation of the throne of religion! O the expressive tongue of religion! Your excellency, Haj Mirza Muhammad Hasan Shirazi! **Allah** has granted you the agency of the Imam of Time... **Allah** has set the chair of your chairmanship in the hearts and minds of the people so that by means of which the pillar of justice may be strengthened, and the straight path may be illuminated, and, because of the greatness bestowed upon you, He also committed to you the protection of religion and the defence of the world of Islam to the extent of attaining to the blessings of martyrdom, like the predecessors. The Islamic nation, the mean and the noble, the urban and the nomad, the poor and the rich, have all

273

acknowledged this divine grandeur and knelt before it and bowed out of respect. In all events the Muslim *ummah* turn to you, and in every calamity they pin their hopes on you. They see their happiness, well-being, salvation and freedom in your hands. Their hopes depend on you and you are their peace.

Such being the case, if you leave them to themselves for a twinkle of an eye, or if you neglect them for turning from one side to another, their thoughts will be confused, and their hearts tremble with fear, and the basis of their faith weakens. Why? Because the ignorant masses, far their beliefs, have no evidence except perseverance and stability which are shown by the learned class in their beliefs. If the *ulama* display weakness in performing their duties, or shrink from forbidding the evil, the working masses will have doubts and suspicion, and everybody will turn away from his religion to his former beliefs, and to deviate from the straight path.

O great leader! The King of Iran is weak and of bad character, feeble-minded and has taken to ill-behaviour, and is incapable of managing the country's affairs and preserving the common interests. Therefore, he has placed the reins of the affairs in the hands of a wicked, evil-charactered and mean man who abuses the prophets publicly, observing no religious instruction and respecting no religious authorities... After returning from Europe he tore off the curtain of shame, took to stubbornness, and to drinking in public. He **makes** friends with disbelievers, shows enmity to the pious people. These are his particularities. What is against the interest of the Muslims is that he has sold out a considerable part of the country and its income to the enemies of religion, as detailed below:"

Sayyid Jamal numbered eight instances of the Shah's betraying the country in favour of Britain for **Mirza Shirazi**[351], the fifth of them being the monopolizing concession of the tobacco. Then he wrote: ─Then this treacherous traitor, in order to please the people, he presents a vain excuse, saying that those agreements were temporary and they do not last for more than a hundred years.[352] The other half of the country he gave to the Russians as hush money (if they do keep silent), in the form of the swamps of Rasht and Anzali up to Khurasan... But the Russian government refused the offer, as it thinks if these agreements remain intact; it will colonize Khurasan and lay its hands on Adharbayjan and Mazandaran ....

O you, leader of religion! If you do not come to help the nation, to collect them, and if you do not powerfully take this country out of the claws of these sinners, in no time this Islamic country will be under the power of the foreigners."[353]

Numerous letters from different quarters reached the late **Mirza Shirazi**, but that of **Jamaluddin** had a different effect. Nevertheless, that authority, by reading that and hundreds of other letters, did not become sentimental, but he acted as **Moses (*a*)** acted against **Pharaoh**. [354]

Today the Use of Tobacco...

A number of tender letters were exchanged between the Court and **Mirza Shirazi**, but the Shah did not come short. Suddenly, on a Thursday morning, a single sentence was cabled to all post-offices, and on the same day its content resounded all over the country, even in the remotest villages: ―**Today using tobacco, in whatever way, is tantamount to fighting the Imam of the Time (*a*)**. Written by the humblest [person] **Muhammad Hasan al-Husayni.**" [355]

This decree stirred an uproar. Its shortness made it firm, and its firmness made it short. Without any introduction it dealt with the original point and the conclusion was hidden in the point. It had no minor and major premises, such that its conclusion might stir any discussion. It was not a decree for *jihad*, nor did it have any smell of gun-powder or of blood.

At that time, about one-fourth of the country's population were addicted to one kind or another of smoking tobacco. [356] How difficult it is for a nation to give up an addiction, especially in such an abrupt way! But how easy it is to carry out a decree if the nation knows its motive.

Breaking the Stems of the Pipes

Thousands of cigarettes were trampled, and the stems of thousands of pipes were broken. Some wholesellers put their stores on fire, and the retailers untied the tobacco bags and emptied them in the water gutters, the teashop keepers stored away the hookas. Strange enough that the soldiers who used to stand against the people so as to force them to sell their tobacco to Talbot Company, now backed the people and enacted the decree of prohibition. Stranger still was that the rascal drunkards stopped smoking, saying: ―The judgement of **Mirza Shirazi** is **Allah**'s". Asked whether **Allah** had not prohibited wine-drinking, they answered: ―That sin is repentable, but this one has no term for repentance." [357]

The text of the prohibition was such that it seemed to be compulsory only to the Shiite, but the Sunnis, too, put no cigarette to their lips. The Zoroastrians, too, observed the decree. The Christians and the Jews spoke of **Mirza Shirazi** with respect, and even in their privacy they did not pollute their throats and chests with smoke.

In an album remained from these days there is a photo of a dervish who had a hooka at his lips. The photographer shot it because the dervish had said: —Uless **Mirza** permits smoking tobacco, I will smoke hashish."

It was a Judgement not a *Fatwa*

It was much regretted that a number of men of religion did not know that it was a decree, not a *fatwa*. One of them, by his own *fatwa*, smoked a hooka on the *minbar*. [358] **Aqa Ruhullah**, who had always respected the *mujtahids* without naming them, by way of a warning, renounced their acts, saying:

—When the late **Mirza** forbade the tobacco the Satans went among the people to the extent of having some of learned men in some towns to smoke the hooka on the *minbar*, as is reported, in opposition to the judgement of the late **Mirza**. But as the **Mirza**'s power was extraordinary, and his supporters were as powerful as the **Mirza Shirazi**, they [the Satans] could do nothing there." [359]

A while after prohibiting the tobacco, the Shah was encountering the people face to face. He humbly asked a *mujtahid* named **Mirza Hasan Ashtiyani**[360]—who naturally undertook the leadership of the people in carrying out the uprising of the tobacco ban—to cancel the decree. He got the reply: —No *mujtahid* has the right to cancel another *mujtahid*'s decree."

An Old Woman With a Poker in the Square

The Shah, through his Chancellor, sent him a message that: —You must either smoke the hooka in public, or leave Iran." He immediately closed his teaching classes and prepared himself to move to the Holy Places. His 200 students, who used to attend his classes, told the population of Tehran to come to protect the **Ashtiyani**'s house. For few days the people watched the streets around his house. In an instance there took place a small conflict between them and the governmental forces[361], which was ended by the falling of **Kamran Mirza** (Nayebus-Saltanah) into the mud. He was the governor of Tehran, the son of the Shah and greatly effective in accomplishing the Agreement.[362] At seeing the people's resolution[363], he knew that to continue the conflict with the people means the destruction of the Palace, as it was the first time in the contemporary history of Iran that the women came to the streets. There was a rumour that **Mirza Shirazi** had issued the decree of *jihad* against the British. An old woman limpingly, with the poker of her stove in hand, came to the street and stood in line with the other women, so as to be armed if the rumour of *jihad* was true.

Shah"s Submission

It happened that the Shah retreated, and how a humiliating retreat! His humiliation reached its peak when he ordered a hooka to be brought to him, but none of the servants was ready to satisfy the Shah's desire in smoking a hooka in defiance of the decree of **Mirza Shirazi**. The Shah bit his finger out of astonishment, because he saw how the soldiers obeyed their immediate superiors in firing at the people, though reluctantly, but no one of his inferiors obeyed his order, even reluctantly, to prepare a hooka for him.

He had no way but to submit. The Shah handed his diamond ring to 'Adudul Mulk so as to give it to **Mirza Ashtiyani** as a tocken of making peace. **Mirza** thanked the Shah for his kindness, but he conditioned accepting the gift on cancelling the Tobacco Concession.

On the 5th of Jumada ath-Thaniyeh the announcement of cancelling the agreement was published in the newspapers and, in the form of thousands of posters, it was sticked onto the walls of the mosques, streets, lanes, bazars, etc. The people, overjoiced, hugged each other and congratulated one another. Many started smoking cigarette after cigarette, and the more committed ones waited for the prohibiting decree to be officially cancelled. **Mirza Ashtiyani, Shaykh Fadlullah Nuri** and **Sayyid Ali Akbar Tafreshi** separately wrote three letters to **Mirza Shirazi** asking the decree of prohibition to be lifted. The answer about cancelling the prohibition was not quite clear.[364] Perhaps this was to consolidate the cancellation of the Monopoly and confirm the impossibility of return. After two weeks the answer to the question of the late **Ashtiyani** about lifting the prohibition was clear: —Yourhonour's telegraph concerning the lifting the Concession of Tobacco, and announcing the permission of smoking, according to my humble letter, was received. Of course, that which you found suitable is quite correct, and from now on there will be no prohibition on tobacoo, as you had announced. In fact, I am grateful to the Royal favours, which caused the consolidation of the religion and the government."[365]

During the Tobacco Uprising, the martyr **Aqa Mustafa**[366] was studying in the holy places. Later, he had told his children: —When the decree of tobacco prohibition was issued, those who were living in the holy places, whether the Iranians living there or the dwellers of Samirra, Karbala, Najaf and Kazimayn, if a hooka was offered to them, they would first ask: _Where has its tobacco come from?' If it was from Iran, they would refuse to smoke it."

277

Broken Hookas in the Store-room of Ruhullah's House
On a shelf in the store-room of **Ruhullah**'s house a number of broken pipes
and hookas were placed and were dusted on the *Nowruz* occasions. They kept
them as a token of the uprising so as not to forget the history of the country.
Aqa Murtada did not remember who threw them away and when they were
thrown away, nor who had broken them, but he remembered that they were
there for more than twenty years, causing childish questions on the part of
Ruhullah, and an excuse for transmitting the history of these days, about
which the aunt and the mother had related tens of exciting stories for the
inhabitants of the house concerning the events of those days, on the terrace in
the hot days of summer, and under the *kursi* in the cold nights of winters.

The Bud of Growing a Fundamental Question
Now that **Ruhullah** is on his way to Qum, he is more or less acquainted with
the orally related history of the life of **Nasiruddin Shah** and that victorious
uprising. So, he must have this question in mind: Why that **Mirza Shirazi**,
that great authority whose decree was so much influential, did not issue his
decree to topple the Shah down and do away with king playing and treason?
If he did not ask himself that question, it would be strange, and if he did, the
replies he had found deserve much contemplation, because, on one hand he
knew that the debauchee **Nasiruddin Shah** had committed many treasons
against the nation, to one of which the Tobacco Uprising was an answer, and,
on the other hand, **Mirza Shirazi** had remedied only one of his betrayals,
while, after his surrender to this struggle, the Shah committed other treasons.

When the sparks of the Islamic Revolution was going to put afire the
hearts of a nation against the Shahanshahi system, and, the leadership of **Aqa
Ruhullah** was being cordially and mentally accepted by the zealous
enlightened fighters, most of the men of religion and the majority of the
people, it was time to answer this question. He delivered an astonishing
speech. The tape of that speech was reproduced in tens of thousands of
cassettes, despite strict watching of the Shah's security system. Those who
had a typewriter, they used carbon papers to type many copies of it. An old
man, bought a typewriter from a retailer for fifty tumans, and when typing
the speech blood dripped from his thin fingers because the keyboard had no
bottons and he had to press his thin fingers on the tips of the sharp keys. It
could have been written by hand on a stencil, and, by way of precaution, it
could be reproduced inside a school house. The photocopying machines were
more used in photographic studios and the government offices. The SAVAK
was watching lest they may be misused. Some government officials used

them properly. Even in a room next to the office of **Ashraf**, the Shah's sister, the son of a gardener could photocopy hundreds of copies of the speech, despite the fact that the security men could have discovered him and shot him with a bullet in his skull. In Isfahan all the pupils of a 3-class school wrote compositions, and each one of them analysed a sentence of the speech. The teacher of the composition had, by this innovation, endangered his life. An Iranian student in Italy paid the largest portion of his monthly allowance to cover a distance telephone call, as he attached his telephone receiver to a recorder so that his friend in America can hear the speech of his leader a night earlier!

The content of that speech was not entirely political, but the politicians described it to be one of his most political speeches. Nor was it historical, as he in many instances repeated: —Ido not know history." But his deep analyses of the depths of history still deserve being analyzed. Nor was it a theological discourse, but it opened new ways of theological discussions among the theologians and the academicians. Nor was it an explanation of the precepts of *fiqh*, but even those who were not of his *muqallidin* realized that they must ask forgiveness for some of their past sayings and deeds.

The concepts of this speech culminated at first, then they descended. As to the culminations, let them be until I reach the culminations of the Uprising. But as to some aspects of their descents we take them to be answers to the questions that whoever looks at the history criticizingly, will take those questions to be sparks of his intelligence.

That speech was delivered because ten days before his eldest son, **Aqa Mustafa**, died in a suspicious way, and mourning meetings were held all over the country. The leader of the Uprising ascended the *minbar* in the Shaykh al-Ansari mosque in an-Najaf al-Ashraf in order to thank the millions of the people who took part in the mourning and reply the thousands who sent him written condolences.[367]

Sincere Complainings

In this speech he expressed his most beautiful criticisms, and so sincerely, of anybody who had an objection against him. He complained against each class or group whom he loved, and what sincere complaints!

—Iam attached to all the exciting wings who serve Islam, whether the wings of the theologians who have been serving from the beginning till now, or the other wings of the politicians and the enlightened who serve Islam, and I have complaints against them, too. As to attachment, every Muslim must feel himself attached to the persons and the groups who serve Islam by pen and foot. Every Muslim, every man, who see them serve humanity, serve Islam, that is, serve humanity (as Islam is the school for making man), when a man sees that some groups are at man's service, at humanity's service, at the service of Islam, which is maker of man, will have but to be attached to them. There is no objection in being attached.[368] And, on the other hand, there are complaints against all groups–sincere complaints![369] Firstly of the enlightened, or, in a sharper appearance, of all their wings."[370]

Later, those whose practical commitment, according to the advices of that beloved, was not little only in their eyes, took this part to be a proof of the basic objections against the enlightened classes, while the enlightened, by way of defending themselves, used to say:

If she had a tendency toward others,

Why did Layli break my pitcher?

A Defence to Protect the Honour of the Sanctuaries

—Butitose groups of the enlightened, the graduates and the new students, and those (may **Allah** support them) who serve Islam, I have complaint against them, because I find in their writings, in some of their writings, about the *faqih*s, about the *fiqh*, about the *ulama* of Islam, there is somewhat extravagance. They said things which were not becoming of them to say... They have no purpose, they have little knowledge. I, too, have little knowledge of history, but I am eighty years old and I was in the scientific circles for about sixty years, and about thirty years I spent in contact with the current events. I myself have witnessed many events, and within the nearest one hundred and odd years we have little, I mean, I have little information about the past. The information which we have about the past, the first times, the early eras of Islam till now, is a general information. We notice that this Islam, with all its dimensions, has been preserved by the *ulama*... Now as you see such rich *fiqh*, for the Shiite *fiqh* is the richest one in the world, it is a law which was explained and declared by the efforts of the Shiite *ulama*. It is the richest law in the world. There is no law as rich as that in the world. The other laws, of course the heavenly ones, were rich, but they did not reach us. The other terrestrial ones made by the people of the earth, they are as weak as their understanding, and made by these brains... That which they did is incomplete... Wherever there are such laws, they are incomplete, especially for a particular condition and a particular position. For example, for managing the affairs of a kingdom, for the politics between a country and another. Others have no other laws. It is Islam which has... All the dimensions of Islam and of Quran, that part which is understandable by man, are, as these people say, made by these turbaned groups—the turbaned and bearded ones. They have brought Islam up to this stage. They wrote books, in all branches, as you notice. They have exerted great efforts till it reached now to this stage... The objective of the *ulama* in approaching the kings was to promote Shiism politically. I said I do not know history, and if I did, I do not remember now. Yet, the history of the past hundred odd years is at hand. We push a little forward and see that a group of the *ulama* gave up some position and joined the kings, although they knew that the people were against that. But they did so in order to propagate the Islamic Shiism, the true religion... They persuaded those kings willy-nilly to promote Shiism. They were not at the court's *ulama*. This is a mistake committed by some writers. They were around these kings. They had political objectives, religious aims. If one hears that, for example, **Majlisi** (may **Allah** be pleased with him), or **Muhaqqiq the Second** (may **Allah** be pleased with him), or, say, **Shaykh Bahai** (may **Allah** be pleased with him), had relations with them [the kings], visited them and accompanied them, one must not think that they felt unable and were in want of post and position. They did not need **Sultan Husein** or **Shah Abbas** to favour them. There were no such things at all. They sacrificed, strove, in order to have this sect prompted at their hands... They struggled before the people who probably had protests against them, out of ignorance. Even now if somebody objects them, he knows nothing about the case... It was a policy above these things. The Imams (*a*) sometimes used to resort to pacification. At times it was impossible, so what could they do? The interest of Islam is above these things which occur to us. This group of *ulama* sacrificed their lives and showed themselves in such a way that you now object them... as you have no information about the facts. This is man-making, not that they became courtiers. They wanted to make men. I complain!

The *ulama* carried up the standards of the uprisings against despotism. This refers to their *fiqh*, to political questions, much as I know now. According to my knowledge about the events nearest to us, the uprisings happened against the events which were against the interests of Islam during the last hundred odd years. One of them was the question of the tobacco which is known to all. **Mirza,** the great **Mirza Shirazi** (may **Allah** be pleased with him) issued an order and the *ulama* of Iran (may **Allah** be pleased with them), at the head of them was **Mirza Ashtiyani** in Tehran, carried it out and brought to life the fallen government of Iran. They had pulled it down for the sake of having a little fun and pedlary. They had sold Iran to the foreigners. But **Mirza Shirazi** (may **Allah** be bleased with him) ordered and the *ulama* of Iran hazarded themselves, suffered a lot, endured hardship, uprose and obliged the people to uprise until it was cancelled.[371]

This uprising against despotism and Constitutionalism started from Najaf by *ulama*. In Iran, too, it took place by the *ulama* who stood against that severe despotism which did whatever it liked, to kill whomever it wished... They brought those unfortunate soldiers from here and there. They did not give them bread. The coach of the Shah was to pass through the town of Shah Abdul Aziim. They gathered there to complain. Someone threw a stone. He ordered them (as is stated in the history) to be brought and choked. They did so to many of them until somebody from **Mustawfil Mamalik**[372] went and cried out: _What is this?', and he interceded. There were such men, and there were such tyrants. Everybody knows that **Muhammad Ali Mirza,** what a monster he was! There were others, too. To face this handful of tyrants, the *ulama* rose up and started an uprising. The *ulama* were at the head of those who wanted it to happen, but it did not. If it had happened it would have been better. They could not, so what could they do? Yet, the situation became better than before, better than the time when someone could do whatever he liked without being questioned, though what they wanted did not congeal."[373]

At that time when he uttered these words by way of complaining against the enlightened, he was starting a big deed, a deed which the *ulama*, along the history, could not implement, the deed of the approach to the Safavid government by the *ulama*, which, as he said: —...They sacrificed, strove... They struggled..." But that which was to happen did not happen. He described all the Shahs of this dynasty, without exception, to be wicked, and had many times referred to their wicked acts so that the scientific and religious flourishing of that period may not be ascribed to the Shahs of that dynasty.

When he said he had complaint against the enlightened, it was mostly because they had taken the approach of the *ulama* of religion to the Safavid Court to mean that the *ulama* were cooperating with the Shahs of that dynasty and they were of the same opinion, not to mean that they sacrificed and struggled in order to put the things right.

The American Islam Beyond Safavid Shiism
He had carefully read *The Alawi Safavid Shiism*.[374] Later on he stepped farther and, instead of *Alawi Safavid Shiism*, he referred to the _pure Muhammadan Islam and the American Islam*.[375]

But he did not agree with **Shari'ati**'s opinion that the **Allamah Majlisi** was a courtier *Mulla*. Not that he did not frequent the Court, but that he did not become a courtier. He was so much disgusted with the courtier *Mullas* and described them with the worst epithets. In this speech he said: ―fiI could put a tyrannical Sultan on the right path, I would have become a courtier, too. You, too, your duty would have been to become a courtier if you could change a tyrannical Sultan to a human being. This is not becoming a courtier, it is man-making."[376]

Of course these expressions came to his tongue when there was nobody and nothing that could change his decision to put an end to the sultanate, the Court and the courtiers. The origin of that decision was religious duty, and these utterances he made to redress the point of view and establish the subject within his time and place.[377]

At the same time as he undertook the leadership of a nation, and as the Revolution was going to give its fruit, he was worried lest the scientific and religious luminaries should be detached from culture and history, and the nation become without an identity, and, by way of imitating that history-versed man, every zealous young man ignorant of history ascribe whatever he likes to whom he likes. It is quite possible that he himself be a victim of those daring speeches. On the other hand, he did not take the already started uprising to be a spontaneous event. To him the nearest start was the uprising of 15 Khordad, 1342 (solar calendar), while its farthest starts he sought in the late hundred years and in 1400 years of history. He also regarded fighting by pen as a part of the emancipating *jihad*.

By this declaration did he answer the question that why a *faqih* like **Mirza Shirazi**, whose brief and penetrating decree rolled off the carpet of smoking the hooka even from the Royal Palace, did not endeavour to overthrow the despotic monarchical regime? If not the whole regime, at least the rule of **Nasiruddin Shah**, which was so bad that **Aqa Ruhullah** called him treacherous.

This is a question which he, in the second part of his speech complaining of the *ulama*, had delicately answered, though not clearly. That which is clear in his declaration is that the *ulama* should learn politics and should not oust out the Muslim enlightened and politicians, who think in a different atmosphere, with the whip of accusing them of disbelief.

Islam in All Dimensions
He believed that all the great Islamic personalities, in all religious dimensions, had exerted fruitful efforts, and that today their valuable

treasures are not merely the cause of pride, but of lofty ideas, too—the ideas which if turned into musical notes, the beautiful resonance of their melody would bring to the ear the sound of the angels' footsteps; and if they went onto painting canvas, they would brighten the eyes; if they flew through the fingers of a little rural girl, they would turn into trans-global carpet-designs; and if they appeared in architecture, instead of luxury, they would create beauty; if they were turned into words paraded in poetic rhyms, their trumpet and drum would be played, not by a ruler like **Sultan Mahmud**, but by a sage like **Firdawsi**, the expert on **Ali (***a***)**, and the hilt of the sword would be grasped by the iron hand of the **Rustam** who, instead of butchery, would do surgery.

He very well realized that the gardeners of a flower garden, from which the green *Bustan* [garden] of **Sa'di** grew out, were the true *ulama* of this upright religion. He very well knew that **Hafiz** [the protector] of the anemones ever adoring the valley of religion, the Tongue of the Unseen, was an upright scholar.

To him **Mawlana**—who said: the legs of the rationalists are wooden— was a rational scholar, a divine philosopher and an intimate gnostic whose moral couplet poems were the unveiled explanation of the truth of existence.

Had the philosophers of the world been shown what a Substantial Movement was, and how **Mulla Sadra Shirazi** connected the reason to the heart, wouldn't the world outlook of the world philosophers elevate up to intuitive understanding of this simple line of poetry?

If you cleave the heart of every atom,
Therein you will see His Sun![378]

The Stature of Political Thought Is Gaunt

Nevertheless, he had found that, despite these valuable treasures, the stature of the political thoughts of the world of Islam, especially during the recent centuries, were still gaunt and thin.

Whatever part of the history he looked into, he found that the *ulama* had been beside the people, if not always, then, mostly. Wherever in the history he looked, he saw the *ulama* rising against the wrongdoers.[379]

Yet, it seems that, due to tens of proofs, a self-evident matter had been neglected, a matter which, probably because of its obviousness, remained unseen. What was it?

A forgotten matter which, despite all the internal beauties of the history of Islam, made its external appearance ugly, disgusting and displeasant, and, of course, the internal was, at times, smeared with hypocrisy, superficiality, meanness and ignobility. A matter as small as the overthrowing of the kingship regime'! A term about which the beloved **Prophet (s)** said: ─No term is as disgusting to me as the term king of the kings'.[380]

The *ulama* who could take the *fiqh* to the wedding bed, too, and exact the religious moral precepts at the sensitive moments of pleasure, excitement and fury, and the time of ecstasy, did not they make easy such difficult things? So, how is that the establishment of a government in accordance with the delicacies of religion is neglected?

What can be higher than establishing a government backed by so much great knowledge?

Was the establishment of an Islamic government always neglected, or only at times?

These are questions if we look for them in his works, we shall very well find them; we sometimes fall in contradiction, and if we try to solve the contradiction, we get to a new discovery.

In the Shiite thinking no government is more desirable than the government of the immaculate Imam. This very fact has led to a general negligence. He many times had thought to himself: Is the congregational *salat* with the Imamate of the **Prophet (s)** more desirable, or a congregational *salat* led by an ordinary *salat* leader in the Prophet's mosque? The answer is clear. But now, is it possible, while performing a congregational *salat*, to abandon the Prophet's mosque? According to his clear *fatwa*-like advice, never!

> Now that no government, except that of the immaculate Imam, is the final desirable, does the obligation for establishing an Islamic government become invalid?

His answer, decisively, is that establishing an Islamic government is at the head of the Muslims' duties. Will it do if any government is established under the name of Islam? His answer is quite astonishing: ─fl a *faqih* committed even a single act of dictatorship, he would lose his position as a guardian."[381]

Consequently, none of the Safavid and the Qajar Kings had the position of guardianship, and their governments cannot be described as Islamic.

But nowadays some of the thinkers declare: ─When a society is religious, the government of that society is, more or less, obliged to observe the regulations of the *shar*, and there will be no need for a religious government." This is not a new idea, nor is it a talk of novelty. Some of the religious *ulama*, along the history, believing in this idea, neglected the establishment of the government—a negligence which brought about **Shah Abbas**, **Nadir**, **Agha Muhammad Khan** and **Rida Khan**.

Great Men Are to Be Regarded Great

Now that **Aqa Ruhullah** is five months and a half short of his nineteen years of age, and is travelling from Khomein to Qum so as to get more acquainted with the Islamic knowledge, his impressions concerning the idea of governorship are this same view. But, when he found another opinion and uttered those complaints, why did not he name any of the past great *ulama* who neglected to establish a religiously legal government? Certainly because —he had weighed their conduct within the conditions of their time and place." Yet, its another reason must also be found in the fact that, as he, abiding by the command of the *shar*, had rolled up his sleeves in order to carry out such a great task, he must regard proudly his own luminaries, and, instead of mentioning their negligences, he must retell their services, so that the great revolution, which is about to take place, may not be void of a historical support. Those who beslight their great men, **Allah** will not grant them the efficiency of undertaking great deeds.[382]

Is My Beard Ridiculous?

When **Aqa Ruhullah** was born, eight years had passed since **Nasiruddin Shah** died.[383] Some people called him the martyred Shah, and every year they used to set up mourning gatherings. This was because he had gone to visit **Abdul Azim**'s shrine in the town of Rey. He was shot dead by a self-bereaved young man by the name of **Mirza Rida Kirmani**, who was an enamoured student of **Sayyid Jamaluddin Asadabadi**. It was as if he had aimed at the Shah's heart by a hint of his teacher. The opinion of **Aqa Ruhullah** about **Sayyid Jamaluddin** cannot be inferred without analysis, because apparently his name was not mentioned in his statements, but, undoubtedly, he ascribes the assassination of **Nasiruddin Shah** to him, since most of the remaining documents about this event point to this idea. He, however, did not regard the murder of the Shah to be martyrdom, because he had jokingly referred to this epithet, and felt pleased with the joke created by **Mirza Rida Kirmani**, and which he had heard as a child. **Mirza Rida Kirmani**, fervently enthusiastic as he was, took part in the riot took place against the disgraceful agreement through which the country became, for the first time, indebted to the foreigners. He was imprisoned in a windowless, dark and damp prison which was very hard for him. When he was once again thrown in the prison and was under severe tortures, somebody told him:

—Younlucky man, you are now a captive, while **Sayyid Jamal** is free and laughing at your beard (= mocking at you)." His reply was: —My beard must be ridiculous!"

Muzaffaruddin Shah

After **Nasiruddin Shah** his son, **Muzaffaruddin**, became king. **Aqa Ruhullah** caught up with nearly the last four years of his life up to the Constitutional Revolution. Before that he was acquainted with the Qajar dynasty and part of his life in history.[384] A part of the effects of the conducts of those last two Shahs of that dynasty he had seen with his eyes and heard with his ears.[385]

Although **Muzaffaruddin Shah** was not, in his eyes, a bloodthirst and treacherous, rather he was kind to some extent, and he was proud not to have polluted his hands with the people's blood, and to have endorsed the Constitutional decree, his travellings to Europe like his father, and loans which he received from the foreigners to spend on his excursions and sensuality, did not draw a lovable and efficient face of him.

Superstitions

This Shah, like many other Shahs, was superstitious. He was so superstitious that although he had waited for twenty years to put the crown on his head, when it was time to wear it, he delayed it for some time. The people were surprised at that. It was later known that he regarded No.13 an unlucky number. Now that there were a double thirteen side by side (1313 A.H.), he had to impatiently wait for the arrival of the month of Muharram and the change of the lunar year, and at least one of the two 13s change to 14.[386]

Is the number 13 really unlucky? Some nations believe it to be so. In some countries the architects could construct amazing architectures. They built towers when you count their stories you notice they were a story more than what was stated on the tableau of the last story.[387]

The Unluckiness of Thirteen

The number thirteen must not be regarded unlucky in Iran. If it was so before Islam, it should not be so now, since the second personality in the world of Islam [Ali ibn Abi Talib], had illuminated the world by his birth on the thirteenth of the month of Rajab. But alas! The superstitions, which are transmitted in the cultures from chest to chest and book to book, mostly remain more obvious than religious beliefs among the superficial classes.

The unluckiness of thirteen is not the most important and the most corruptive superstition found its way into Iran's culture, even if a day is called *sizdah bedar* [the 13th day out of doors], but before thinking about its unluckiness, it was thought of as the displeasing end of the pleasing holidays of *Nowruz*, the holidays which please the children more than the three months of summer. If we ask the children: —s thirteen unlucky?" The majority will reply: _It is the most unlucky day of the year," especially the children who failed to complete their homeworks, and particularly the children whose dresses are not quite new, who will feel ashamed next day on facing their classmates who wear better clothes.

The unluckiness of the thirteenth of *Nowruz* is the most tangible superstition which the children, nowadays, within the tumult of the personality formation, feel its unluckiness in the depth of their souls. If the *Nowruz* holidays in Iran become nineteen days, will not *nuzdah bedar* [the 19th day out of doors] be unlucky?

Now according to this analogy, don't the superstitions believed in by a nation have their roots in the realities, through a final analysis?

Qawamul Mulk was arrested by the coup d'état on *sizdah bedar*. He had reason for believing in the unluckiness of thirteen. But why should **Muzaffaruddin**, who neither went to school, nor was in such a difficulty, be superstitious? Undoubtedly, every superstitious can find agreeable reasons for himself. But alas! It is regrettable and painful if the misinterpretings of religion should be used as evidences for justifying superstitions and worshipping falsities, as in which case, even the divine *ayah*s and the traditions of **Allah**'s prophets and the gnostic invocations of the pure Imams would, with tens of interpretations, put the stamp of endorsement upon the superstitious beliefs.

The Anti-Superstition Devious Thinkers

Among each nation there appear, at times, individuals who resolve on fighting superstition. Sometimes they succeed and knock down a superstition, and sometimes they themselves are knocked down and the superstition triumphantly proceeds forward on its way. Among the superstition-combatants numerous individuals can be seen who cannot distinguish between the superstitions which found their way into religion, and the niceties created by religion, and, in weeding the vegetations of the garden of religion, they not only do not uproot the weeds, they rather break the roots of the delicate stems of the beautiful flowers.

288

Ahmad Kasrawi[388] was one of those superstition-combatants who joined the book-burners. **Aqa Ruhullah** heard about him in Khomein, and in Arak read some of his articles, and in Qum he followed up his ideas. In his book, *Kashful Asrar*, he criticized some of his ideologies. After the Revolution he referred to some of his misunderstandings and said:

—Ofourse **Kasrawi** was an able writer, but of late he became lunatic... [some people] have high claims. **Kasrawi** claimed to be a prophet, but as he could not reach so high, he tried to pull it down. This book, *Mafatih al-Jinan,* is not by **Haj Abbas Qummi**. He compiled it[389]... He collected the invocations in it. This man who burnt *Mafatihul Jinan*, or appointed a day for burning books like *Mafatihul Jinan*, did not know what was there in this book. Perhaps he never read the Shabaniyyah Invocation. His thinking was not such [as to read it]. These invocations which belong to the months and to the days, especially the months of Rajab, Shaban and the blessed month of Ramadan, grant man spiritual strength if he is worthy of it, but we are not. They open the road before him. They are searchlights in order to bring out man from darkness into the light. These are miraculous. Take care of these invocations."[390]

A Superstition-Combatant Should Be a Superstitionist

In another speech, in a reference to **Kasrawi**, he stressed that if being a superstitious means being a misthinker, and if superstition-combating is an obligation, then superstition-combating requires superstitionists. How often numerous superstition-combatants are themselves misthinkers:

—There are in man misunderstandings which sometimes increase. They do not know what a *dua* is. They think: Well, we shall now take the *Quran* and leave the *dua*. They do not know what the du‹a originally is. They do not try to find out what the contents of the *dua* are, what it says to the people, what it wants to do. If there was nothing in the *dua*s except the Shabaniyyah Invocation, it would have been sufficient to prove that our Imams are true Imams, those who composed this *dua* and followed it up. All these questions which the gnostics say in their lengthy books, are, as they themselves say, expressed in few words of the Sha‹baniyyah Invocation. Rather the Islamic gnostics used these very *duas* stated in Islam. Gnosticism of Islam is different from that of India and other places. It is these *duas,* which, according to some of our teachers, are (ascending) *Quran*. They said: The *Quran* descended, it came down, while the *dua* ascends upwards. It is the ascending *Quran*. The moralities in these *duas* want to educate man, who, if left to himself, would be more rapacious than the rapacious animals. These *duas* have a particular language. They take man by the hand and lift him up, the _up' which I and you cannot understand. There are those who can. Once one sees that **Kasrawi** came and started book-burning. *Mafatih al-Jinan* was one of the burnt books. He also burnt the gnostic books."[391]

Pouring Water into the Ants" Hole

Later, when **Ruhullah** married and had children, one day his son, **Mustafa**, emptied a pitcher of water in the earthy ground of the yard. The water ran a yard forward and poured into an ants' hole. **Aqa** told his son: ─When I was a child we were told not to pour water in the garden at night, otherwise the jinn would come upon us. I did not believe that, and now I do not believe in such things, either. But now I think that the wisdom in that was to teach us that one must always know what one is doing. When one, in the dark of the night, pours water, how would one know where to that water goes and what would it do. If it was winter, it would freeze on the ground and cause someone to slip. Now you, in the light of the day, poured the water and caused the helpless ants to be hurt!"

Cause of Superstitions

These stories indicate that he did not think the superstitions to be rootless. Yet maybe he thought that the superstitions were like the dried or diseased leaves and petals of the trees which had dried of thirst, or became yellow and sick because of excess watering, or their living period had reached their end and they became no more beautiful. He, who, in his old age, was well-versed in the art of gardening, never stroke with his axe at the roots of the stout trees which had dry ugly branches. He rather irrigated the roots, cut off the dried branches and even turned the leaves into powerful fertilizer. Thus, without directly criticizing some forms of mourning the anniversary of the Master of the Martyrs, which had become too much superstitious, even from among those who wounded their heads with swords, daring to strike their [shaved] heads with sharp swords, he made fighters in the battlefield, fearlessly walking on the enemy's fields of mines, afraid of no power, even at the peak of fighting, when the whistling mortar shells pierced the ears, at which a fighter, jokingly said: ─flone of these shells strikes my head it will throb till morning."[392]

Is wounding one's head with a sword not now a disgusting, ugly and repulsive superstition?[393] If it is, doesn't it, in its root, mean: ─W are the self-sacrificers who are not afraid to have sharp swords come down upon our heads for the sake of **al-Husayn (a)**! If you do not believe us, here is the sword and here is our shaved, naked and helmetless heads."?

Nice Superstition-Combating

It is not idle talk to say that, during the last decades, no philosopher was so successful in removing superstitions from the religion as he was. This denotes that he knew very well the roots of the superstitions.

In the very expressions by which he described **Kasrawi** to be lunatic because he burnt *Mafatih al-Jinan* and gnostic books, he also attacked superstition, and without injuring the feelings of anybody, guided them to the depths of the *dua*s, and of those who used to recite the gnostic *dua*s to expel the jinn, the fairies, toothache, gripes and colic, he could make gnostic people who woke up in the middle of the night to demand from **Allah**, the Beneficent, the Forgiving, to eliminate injustice, darkness, poverty and debauchery from the earth, and to make the people tactfully try the sweet taste of pure love, sincere sacrifices and purities.

Within the last ten years of his life his superstition-combating crossed over the national borders and the religious concepts of the Islamic *ummah*. Is not it a fable to say that the globe revolves on the horn of an ox? If it is, then in his eyes it is also a superstition to say that the world revolves on the finger tips of the monster of the upper powers. In his opinion, each nation, in accordance with its high ambitions and intelligence, plays its role in the international system and is effective, disregarding the desire of the upper powers. **Galileo** was the first person who eliminated the first superstition from the astronomic culture. He [the Imam] is the first to eliminate the second superstition from the political culture. Nevertheless, he never claimed that if a garden was weeded once it would not need weeding again.

Superstition-Combating a Desire and a Duty

If the gnostics had the right to desire, one of his lofty desires was to sacrifice himself in the fight against ignorance and superstition.

Let us see:

In the name of Allah, the Beneficent, the Merciful.

His Excellency, **Hujjatul Islam Mr. Qadiri**, may the flow of his favours be continuous. With greetings, wishing good and desiring success for you at enacting the precepts of Islam. Your first letter and my reply were about the conditions of the school and the lessons and discussion; otherwise, I take you as a *mujtahid* and an authority in the *fiqh*. I have always been asking **Allah** that you, the youths, would be able to solve the difficulties of the country in different fields. I regard you one of my best old friends. I will not forget your efforts in teaching, discussion and your assistances in all levels. We must try to break down the blockades of ignorance and superstition, so as to attain to the clear fountain-head of the pure Muhammadan Islam. Today the lonliest thing in the world is this Islam. Its salvation requires sacrifices. Pray that I may also be one of the sacrifices. May **Allah** confirm your excellency. May peace and **Allah**'s mercy be upon you.

Ruhullah al-Musawi al-Khomeini.[394]

IN QUM

Qum is a historical city, around it is a desert. Its water is salty. A river divides it into two parts. In spring its water is muddy, and in summer it is dry. The sun of July pours fire on the city. Winter slaps the face with its burning cold. Many times earthquake deposited it, then once again, bricks raised out of the earth upon bricks. One time Sawah was the center and Qum was a suburb. Before recently becoming a province, it was a part of Tehran. Near it is a lake with variable width of 30 to 60 kms., and a length of 80 kms., with an average area of 2400 km^2. On the road to Tehran a part of it can be seen. Its dawn is extremely beautiful and its sunset is spectacular. From a distance it stirs in the stranger the desire to swim, and from near-by its swampy shores beat the drum of death. No one stretches a leg to its shore, and if one did, no return will be probable. It is as if a mountain of salt is solved into the bitter water of a pool. Its geographical name was —The Sultan's Pool", which was derived from history. Its historical name, taken from its own geography, was —Swah Lake". It is narrated that in the night on which **the Prophet (s)** was born, the Satans were prohibited from going and coming to and from the heavens, 14 crenations of the Ctesiphon fell down, the Fire-Temple of Pars died off and the lake of Sawah dried up. This white desert, which is wetted by vernal rain, is the remaining of that lake which dried up. Its third name is the lake of Qum. But, in fact, the lake of Qum, which is of very little width and has an island floating in it, was in its neighbourhood.

The name of Qum is stated in the narratives. It is a Persian name. In Arabic it means _Stand up' or _stand errect'. It is known for its sweet _suhan'. It exports cotton and pomegranates. This city is distinguished from other similar cities by the fact that a girl is buried there preventing it from being neglected. She is **Fatimah Masumah (a)**, the sister of the **Imam Rida (a)**, the eighth of the Shiite Imams, and her shrine, like her brother's, is a place of animating visits.

Masumah (a) was 18 years old when she left al-Madinah, heading for Khurasan, prompted by the desire for seeing her brother. Her father, **Musa al-Kazim (a)**, the seventh Imam of the Shiite, was imprisoned for 14 years with chained hands and feet, by **Harun ar-Rashid**, the sixth Abbasid Caliph. But his spirit could never be chained and flew away from the dungeon and climbed up the walls of the prison, mingling with the people so that religion may not leave them and justice-seeking remain stable among them. The Caliph became feeble and thought that by murdering him the people's love for justice would subside. When he gulped down the *sharbat* of martyrdom brought to him in a poisonous cup, the burden of the Imamate was shouldered by his first son, **Ali ibn Musa (*a*)**.

The Shiite believe that the Imams of Guidance are of a single light, but, among the people, each becomes a certain manifestation of the Truth as a guide. **Ali ibn Musa (*a*)** illuminated in the manifestation of **Rida**, which means being pleased with **Allah**, and this is above the state of reliance and submission[395], because in submission one submits to **Allah**'s command with full desire and acceptance, but **Rida** means that whatever man sees from **Allah**, even a calamity and a difficulty, it is nothing but good. One of the great tortures of **Ali ibn Musa ar-Rida** was that his bitterest enemy, **Mamun**, the seventh Abbasid Caliph, who was the most powerful Emperor in the world of that time, showed extraordinary attachment to him. **Harun**, **Mamun**'s father, imprisoned **Musa (*a*)**, **ar-Rida**'s father, and chained his hands and feet, but no chain could tie the hands of the Imam. But **Mamun**, son of **Harun**, invited **ar-Rida (*a*)**, son of **Musa (*a*)**, to accept the position of the Crown Prince of the greatest Empire of the world. It was the most ingenious trick on the part of the most ingenious Abbasid Caliph. It meant that refusing the post would mean that he did not care for the lost government, for reviving which the impeccable Imams offered many sacrifices, and which now was readily offered. What reason could there be for refusing? Accepting meant endorsing the Caliphate which had the color of religion, but was worse than disbelief. Rejecting the post also meant the general homicide of the Shiite. Acceptance also indicated that the two centuries of struggle of the offspring of the **Prophet (*s*)** was for nothing but to attaining to power, and Imamate and equity, which are the first two principles of Shiism, would change their meanings according to the Empire's style. Consequently, the story of inviting the Imam **Rida (*a*)** concerning accepting the Caliphate and the position of Crown Prince is one of the most complicated section of the Shiite political thought which remained as a source, though not yet strictly analyzed. At any rate, **Rida (*a*)**, had, at last, to accept and had to leave al-Madinah to Khurasan as slowly as he could, so that those who loved the offspring of **the Prophet (*s*)** may have time to join him on the way. Wherever there was an inhabited village he delivered a clever speech. The deepest of his speeches was called *Hadith-e Silsilatudh-Dhahab*, which he delivered in Nayshabur.[396]

On leaving al-Madinah he said: —Wep for me." That was because weeping, at the time of strangulation, had a clear and deep concept. After that, the other thirty-six sons of the seventh Imam realized that there was no way but to migrate to other parts of the Islamic world, so that if martyrdom knocked at their doors there might be —no death in silence, which would only benefit the enemy."

Masumah in Qum

One of the sisters, **Fatimah Masumah** by name, prompted by her desire to see her brother, set out of al-Madinah. When she arrived in Sawah, she fell ill and could not stand the fever. She understood that death would prevent her from seeing her brother, but she had in her mind a saying from her father. So, she said: —Befre it is too late, take me to Qum speedily, disregarding my illness." Her father had said: —A man from Qum will invite the people to the truth and freedom. The people, who possess powerful will and an iron determination, will accept his invitation and gather around him, they are not afraid of the events and the adversities, and will not get tired of fighting and struggling. Their only hope and support is **Allah**. Victory belongs to the people of *taqwa*."[397]

When she arrived in Qum, death arrived, too. She was buried there so as to be the ever kindling light of the city, which, as a result, got its fame. Despite the fact that this city's water and weather were not satisfactory, but every time nature opposed it and ruined it, it stood again on its feet.

Visiting Ghusl in the Public Bathroom

When **Ruhullah**'s carriage arrived in Qum, he went to a public bathroom in order to wash off the travel's dust, as well as to perform the *ghusl* before visiting the shrine of **Masumah** (*a*). From then on it became **Ruhullah**'s habit every day to kiss the door, the wall and the shrine of this girl who was, in a way, his historical aunt. Later, when he saw the common people, in certain easy acts, outran their elders, he took care that when the eager ones exaggerate in showing out their love for **Masumah**, he, on entering the sacred place, greeted her, read the suplication, performed the *salat* and left without putting a hand on the shrine or kissing it.

Qum's Attractions

Qum had no attraction other than the visiting of **Masumah**'s shrine. But what kept it alive was the seriousness of the teaching centers after the settlement of **Ayatullah Hairi** in it. Perhaps seeing that narrative from the father of that girl, who has become now the eye and the light of the city, and several other *hadith*s from the infallibles (*a*) not only increased the attraction of settling in the city of Qum, but made quitting rather impossible. If at the beginning of studying in Qum he had seen that narrative, he would have, undoubtedly, wanted to stay so that if that man, in his life, rose from that city, he would be among those who gather around that truth-seeker.

The Evidence of a Hadith

Had it ever occurred to him that after half a century, the people would look at him—not at another one—as an evidence of that noble hadith? How hard was upon him this belief of the people if he was sure that, that man was another one, not he, since whenever great men like him become the topic of exaggeration by the people, their effort in cleaning off the fanciful minds of the people would have a contrary result. When he used to feel that the people were lauding him with big and sacred terms, he trembled and, to redress the people's opinion, he used to say: —am no more than a *talabah*." In his vocabulary, a *talabah* meant a student. It was a good epithet, but not great in position. Yet, by saying it, his status did not come down. The term _student' rose to the highest scientific, gnostic, philosophic and *fiqhi* states, and covered the same stages which the term _philosopher' covered.[398] Nowadays, when someone wants to praise himself, or unknowingly praises himself, says after him: —am no more than a *talabah*."[399]

It would have been much harder to him had he known that he himself was the evidence of those *hadith*s, not anyone else, because undertaking the message of religious awakening is a burden which man had been shouldering for long years. But just knowing that such a burden must be shouldered is, in itself, a burden which is, at once, placed on one's back. If really he is the evidence of that *hadith*, when did he realize it?

Attraction of settling in the city of Qum, but made quitting rather impossible. If at the beginning of studying in Qum he had seen that narrative, he would have, undoubtedly, wanted to stay so that if that man, in his life, rose from that city, he would be among those who gather around that truth-seeker.

The Evidence of a *Hadith*

Had it ever occurred to him that after half a century, the people would look at him—not at another one—as an evidence of that noble hadith? How hard was upon him this belief of the people if he was sure that, that man was another one, not he, since whenever great men like him become the topic of exaggeration by the people, their effort in cleaning off the fanciful minds of the people would have a contrary result. When he used to feel that the people were lauding him with big and sacred terms, he trembled and, to redress the people's opinion, he used to say: —Iam no more than a *talabah*." In his vocabulary, a *talabah* meant a student. It was a good epithet, but not great in position. Yet, by saying it, his status did not come down. The term _student' rose to the highest scientific, gnostic, philosophic and *fiqhi* states, and covered the same stages which the term _philosopher' covered.[398] Nowadays, when someone wants to praise himself, or unknowingly praises himself, says after him: —Iam no more than a *talabah*."[399]

It would have been much harder to him had he known that he himself was the evidence of those *hadiths*, not anyone else, because undertaking the message of religious awakening is a burden which man had been shouldering for long years. But just knowing that such a burden must be shouldered is, in itself, a burden which is, at once, placed on one's back. If really he is the evidence of that *hadith*, when did he realize it?

Aqa Ruhullah's Acquaintance with Mudarris

Qum had another attraction. The political believers in religion, and the religious believers in politics were sometimes taking refuge in the shrine of **Masumah (*a*)** owing to the current policies, or they used to visit the holy shrine, which was a chance for him to get acquainted with the politicians who were breathing in the atmosphere of their own time. Perhaps on a visiting day he got acquainted, in a corner of the sacred place, with the martyr **Mudarris**—a man full of vividity and enthusiasm. In his time he was one of the few persons who, from the inside of religion looked at the current social affairs. He was one of the *'ulama* who dignified politics. He, from among the twenty *ulama* introduced by the Great **Ayatullahs Khurasani** and **Mazandarani** to be admitted to the Parliament, was chosen by *qurah*, with other four persons, so as to supervise the Parliament's ratified laws lest non-religious terms should enter the law. The day when the announcers called out in Khomein that the Constitution had come, while **Ruhullah** of four years could not know well what did it mean, this man was a defender of

297

Constitution, and in Isfahan he heartily defended it. But after the first term, he entered the Parliament when **Ruhullah** started attending school.

After the second term the people of Tehran voted for him for five terms, but his votes for the seventh term were not counted, to which he jokingly said: —had given my vote to myself, why did not they count it?" Now this man is in the fourth term of the Parliament representing the people of Tehran. Many of the English and Russian politicians know him very well, because several of his short sayings had crossed the borders to the outside.

He was a man not so much handsome, but in politics he had nice features. He was lean and slim, but experienced and fond of satire. Many of his criticisms were sarcastically expressed. As a child he was afflicted with malaria. When he was caught by the fever's quivering, he used to say: —I want to quiver a cauldron, so do not tease me!" If it was sunny he used to cover his head with his *aba* and sit in the sun, quivering. When he used to go to the *haram*, the other visitors pointed him out to one another. Now **Aqa Ruhullah** is acquainted with his name. Probably he had also seen his picture in the newspapers. Talking to such a man, who is a scholar and a famous man of politics, by a young student who wants to be a scholar yet not ignorant of the people's political destiny, is quite an important event. Of course, before being important it will be interesting.[400]

The circumstances of the meeting are unknown, but **Aqa Ruhullah**, nineteen years of age, met a man of about fifty years, half of which he had spent in the current of politics. **Mudarris** was acquainted with the martyr **Mustafa** since they both were students studying together in Isfahan. Now that he is meeting his son he is very pleased, and he would not refrain from teaching him the tricks and secrets of the pottery of politics.

Sometimes in the Parliament

The result of that acquaintance was that whenever **Aqa Ruhullah**, for an excuse or another, visited Tehran, he also called on **Mudarris** in his house.[401] Sometimes he went with him to the Parliament as a spectator. He noticed how the debates were conducted by the deputies. In several sessions he could notice **Mudarris** how seriously and firmly he delivered his speeches, while those in front of him were indifferent. Probably he wanted to know strictly, for what reason and on what mental and ideological bases **Mudarris** took the Parliament so seriously. When in some sessions the oral debates went so high, and such speeches were delivered by **Mudarris**, he realized the reason for his being serious concerning the work of the Parliament: —am serving the people. Quibbling one another, and indulging in trivialities, which are not in the public's interest, are useless. They waste the Parliament's time. Each one of its sessions is estimated to cost seven hundred tumans, while each minute of it worths the value of the whole world, because in this one minute one can say something, exact a law, manage a matter or do something. Spending the time in such deeds has so many results in this world and in the hereafter."[402]

Teaching and Parliament Sessions Must Be Serious

The personality and the speeches of **Mudarris** in the Parliament stirred in him serious mental crises. On one hand, he had come to Qum to study, and learning besides being a duty, according to the saying of **the Prophet (s)**, is also a high act of devotion with its own originality. Someone asked **the Prophet (s)**: ─"If I had only one hour left of my life, which devotional act is better to do?" He said: ─"Acquiring knowledge". Now, here is **Mudarris** saying that a minute spent in the Parliament for arranging an affair or enacting a law is more valuable than the whole world. Is it more approved to take to politics or to acquiring knowledge? The final result of his lengthy and quarrelsome discussions with himself was that a minute in the Parliament to legislate correct laws, which are fruitful for the people, is better than a thousand learning session, but there should be thousands of learning sessions so that the legislated law must have a root in the tradition of creation and legislation. The Parliament whose members are of illiterate deputies is better for the enemy than for the friends. So, learning classes should be taken more seriously, so seriously that fifty years later, when his son, **Aqa Mustafa**, was martyred he did not stop the classes.[403]

Impacts of Mudarris's Political Ideas on Ruhullah's Speech

The impacts of the political opinions of the martyr **Mudarris** on **Aqa Ruhullah** can easily be traced, particularly in his saying: ─"Oupolitics is our very religion, and our religion is our very politics." If the names are cared for in creation—which certainly are—martyr **Mudarris** [= teacher] was the first teacher who taught **Aqa Ruhullah** his deep lessons in politics and its inseparability from religion. Probably the first lesson he learnt from him turns back to the years when he was exercising penmanship. One of the sarcastic sentences ascribed to **Mudarris** was given by his teacher as a model with large letters at the head of the page: ─"They do not commit suicide for fear of death."[404] The content of this sentence which was circulated, in different expressions, on the tongues quoting **Mudarris**[405], and which had become a model of large letters to be copied by **Ruhullah**, must have, as a rule, placed the name of **Mudarris** in the central circle of his political imaginations and ideas, since on those days when **Ruhullah** was stepping into his ninth year of age, the government, in order to reform its pecuniary affairs, entrusted the post of its general treasury to **Morgan Shuster**, the President of the Pecuniary Board of America. But the Russians opposed it and sent a 48-hour ultimatum to the government of Iran. Some of the deputies seriously stood against the Russians. Some women entered the Parliament with firearms, threatening that if that disgrace was accepted they would kill their families and themselves. In this instance, **Mudarris** had said something like this: ―We do not commit suicide for fear of death. If we are to be annihilated, why should we do it by our own hands?" The Parliament, however, was dissolved, and the people hurried to the streets in a demonstration against the Russians. The Russians, as was common to them, dispatched fresh forces to Tabriz, Rasht and Mashhad to kill the people. At last a court martial government was formed, and the Russians brought their word home. [406]

68 years after the enactment of the ultimatum, when the Imam was in Neauphle-le-Château pulling the warp of the kingdom out of its woof, he renewed his attachment to **Mudarris**, and showed how much that sentence, which had been boldly and nicely written and used as a model for good penmanship, was placed deep in the lines of his political ideas: ―When Russia sent its ultimatum to Iran, concerning a question which I do not remember now, and their army was proceeding to such-and-such place, they brought the ultimatum to the Parliament... A sayyid, a turbaned man, a *mulla,* with trembling hands, came there and said that if we were to be annihilated, why should it be done by our own hands? No, we reject it. It was rejected, and they could do nothing about it. They were encouraged and voted against it. They did not accept their talk, and they did nothing." [407]

As a matter of fact, it was not that the Russians could do nothing. It was not precisely so. They conducted a massacre, dissolved the Parliament and brought their word home. [408] Maybe the same sarcastic, wise and meaningful sentence, which being ascribed to the loved person of **Mudarris** doubled its sweetness, caused the event to be pushed aside and to get pale such that the other victories of the people and the Parliament at other instances were mixed in his mind into a single one with the results of the ultimatum.

He always Respected and Esteemed Mudarris
Thus, **Mudarris** and official and non-official teachers of **Aqa Ruhullah** had always been respected by him, but not absolutely. Whenever a teacher stood

to leave, he, too used to stand up in respect. But if knowledge was slow in the teacher, the student would permit not even a moment's hesitation and would swiftly outrun him. Sometimes the thoughts of the student and the teacher faced each other, as it happened in the session No. 280, when **Mudarris** uttered words which he thought to have come out of the text of religion, but his understanding of religion in this respect was quite on the other side of the **Imam Khomeini**'s understanding during the blessed years of the consistency of the uprising. Then, there was no talk about whether women can be elected as representatives in the Parliament or not, nor was it about whether they can vote. In fact, in the bill of the Committee, among those who were not allowed to vote, the name of women was stated. **Mudarris** delivered a speech in which he agreed with that bill.

Ruhullah's Initial Opinions about Women

At the beginning of studying *fiqh*, **Aqa Ruhullah** could think about the kinds of impressions of the noble *ayahs* of the Glorious *Quran* and the belief of some *faqihs* concerning women's legal rights. But it took him forty years to become well versed in this subject and to be able to fish out of the depths of the seas of narratives and *ayahs* the religious precepts concerning women's rights in Islam. When in 1341 S.H. the question of the women elections was discussed, in his most exciting statement, under the title: ―The *ulama*[409] of Islam Will Have No Feast This Year", he said: ―The despotic regime is intending to ratify equality in men and women rights and exact it. That is it wants to tread upon the necessary precepts of Islam and the *Quran*, that is, the 18 years old girls are going to be summoned to military service and dragged to the barracks, that is, they will force the chaste Muslim girls into the centers of adultery."[410]

One thing was quite clear, ie, the mooting of the election of women in Iran was initiated at first by an open anti-religious movement, and the imposed renewal had come to interpret the concept of civilization as was agreeable to the westernized, not that civilization had by itself changed its opinion, creating a modernism to comply with the religious concepts. So, some of his students, with the help of some persons who were sensitive to the time's social affairs, and inspired by him, wrote the book *Women and Elections*[411], under the suffocating publishing conditions, and they did get the regime's full punishment. Now as all the writers of that book have, to some extent, carried out their duty against the extreme westernization of the government's employees, feel pleased. But if a publisher suggested reprinting it, they would certainly take him to be the enemy of their scholarly dignity.

Women's Rights in Latest Opinions

Despite the fact it took some forty years for **Aqa Ruhullah**'s *Fiqhi* opinions concerning the multilateral participation of women in their own political destiny to stand right against the opinions and ideas of the martyr **Mudarris** and many of his own notable teachers, to the extent of saying: —Women, in the Islamic system, have the same rights as men have—the rights to education, to work, to possession, to voting and to be candidate"[412], yet, during his studies in non-political matters, personally, he completely recognized the admitted rights of women. Although the above words were his *Fiqhi* judgement in this respect, he had even gone further than that. In another instance he was inspired by another statement and played another tune: —Women are the leaders of our uprising, and we are their sequel. I accept you as leaders and I am at your service. May **Allah** preserve you for Islam."[413]

Perhaps the woman had no such high position in **Aqa Ruhullah**'s heart, mind and thought during his early days in Qum, because some *ulama* took her to be —daifah".

He was, then, a young man and had climbed only a few steps of the ladder of knowledge, and his picture of woman was that of a wonderful existence of affection. She is as if her clay has been kneaded with kindness and love. In fact, Mother's practical affection, the aunt's courage and perseverance, **Naneh Khawar**'s merits and multi-knowledge, the knowledge and method of **Iftikharul ulama**'s mother in teaching him, as a child, astronomy, astrology and arithmetic, as well as the names and biographies of some great women, all put hand in hand to convince him not to believe in the women being a —daifah". In this connection we shall once again sit at the stream of his thoughts and will search for the source of that *fiqhi* judgement, and this candid praise, so as to know how Iran's men were indebted for the victory of their Revolution to the women of their time.

He Had Come to Learn Fiqh, Not Politics

It must not be forgotten that he had not come to learn politics. He had come to complete his lessons in *fiqh*. Later on he become certain that politics and religion were inseparable. He had to find a room (to live in). He had found a room in Darush-Shifa school before being attracted by **Mudarris** to frequently visit Tehran. The room was so small that its area was equal to the area of his house in Khomein divided by all the days of the year. However, he had to stay in it, but for how long? Till his marriage. Worse than that, they believed that a room was too much for one man. Mostly four students lived in a room, and some times, six. From then on he had many remarks. He was a young man who had, from childhood, been brought up ethically, so, he had but to sit politely and to have his food plate alone. If others liked to wash a single large plate, they must be convinced, not in an impolite way that the trouble of washing some more plates was preferred to washing a single one. From his early adolescence he had experienced the nicety of nocturnal ascending in nightly invocations, and he regarded abandoning it a kind of deprivation which turned life void of blessings. So, in the middle of the night he had to so slowly get out of bed that if somebody liked to sleep more he might not be awakened. The ration and allowance of a theology student did not exceed 50 rials. He must put up with it. A part of it went to the bathroom keeper and his attendant. The rest remained for food, clothes, books and notebooks. His heritage from his father was not little, so, he could take no monthly allowance, and spend the incomes of his estates to eat well and to wear better and to buy nicer perfumes, following the tradition of **the Prophet (s)**. Even if his room-mates became his permanent guests, he would not be short of money. A generous one is he who, in cases of abundance, shares his money with the others, as did his father and grandfather. So, the room-mates were pleased because he was their room-mate. Yet, tens of other moral instructions paraded in his mind, and a difficult result came out: To put up with the alloted monthly allowance, like all other students. [414]

Adib Tehrani, Teacher of al-Mutawwal

After arranging the question of the room, he anxiously turned to studying.

Mirza Muhammad 'Ali Adib Tehrani, a man of literature, was teaching *al-Mutawwal*, a book on rhetoric. He became his first teacher in Qum.

The Second Teacher Who Prayed for Rain

The first level of learnings he had finished in Khomein and Arak. Now, for the completion of methods, he was attending the lessons of a man whose holy complexion was stamped in the minds, **Ayatullah Sayyid Muhammad Taqi Khansari**. He was the man who put an end to the drought during the Second World War, which had brought the people to their wit's end, by a *salat* of rain.

Ayatullah Yathribi Kashani, the Third Teacher

The lessons of the primary level were completed with **Ayatullah Sayyid Ali Yathribi**. He is now 25 years old, and from then on he could attend the lesson of **Ayatullah Hairi Yazdi** and start the higer stage of *fiqh*.

Fervency for Learning Fiqh

So far, as from his childhood, the conditions were such that his talents found ways to show up. But when he attended the lessons of **Ayatullah Hairi** the situation was different. Certainly a big event must have happened. Perhaps getting a small room, fighting against poverty, long nocturnal prayers, insufficient sleep, curbing sexual desire, enduring lacking family life and being away from his own town or being worried about the dark fate of the people, which showed its teeth on the last day of **Rida Khan**'s coup d'état, each of which can sometimes kill one's talent, and, on the other side, each one of them can be a factor for the dorment talents to raise their heads. Maybe all these or other things, hidden from us, put hand in hand to bring up his hidden talents in such a way that if it was said that in learning he was an amazing man, less was said. He was talking and arguing in a way that the word genius was insufficient to describe his talent to take in *fiqh*. Was he inspired by the *ghayb*? If one was not afraid of saying that a real man had become a legend and could not but be praised, would the answer be —Yes"? But now the answer is —Yes", with the explanation that whoever washes himself likewise in the wine fountain of sincerity as he did, his heart will be lusterous and becomes the mirror of the truth.

Shahabadi, Shams Tabriz of Ruhullah

When we look back at those years our eyes fall upon a tall lean man who walks like all other men, eats like them, kisses his children, at some dawns goes to the bath so as to perform the *salat* purified. But should we be able to call upon his heart, there we would see a turbulent ocean which discerns multitude and hears the famous tune of unity out of the lips of the multitude. He blends with unity and from his roaring waves he hears the call of *ana'l-haqq*' (I am the truth) (as said by **al-Hallaj**), but he is not immature to expose the secrets and, like **al-Hallaj**, ascend the gallows. In him gnosticism is so far from Sufism that he knows that a common life among the people, without letting the aliens know who he is, is the most correct way of living. All know him to be a great and honourable man. But not all of them know how far greatness extends in him. He himself chooses his students. Now it is the years in which **Ruhullah** learns higher *fiqh* at the class of **Ayatullah al-**

Hairi. Yet, before the teacher teaches, he himself learns, because that tall man whose sacred name was **Muhammad Ali,** but as he bought a house in Tehran's Shahabad quarter[415], he was surnamed: **Shahabadi**, has chosen himself to teach theoretical gnosticism to this lovesick young man.

First Lesson in Gnosticism

In the first gnostic lesson he primarily learnt: —Get out of yourself. When you are there, there will be no vacant space in your heart. But if you take you out of yourself, the light of wisdom will sit where you had engaged." **Ruhullah**, in this first lesson, was practising to take _his self‛ out of himself.

For six years he used to visit him, sometimes every day and sometimes once a week, to be acquainted with the theoretical gnosticism and swim in the practical gnosticism. Theological gnosticism taught him that in every thing he sees, he sees **Allah**, not His manifestations, as this is usual for everybody who looks at anything. In the practical gnosticism he was learning a way which took the disciple [*salik*], through the Shari‛ah, to the streams of knowledge.

Covering Several Years‛ Distance in Few Months

Now **Ayatullah Hairi** realizes that this young man is covering several years‛ way in few months, such that after a few years **Ruhullah** got the licence of *ijtihad* and himself became one of the best teachers of high subjects. But politeness required that as long as the teacher was able to sit on the teaching chair, he must not be impatient, and regard sitting at the teacher‛s chair a duty, being a condition of politeness as well as a practice of modesty. More important than that, however, was being a permanent attendant at the class of the founder of the new *hawzah* as blowing the scent of hope in the heart of that old man. The *hawzah*, in order to be firmly established under those difficult conditions, needed even that amount of support. To him, how quickly it passed! And how quickly did the teacher close his eyes! The fifteenth year of his moving to Qum had not come to an end when in a cold dawn his body became cold and lifeless. [416] On the tenth of Bahman, 1315 L.H., the people were informed that the old man of Qum had closed his eyes forever. Countless people came from everywhere. His body was taken round the shrine of **Masumah (*a*)** and was buried there.

Ruhullah in the Eyes of Ayatullah Hairi

In the second year of attending the class of **Ayatullah Hairi**, the teacher‛s look was not equitably distributed among the students, as the larger share

305

was given to the more eager one. So, he tried to sit where the teacher could not easily give him a larger share. This procedure required three delicacies: first, to sit where the lazy students would not sit; second, not to disregard the elders' respect by sitting in prominent places; third, not to get the habit of always sitting in the same place. So, during the first year he continually changed his place. But during the last years of the teacher's life he used to sit beside him, as if the teacher felt calmness from the sitting of his own hand-educated man next to him.

Philosophy at the Presence of Najafi Isfahani
In his second year of studying high *fiqh*, he encountered a man who was acquainted with western philosophy. How and to what extent? There are no enough signs of those discussions to make judgement easy. The name of that philosopher was **Haj Shaykh Muhammad Rida Najafi Isfahani** who, due to the migration of **Aqa Nurullah Isfahani**, had moved to Qum and started giving lessons on Darwinism and criticizing it, because it was based on irreligiosity. By presenting such kind of discussion it can be said that the *hawzah* in Qum had taken a step forward on the direction of getting more acquainted with the scientific world outside itself, but as to how much those discussions could inform the students about the essence of western philosophy, is obscure, because very few knew languages other than the Arabic and the Turkish. So, only the amount of the western philosophy which had been translated into Farsi, Arabic and Turkish could be the basis of any information.

Referring to the papers of those days and the translated books, it can be said that, it was the same amount which the West was acquainted with the spirit of the Islamic philosophy[417], though our *ulama* knew less about the philosophy of the West. The style of the writings of the Islamic philosophers especially that of the philosophers of Iran within the last three centuries, was such that reading philosophy without the help of a teacher was useless, and sometimes harmful. But the style of writing the philosophic books of the West did not need any teacher, but it needed considerable time so as to uncover the spirit of the new philosophy from among hundreds of novels and plays. Our philosophers did not allow spending so much time. But some genius men, like **Allamah Tabatabai**, who was a deep-thinking philosopher, like **Covier**, the French biologist who could draw the sketch of any animal on the basis of a piece of its bone, he, too, could, from a few expressions of the Western philosophers put the foundation for the construction of their thoughts, and, surprisingly, he was proportionally successful.

Acquaintance with Western Philosophy

At any rate, without consulting his teacher of *fiqh*, **Ayatullah Hairi**, prompted by his eagerness to understand western philosophy, **Ruhullah** sat humbly before **Aqa Najafi Isfahani**. Perhaps this lesson of an incomplete ultra-program was a spark which made him realize that to know at least one western language was necessary. He chose the French language which was in those days more international, but he was not successful in this respect.[418] Later he learnt a little English at the level of a secondary school. Nevertheless, in that language he had not much progress. When the discussions concerning Darwin's theory of evolution, which confused the minds of many academians, were brought up, it undoubtedly engaged **Ruhullah**'s mind considerably. But it seems quite difficult to trace in such a look to the living nature in the thought of **Aqa Ruhullah** whether he is for or against that, because if he generally agreed with it, he could not reveal it, since this was originally brought up to be denied. The time in which **Ruhullah** was living was engaged in more serious questions. So, to show up one's support of such a theory could have no result but to be beaten by the stick of disbelief, and if he disagreed with it, then his disagreement had a style and a context behind the hot discussions of the day.[419]

The Theory of the Evolution of the Species

In the enlightened circles of that time in Iran the door of the theory of the evolution of the species remained wide open for many decades, and it entangled in that tumult raising argument anyone entered the university. The Marxists, who were its firm supporters, described the religious people, who looked differently at the creation of man, as to be reactionarists, as they took Darwin's theory to be scientific, and to oppose any scientific theory, for any reason, was a proof of reactionism and superstition. The students, before entering the university, used to take lessons on _Geology and Evolution', which was a basic subject of the faculty of natural sciences. In that subject, by studying the theories of Lamark, Darwin and the scientists who came after them, and by getting information about the genes and heredity, the way was paved for accepting the theory of the Evolution of the Species. The student was bewilderedly standing at a cross-road of either accepting the science or remaining loyal to his traditional religious beliefs. It was as if the thin thinking stones of the young student in the fourth class of the secondary school were crushed under those two millstones.

Science and Religion Face to Face

For many decades this subject, and in different branches other lessons were, quietly and creepingly, placing religion face to face with science. Most of the religious propagandists were unaware of this encounter whose result was mostly alienation and even hidden opposition to religion. Some others, who recognized the problem, dragged it to the philosophic field, because they were ignorant of its scientific bases. **Aqa Najafi Isfahani**, who had invited **Aqa Ruhullah** to his class, was among the clear-sighted ones. But some of the enlightened *ulama* gave priority to the union between politics and religion and to face the system of the political rule over facing the system of the political rule over facing the system of cultural rule. Those two groups had sometimes hidden argument. One of **Aqa Ruhullah**'s particularities, after being well acquainted with philosophy, astrology, astronomy, mathematics and politics, was that he was getting his full place in both these two visions at the same time. After the appearance of **Aqa Ruhullah** in the hot arena of politics, some political parties and individuals were not quite in compliance with his ideas. So, they were insulted by some of his political students, unknowing that those who, in the field of encounter between religion and science, found ways of unity between the two for the irreligious educated young generation, were on the same mental battleground with him. Among these individuals was the engineer **Mehdi Bazargan** of *Nihdat-e Azadi* party, who, after the victory of the Revolution, was entrusted by **the Imam (a)** with the premiership of the temporary government, who, after the occupation of the American Embassy in Tehran, resigned. **Imam (a)** respectfully accepted his resignation, as he tried to move and to manage the country within the conventional frames. But some students, who were called _The Students Following the Line of the Imam', realized that the American Embassy had passed over the limits of an Embassy, and had become a center for overthrowing the newly established Islamic Regime. So, they named it as —the nest of espionage" and occupied it. This caused the engineer **Bazargan** to present his political theories in a different form and to start opposing some revolutionary methods. He used to say: —Imam is a bulldozer and I am Volkswagon". Nevertheless, during the onslaught against religion, he had many fights, situated under the shadow of **the Imam (a)** and used to praise him. He, having got his highest level at his specialty course, had a message for the new generation. He could answer a part of the scientific questions of a generation who wanted to settle its duty towards religion. Probably today his answers, which came out of his pen to any question, are once again questionable, but at his time they were approvable and fruitful fightings.

The Book *Creation of Man*
A friend of him, named: **Dr. Yadullah Sahabi**, had a geology doctorate and wrote a book titled: *Khilqat-e Insan* [Creation of Man] in which he treated the theory of the Evolution of Species through a new look at the noble *ayahs* of the *Quran*. By the encouragement and protection of Engineer **Bazargan** he published his book. Fortunately, without much ado against him, his researches were studied and criticized by **Allamah Tabatabai**, and from among those researches tens of viewpoints boiled in the boiler of thought, and the theory of the Evolution of Species, which caused so much disturbance in the minds, was resolved in the university sanctuary in a most delicate way. Of course, not to mean that all men of religion became supporters of the said theory such that to take man to be a hairless monkey, but to mean that religious faith requires neither to confirm nor to deny the theory of the Evolution of Species. Every expert in any scientific branch may by himself reflect upon the *Quranic ayahs* and believe in whatever he understands, under two conditions: being specialized in the relevant branch, and having knowledge of the *Quran*.

When the book *Creation of Man* was published[420], his Excellency **Ruhullah** was living in his exile, in Iraq. When he saw it he read it carefully, but did not comment on it. One of his close friends, **Ayatullah Mishkini**, after the publication of the book, commenced a discussion on evolution in Islam. He chose Friday so as to provide a chance for the students to attend it in Qum. As **Ayatullah Mishkini** was a student of **the Imam (*a*)**, one can infer that **Aqa** was pleased with rediscussing the question of evolution from Islam's point of view in the *hawzah* and the university, and he did not regard it a deviation from the course of the struggle already started.

Leap in the Evolution of Species
When **Aqa Najafi** was informing **Aqa Ruhullah** about the philosophy of the West by means of refuting **Darwin**'s theory, probably discussing the leap in the Evolution of Species had not yet seriously been started in the science of biology. But later he very much wrestled with this concept. He knew that evolution in civilization was gradual, but revolution was a leap, like the leaping effects of the revelation. Darwin's theory was more a stand of a world looking than a biological view, and got more a philosophical nature. The Marxists paid more attention to this theory than others, connecting everything in a way to the Hegelian dialectic. Yet, if they could claim that the rise of **Moses (*a*)** against **Pharaoh**, and the flowing of **Jesus**' soul (*a*) in

309

the rough body of the worldly ancient Rome and Greece, on the basis of evolution, were products of dialecticism, they would have been helpless in justifying the inspired revolution of **Muhammad (a)** in the dry, burning uncivilized Arabia, laying the foundation of a great and worldwide civilization. Thus, the theory of a leap in the Evolution of Species was just a pretext for them. Such type of discussions, before and after the victory of the Islamic Revolution, got once again a hot market, but this time they were many times deeper in political color than fifty years earlier, and their life was many times shorter than fifty years before. Surprising is the fate of some theories, from experiment and witnessing nature, till becoming the theory of a scientific finding, entering the arena of philosophy and rising out of politics! Was the necessity and the attraction of such a discussion, which **Darwin** was its pretext, and by raising which the sperms of tens of other philosophic questions were clotting, the reason for **Aqa Ruhullah** to turn to the Islamic philosophy?

With Another Teacher of Philosophy He Learnt Mathematics and Astronomy

We still do not know which one of his teachers of philosophy—the second being **Haj Sayyid Abul Hasan Rafii Qazvini**—was the first and which was the last. But we do know **Qazvini** had taught him three subjects: mathematics, astronomy and philosophy[421], whereas **Aqa Ruhullah** himself thought him discipline many years later.

Aqa Qazvini used to visit Tehran during summer seasons. In the year during which he used to perform the *maghrib* and the *isha salats* in the Masjid-e Jumah in Tehran, he used to come to the *masjid* any time he liked. Perhaps when he was solving an equation he did not remember that the people were waiting. One night, like many other nights, some time passed after the *maghrib*, and he did not show up. **Aqa Ruhullah**, in a summer when he went to the masjid, he, too, saw that his former teacher had forgotten that the time of the people in the bazar is not of little value. He stood up and, addressing the people, said: —W must together tell him to be punctual in coming. This disregard of coming in time wastes the time of many people." When the **Aqa** came and performed the *salat*, somebody came and sat before him and told him what had happened. The **Aqa** asked: —Who was that man?" The pointing finger pointed to **Aqa Ruhullah**. Those standing near him heard him say: —Heis **Haj Aqa Ruhullah,** a man of merits, upright, pious, regular and polite. He is right. If one day I came late, perform your *salat* after him." It seems, however, he observed punctuality afterwards, because **Haj Aqa Ruhullah** never stood in that *masjid* as a leader of the *salat.*[422]

The Complicated World of the Nature of Line and Figure
The late **Rafii Qazvini** was a man of taste. He felt no shame of reading the latest information about philosophy, astronomy, astrology and mathematics, and he did not think the time spent on that as wasted. If somebody claimed to know philosophy, but no mathematics, one can guess how much his philosophy is mixed with illusions, and if he knows no merits, upright, pious, regular and polite. He is right. If one day I came late, perform your *salat* after him." It seems, however, he observed punctuality afterwards, because **Haj Aqa Ruhullah** never stood in that *masjid* as a leader of the *salat.* [422]

The Complicated World of the Nature of Line and Figure
The late **Rafii Qazvini** was a man of taste. He felt no shame of reading the latest information about philosophy, astronomy, astrology and mathematics, and he did not think the time spent on that as wasted. If somebody claimed to know philosophy, but no mathematics, one can guess how much his philosophy is mixed with illusions, and if he knows no astronomy, it shows how much he sentimentally knows about the extension of existence and existing, i.e. the most original topic of the Islamic philosophy. The late **Qazvini** learnt the three of them together. But as to the mathematics of the *hawzah*, it was very much far away from what we nowadays learn of mathematics. The original four operations, finding the square and the cubic roots, and some geometry, were the primary lessons. Then, all at once, and without knowing enough about algebra there appeared the complicated world of the nature of Line and Figure. Naturally, to know little mathematics, then to claim knowing it well, is an invalid claim. Of course, there were individuals who had some knowledge of strange sciences, such as arithmomancy and the properties of the alphabet, whose root was in arithmatics. **Aqa Ruhullah,** like a fish out of water, was restlessly anxious to learn these sciences, especially mathematics, and, with all difficulties he could take in, up to the limit which the teacher said that he knew no more. Of course, that much of mathematics with the same teaching method, could make the one, who had patience capable enough, if provided with sufficient respite to calculate, with the help of astronomy, the solar and lunar eclipses. Strange enough that the astronomy studied by the students of that time was the same Ptolemaic system, and by that very old and refused science the

eclipses of the moon and the sun, and the correspondence of the lunar months to the solar months, they could calculate, and mostly correctly.

Ptolemaic System

The Ptolemaic system believed that the earth was the center of the universe. But in those years in which **Aqa Ruhullah** started studying astronomy, suddenly and without much ado, this subject wore new dresses. That which the Western scientists used to discuss under the name of new discussions about astrology, wrote and published, found its way into the scientific *hawzah*s. **Aqa Ruhullah** had studied the Ptolemaic system as a history of astronomy, but that which he learnt of astrology was the new discourses.[423] Undoubtedly, he, like other young men, in studying astronomy, which was mixed with astrology, remained sleepless for many nights, especially if the teacher had reached the information that: The expansion of the material existence extends to infinity. What we know about it is like a drop of an ocean, and that very drop, which is a sea, is an unseen world. The sky which we see at night and which we do not know well, includes milliards of galaxies, one of which is the Milky Way. This galaxy is neither the biggest nor the smallest one in existence. To imagine its smallness it is sufficient to know that in the Greek mythology it is said: —When Heraclius's mother was suckling her child, some milk of her breast sprinkled out into the sky, and there was the Milky Way." To imagine its bigness it is enough to know that if someone gets on board of a spaceship whose speed is 300000 kms per minute, then a life of 100000 years is required to cover the diameter of this galaxy. Such being the case, in this spacious sky, if we know it all, we will only know a single sky. Are we the most honourable creatures of existence? Knowing astrology takes man out of his country which, at times, he thinks that there is nothing larger in the world. At times it causes him to be disappointed of himself. At times he is united with it and feels big. These depend on the stage of knowledge the man is in. Some students, when get to know about galaxies tremble and feel themselves in significant and trivial compared with the sky so high, wide, full of stars, clamorous and great. Those who are more delicate, their inclination to talkativeness and gluttony and pleasure declines. To some others, however, these are but a pack of information which must be learnt to get good marks. Knowing astrology is a good example to realize that science, to some people, is a handful of formula which if they learnt or not would affect their position, but not their talk and behaviour. As the *Quran* says, they are: —...like the ass carrying books..."[424] Others are changed by any scientific finding. Sometimes it puts their inside aflame, and sometimes pours water of tranquility and assuredness on the flames of their fire. Knowing astrology, not for getting good marks, but for getting good knowledge of the greatness of creation and the infinite expanse of existence, is a great lesson for knowing **Allah**. Perhaps this is why the Glorious *Quran* swears by the places of the stars and says: —..and it is a very great oath if you only knew." [425]

The Seven Earths and Skies

Providence ordained that **Aqa Ruhullah,** mounted on the wings of astrology, should travel to some galaxies, and get some knowledge about the secrets of the earth's sky, inside which the earth is lost. This little knowledge became an opening through which witnessing the endless truth of existence, in his long journeys into the depths of the galaxies of the *ayahs* of the stars, become deeper. Now he better understands why he recites in the *qunut* [426]: —Glry be to Allah, the Lord of the seven skies and the Lord of the seven earths." Undoubtedly, this invocation clearly states that the earths are also seven in number. But what is the earth? Is it the terrestrial globe which is countless? Those who knew nothing of astrology thought it to mean that the crust of the earth was of seven strata. But those who knew about astrology knew that it meant other earths, and that **Allah** was too great to have only one earth.

After the repetition of the word _Sky' 297 times, and the word _earth' 440 times, in the *Quran*, is it sufficient to know that the earth and the sky of the visible world, which is infinitive, are all that intended by the *ayah*s of **Allah**? Or in the valley of the invisible, where there are other earths and skies, the world is different. Paradise is described to be —a wide as the heavens and the earth." The minds which are accustomed to believe after the disclose of facts, cannot understand these. The new astrology is not yet so advanced to be able to count the number of the earths of the visible sky. But it is worthy, as a clear *ayah* of **Allah** to guide the mind to deeper *ayah*s.

The Wonders of the Skies in Nocturnal Ascensions

Some people like to kiss the hand of their leader. Others love to kiss his forehead. The love of others goes beyond that, they look for his will. Some fly from the summit of love to be lost in the sky of his thoughts. Others impatiently want to penetrate into his ocean-like heart to find out what was there. But alas! Except by mounting the horse of imagination and comparison one cannot find a way into his heart. Even if imagination and comparison came to our assistance, we can only guess that when he was getting acquainted with astronomy, astrology, mathematics and philosophy, how

313

difficult for him his return to *fiqh* was! At his later years, when he was asked:
—Wich branch do you like best?" —*Fiqh*", he said. It is difficult to believe
that one goes to ascension of the *salat*, looks for the God who is the Creator
of the galaxies, and glorifies the Diety who has countless skies (Perhaps he
had attained to the concept that our sun is but a tiny atom in a big molecule
for a bigger sky, and that the fable of —The Milky Way" or something like
that, was the figurative tongue of the truth, and man is to worship that God,
not a God who is a little bigger than Khomein, Qum, Iran, Asia, the globe,
the sun, the sky of the nights of the deserts of Yazd and the known galaxies),
and after finishing the *salat*–which is a clamorous trip–some one may ask:
—Can afasting person brush his teeth?" and he, without frowning or critcizing
the asker, replies: —flthe wetness of the brush does not slip into his throat, it
is allowed," and again he stands for another clamorous trip!

Man's Smallness in Face of the Sky's Greatness

When the torch of religion is out, stars, which are millions of times brighter
than the sun, humiliate man, especially the one who sees himself bigger, will
be more humiliated. Even its image makes one tremble by humiliation.
Alexander thought that the east and west of the world were under his feet. If
an intelligent person could tell him what his address was in the world of
creation, he would have been attacked by the fever of shame. Was his
address anything other than: One of the visible worlds, the 1st sky, the galaxy
of the Milky Way, the Solar System, the 3rd Planet, a part of land on the
earth, among thousands of tents and cottages?

How much the knowables of astrology are necessary for the monotheists!
Why some *hadith*s quoted from the Imams of guidance (*a*) prohibit
astrology? Isn't it that **Allah** is great, too great to be described? *Allahu Akbar*
[**Allah** is Greater]. But **Allah**'s greatness to the one who takes the earth to be
the biggest existing creature, how small it will be! **Aqa Ruhullah** had
realized that the prohibited astrology is not these lessons. Servitude had been
so much strengthened in him that he would approach no desire disapproved
by the *shar*. So, what did those *hadith*s point to? They point to the fact that if
we believe that the stars have effects on man's fate, and instead of knowing
their states and discovering the reciprocal effects of anything in anything we
are led to fortune-telling, in that case we would be destroying science and
will. On the other hand, he knew that **Allah**, in a kindest expression in the
Glorious *Quran*, asks man: —Dahey not consider how camels are created?
(biology). Nor how the sky has been lifted up? (astrology). Nor how the

mountains have been erected? (orology). Nor how the earth has been expanded flat? (geology).[427]

Although astrology and astronomy widen man's world look, yet, before that, they humiliate him. Biology, on the contrary, by announcing that it is only man who stands on the summit of evolution, and the distance between him and the most evolved living creature which we know is several million years, causes man to be proud. With a biologist look, countless atoms are needed (much more than the stars of a galaxy) to come together, and through their complicated combinations, in order to put into motion a single cell, and billions of cells—each of which is in itself a wonderful world—must collect together so that man may stand erect, and what a wonderful creature he is! Even in a single millimeter of his red blood there are four million globules carrying air. The stars are the contrary. It is said: —All men in all lands and in all eras lived, and are living, on a globe which is lost in the Milky Way galaxy, and its sun is no bigger than a particle of dust, and this galaxy, in the limitless space, is no bigger than an atom. The Glorious *Quran* goes even farther to say that this sky, which we see only a part of it by means of the strongest telescopes, is only one sky of the seven skies, and if seven implies multiplicity, it means countless skies.

Astrology as a Fire on the Heap of Proud Thoughts

By learning astrology, the following sarcastic lines are the elegy of man's humiliation:

> The world, beside these nine blue ceilings,
> > Is like a poppy on the surface of the sea.
> See how much you are of that poppy;
> > It is deserving then if you mock at yourself.

Aqa Ruhullah liked this poetry. He once recited it in the class of ethics in such a way that those who knew it by heart were as if they were hearing such a wise saying for the first time, because the tune of the poetry of gnostics cures the soul which becomes sick by the fuss of praisings and loses itself. The awe of astrology and the new astronomy is a fire on the heap of man's proud thoughts. But the monotheists would not be humiliated in the astrology class, because the Diety who is closer to man than his jugular[428] vein, hears his voice, sees him clearly and is aware of the secrets of his heart. In this science He becomes greater than that which can be imagined, and, together with the greatness of the worshipped, the worshipper becomes

315

elevated. Psychologists say that the forsakers of the world and the ascetics are prouder, in a complicated way, than the others, and that is because their world is quite small, and they see themselves big in that small world. The old psychology, which was, in a way, ahead of the new psychology, redressed this theory by saying that if asceticism is the product of inabilities and unknowings, it gets proud, since negligence and pride are identical in meaning. But if asceticism rises from knowledge, humbleness affects one's soul not only towards other men, but towards the whole existence. That which is more deserving to be said is that acquaintance with astrology humiliates the mind of the materialist, though materialistic outlook is itself a step of knowledge, but it is regrettable if man is marking time on that step.

Where is the Center of Existence?

Aqa Ruhullah, with two other kinds of knowledge followed up studying astrology and astronomy as is required by the quest of the truth. One was in philosophy and the other in gnosticism. In philosophy he found the answers of his questions—the questions which inevitably occur to every young man who is not engaged in daily life—by spending years in learning, searching, thinking and exerting efforts. Within the multitude of what has been created, and everyday **Allah** has a new creation, how much do I (in kind) amount? Where in the existence do I stand? If I (in kind) am not the center of existence, where is its center?[429] The earth, which is lost in the space, how much does it deserve that **Ibrahim (a)**, who had his root from the earth, should rise from it and become the friend of **Allah**, and **Moses (a)**, out of all creatures, should be the interlocutor of **Allah**, and **Allah** Himself should call **Jesus (a)** His own spirit, and **Muhammad (s)**, this wonder of creation, should be called the beloved of **Allah**? Inspired by a narrative, a poet, quoting **Allah** addressing the honourable **Prophet (s)**, said: —Had it not been for you, I would not have created the Heavens."[430] Now, where in philosophy can one find the answers to these questions? I think one can find the first simplest answers in the deductive discussion about the unity of the intelligent, intelligible and intelligence, but to believe them by heart one must use effort.

The Unity of the Intelligent and the Intelligible

The argument of the unity of the intelligent and the intelligible has long been conducted. The first time, a philosopher by the name **Porphyrius**, three centuries after the birth of **Jesus (a)**, tabled it. The Islamic philosophers fattened it. In fact, **Avicenna**, a genius as he was, could not understand a section of it, concerning acquired knowledge, and he denied it. But **Farabi**, **Mulla Sadra** and **Mulla Hadi Sabzawari** could quite deductively prove it. **Aqa Ruhullah** accepted their deduction. The title of this philosophic topic is that the one who thinks and that which is thought are one. In the intuitive knowledge it is easy to believe it, but in the acquired knowledge much difficult.[431] An example of the acquired knowledge is that when one thinks of himself as to how he should construct himself, or when he praises himself, or when he sits aside cursing his envy, anger and hatred, is the one who is to construct himself, and the one to be constructed, two beings or a single one? And the one who praises or curses himself, and the one who is praised or cursed, are they two or one? Believing that when the object of (the thought of) a man is something in himself, both are one, is easy. But believing that when we think about the galaxies, or about existence, that which is thought about and one who thinks, both are one is not so easy to be, by a simple deduction, acceptable to the mind and endorsed by the heart. But **Ruhullah** was quick in accepting the unity of the intelligent, the intelligible and the intelligence, and in that he found the answers to many of his philosophical questions. Actually, it took him years to tie the deductional thinking of this thought to the gnostic intuition of —presence" and to make both identical. By lowest understanding of the intuition of presence one may say that time and place are accidental in respect of existence, and ignorance is a fetter on thought's feet. If we break down these three we will be everywhere in existence. This line of his poetry indicates this concept:

Open this cage, tear this snare off the feet,

With flapping wings, ripping the curtains away to the beloved's abode.

A line from **Mawlana** is a simple expression of the other side of the meaning that a man's soul is the amount of his knowledge. The more one's knowledge concerning existence, the more the expanse of one's existence, or, in other words, the amount of the intelligibles of an intelligent represent his existential vastness.

The soul is nothing but knowledge when examined,

Whoever has wider knowledge has a wider soul.

Did he learn only this in the philosophy class, or more? When he learnt he knew what he was learning, and when he taught, he knew what he was teaching, but when he was neither learning nor teaching, but in his loneliness he used to be in seclusion with himself, it was difficult to follow up his philosophic knowledge, because the mixture of *fiqh*, *Usul*, gnosticism, philosophy, politics and ethics is such that his talk was a compound of all of them.

317

Fati, as She Says, Is a Clear-Sighted One

His daughter-in-law, **Fatimah**, the wife of **Haj Ahmad Aqa** [his son] had become, like his own daughters, his beloved. She did not lose the chance to pick flowers from the garden of poetry, gnosticism and thoughts of her father-in-law. This woman, who knew the merits of her father-in-law very well, was studying philosophy. Naturally, what she was looking for in philosophy was that which was blacking most of the books. The **Aqa** in order not to hurt the philosophers, addressing his daughter-in-law, recited:

> **Fati**, as she says, is a clear-sighted one,
>> Philosophy needs much more effort.

> Let her come to herself and wake up,
>> And know that the torch of her disposition is endangered.

The Greater Veil

He who studies philosophy becomes, more or less, proud, and thinks that he can answer any question as best as possible. Philosophy sometimes causes one to be needless of strict sciences, not actually, of course, but as a feeling. When the philosophic spirit of the middle ages mixed with Christianity, it got the color of theology, and the strict sciences were, for centuries, devalued. But if one reads the philosophy deeper, he will become humble towards the other sciences. His following couplet may be an evidence of this, of course with the reservation that by —dter sciences" he may not only mean gnosticism:

> **Fati**, who is proud of philosophy,
>> Openly attacks other sciences.

> I am afraid that, in this greater veil,
>> She may be heedless and lose her existence.

Those who attended his class of philosophy must have noted that he, like **Socrates** the Wise, knotted the earth to the sky and described the existing as if he was describing the existence. But this line of poetry—which was said late in his years, not as poetry, since it lacks poetic delicacy, but as rhyme—addressing **Fatimah**, warns all those who agree with her on the talent of philosophic knowledge:

Fati who studies the arts of philosophy,
Knows of it -ph", —¹l and -s".

My hope is that, by the light of **Allah**,
She may deliver herself from the veil of philosophy.

Strange is this line of poetry, because he, too, late in his years, repeats the same words which, during the early years of teaching philosophy, others used to say! What does this mean? Somewhere in respect of the fate of philosophy and the philosophers of the *hawzah*, not as a blame, but as a description, he said: —The state of philosophy was not like that of today. **Aqa Shahabadi** (may Allah have mercy upon him) used to say: _The late **Aqa Mirza Ali Akbar Yazdi** was one of the great philosophers, a scholar, a truthful and a pious man. When he died someone, by way of praising him on the *minbar*, said: _I myself saw him recite the *Quran*.'[432] He himself had a similar difficulty. In the days when he was teaching the *Asfar* of **Mulla Sadra**, the narrow-minded, allusively, broke the jug from which his son had drunk water! Nevertheless, despite this ugly play, he continued to deliver his lessons, scrutinizingly, to his select students. So, what does this contradiction mean? Does it mean asking forgiveness and repenting getting close to this knowledge?[433]

In a way, it is nothing but this–a usual repenting and asking forgiveness, a forgiveness which is demanded even from the prophets. In the last *surah* revealed to **the Prophet (s)** there is a good tiding, and then a command to ask forgiveness! Repentance is essential in asking forgiveness, but asking forgiveness (by the Prophet) for what? Strange enough is that in this *surah* man is ordered to ask forgiveness, and **Allah** is Oft-Returning![434]

Not All Knowledge Is in Philosophy

There come indications to our help to show us that his advice to **Fatimah** (s) to deliver themselves from the veil of philosophy does not mean neglecting philosophy. Perhaps we are guided to notice that we have seen philosophers who, with the philosophic reason, had rationalized the existence. Hence, according to the rule of the unity of the intelligent and the intelligible, existence is their very entity, but they are bigger than the existence, because existence is their intelligible, and they, in addition to the intelligible, are intelligent, too! And this, without logically negating the unity of the

319

intelligent and the intelligible, causes the mind to be arrogant. Is not it the greater veil to see oneself so big to this extent?

Aqa Ruhullah, who did not only philosophically understand the unity of intelligent and the intelligible, but also through theoretical gnosticism, and believed in it, he regarded not only himself, but the whole visible world, not just an atom, but naught, in respect of the greatness of **Allah**. Strangely, in understanding these concepts he dragged science to the field of gnosticism. In other words, he made science gnostic, and still in other words, when he says: —Openly attacks other sciences", he does not separate _other sciences' from gnosticism. He, who apparently knows only little—and as possible, much more than comes on his tongue—of astrology and astronomy, sometimes has so surprising talks that believing them is possible only by the natural (common) people, especially when we remember that those talks were uttered when there were two great events, one had passed and the other yet to come: The passed one was the martyrdom of his beloved son, **Aqa Mustafa**, ten days earlier, and the other event yet to come was that a great nation was going to live under the shade of his leadership. Let us see what he said in those conditions:

Surprising Sayings Under Difficult and Complicated Conditions

—Such events are not very important. They may happen. They may happen to everybody. **Allah**, the Blessed and High, has manifest favours and hidden ones. He the Blessed and High, has a hidden favour about which we have no knowledge, no information. Since we have incomplete knowledge, we are incomplete in knowledge, in act; in all aspects we are incomplete. That is why, in such incidents which may happen, we show impatience and fear. We do not show forbearance because of our incomplete knowledge of the status of the Creator, the Exalted. Had we known the hidden favours which **Allah**, Blessed and High, bestows upon His servants (He is Kind to His servants), and had we information about them, we would not have shown so much impatience in such trivial and unimportant incidents. We would have realized that there must have been some interests, some favours, some education, in them.[435] This world of ours is to be crossed over. It is not a world to stay in. It is a passage, it is a path. If we could, we may directly cover that road, as the holy men did: —We passed it while it was calm". If we could pass it safely, we would be happy. If on this path we slipped, God forbid, the slip would appear there, too. There they would cause other slips and more troubles. I implore **Allah**, Blessed and High, to wake us, to inform us of the hidden favours which we do not know, so that, like the ones who know the status of

Divinity and the high degrees of humanity and who give no heed to the world, nor regard it independent, and they pay no direct care to the mundane affairs, and they take this world to be a passage to somewhere else, to other big happinesses, we, too, *inshaallah*, may attain to such a stage, to the stages which we cannot comprehend as we are still in this world. We cannot understand what stages, what worlds, what stands they are. This stand, this world, we have opened all our eyes to this world, —**Allah** did not look at it ever since He created it" (according to a narrative), the world of substances, at which (as a narrative says) **Allah** did not look since He created it, despite the fact that this world of substances, the world of nature, as so far understood and as so far discovered, astounds the minds. Our reasons cannot comprehend even what has so far been discovered, while the rest of it is as **Allah** wills, at whose light no hand can reach. There are stars whose lights reach the earth after six billion years. This figure we cannot comprehend. Some writings say that if the inside of some stars is cut open, 500 million suns can be accommodated there. Other stars are so large that if one of them is put in the center of the sun, it will reach the earth, such is its largeness. This vastness, which minds cannot comprehend, and no one knows about them, they all belong to this world, the low world. Some people of knowledge said this world was called _dunya‘_, because it was shameful to tell the reality of the case, the actuality of this world. That is why this world is called _dunya‘_. The world, wide and complicated as it is, is called the low world. These skies, with all the things which have so far been discovered, according to the tongue of the *Quran* which says: —**We have adorned the lowest sky with an adornment: the stars,"** (37:6), are the lowest sky. Those which have so far been discovered are all, in the language of the *Quran*, low. The higher skies have not yet been discovered to know what is there. Yet, as the narrative goes, —He did not look at it with kindness ever since He created it". And, according to the *Quran*, this lowest life is described as *mata‘*. Life in the Hereafter is the life, the living. The life here is not life: —**The Last Abode is the [real] Life"** (29:64), about which we have no information. Do not neglect the divine duties which are divine favours. During our stay here we are put by **Allah**, Blessed and High, in charge of duties. As long as we are in this worldly life, as long as we are here, we are charged by **Allah**, Blessed and High, with duties, and we have to perform them. We must not forget the divine duties. All the divine commands are divine favours, while we think them as impositions. All of them are divine favours, whether individual duties—which are for one‘s education and perfection, since there is no other way for perfection and progress, as there are (high) stages which cannot be

321

reached but through this way—or social duties. We have duties towards the society, and we have to carry them out for the sake of regulating it."[436]

Inviting Ayatullah Burujerdi (to Qum)

Qum, like any other city, had theological schools, but it was announced as a big center, like Najaf, when **Ayatullah Hairi** moved to it. He was a man accepted as the head of the *hawzah* by all the teachers of Qum, when they knew that he had come with the intention of establishing such a center. This was so naturally accepted that there was no need for him to quarrel with anybody, and there were not many questions to be answered. It seems that what he had in his mind, without announcing them, were known to the others in their heart, and a conscious silence spoke of a big work. Apparently he had nothing to do with politics—a procedure which was intended not to attract the attention of the statesmen to the establishment of the *hawzah*, as at those days they were engaged in tens of other subjects. Had he taken to the usual political ways, probably the Freemasonry—which was a strong and secret political establishment, effective in the political change of Iran at that time— would have also formed a lodge there, and from then on tens of religious sects would have been formed. Perhaps, if in those days, this sharp-sighted *Mulla* had a little sharp-sightedness in the day's political career, a good many of the *ulama* could have now delivered speeches in English. This strict and intellectual position guaranteed the life of the *hawzah* during the most difficult time of irreligiousness. Although, on the other hand, the policy of apparently running away from the politics of that honourable and perspicacious man became an endorsing signature on runnings away of a different kind, which, before being fundamental politics, were crafty welfare-seekings, and that asceticism and *taqwa*, polluted with hypocrisy, shadowed the *hawzah* for tens of years. It so filled the atmosphere with running away from politics that afterwards it was difficult for **Ruhullah** to teach ethics in the same *hawzah*. Nevertheless, after a while **Aqa Ruhullah** could find its depth. If he, during his youth, sometimes objected his teacher's political viewpoint, but till the end of his life whenever he mentioned his name he added —may my soul be his ransom." This he often repeated after mentioning the names of three personalities. The first personality was the twelfth Imam (*a*) after whose name he used this expression for two reasons: One because he is the leader of the leaders, and the other was to break down the greatness of the **Imam Knomeini** in the eyes of the others in the face of the greatness of the last infallible Imam. The second was the one who, for the first time, put hand in his hand up to the shore of gnosticism. The third personality was his teacher of *fiqh* who sometimes disagreed with him in matters of politics.

Although that great man had apparently nothing to do with politics, yet he had a strong smelling sense in politics. **Ahmad Shah**, the last Qajari King, intending his last abroad journey which caused him to lose his throne, went to Qum to say farewell. He met **Ayatullah Hairi** at Darul Hukumah in Qum. **Rida Khan**, who was among the king's attendants, was standing at the head of the king during the meeting. From the way of his standing and his conduct, **Ayatullah Hairi** understood something, to which he alluded after their departure. He said: ─May **Allah** protect the country from that Cossack." [437]

When the torch of the *hawzah* went off[438], **Aqa Ruhullah**, the *faqih*, was a man with nothing short of the scholars to be an authority, though he was only 33 years old. Alas! Age was part of the unwritten conditions of becoming an authority, as it is the same now. The people of the *hawzah* took maturity to be in age, which requires hesitation and ponder. But some of the pseudo-scholar common people, following up their more commonly disciples, looked for the quality of equity in ages when one's desire for mustering wealth and position had become dormant, and the sexual desire had been put off. Yet, the carnal desire for fame, which remains aflame till the moments of the last breath, does not attract general attention. Many like to imitate the one whose ears are hard in hearing sportiveness, and whose eyes are so poor in sight that they do not see an alien woman. They looked for the asceticism which brings about equity in the inabilities. The conditions were such that even the martyr **Mudarris**─who went to the Parliament as a *faqih*, and who, in *fiqh*, in the religious precepts and in sociology and politics, which is the other side of the coin of religion, incited the approval of even his enemies─could not be suggested as a *marja*, let alone **Aqa Ruhullah** in his age, who, despite all his scholarly fame in the *hawzah* of Qum, was not so much famous outside the *hawzah*. Although lacking favourable conditions for accepting him as a conventional *marja* hurt, in a way, his disciples, yet it was, on the other side, of his good luck that he knew very well and seriously believed that to be a *marja* is a difficult religious duty, not a privilege. If anybody regards it to be a privilege, he will be destroying the religion and the life of the people and of himself.

For eight years afterwards, the *hawzah* was under the supervision of the *mujtahid*s by the names: **Sayyid Muhammad Hujjat, Sayyid Sadruddin Sadr** and **Sayyid Muhammad Taqi Khansari.**[439] Late in those years, Pahlavi government put in its intention to close down the *hawzah*, whereas

323

the students of the great **Hairi**, including **Aqa Ruhullah**, decided to protect it. The Shah had clubs, boots, claws and teeth, but he had no sound and proper intellect. So, if the people of the *hawzah* had acted wisely, he could have been disarmed. Here the case was handled quite wisely. At first the students went to the elites of each city, asking a question whose answer was known: —What kind of a *marja* is **Ayatullah Burujerdi**?" The answer was nothing but: —He is an upright *faqih* and versed in theology." After this question and answer, inviting that great *marja* to accept the leadership of the *hawzah* of Qum suddenly became the duty of every intellectual hearer. But the *ulama* of Hamadan did not accept **Ayatullah Burujerdi** as a general *marja*. **Aqa Ruhullah** undertook to go himself to Hamadan and talk to its *ulama* about the matter. He came back from the journey full-handed.[440] Within a short time a flood of letters and messengers flew towards **Ayatullah Burujerdi**, who was taken to bed for treatment in Firuzabadi Hospital in Tehran. Recovering, he returned to Burujerd in order to prepare for moving to Qum. The flood of letters continued to flow to Burujerd, and then they drove him to Qum. On his way, at every village and town cows and sheep were sacrificed. A poor old woman, who lived alone, brought a hen and slayed it at his feet. When the news of the popular reception of **Ayatullah Burujerdi** reached the court, the Shah ground his teeth.

When the walls of Qum became visible, this *mujtahid* entered the city through the same gate through which twenty-two years ago the young **Ruhullah** had entered it. Now, that young man of yesterday, the *faqih* of today was at the head of the pressed rows of the people coming to receive that *marja*. His stature was like a cypress tree, growing tall, and his face, like moon, emitting light. His two eyes, once this way and once that way, flashed in a moment, and from then on, this young *faqih* became the companion, overtly and covertly, of that old man. He started attending his class, without needing it, but just to support him, as supporting him meant supporting the *hawzah*. Although the high spirit of **Ruhullah** knew that it would also strengthen superficiality and bigotry in the *hawzah*, and that superficiality, in order to sterilize and curb religiousness, would become more effective than aqua regia, yet he believed that strengthening the *hawzah* was necessary. He set to action, and with the help of two **Murtadas**, one was the son of **Ayatullah Hairi**, and the other was the best of his students, **Mutahhari**, and a number of the devotees, he presented, in 1328 S.H., the suggestion of reforming the *hawzah*, to **Ayatullah Burujerdi**.

Ayatullah Burujerdi was a man of clear conscience. In his talk there was a tune of self-possession, which, despite his being deeply aware of the disturbed world of Islam, permeated his speeches. At the time when the world of Islam was being cut into pieces, the devils of the time tried to display that there was nothing with greater reward than cursing the Caliphs, while he, in such conditions, used to support —Approximation of Sects", to send representative to al-Azhar [the Egypt University of Religion], to build mosques abroad, to send propagator and to encourage the students to learn foreign languages. He was not afraid of rumours that whoever learnt English would be deviated.[441] When he received the suggestion of reforming the *hawzah* in the legible and efficient handwriting of **Aqa Ruhullah**, his skin could not contain him, because he, too, deeply believed in it. But alas! It was much regretted that the pseudo-holy men, who, without exception are, psychologically, the most safety-seekers, regarded reforming the structure to be contrary to their calm, easy going, worry-free, well-paid and dignified life, hence the ugly obstructions started. **Ayatullah Burujerdi**, commenced a slight running fight, then retreated. **Ayatullah Murtada Hairi**, angrily migrated to Mashhad. **Ustad Mutahhari**, despite his great attachment to **Aqa Ruhullah,** went to Tehran so that he may not remain there and be dissolved in the superficiality of the *hawzah*. This was **Aqa Ruhullah's** first defeat, and a big test. The students kept asking: —Has a great *marja*, who is aware of the shortcomings of the *hawzah*, the right to surrender to falsity?" It was a rightful question which had an explicit answer. But **Aqa Ruhullah,** with a thorn in the eye and a bone in the throat, was watchful lest respect for that great man, who had committed a mistake in his retreat as big as himself, should be lessened. He had no way out except in promising the clear-sighted ones in the *hawzah* to exert more efforts so as to make up for that defeat. He also severely warned himself lest he should be short in offering his attachment to that old scholar who had caused the defeat. This was his conduct and till the end of his life he preserved his manly behaviour and continued his manly steps. Even when he insisted on **Ayatullah Burujerdi** to take a step forward to prevent the execution of **Nawwab Safawi** and his group, and the prudence of **Ayatullah Burujerdi** turned his insistences futile, he burst into tears for the martyrdom of those four persons, yet he did not pollute his lips with an abuse against **Ayatullah Burujerdi**. To support him even more, he took up paper and pen and wrote down the oral lessons of **Ayatullah Burujerdi** on *fiqh*. For five full years he patiently listened to his lessons and took notes. Later on he compiled those writings in a volume as a text book.[442]

In those years two points in respect of knowing his political ideas are important: One is that although he regarded the government to be corrupt, yet he wrote three letters to three governmental personalities warning them against the consequences of executing *Fedaiyan-e Islam* under the leadership of the martyr **Nawwab Safawi**. The other point was that although he believed that **Nawwab** was a clean-thinking man and that their zeal was praiseworthy, yet he did not join Fedaiyan-e Islam, though he did not deny their armed actions, nor did he say anything to be a complete support to their armed fighting.

BLESSED DREAMS

After eight years from his moving to Qum, in his 27th year of age, **Aqa Ruhullah** married. The result was two sons and three daughters, and a son and two daughters closed their eyes forever after a while of opening them. He had not yet got the degree of *ijtihad*, but he, hand in the hands of **Ayatullah Shahabadi**, had wondered in the lanes of the gardens of gnosticism in two or three cities of love. Therefore, his proposal, before being a performance of a *fiqhi* precept, or a submission to a social custom, it smelled of an old friendship.

After marriage, beside observing all the *fiqhi* precepts step by step, he also observed the delicate moral instructions so that his followers may know that the one who is more religious has better behaviour with his family. The story of his marriage and consortship is so beautiful and instructing that it is regretful not to allude to it briefly.

Wife-choosing appears to be a completely optional and elective matter, unless culture and religion limit its scope. Islam does not regard singleness a choice, and for selecting a spouse it divides the limitings into two groups: One covers the limits of the allowed and the not allowed. The other covers the supererogatories and the disapprovals in this great event of life. After choosing a religion, there is nothing more difficult than choosing a spouse. After choosing the religion, one has, till the end of one's life, to lovingly observe its musts and must-nots. The spouse, too, has orders covering a handful of musts and must-nots, which if cordially observed, life, with all its hardships, turns kind and delicate. Otherwise, the house will be hell. Thus, finding a spouse whose orders coincide with the orders of religion, adds to the difficulty of choosing, especially that people, under intricates and complications of life, get twisted, and mostly they will not remain the same as they were at the time of choosing.

Marriage divides one into two halves, a half for oneself and one half for the other. Yet, at the beginning, it makes man twice, and later hundreds and thousands of times as much. This is the miracle of marriage that when one's age comes to an end, one's genes remain in all the bodies of one's children and life continues, as the children are the continuation of man, otherwise,

Allah would not have said: ─**We have given you plenty**."[443] Half of the children the woman offers from herself and the other half man adds to it. So, if somebody likes not to be completely void of his option, choosing the spouse will be the first step. Taking care of these obligations makes the case so difficult that the fastidious will remain single, whereas the nonchalant after a while feels being cheated. Nevertheless, in choosing the spouse **Allah** guides one as he does in choosing the religion. Commonly this surprising event of life goes forward so automatically that many see it like a dream. Sometimes the flash of a look, hearing a name, or the inclinations of the mother, sister, father, relatives or the friends settle everything. The children, before reaching puberty, also engage their imagination excitedly with thought of their tomorrow's joint life, but at the moments of choosing, invisible things tie one's hands and feet, and throw one where one can little guess where it is. Sometimes it is a fearful valley, and sometimes it is a stormy sea. One mostly thinks that it was his own choice and voluntarily submits to it. Spouse-choosing of **Aqa Ruhullah,** was like other marriages. He had no father and mother to choose for him so that he may approve their choice. The brothers and sisters regard him a grown up person who knows what to do. He himself was so shy that he said nothing, and was so bashful that he never followed a girl with his eyes, even in his imagination. Now he is 27 years old. According to the customs of nowadays it was time for him to marry. But in those days he must have been ten years late.

Aqa Ruhullah's joint life was the most delicate part of his actual life. The one who, from that year afterward, became his wife, and after the departure of the Lover was given the title of _The Sun's Beloved' *(Yar-e Aftab)* describes the story of their marriage. It is a wonderful description. It is so truthful and candid that if somebody reads it, if not like her who, while telling the story, the stream of her tears for the separated lover, never dried, at least, in certain expressions, tears of eagerness will veil his eyes from reading. Words dance naked on the stage of her mouth. It seems as if she has attained to such a magnanimity that expedience becomes mean in her expression. I wish the context of the pen in portraying the apparent life of that beloved was such that the sun's beloved said this part, exactly as she said it. Inspired by what she[444] recited and by what others had, the story went as this:

On a school day, there appeared a handsome, smartly dressed student, wearing a valuable Istambuli fur cloak. He joined the students in the class of **Ayatullah Hairi**. The students' attention turned to him. Despite the fact that that way of joining a class was almost unprecedented, yet it was not blameworthy. Blame was directed to the unclean ones. Of course wearing nice clothes is recommended, but to wear costly dresses was subject to criticism. Perhaps **Aqa Ruhullah**, who was much neater than others, wished to say something, but he was some seven years older, and to practise forbidding this disapproval in respect of the elders, required a double delicacy. It is unknown what debate was exchanged. Whatever it might have been, that meeting had no effect, whatsoever, on the dressing of the new coming student. Perhaps the preliminary steps for knowing each other blocked the way of argument. Or perhaps the new comer had said: —have come from Tehran. In the Capital there have recently appeared a handful of dandies who stroll in the streets, and whenever they encounter a man wearing a turban and an *aba*, they (mockingly) say: _O you Aqa Shaykh…!' So, by dressing myself in this way, I wanted to punch them on the mouth."

In fact, in **Aqa Ruhullah**'s dictionary, this reasoning was not so strong, and the argument and discussion on this subject was equally valueless. Later, **Aqa Ruhullah** told the son of that well-dressed student: —You father is very much *mulla*, very much merited and versed, but it is a pity that he does not keep to the line of being a *mulla*." From that meeting a deep friendship resulted. Later, **Aqa Ruhullah**, together with another friend by the name of **A Sayyid Muhammad Sadiq Lawasanii**, who had also come from Tehran, used to call on the new coming student at his house. His name was **Haj Mirza Muhammad Thaqafi**. His house was near the school. It was a house in the bazar of Qum, Sayyid Ismail Alley, a good house with *andaruni* and *biruni*, which he had rented from a well-known merchant. They also had a servant by the name of **Dhabihullah**, who was in charge of bringing tea and hooka and laying the table. He was ready at service. **Aqa Ruhullah** never said to him: My house in Khomein is longer than yours, and my financial standing, if not better, is not less than yours, yet I live like other students live, while you live differently. How bad would it have been if he had said it! **Aqa Ruhullah** had found in him tens of good merits that disregarding this disapproved conduct was forgivable. Whenever now and then he invited him to a lunch, dinner or to an afternoon talk, he would accept without any excuse.

One day **Aqa Thaqafi**, who was a student in Qum and rather a famous Ali*m* in Tehran, decided to go to Tehran. He invited his close friends to his house. After the usual greetings, tea-drinking and hooka-smoking, **Aqa Lawasani** turned to **Aqa Ruhullah** and, without any premise, said: —Dea **Aqa,** you are now twenty-six-seven years old. You are now quite a man. Why don't you marry?" Gross beads of sweat appeared on **Aqa Ruhullah**'s forehead. After a short pause, in a tune dripping shyness, he replied: —Sdar I have not yet approved of any girl to marry. I do not want to marry from Khomein. No one has come to my attention." It is doubted whether it was predetermined that **Aqa Lawasani** should suggest, in the presence of **Aqa Thaqafi**, a proposal: —**Aqa Thaqafi** has two daughters. My brother's wife says they are good.[445]" If he had said something in addition to that, **Aqa Ruhullah** did not hear it. His heart started throbbing for a girl he had never seen. How embarrassing it is to hear such talks at the presence of one's would-be father-in-law, and how easy was one of the most difficult elections in one's life which requires years of thinking. His answer was silence, and the reply to his silence was a smile of content on the lips of his future father-in-law. He went to Tehran and frankly talked it over with his daughter. But alas! The daughter's reply was in the negative.

Aqa Ruhullah was 27 years old, but the daughter of **Aqa Thaqafi** was only 15 years old. The difference between the two ages was not small. Moreover, she was brought up in Tehran and tenderly cherished. She did not like the life of a student in Qum, that is, she did not like the climate of Qum. Furthermore, she was a student in the secondary school. At that time few of fathers allowed their daughters to go to the primary schools, let alone the secondary schools, where the teachers, the footman, the director, the supervisor, were men. He had even employed a private teacher of French language to strengthen her in that subject. This girl was quite a modern-minded, much as her father was. Naturally, her father's modernism was slightly different from that of hers. Under the conditions of that time he did not like her daughter to go to the secondary school. It was imposed up on him, and, on the other hand, he imposed that he should protect his daughter beyond merely the Islamic *hijab*. She must wear knickerbockers, with plain black shoes. But he had a luxurious life. What a suggestion that of **Aqa Lawasani** was! Now how could he convey the girl's refusal to **Aqa Ruhullah**. **Aqa Ruhullah**'s heart was big enough to bear the refusal of a girl whose name he even did not know. But, on the other hand, big as his heart is, it is so delicate that sometimes a small wave may break it. His close friends, who had, to some extent, gone deep into his soul, knew that the love of **Allah** in his heart so engaged it that there remained no vacancy for any other love. Yet they did not know that in the lessons of gnosticism he had taken a step ahead. Any love which makes his heart throb, he takes it to be divine, and the daughter of **Aqa Thaqafi**, without knowing her name and recognizing her complexions, had settled in his heart from the first sign.

330

The question, however, could not remain without an answer. Strange enough that when **Aqa Ruhullah** heard about the refusal of the elder girl of **Aqa Thaqafi**, this bashful man pushed shyness aside and asked **A Sayyid Ahmad Lawasani**, his intimate friend, to go to Tehran and officially propose, on his behalf, to that girl. Once again, on return, the answer was even more decisive in refusal. The second time, the third time and the fourth time, the answer came that the partner in the properties of the girl's grandmother had proposed to her. He, too, remained without an answer. What could **Aqa Ruhullah** do more than that, except lessening his visits to **Aqa Thaqafi** so that they may not be ashamed at seeing one another.[446]

Others were wondering what caused that obstinacy. How could it be known that if **Aqa Ruhullah** had seen her he would approve of her, and how could it be known that if she had seen **Aqa Ruhullah**, she would not approve of him? For the fifth time when **A Sayyid Ahmad** visited **Aqa Thaqafi** to find out, for the last time, what the girl had to say about refraining even from coming and seeing, he had a row with his intimate friend and said to him: —Why don't you convince her to accept?" The answer was: —tlis the girl who wants to marry, not I. I take **Aqa Ruhullah** to be the best husband for my daughter, but she does not agree, nor do the relatives, and the most important point is that this girl from her infancy lived with her grandmother, and she loves Tehran. Many times she was forced to visit Qum, she did not like it and restively returned. She wants to continue her studies. She is young. Her grandmother does not allow..." Despite his friendship with him, **Sayyid Ahmad** changed his anger into rough words and abused his friend who had kept on a crossroad. **Aqa Thaqafi** liked **Aqa Ruhullah**, and he was bound to his behaviour, morals, knowledge and disposition. On the other hand, he had no religious permission to impose his own inclinations and interest upon the girl and stir **Allah**'s anger. Now he was hearing from the tongue of a friend, decisively, firmly and roughly: —Yes, say that she was brought up luxuriously, and cannot put up with a student's living. This is a talk uttered by those who disagree." **Aqa Thaqafi**, helplessly, was pressed by his family and his friend. The suggestion of this marriage and the heart breaking answers, were, like a bitter medicine, pouring into **Aqa Ruhullah**'s throat. The event which was caused by intimacy, the very event drew the warp out of the woof of friendship. It was a bitter event, and it was like a medicine because it brought **Aqa Ruhullah** to his senses. He was so indulged in his studies, discussions, readings, researchings and following up the news of politics and the wonders of theoretical gnosticism that he had completely forgotten that marriage, in the view of the pious men, is the other half of faith, not just because it pours the water of purity on the flames of the sexual desire of the body, but more because it is a response to the call of nature. Forty years later, concerning this, he said: ―The woman is the manifestation of the implementation of the hopes of humanity."[447] He, who was going to bring out many of man's hopes from the subterranean canal to the manifestation, took, from then on, the question of getting married a very serious matter, as serious as the *salat*, as gnosticism and as politics. Days passed by, and weeks and months, too. Studying, discussing and classes went on as in everyday. But to the long nocturnal invocations another invocation was added, perhaps saying: ―Othe Holy Being! Grant me a holy wife!" **Allah** leaves no invocation without response. He ordered the angels to go to the house of a girl with a pure nature, and, when she closes her eyes, they are to quietly enter her dream and give her wakefulness. Several times the holy ones entered the sleep of a girl whose holy name was **Quds Iran**.[448] The last ignition, which put the tent of her children fancies aflame, and burned her desire for a luxurious life, was a bewildering dream. In the morning, when she sat at the table, she related her dream to her grandmother: ―Iwas there with an old woman wearing a *chador*, which resembled a wrapper for bedclothes, with small dots. The old woman was small and I did not know her. We were sitting behind the door of the room which had glass panes. I was watching the other side [the facing room]. I asked her: ‗Who are those there?' The old woman, who was sitting beside me, said: ‗The one facing us, with the black turban, is **the Prophet (s)**. The other one, with the small green turban and a red cap with a shawl tied to it, is **Amirul Muminin (a)**'. On a side was a young man with a black turban. The old woman said he was the **Imam Hasan (a)**. I said: ‗O, this is the Prophet and this is **Amirul Muminin!**' and I was overjoyed. The old woman said: ‗How, it is you who dislike them!' I said: ‗I do like them. They are my Prophet, my Imam! That one is my second Imam! That is my first Imam!' The old woman said: ‗Why, you do not like them'!"

Grandmother, assuming to be Joseph (the prophet) (*a*), interpreted the dream as follows: ―Itseems that this [**Aqa Ruhullah**] is a real Sayyid [of the Prophet's offspring], and the Prophet and the Imams are not pleased with you. There is no other way. It is your fate!"

This last dream had taken place the very night on which **A Sayyid Ahmad** had, for the last time, come to Tehran to repeat his proposal, and on which had a row with **Aqa Thaqafi**. When the breakfast was over and the table was removed, the father of **Qudsi** came in. It was winter and he sat under the *kursi*. **Qudsi** went to bring her father a cup of tea. **Aqa Thaqafi** started talking softly and calmly: —. **A Sayyid Ahmad** came. It is his fifth time. He said something which I am unable to repeat. When I said: _No, the women did not agree', he firmly said: _Yes, say that she was brought up luxuriously and cannot put up with a student's living'. Now it is up to you, but I believe him [**Aqa Ruhullah**] to be a good, educated and pious man. His piety will cause him to treat **Qudsi** well."

The last part of his talk was almost addressed to his daughter when she was offering tea. It was the first time that the tone of the father was blameful. Although grandmother had brought her up, the fatherly love in the separation days during which he will not see her appears (to him) in the halos of embarrassment which twist into each other. The girl, too, used to take her respect for her father likewise to the halo. Whenever the father used to call her, she would never go to him without wearing her *chador*. Now that she is directly addressed and blamed, finds no better way to defend herself than to practise silence: —flyou will not marry, I will, from now on, have nothing to do with your marriage." Her answer to her father was silence and silence. The first silence was an objection against the father's tone, and its extension was a meaningful answer to what the old woman in the dream had said.

The grandmother brought a box of sweets. The father took one and, before putting it in his mouth, said: —SoJ will eat the sweet as a token of **Quds Iran**'s consent."

A week passed. Two stage coaches stopped at the door of **Aqa Thaqafi**'s house. From the first three brothers landed: **Aqa Murtada Pasandideh** and **Aqa Nuruddin Hindi**, the brothers of bridegroom, and **Aqa Ruhullah Mustafawi**, the bridegroom himself. From the second coach two **Lawasani** Sayyids got down, and **Aqa Musayyib**, a good-hearted employee. Perhaps an army officer, a Tehranian friend of **Aqa Pasandideh**, could join them. After the usual greetings, **Aqa Thaqafi** sent his servant, **Dhabihulah**, to tell **Qudsi Khanum** to come, without telling her who the guests were, lest she may refrain from coming. Grandmother asked: —Who is the guest?" She received no clear answer, but she, together with **Qudsi Khanum** and her sister **Shams Afaq** came. All of them had smelled something. **Shams** went a few steps ahead. Becoming assured, she hurried back to **Qudsi Khanum** and excitedly said: —tIs the bridegroom! It's the bridegroom!"

The would-be bride looked through the pane of **Dhabihullah**'s room into the room where the bridegroom was shyly, calmly and silently sitting. At this first look she noticed a man whose stature was unknown, because he was sitting at the *kursi*, his complexion was yellowish, like his short hair. After the departure of the Lover, the Beloved of the Sun, asked whether she had approved of the bridegroom, she said: —Ididn't dislike him, but I was too young to know what I was to do. I myself was a simple girl. My father quietly came and asked my grandmother: _What did **Quds Iran** say on her return?' My grandmother said: _Nothing. She is sitting there.' Later I was told: _When you were sitting silent, he fell down on the ground in praise of **Allah**.' My father always used to say: _I desire to have a son and a son-in-law, both to be of the people of knowledge'."

The eyes of many people have the habit of looking for asceticism and piety accompanied with shabby clothes. They do not usually recognize them in more delicate beauties. That student of **Ayatullah Hairi**, whose external dresses attracted attention and whose nice perfumes went ten paces ahead of him, now is performing a thanksgiving *sajdah* because the spouse of his delicately brought up daughter was of knowledge and piety. He knew nothing of his financial standing. He thought that his elegant and modern daughter must from then on put up with an insignificant monthly salary paid by the *hawzah*. But not all of the relatives pay tribute to knowledge to this extent. They have three basic questions, and the first understanding of the *shar* coincides with the customary, turning the right to their side. The first: —Hasthe bridegroom anything of his own? If it is the spending of the monthly salary paid by **Haj Abdul Karim**, then she cannot put up with it. If not, has he any capital of his own or not." The second and third questions were: —sl the bridegroom already married or not? Perhaps he has a wife in Khomein and he may have children. Maybe he practised the *sighah* till finishing his studies and manages to find a capital. Perhaps he got one or two children from his *sighah* marriage. The first question and the question about having wife and children were basic. As to the question about the temporary marriage, even if in the affirmative, it seemed not to be so much negative, and they could pass by it unnoticed, because during the period of singleness, there is no remedy for those fiery temperaments against polluting themselves with sinning, except temporal marriage.

But it is much regretted that some people prefer the *haram* in the society to the *halal* of **Allah**. More regrettable is that this permission, or rather this religious realistic decree is mostly so basely and ugly used that the term *sighah* became more abusing and indecent than any other abusive term. However, after much investigations by **A Sayyid Ahmad** and others of the relatives of **Aqa Thaqafi** it became known that **Aqa Ruhullah** not only did not submit his body to any *sighah* woman, but even his room-mates, by way of respecting him, never talked about this subject. However, disregarding the investigations of the relatives, the wife also likes to know the true nature of the youth period of her husband. So, at times, she, in a way known better by the women, asked him too many questions, and each time he passed it honourably. The Beloved of the Sun, from then on, believed in whatever her husband said. The biggest evidence proving that he did not practise the *sighah* was that she said: ―He had never seen a woman, as he had later told me." It was a wonder that the beloved believed in her beloved, as the investigations of the others were believed by themselves, and ―He himself told me" was the strongest proof!

Stranger even was that the **Aqa"s** forbearance, and the plans of those who understand the realities according to their own inclinations and disinclinations, none of them prevented him, when teaching the precepts of the temporary marriage, from going into its details to the full.

But following up two other questions by the women of the family, reason judged that since he had no connection with any woman, it would be nonsense to ask about children. Yet it was imperative to have a call on Khomein to complete the investigation. **A Sayyid Ahmad** accepted to undertake that trouble, and brought the answer: ―Their house is large and respectable, with two connected and very nice yards... He is good and gentlemanly in behaviour. His monthly allowance is 30 *tumans* out of his fatherly heritage." The wife's father said: ―Well, if he pays 5 tumans as rent, there will be no problem."

The bride had seen the bridegroom from behind the pane, but he had not seen her. Why from behind a glass pane and not face to face? Why did not they talk to one another? The bridegroom is shy, but marriage is the most difficult choice. The religious precepts in this respect are not ashamed. The author of *ash-Sharai*, in the chapter on marriage says: ―He who really intends to marry, is allowed to carefully see the fiancee." Two *hadiths*, both authorized, concerning shame, stand facing each other. One says: ―There is no shame in the religion." The other says: ―A pious man is bashful." Marriage is half of the religion and half of life. So, shame is out of question. **Aqa Ruhullah** is innately shy, and it was doubled by his piety. The others forgot that he, too, must see his fiancee, perhaps after seeing her he might have something to say. But he need not to see. Had he seen his wife in a dream? He was not used to relate his dreams to anybody, so that the common dreams may not become a cause for taking big decisions. Didn't he believe in dreams? This can't be! There are many true stories in the *Quran* based on dreams. Dreams, in the eyes of the believers are the second face of the truth. Even the dreams of ill-behaving persons manifest sometimes their realities. Pharaoh dreamt that his throne was overthrown, and consequently he started to kill the sons of Bani Israel. His dream was interpreted by the arrival of **Moses (a)**. **Yusuf (a)** dreamt that the sun, the moon and eleven stars bowed to him, and it was interpreted. The ruler of Egypt dreamt that seven fat cows ate seven lean ones. **Yusuf (a)** interpreted it and himself became the ruler of Egypt. **Allah**, the Exalted, regarded the interpretation of dreams as a favour bestowed upon **Yusuf (a)**. How horrible the dream of the champion of monotheism, **Ibrahim**, **Allah**'s Friend, was when he saw his knife on the throat of **Ismail**. He obeyed what he had dreamt, while Satan was shouting at him: —OIbrahim! Does a dream deserve slaying your son?" And he was stoned three times. So, dream in itself is a knowledge when the eyelids draw the curtain on the eyes, the mind draws the curtain off the past and and future secrets... But **Aqa Ruhullah** did not speak about his dreams. Probably he had seen in his dream his Jacob advising him not to tell anybody about his dreams.[449] Yet, **Aqa Ruhullah**'s life was a strange one. Whenever we find a questionable thing, if we carefully investigate we find somewhere a clear answer to the effect that he had no need to see his fiancee's face. A short expression appeared on the tongue of **Yar-e Aftab** (The Sun's Beloved), saying: —Ihese things had later been told to me by **Aqa** who said: _When **Aqa Lawasani** said: **Aqa Thaqafi** has two daughters who are praised', it was as if my heart was beaten down'."

Half of the process of choosing the wife is the mind's job, and the other half is done by the heart. As to its rational side, it is sufficient to be satisfied with a many-years friendship with a handsome, good-talking, good-behaving, reasonable and amicable man. This was because if there had been any external or internal defect in the girl, the father must be aware of it and he would not hide it from his friend. As to the part concerning the heart, it is because his heart was not dissolute nor vagrant, so a hint from the heart was enough. **Aqa Ruhullah**'s heart was beaten at the first short hint. So, the girl is that whom he wants. But is such kind of choosing a completely personal matter? Or is it a type which can be imitated by anyone? Undoubtedly, imitation in this important matter is dangerous. The **Aqa,** who was in this marriage the most successful person, did not allow his sons to imitate him.

From the suggestion of the marriage of **Aqa Ruhullah** in **Aqa Thaqafi**'s house in Qum, till the official proposal presented in his house in Tehran, **Aqa Ruhullah** had to wait ten months for the _Yes' to be uttered by **Quds Iran**. After the _Yes', everything went swiftly forward. The rest of the story is better to be heard from the tongue of **Yar-e Aftab**: —The wedding ceremony was not extensive. My father was sitting in the large room in the *andarun* named the saloon. He told me to come. I had just returned from the school, and as I was not used to go to him without *chador*, I borrowed my younger sister's, threw it on my head and went to him. He said: _Sit at the other side of the *kursi*.' The family of the bridegroom had come on the 1st of Ramadan. It was then the 8th. In those days they were guests in my father's house, and my mother had very well entertained them. Within those eight days during which **Aqa** [the bridegroom] stayed in my father's house, **Aqa Kashani** [a well-known struggling *Alim*] came and they met one another. The houses of my father and of **Aqa Kashani** were in the same alley and they were friends. **Aqa Kashani** had said to my father there and then: _Where did you find this wonder!?' They were looking after a house to rent and take the bride there. It was decided to marry in Tehran, and then go to Qum. After 8 days a house was found. It was the same house with exactly the same rooms which I had seen in my dream. Even the curtains, which they brought for me later, were the same that I had seen in my dream. My father said: _Appoint me as your agent so that I can appoint **A Sayyid Ahmad** as my agent to go to the shrine of **Abdul Azim** to conclude the text of the marriage contract. The bridegroom will give his agency to his brother, **Aqa Pasandideh**.' I paused a little [as was usual at that time], then I said: _I agree.' They went and concluded the contract. On saying that the house was ready, my father said: _Give them furniture [trousseau] as they want to go to the other house.' The preliminary furniture, such as carpet, kursi-quilt, kitchen utensils and other things, like kerosene-cooker, were sent ahead. We had a **Naneh Khanum** who was my mother's nurse. She and her daughter, „**Udhra Khanum**, were sent there for reception and cooking. On the night of the 16th or 15th of Ramadan, the friends and the relatives were invited. I put on a white and modern dress, on which my aunt's daughter had, with her taste, painted flowers."

The house which they rented could not be compared with the house in Khomein. Nevertheless, it was more comfortable than the single room, and, moreover, the young wife, who keeps her eye on the door, every noon and sunset, waiting for **Aqa Ruhullah** to come, makes the **Aqa**'s house quite warm. This is the wife he desired, and what makes the **Aqa**'s heart quite warm is her truthfulness. When she had decidedly said: —No, to the proposal, she said it with truthfulness. When she said: —Bo not like Qum", she truthfully said it, till she, from behind time and place, saw this very house in blessed dreams and in which the beloved slept. Now if she says: —love Qum only because of you, because I heartily love you," then these expressions are so clearly uttered that from behind of them her naked and pure soul could be seen in the hands and the bosom of **Aqa Ruhullah**. Quite assuredly, due to her sincerity, **Allah** rewarded her with the **Aqa** as a gift, and also he gave her to **Aqa Ruhullah** due to the pure eyes of him.

It seems that the human disposition indicates that women are to undertake the domestic work, leaving the outside work to men. If a woman wanted to undertake a role outside the house, she has first to obtain the man's consent, except the obligatory acts [*wajibat*] for which man's consent is not necessary. Islam has, in this respect, delicate instructions. Isn't it that a woman has her own taste, and has, in domestic matters, better experience than man? Isn't it that she is more worried about the constancy of the family than man? Isn't it that even if man's love for his children is deeper, but the child feels the love of the mother more and at the beginning needs it more? Isn't it that in the creation of the child both of them are needed, while man's effort is less than an hour, and the woman's toil is for more than nine months? And tens of other —sh't it"s, from whose collection this fact manifests that as far as the domestic and family affairs are concerned, the woman is more sensitive, more worried and accepts more responsibilities than man. This is a rule, and other than that is the exceptional. A rule does not need any bringing up. It manifests itself. Exceptions in this question are the result of incorrect and rough education of the society and culture. If the disposition of a society is not polluted with incorrect educational norms, it will be natural, more natural than to be even noticed, that the management of the house will be undertaken by the woman. Strange enough that the woman in the house is both the mistress, without lowering the high authority of the man, and being under the man's authority without reducing her authority as mistress. The woman is capable of keeping her delicate pride, even when she does mean works, such as cleaning the foul smelling nappies of the babies, such jobs appear to be more artistic than to be management. So what room can there be for biddings and forbiddings of a man whenever he likes? The biddings and forbiddings of a man, who is a manager in the outside, and a successful one, put in disorder the house management, because the house is not a factory. Here profit and loss count, but there love, feelings and affection count. Therefore, in order to protect the calmness of the home against man's disorderly behaviour, Islam, in addition to its delicate moral instructions, issues rough legal instructions, too. Sometimes these instructions are quite unbelievable to the non-Muslims. If some men and women of the believing society do not apply these frank precepts, they must not suspect their own piety, they must be sure of their irreligiousness. One of these precepts say: —The husband has the right to order his wife not to leave the house except for performing a duty." Is there a sane man who would bind his wife such? No one! But if there was a corruption ahead, reason would judge that man should apply the precept, and the *shar'* would judge that she must obey, even if the man's reasoning could not convince her. It is better for the wife to obey this temporary order than permanent separation. If the man had lost his mind, what would the judgement be? The elders of both families would intercede and solve the question.

A woman has another right of which man is deprived–the right to receive the common expenditures of life, even if she had no real need of them. Moreover, any want by the man and the woman is to be put in the form of a kind request, not in the form of a rude order. If a man knew the rule of being manly, he would cast off, at the threshold of his house, all the business problems, and would get in with a warm greeting, an open face and full-handed, and be received by a warmer smile and a cup of hot tea or a cold *sharbat*, with an agreeable answer. Cooking, washing the plates, laundering and tens of other works which are generally considered to be housework can be done better by the women than by men. In any house where the relations tend to soundness, the woman undertakes, normally, all these works. The pleasure of life depends on man's help, at times, in the woman's works, in order to feel her bodily toil and to atone for her spiritual boredom of the everlasting repetition of these ordinary and unpleasant works. If any woman was aware of the custom of managing the house, she would do her best to do what she takes to be her duty, even if she worked outside. Now the more the woman exerts her efforts, the more the man indulges in the false imagination that all these works are in fact the real and undeniable duties of the woman. So, if one day the food was delayed, or a shirt remained unironed, or the child's snot made ugly his face, then the ungrateful man would become tyrannical and arise a great fuss, and a one-sided court would be set up, in which he himself would be the judge, the claimant and the executor. The ungrateful man would become so blind-hearted that he disregards hundreds of her favours, and sometimes her shortcomings would be responded by slaps. Thus, in order to kill in man his unfounded expectations, Islam issued a judgement which is mostly not practically needed, unless the secrets of the house were disclosed in the court. The judgement is this: The man not only has no right to force his wife to do household works, but even for suckling the child she has the right to ask for a nurse, or demand a wage for feeding the child with her milk. Is there any such heartless mother to put leg on leg and insist on misusing her legal right and leave her children without clothes and food? The answer is: –No!", unless when she is ill. Where can you find a man who, all along his life, always remembers this right of the woman? Had it not been for the holymen, one could also say: ―Nowhere!" It is incredible and is more like a legend that it deprives one from one's courage to retell it lest one is accused of exaggeration. But the truth is to be said, even if some hearts hardly believe in it. If this question: ―Dd̵he holy people, too, have miracle?" is answered in the affirmative, then one can say that **Aqa Ruhullah**'s astonishing miracle was that for more than half a century, from the moment of the coming of **Qudsi** to his house, to the moment of his departing the house of **Qudsi Khanum**, his lips never parted in an expression bearing a smell of a command. Even the simple requests never appeared on his tongue. Whenever **Qudsi Khanum** was spreading the *sufreh* and could not close the door behind her as her both hands were engaged, and if it was winter and the burning cold slapped him in the face, he used to calmly stand up and close it even if it was repeated twice, thrice and many times, in several goings and comings. He believed that the lamps must not remain uselessly lit. If nobody put them off, he used to remind them of that, but if it was **Qudsi Khanum** who forgot them she would not remind her, but he would himself go and put them off. Even during his old age and cardiac sickness, he never ordered his wife to fetch him a glass of water to swallow his pills. He used to fill a cup of water, drink some of it, cover it with a tissue paper, so that he may not bother anybody, especially **Qudsi Khanum**, when it was time for the next pill.[450] He sometimes would bring half a glass of water to his wife. **Qudsi Khanum** would remember that it was time for her to have her pills. She would get the glass and thank him. Of course sometimes he had some orders, but he so cleverly issued them that the ordered was so much pleased with them and laughed at heart. For example, when there was a tear in his dress, or if a botton fell off, he would say: ―My you please give this to be amended?"

Study, discussion, work and engagement could not prevent the **Aqa** from knowing who washes the clothes, who puts the heavy cooking pot on the stove and who cleans the rooms. But all these were done while the **Aqa** was not in the house. In front of him the mistress of the house was only the mistress of the house. But how long can this situation continue? For some people, ten days; for others ten months, and for those with strong will, ten years. But for the **Aqa,** till the end of life: ―Ifhe saw me at the pond trying to wash a piece of the child's clothes, he would come and say: ‗Get up. You must not wash.' I used to sweep his room after him. When he was not there I used to wash the children's clothes. One year when the woman-worker, who worked in our house, was not there, we were in **Imamzadeh Qasim**. It was about that time[451] when the girls had grown up and married. After the lunch, I sat at the pond to wash the dishes. As soon as he saw me trying to wash the dishes, he called **Faridah**, who was there, and told her: _Faridah, hurry. **Khanum** is washing the dishes.'"

How insightedly the father of our **Quds Iran** and of the **Aqa"s Qudsi-jan** had seen: —It is up to you, but I believe that he is a good man, learned and pious, and his piety will cause **Qudsi-jan** to be comfortable."

On his coming home, the **Aqa** used to present to her a greeting, throw a few buds of smiles in her lap, hang his *aba* on the hanger, go to the kitchen, come out with two cups of tea and sit beside her. Sometimes he would roll up his sleeves and help her in arranging the *sufreh*, and the wife, used to shyly say: —Why you?", and, with a smile changing the depth of the soul into spring, she used to hear the answer: —He is from Paradise." In such apparently calm times, the *ghayb* was also calmly doing its job. It photographed these candid conditions, which **Allah** knew and the wife saw, so that, without letting anybody know about them, make them a tune in his speech, and when he talks about the right of the wife, the heart may accept it without having to get from the customs and reason any permission. Man, in moments of sincerity becomes so big and beautiful that whatever is hidden behind his privacy becomes the manifestation of visibility. One of the secrets that in a great Revolution and for the first time along history the woman had the larger share was that the vanguard of the Revolution paid, to the full, the rights of the woman he had in his house. These rights were not confined only to refraining from issuing orders. Actually they also concerned sincere love, a love which seemed never to end in a union.

It is a mental custom to have someone be the original actor in a story. But in the warm house of **Aqa Ruhullah** there were two original persons–a married couple. If we look deeper, in the house the more original pesonality is the wife. Women are more jealous than men. **Allah**, for the sake of a longer life, poured one more measure of this instinct into the clay of the women's disposition. When she realized that the **Aqa"s** eyes and heart were too pure to be possessed by another woman, she did not use the feminine jealousy for other purposes. She had the art of recognizing beauty such that she knew that the one beside her is so beautiful that the beautifying of childhood and youth became mean in her eyes. In short, her soul became so big that to pretend bigness turned to smallness. When with a sign from her husband a nation offered their souls as a gift, she, too, was so drown into the perfections of the husband that she forgot who her husband was. She attended women meetings so unaffectedly that those who did not know her thought her to be an ordinary woman. In a party for *iftar*, the wife of an employee was also invited. She did not see it becoming to sit beside the women from whose dresses and behaviour it was clear that they were the wives of director generals and up. In a corner of the place she saw some women sitting dispersed. She went there and asked a woman to make room for her. After a while of hearing the exchanged talks she realized that she was sitting beside **Yar-e Aftab**, who was so amicable that to leave her was difficult.

Nowadays pretending to be pious is not so difficult in Iran, but it was difficult in few decades before. But sometimes it is not so easy to expose certain facts, such as when the children are careless in performing the religious duties, and she does not refrain from admitting that her children were not exceptional: ─The **Aqa**"s morals, movements and talks all had their effects on the children, especially in respect of religion. My children are very much religious. His religiousness and piety had their effect on me as on my children, but his morals and behaviour were more effective on them. I am as I was. The **Aqa** seldom advised. He was careful about their religious education when they were seven years old. He used to say: ‿Start performing the *salat* when you are seven years old. Make them [the children] do the *salat* so that when they are nine years old they become accustomed to it.‘ I used to tell him: ‿Other aspects of their education are up to me, but their *salat* is up to you. You tell them. They do not listen to me.‘ So, he attended to that. He used to ask them. If they said: ‿We performed it‘, he would accept and stop at that."

Splendour in simple sentences, like a blossom, is nice. How splendid and artistic this simplicity is, not because she is naive, but because the reins of the self are in her hand, and the weak expediences are but mean in her eye.

The family identity card of **Yar-e Aftab**, as much as she knows, is, in short and with alteration, as below:

─Ṃ father, **Haj Mirza Muhammad Thaqafi**, was of the *ulama* of Tehran. He mostly wrote books and was less interested in the *akhundi* practices, such as receiving religious taxes and having connections with the businessmen. Of course he was a leader of a congregational *salat*, and he gave lectures. He had a large library; a part of which he presented to the former Sepahsalar School (now called Shahid Mutahhari School). Its smaller part filled a room up to the ceiling. A few volumes of his *Tafsir-e Nuwin* still survive. My mother[452] was rich and she paid his expenses. My grandfather, **Mirza Abul-Fadl Tehrani**, was a genius in his time. He wrote *Shifaus-Sudur* which is an explanation of *Dua* Ashura. He also composed an Arabic collection of poems. He died over forty years of his age. The grandfather of

342

my father, **Haj Mirza Abul-Qasim Thaqafi**, was known as **Kalantar**. He was a *mujtahid* in his time, and wrote a few books. One of them is exposition of the late **Shaykh Ansari**'s lectures. The grandfather of my grandfather, **Haj Mirza Mahmud**, was a personality of the era of **Nasiruddin Shah**. It seems that when the Shah left Iran for a visit to **Karbala** [Iraq], he appointed him as the governor of Tehran. For this reason he got the nickname: **Kalantar**, which was, later, left for his son."

The mutual life of the **Aqa** is one of the most beautiful manifestations of his life, and the most successful part of it. Perhaps this was a reason, other than glory and pride, which attracted marrying couples to his house, asking him to conduct the wedding ceremony, and he, modestly, would accept the agency from the girl or the boy for reciting the text of the marriage contract. Even during the clamours of the war he rejected no one.

NOTES

1. **Bahman**, son of **Isfandiyar**, a famous king of the **Kiyani** dynasty. A part of his biography is stated in **Firdawsi**'s *Shahnameh*. Around the end of his years he abdicated the throne to his daughter, **Huma**.

2. Extracted from the *Zindeginameyeh Siyasiyeh Imam Khomeini*, by **Muhammad Hasan Rajabi**, vol. 1, p. 115.

3. On p. 358 of *Guzareshnameh* or *Fiqhullughah Asamiyeh Amkinah*, by **Ibrahim Dehgan**, under the above name it is said: ─It is the name of a quarter in **Iraq-e Ajam** whose central town was **Khomein**, which, originally, was called **Taymareh**, or **Big Taymareh** and **Small Taymareh**, or **Taymaratayn** [the two Taymarehs]. **Taymareh**, or **Kamareh**, consisted of the two upper sections, which are now called **Kamareh**, or **Khomein**, and the lower section, or **Taymareh**, which is now called **Mahallat**. The word ‚Kamareh' was certainly taken from the root ‚Kamir'', who were of the olden Aryan clans, who, according to **Sennakherib**, used to press, from the north, upon the kingdom of ‚Wan'. They were called ‚Cambra'. The Torah called them ‚Jurt', while the Greek historians called them ‚Kaymari'.

In the book *Bustanus-Siyahah*, ‚Kamareh' is stated to be: ─a pleasing district, a joyful quarter, covering prosperous places and famous plantations. The weather of that land is quite convenient, with plenty and continuous orchards. It is connected to **Kazzaz** region, and its people are affable, and its fruits are excellent." Re: **Zayn al-Abidin Shirwani**, *Bustanus-Siyahah*, with the help of **Sayyid Sa'id Tabatabai Naini**, Tehran, **Mirza Ali Asghar Khan Atabak**, 2nd ed. Lith., 1342 A.H., p. 472. (The Late Imam had signed some of his declarations as: **Khomeini Kamarei**.)

4. The mountain of **Alwand Lakan** (Alwand Saki) is situated in the north of **Lakan**, in the rural district of **Dalaiy**. It is 3065 m. above sea-level. One of its peaks is called **Bigham** [worriless]. (The name of **Alwand** is a repeated one on the mountains of Iran, the most famous of which is the **Alwand of Hamadan**.) *Nameyeh Kamareh*, vol. 1, p. 298.

5. *Tarikh-e Kamareh*, vol. 1, p. 52.

6. At 23 kms. to the east of **Khomein**, near **Gulmagard** village.

7. Nowadays it is called: **Razi** quarter.

8. On those days the doors of the nobles used to be built in a recess of two metres deep in the wall, with two [brick or stone] seats on its both sides, on which the servants of the guests would sit waiting for them to come out, as it was common for every person of high social rank to take with him a group of retinue accompanying him here and there. Such a group consisted of the coach driver, the muleteer, lamp-lighter, a foreman and sometimes a number of riflemen. Some houses, however, had those brick-seats for the old and feeble passers-by to have a rest, since they had to rest for several times to refresh themselves during their moving from one district to another.

9. To get acquainted with the architecture of the houses during the Qajariyan era, please look up: *My Autobiography*, by **Abdullah Mustawfi**, also refer to *Khatirat and Khatarat* by **Mukhbirus-Saltanah Hidayat**.

10. Her marriage-portion consisted of: twenty tumans in cash (equivalent to 75 grams of gold), a set of mattress and cover costing five tumans, a rug costing five tumans, one sixth of the said house, one-sixth of an orchard in **Khomein** and five *mans* [a weight which differs from place to place] of copper utensils costing five tumans. **Ayatullah Pasandideh,** *Pasdareh Islam* magazine, 7th year, No. 84, p. 26.

11. Tea-seeds were brought from India to Iran in 1283 [1904 A.D.], and were planted in the northern provinces. **Kashifus-Saltaneh**, Iran's Consul in Bombay took a quantity of it to **Muzaffaruddin Shah**. Before that, drinking tea was not so common in Iran as it is now, while drinking coffee was more common. For this reason when places for diversion and resting, offering breakfast and lunch together with tea appeared, they took the name of coffee-shops. As such, at that time, the **Aqa**'s relatives and friends sometimes sent to him bags of tea from India, and he used to brew of it for the guests.

12. One of the ancient towns of Iran in the Province of **Khurasan**, which presented great men, like **Attar** and **Khayyam**, to humanity.

13. The **Sayyids** in **Kashmir** are also called —Shah".

14. It is a deep book explaining the noble *hadith* of *thaqalayn* in Arabic, which has lately been translated into Persian.

15. This migration must have taken place within the years 1240 to 1250 A.H. **Ayatullah Pasandideh**, *Memoirs*, p. 9.

16. The marriage took place on 17th Ramadan, 1257 A. H. Ibid.

17. 29th Rajab, 1278 A.H.

18. More information about these two are available, except that on the 12th of Dhulqa'dah, 1254, she reconciled her marriage-portion to **Sayyid Ahmad**.

19. It is not known that **Murtada**—who, in his early youth, was called **Sayyid Aqa**—was the son of which one of the two wives. He died either in 1287 or 1288 A.H.

20. The date of her birth is not clearly known. She married **Karim Khan Qalahi** and gave him four children: two sons, named: **Mirza Yahya Khan** and **Imamquli Khan**, and two daughters, named: **Tajunnisa** and **Maryam**.

Mirza Yahya went to Tehran where he became a teacher of penmanship. We know nothing of the number of his children. One of his sons, however, went to Europe where he was lost. **Imam Quli Khan** married twice. First with the sister of **Haj Jalal Lashkar**, then with another girl whose name we could not know. But he got no child from either of them. He quarrelled with his brother-in-law about the heritage of his father-in-law. **Imam Quli** entrenched himself in the very house of **Aqa Mustafa**, but **Jalal Lashkar** could overcome him and, with the bastinado made bruses on his soles. When one of his acquaintances, by the name of **Amir Mufakhkham**, became the governor of **Kirman**, **Imamquli**, accompanied by his horsemen, went to **Kirman**. He had the intention to return to **Khomein**, but he died near **Yazd Uqada**.

Tajunnisa married **Shukrullah Khan**. She had no child from this husband. When **Shukrullah** died, **Shamsul Ulama** proposed to her. **Shamsul Ulama** left several children. One of them, by the name of **Baqir Shams**, was married to one of the sisters of the Imam and formed a large family. One of his grandchildren was **Ahmad Shams**, who finished his studies of aviation and was favoured by **Muhammad Rida Pahlavi**. Then he resided in the USA and worked at an arms manufacturing factory. After the Revolution he returned to Iran, but as no one cared for him, he went back to the USA.

Maryam was married to **Mirza Muhammad Kamarei**, son of **Sayyid Mehdi Kamarei**, and went to Tehran and dwelt in Abbas Abad district. **Sayyid Muhammad Kamarei** was a constitutionalist and against **Shaykh Fadlullah Nuri**. **Ayatullah Pasandideh**'s *Memoirs*, p. 39.

21. Birthday: Thursday, 18 Jumadal ula, 1272 A.H. The birthday of the other girls are unknown.

Agha Banu married **Jawad Mujtahid Khomeini**, resulting in three boys and three girls. **Mirza Rida Najafi**, who later became a *mujtahid* and had a book of *fatwas*, once for the publication of such a thesis under the title —Congregational Salat," he gave 25 rials to **Ayatullah Pasandideh** who had large copies of it printed in **Isfahan**. **Mirza Rida**, a cousin to **Ruhullah**, married one of the Imam's sister. **Mirza Abdul Muhammad**, was given the title of *Imam Jumah* by the government despite the fact that he never led any *Friday Salat*. He married the daughter of **Muhammad Husayn Khan**, one of the Khans of a village near Khomein. **Sadruddin Najafi**, who was known by the name **Haj Aqa Sadra**, established a Marriage-and-Divorce Office.

Agha Banu's daughters: **Shayesteh**, who had a strong personality and a sturdy tall stature, was famous among the women relatives. She married **Mirza Khalil Mahurzani** and lived with him in Khomein, in Hamzelu district. Her first husband died and she married **Aqa Sayyid Turab Rayhani**. Most of her children and grandchildren inherited intelligence from their mother, advancing to high education, mostly moving to Tehran and Shiraz.

Farkhundeh, **Agha Banu**'s second daughter, was married to **Sadra**, the son of the Friday *salat* leader of Jafar Abad. She had several children, one of whom was lost and there was no trace of him.

The third daughter, **Halimeh**, married **Aqa Ruhullah**'s uncle, **Mirza Abdul Mahdi Mujtahid**, who, when fifty, was the most famous scholar in Khomein. She got several children from him.

22. It is the name of a rural district in a mountainous region in the south of Arak, to which the town is connected, with some 45 or 46 villages. ‿Qareh', in Turkish, means black, and ‿kahriz' means ‿kariz' or canal. *Guzareshnameh*, by **Ibrahim Dehgan**, Arak, 1342, p. 192.

23. The daughter of Ali (*a*), the sister of **al-Husayn** (*a*), who gave to patience and forbearance their meaning.

24. Most of the Shiite had the desire to be buried near the graves of the pure Imams or their offspring. Their financial condition and their wills determined where they were to be buried. The *Baqi* cemetery in al-Madinah al-Munawwarah, and those in Najaf, Karbala, Kazimayn, Sacred Mashhad and the graveyard of **Zaynab** in Syria considered no border. When the Saudis became the rulers of the Hijaz, the flower-garden of *Baqi'* became stranger, and in the late decades Najaf, Karbala and Kazimayn used to receive only those who died in Iraq. In the past, when the frontiers between the Islamic countries were not regarded as impenetrable barriers, everybody could live in whatever place on the Islamic lands, and he could will to be buried wherever he liked. It is now quite difficult even for many of the students of politics to understand how it was possible, on those days, for the Islamic countries to be so borderless that one could live wherever one liked and be friendly received, despite the existence of numerous governments, with distinguished frontiers and fortified gates and sometimes bloody wars on small lands. More important was that along the history it frequently happened that two armies faced each other on both sides of the Tigris, killing

one another at daytime, but at night the bodies of the dead were sent from this side of the border to the other so as to be buried in Najaf and Karbala. Probably it will be possible, in this biography, to explain, to some extent, this complicated conduct. Generally speaking, one of its causes was that the mutual Qiblah and the existence of the shrine of **the noble Prophet (s)** and those of the pure **Imams (a)** had so joined the world of Islam that the borders were incapable to cleave everything on this side and that side.

25. —Aman, named **Khwajah Nasiri Mahallati**, wrote a book against our uncle accusing him falsely. He wrote that **Sayyid Aqa**, i.e. **Sayyid Murtada** had acted contrary to the *fatwa* of **Mirza Shirazi** concerning the tobacco as he smoked a *hooka* in the market of Qazwin, whereas our uncle had died ten years before the Tobacco Prohibition, and as such he was not living at that time." *Memoirs*, **Ayatullah Pasandideh**, p. 31.

26. From the year 1254 to 1285 or 1286 A.H.

27. From the year 1264 to 1282 A.H.

28. —W have not got the documents concerning the Nazi properties." *Memoirs*, **Ayatullah Pasandideh**, p. 12.

29. —Afer settling the heritage of our father, our monthly income from those properties was 100 to 200 tumans." *Memoirs*, **Ayatullah Pasandideh**, p. 12.

30. The year 1283 A.H.

31. The *Quran* (2:261).

32. The 6th of Safar, 1312 [1933].

33. 49 years, one month and 3 days, from the 14th of Shawwal 1264 to 17th Dhul-Qa'dah, 1313 A.H.

34. **Amir Kabir**, the Chancellor who was given the title of the hero fighting imperialism. There are many documents which testify that the British and Russian Embassies had played a role in instigating the courtiers, the First Lady and the beauties of the *harem* to do away with that efficient manager. Look up *Amir Kabir and Iran*, by **Faridun Adamiyyat**; *The Hidden Hand of the British Policy in Iran*, by **Khan Malik Samani**; and *Amir Kabir or the Hero of Fighting Imperialism*, by Ali **Akbar Hashimi Rafsanjani**.

35. **Ayatullah Pasandideh**: —The tower was built in the days of **Muhsin Khan**. When we were children, the upper story was ruined, and our father rebuilt it. I built the rampart. It was a wall of about one *zar* and a half (about 1m and 60 c.m., the height of a common person) for the sake of fortification, with small holes through which the riflemen shot at the wicked."

36. Ayatullah Pasandideh: —He was very influential, with attendants and riflemen. He was engaged in managing the people's affairs. He also used to look after the affairs, but as regards religious lawsuits he handled them with caution. Such religious cases were mostly handled by the late **Akhund Mulla Muhammad Jawad**, our mother's uncle, and other conservative *ulama. Pasdar-e Islam,* 7th year, No. 84, p. 28.

37. The very great man who issued the decree of Tobacco Prohibition.

38. **Hujjat al-Islam** and **Ayatullah** are two terms which show, to some extent, the scholarly level of the *ulama*, though they have no strict limits as the university degrees have. It is quite possible that a Hujjatul Islam may be at the level of a master's degree, and another may be at the level of a doctorate, as far as religious knowledge is concerned, though both bear the title of **Hujjat al-Islam**. But Ayatullah is the person who has studied the high levels of *usul* and *fiqh*—which are termed as seminary study—under a *mujtahid* or many *mujtahid*s, and has received permission to act, in the religious subfundamentals, according to his own *ijtihad*. (Probably on those days the term Ayatullah was still not known).

39. 1319 to 1320 A.H.

40. —**Aqa Sayyid Ruhullah** is the last son of **Aqa Sayyid Mustafa Hindi**. He was the scientific head of the town of Khomein and its suburbs." *Aineye Daneshwaran*, **Sayyid Ali Rida ibn Muhammad Yazdi Husayni**, known as **Sayyid Rayhanullah**, vol. 1, Tehran, 1353 [1974].

41. 1305 A.H., **Ayatullah Pasandideh**, in his *Memoirs*, p. 15. He calls her **Awliya Khanum**.

42. 1312 A.H. (1274 S.H.).

43. **Hajar Khanum**.

44. By Nazmiyyah they meant the police forces on those days. The Government Deputy, who was assigned by the Capital to be governor in a town, had a Sheriff and a headservant. Preserving security and order was the task of the Government Deputy. In the year 1288 [1909], on the days of the chancellorship of **Mirza Husayn Khan**, **Mushiruddawlah Qazvini**, an army regiment in Tehran was named —The Nazmiyyah Regiment". After the second visit of **Nasiruddin Shah** to Europe in 1295 A.H., **Conte de Mont**, an Italian by origin and Austrian by nationality, came to Iran. First he established the office of *Nazmiyyah*, then its Ministry. However, the Nazmiyyah got its administrative offices as from 1290 [1911] on, by the Swedish counsellors.

45. *Memoirs*, by **Ayatullah Pasandideh**, p. 16.

46. **Ayatullah Pasandideh**: ―The Dalai Khans, including **Haj AbbasAli Khan** and **Haj Jalal**, did not wrong the people, except in one way, the way of giving usurious loans to the merchants through religious tricks of conditions, reconciliation, property and the like. By this means and properties they got their income. *Memoirs*, p. 66.

47. ―**Muhammad**'s *halal* is *halal* till the Day of Resurrection, and **Muhammad**'s *haram* is *haram* till the Day of Resurrection."

48. The concept is **Aqa Mustafa**'s, but the phrasing is the writer's.

49. Born in 1305 A.H.

50. In *Pasdar-e Islam* Magazine, **Ayatullah Pasandideh** refers twice to this child, yet it was not known whether he was born in Najaf, in Isfahan or in Khomein.

51. Born in 1312 A.H.

52. Born in 1313 A.H.

53. Born in 1315 A.H.

54. Born in 1318 A.H.

54/1. According to some comparative calendars it was on Monday.

55. It is more probable that he was born at dawn.

56. *Hudur* Magazine, No. 1, year 70, quoting him: ―18th Jumada ath-Thaniyah, 1320 A.H. is correct."

57. ―**Ruhullah**" is the title of the Prophet **Isa the Messiah**. In the prayer recited on visiting the shrine of **Abu 'Abdullah al-Husayn (***a***)**, it is stated: ―Peae be upon you, O the heir of **Isa, Ruhullah**."

58. **Ayatullah Pasandideh**: ―Hewas born in 1320 A.H., the 18th or the 20th of Jumada ath-Thaniyah, as inscribed by his own hand on the back of the book *Jannatul Khulud*." The Memoirs Section at the ICPIKW.

59. **Behjat Khanum**, foster-sister of **Ruhullah**. *Neda*, a periodical issued by the Society for the Women of the Islamic Republic of Iran, Spring of 1369 [1980], p. 140.

60. Wheat is soaked, when it buds, it is minced, mixed with flour, put into a large pot on fire, and stirred from morning till midnight. When it browns, more water is added and left to brew on a slow fire till morning.

The *Samanu* was originally prepared as a dessert dish on the *Nowruz* table of *Seven Eses*'. Later it was introduced to large banquets of the Iranian celebrating customs. Then it acquired a sort of sanctity. It is now many centuries that some persons vow to cook it every year in remembrance of **Fatimah (***a***)**, sending a quantity of it to the relatives, friends, neighbours and those who helped in cooking it.

61. The census provisions in 1297 [1918], were enacted on the days of the premiership of **Wuthuquddawlah (Hasan Wuthuq)** in Tehran. Their enforcement was entrusted to commissariats (police stations), which were pronounced by the common people as *comisary*. (*Iran* newspaper of the same year). Its relevant law was certified by the *Majlis* in 1304 [1925].

62. The law concerning military service was enacted as from 1307 [1928], but in 1304 [1925] when they distributed identity cards, there was a whisper that those cards were to be used for levying taxes and compulsory recruitment. It took years for recruitment to become ordinary, because the disgusting conduct of the cossacks, their corruption and bad-temperedness resounded even in the remote villages. People tried at every cost to avoid sending their youths to military service. The easiest way was to report the ages of their sons higher than their real ages in the identity cards. If the age, on applying for the card, was near that for going to military service, it was increased. But the relevant officers, by way of being serviceable or expecting bribes, used to increase the ages of even the small boys, thus, they would later on face difficulties, because the officers came after the young boys of, say, 15 years old whose identity cards showed them to be of 18 years old and suitable for military service.

63. Even when he redressed the date of his birthday, an expression made it vague: —Accrding to the identity card No. 2744, born in 1279 solar year [1900] in Khomein", while in fact it was on the 20th of Jumadi ath-Thani, 1320 A.H. The decisive date: 20th Jumadi ath-Thani = 1st of Mehr, 1281 solar year (18th Jumadi ath-Thani, 1320 A.H. = 30th Shahrivar, 1281 [1902] is correct). *Hudur*, Khordad, 1370, p. 5.

64. Such as: **Mirza Qummi, Shaykh Ja'far Najafi** and **Wahid Behbahani**.

65. Such as: the authors of *al-Jawahir*, *al-Makasib* and *al-Qawanin*.

66. Such as: **Mustawfiyul Mamalik, Malikul Mutakallimin, Atabak-e A'zam** ....

67. **The Imam (S.)** in his lyric poem ‚Pir-e Mughan' in his collection of poetry, calls himself ‚Hindi':

The covenant I had concluded with the old vintner

Last year, I renewed once again last night.

From the lips of ‚Hindi" hear you no talk

Other than that clear wine and the talk of the vintner.

68. ↓; Sayyid „Murtada Hindi", was, according to the (governmental) Friendship Committee of Iran, forced to change my family name from ‚Hindi" to ‚Pasandideh".

The justice authorities refrained from changing the (**Imam**'s) family name to ‗Mustafawi' or ‗Ahmadi' because these were Arabic." *Ganjineh Dil*.

69. On 22/12/1358 solar year, a foundation was established under the name of **Bunyad-e Shahid** to take care of the families of the martyrs of the Islamic Revolution. As the imposed war [by Iraq] started, that **Bunyad** extended its activity to cover the families of the martyred in the war as well. Now it is one of the most important establishments of the Islamic Revolution. It is not governmental and its chairman is appointed by the Leader of the Revolution.

70. **Ali Dawani**, *Nehdat-e Ruhaniyun-e Iran*, vol. 6, p. 76.

71. *Kalimat-e Qisar, Pandha wa Hikmatha*, p. 228.

72. **Mirza Ali Asghar Khan, Aminus-Sultan**, the Grand Minister of **Nasiruddin Shah**, and who got the post of chancellorship in 1310 lunar year, after the assassination of **Nasiruddin Shah** in 1275 solar year, kept his post under **Muzaffaruddin Shah**. Later he was also put in charge of the Foreign Affairs. In the year 1276 [1897] he was deposed and sent to exile in Qum. In the year 1277, **Muzaffaruddin Shah** demanded from **Sayyid Ali Bahrayni** to do *istikhareh* to augur whether he may return back the **Mirza** from Qum and return him to chancellorship. The answer was in the affirmative. In 1279 **Muzaffaruddin Shah** travelled to Europe and stayed there for six months. Returning home, he bestowed upon his good-looking Chancellor the title of ‗Atabak-e Azam' [Great Chancellor]. In 1283 [1904] he was once again deposed from his post of Chancellorship. He travelled to Europe and from there he went to pilgrimage. On the 8th of Isfand, 1286 [1907] he was invited by **Muhammad Ali Shah** to accept the post of Chancellorship. Although he had a comfortable life in Europe, yet on the 30th of Farwardin, 1286, he came, on board a Russian warship, with extraordinary celebrations, to Anzali Port. But the Gilani fighters prevented him from landing, until the National Assembly announced that there was no objection against his entering Iran. On the 12th of Ordibehesht of the same year he became the Premier and on the next day he explained to the Assembly the future program of his cabinet and recollected that his travel to Europe had changed some of his ideas, and that from then on he would do all the affairs of the country according to the consultation of the Assembly's deputies. On 8th Shahrivar of the same year, the British Minister handed over to the Ministry of Foreign Affairs a note about the agreement reached at by Britain and Russia about dividing Iran into two parts under their influence. The Chancellor went to the Majlis where he delivered a speech. When, at 2 o'clock at night he left the Majlis, engaged in a conversation with **Ayatullah Behbahani**, three bullets were shot at him.

The murderer, by the name of **Abbas Aqa Tabrizi**, committed suicide as they were arresting him.

73. The year 1322 A.H. *Mishkat*, Nos. 23 and 24, Summer and Fall of 1368.

74. "And of His *ayahs* is that He shows you the lightning for fear and for hope and sends down from the sky water, and thereby revives the earth after its death. Surely in that are *ayahs* for a people who understand." The *Quran, surah* of *ar-Rum*, 24.

75. Oral reference: **Dr. Mahmud Burujerdi**, the Imam's son-in-law.

76. Many of those who had seen his swimming, even at the threshold of old age, told legendary stories about the elegance and artifice of his swimming. **Ayatullah Khalkhali** relates: —Before 1342 [1963] in some summer seasons we used to climb the mountains of Darakeh with **Aqa Mustafa** to swim in the river. At times **the Imam (S.)** used to come with us. How good he was at climbing the mountain! He was so excellent at turning somersaults in _haft-hawd_ that I feared he would strike his back at stones of the river-bed. But he was so clever that in a river of no more than half a metre he never had his back injured." Nevertheless, when the late **Ahmad Aqa** was asked whether **the Imam** had good knowledge of the art of swimming, he said: —He had no knowledge of the art of swimming, but he had ordinary knowledge of it." *Pa beh Pay-e Aftab*, vol. 1, p. 80.

77. On the 23/3/1358, **the Imam (S.)**, in a student gathering in the University of Tehran, answering a question put to him by a group, he referred to the group's affliction, and mentioned a person by the name of **Amir Mufakhkham** who, most probably, was the same person. From his statement it can be derived that **Amir Mufakhkham** was a Bakhtiyari living in Khomein and was the governor of Kerman for a while. However, in his opinion, if this man was not very bad, he was not good either: —Yes, their affliction was worse than the other's. It happens that somebody comes and is known who he is. At that time I was a child, when in Khomein they talked of **Amir Mufakhkham** (He was of the Bakhtiyaris. He was a chief there). He said **Sardar Hishmat** (a khan, a prince), his position is known. His hostility is known and his amity is known, too. But so-and-so had said: _Save me from this man! Seemingly he is friendly, but he breaks one's back.'" *Sahifeh-ye Imam* vol. 7, p. 106.

78. The _khalili_' was a board with several holes, and with a rod, by sending it through the holes, the prisoner's feet would be locked.

79. **Qara Suran** was the name of the private army under the command of local governors. They undertook keeping the order of the region. For the

first time, on 25 Khordad, 1290 [1911], **Morgan Shuster**, an American, formed an armed force for the purpose of levying taxes, and called it _Gendarmeri.e.' Two months later, on the 23rd of Murdad, three Swedes, headed by **Colonel Yalmarson**, came to Tehran to organize a police force. We do meet the word _Gendarmerie' in the historical sources, such as *Afdalut-Tawarikh* and *Tarikh-e Bidariye Iraniyan*. It was decided to be established in the days of **Muzaffaruddin Shah** by an Italian emigrant living in Tehran, named **Malta**, but he did not succeed.

80. Probably the following expression refers to the above story: —When I was young, there was in Khomein a governor who arrested one of the khans of that region and imprisoned him. Then a number of the khans with their riflemen came and arrested the governor and took him. The people showed no reaction, rather they were pleased." *Sahifeh-ye Imam*, vol. 8, p. 146.

81. **Sadr al-Ulama** and his brother, **Mirza Muhsin Mujtahid**, were of well-known *ulama* in Tehran. **Mirza Muhsin Mujtahid** was assassinated by the Punishing Committee in 1295 [1916]. Look up: *Rijal Iran*.

82. **Colonel Kasakovski**, in his *memoirs*, says: —Iwent forward and reported: _The town is completely secured.' The Shah once again asked: _Is security established?' Then he asked: _How are you? How are your cossacks? His Excellency the Chancellor has written to me about all things. I am grateful. I thank you for your efforts... I will try to practically prove my gratitude. Now I submit myself to you. Take me to the palace.'" *Memories of Colonel Kasakovski*, translated by **Abbasquli**, 2nd ed., 1355, pp. 82-83.

83. Ali **Akbar Wilayati**, *Tarikh-e Rawabit-e Kharqjiy-e Iran dar Dawran-e Nasiruddin Shah wa Muzaffaruddin Shah*, p. 469.

84. Concerning **Muzaffaruddin Shah**'s temperament and conduct, look up: *Memoirs of Sergent Hardinig*, the then British Minister in Iran, translated by **Jawad Shaykh al-Islami**, and *Tarikh-e Bidariy-e Iraniyan*, **Nazim al-Islam Kirmani**, *Afdalut-Tawarikh*, by **Afdalul Mulk Kirmani** and *The Memoirs of Tajus-Saltanah*, Muzaffaruddin Shah's sister, and also *The British Secret Documents about Constitutional Events of Iran*, translated by **Hasan Muasir**, and *Khatirat wa Khatarat*, by **Mahdi Quli Hidayat**.

85. The investigation about whether the daughter of **Sadrul Ulama** was the wife of **Jafar Quli Khan** or of **Rida Quli Sultan** has not yet been cleared, but possibly she was **JafarQuli Khan**'s wife.

86. —And there is life for you in retaliation, O men of acumen! That you may practise *taqwa*" The *Quran*, 2:179.

87. The last chancellorship of **Amin as-Sultan**, in the time of Muzaffaruddin Shah, came to an end on the 22nd of Jamadiyul akhar, 1321.

88. Concerning whether **Rida Quli Khan** died in the **Qal'ah** or in prison, **Ayatullah Pasandideh**, in his *Memoirs*, p. 23, says that he died in prison. But from his interviews with the *Pasdar-e Islam* magazine, it appears that he died in the **Qalah**. Also concerning whether there was a woman in the **Qalah** who was arrested with the other members of the family, is still disputed.

89- The Minister of Court was called Vazir-e Khalwat [Minister of Privacy]. Perhaps, he was, then, **Wakilul Mulk Tabatabai**.

90- —In those days His Royal Highness decided to travel to Europe, and he did travel. Thus, all the efforts of the merchants, the exchange and the guilds turned fruitless, and **Monsieur Noze**, too, behaved powerfully. Two days after the travel of His Royal Highness, at the order of the Crown Prince, because of killing **Sayyid Mustafa Kamarei**, they killed **Mirza Jafar Khan Kamarei**. This stirred general fear, and particularly bread and meat which were difficult [to find] became abundant." **Muhammad Mehdi Sharif Kashani**: *Waqiat Ittifaqiyyah dar Ruzgar*, [published] with the help of **Mansureh Ittihadiyyeh wa Sirus Sadwandiyan**, Tehran, Nashr Tarikh-e Iran, 1362 [1983], vol. 1, p. 22.

91- *Memoirs* of **Ayatullah Pasandideh**, pp. 23 and 24.

92- Abdul Majid Mirza was son of Sultan Ahmad Mirza (Adududdawlah), grandson of **FathAli Shah**. He was born in 1261 A.H., corresponding to the solar year 1224 in Tehran, and started his activity in the administration and politics, as the secretary of the Crown Prince, **Muzaffaruddin Mirza**. Then he was prompted to Amir Akhuri (head of the stables), ending with the post of premiership. During his life he occupied diverse posts, including the governorship of the towns of Urumiyeh, Mahabad, Tabriz, and the Provinces of Mazandaran, Lurestan, Khurasan, and for a while he was the governor of Tehran, and then he was appointed as the Minister of Interior. One day, after the resignation of the Chancellor (Atabak) on the 25th of Murdad 1282 [1903] (when **Ruhullah** was only 13 months and 5 days old), **Muzaffaruddin Shah** appointed him as Prime Minister. In the administration of the government he was so despot that it accelerated the speed of the Constitutional Revolution, and by deposing and exiling him, Constitutionalism was endorsed. Strange enough that although the Crown Prince (Muh. Ali Mirza) believed that his efforts were to abolish his succession to the throne, and, consequently, he regarded him his enemy, yet this open enmity was neglected in order to suppress the uprise of Adharbaijan, led by **Shaykh Muhammad** Khiyabani, and he got the Shah's decree for that. So, once again, in Ordibehesht of 1294 [1905], he was introduced by **Ahmad Shah** to the *Majlis* as Prime Minister. He introduced the members of his cabinet. At last, in Aban of 1306 [1927] he died in Aynuddawlah Street. He was not a complicated person, but the complicated political situations of Iran complicated him. At times he acted with little patience, at times he was tolerant, mostly incredulous and some times confused. He behaved roughly with the people, yet he was kind to some of his friends. He was resolute in issuing orders, irresolute in thought. He was keen on acquiring wealth, but in spending it he was not stingy. The family and the environmental education in which he was brought up made out of him a daring, decisive, obstinate and despotic personality. It, thus, happened that during the different posts he had, most of the people, though not so deeply disliked him, they were displeased and objecting. Despite the fact that he had many posts and seriously managed them, he was registered in history as a disgusting personality.

93. He was **Nasiruddin Shah**'s son-in-law from whom he received the title of *Imam Jumah.*

94. **Sayyid Hasan Imami** got his doctorate in law from Switzerland, and after returning to Iran wore the turban. As from 1324 to 1357 [1945-1978] he retained the title of *Imam Jumah*, without leading any Friday *salat*. After the victory of the Islamic Revolution he got asylum in Switzerland and died there.

95. *Pasdar-e Islam*, 8th year, No. 85, pp. 27 and 28.

96. **Mrs. Zahra Mustafawi**: ʽThe **Imam (S.)** used to say: ʽThe place of execution was at the entrance of Bab Humayun St. at the former Tupkhaneh Square (now Imam Khomeini Sq.). A pocket watch was presented to the executioner by Ammah Khanum.ʻ

97. *The Memoirs*, by Ayatullah Pasandideh, pp. 24-29. Words slightly altered.

98. Ibid., p. 45.

99. 1293-1298 (S.H.).

100. Kaftar = pigeon. Khan = house. Kaftar khan means pigeon-house of which there were plenty in Khomein. In *Nameyeh Kamareh*, vol. 2, pp. 11-30, the names of their most famous ones and the way of making different kinds of them in the town and the villages, are stated.

101. Refer to *Hilyah al-Muttaqin*, Ch. on keeping animals, especially birds and cocks.

102. *Sahifeh-ye Imam*, vol. 1, p. 46.

103. Ibid., vol. 6, p. 21.

104. I could not find this man's name.

105. The *Quran, Surah Al-e Imran*: 92.

106. Quoting the concept from several quotations.

107. *Kawthar*, vol. 3, p. 38.

108. *Sahifeh-ye Imam*, vol. 8, pp. 86-87.

109. Ibid., vol. 11, p. 24.

110. On the 9th of Deymah, 1285 [1906], Constitutionalism was ratified and received its formality when the Shah endorsed the Constitution of Iran, which was inspired by the Belgian Constitution. Nine days later the Shah died and **Muhammad Ali Shah** succeeded his father.

111. The Constitutional uprising of Iran, based on the documents of the Ministry of Foreign Affairs, pp. 154-160, quoted from *Tarikh-e Rawabit-e Kharejiy-e Iran*, **Ali Akbar Wilayati**, p. 520.

112. —Constitutionalism was also one of the British Imperialistic tricks in the first decade of the 20th century in Iran." **Muhammad Turkman**, *Shaykh-e Shahid Fadlullah Nuri*, vol. 2, p. 11.

113. —...Constitutionalism, this uprising, started from Najaf by the *ulama*... The severe despotism, doing whatever it liked in Iran... In the face of a handful of despots, the *ulama* revolted and brought about an uprising, with the *ulama*, at its head. They wanted to implemented it, but they could not. Had it been implemented it would have been good. They could not. Well, as they could not, what could they do?" *Sahifeye Imam*, vol. 1, pp. 255-266.

114. In his political thought, rulership belongs to the law, and legitimacy returns to the law, not to the government. In the course of the development of his political thoughts I shall take up this question at length. Look up: *Wilayat-e Faqih*.

115. *Asnadi dar Bareyeh Hujum-e Inglis wa Rus beh Iran*, [Documents Concerning the Attack of the British and the Russians on Iran], **Muhammad Turkman**, Published by the Office for Political and International Studies in the Ministry of Foreign Affairs, pp. 51-52.

116. From the report of a *Majlis* Deputy to Churchill, the British Embassy's oriental attaché, at the meeting of a delegation of the *Majlis* Deputies with Muhammad Ali Shah Qajar, on Wednesday 3rd Sha'ban, 1325 [1946], it becomes clear that in the said meeting, the Agreement of the British and the Russians was also discussed. Ibid., p. 54.

117. Ibid., p. 56.

118. Ibid., p. 49, quoted from **Mahdi Quli Hidayat** (Mukhbirus-Saltaneh). *Iran Report*, by the care of **Muhammad Ali Sawti**, Tehran. *Nashr-e Nuqreh*, 1363 [1984], p. 199.

119. **Ayatullah Pasandideh**: —Some 60 deputies had been elected for the First Term of the *Majlis*. From Khomein, too, our uncle, the late **Aqa Mirza Abdulhusayn** was elected to the *Majlis*, the very *Majlis* which was bombarded by **Muhammad Ali Shah**." *Memoirs*, p. 66.

I could not trace back the above name in any source registering the names of the deputies from different regions covering 24 terms. In the First Term, Gulpaygan and Khansar had two deputies by the names of **Mirza Muhammad Baqir Adib Gulpaygani** and **Shaykh Muhammad Baqir Mashayikhi Khansari**, but Khomein had no deputy. In the Second Term of the elections in Kamareh, Gulpaygan and Khansar, there was a deputy by the name of **Haj Buyuk Khan** (Liwauddawlah). As from the Third Term onward, Khomein (Kamareh) and Mahallat used to send a deputy to the *Majlis*. Probably the late **Mirza Abdulhusayn** was a candidate who did not win in the elections, and possibly his distinguished social status and his frequenting the deputies gave **Ayatullah Pasandideh**, as a child, to think that he was actually a deputy, then the thought became a certainty with him.

120. The first session of the *Majlis* was held on the 14th of Mehrmah, 1285 [1906] in Gulestan Palace or Madrese-ye Nizam.

121. —fiI wanted to write down all the lies I hear, a quantity of 70 *mans* of paper would be needed. There is talk in Tehran as much as there is snow on the Shimiran Mount. They tell such lies that one grows feathers." The newspaper: *Akhbar-e Mashrutiyyat wa Inqilab-e Iran, Notes of Sayyid Ahmad Tafrishi Husayni*, with the help of **Iraj Afshar**, [published by] Amir Kabir, 1351 [1972] p.194.

122. Even the researchers who believe that **Muhammad Ali Shah** was not as bad as he is reported, they do admit that he had no good reputation.

123. Most of the parks had Persian names, such as Bagh-e Milli. But this one was called Aminuddawlah Park.

124. According to a surviving document about the events of 23rd Jumada al-ula, 1326 A.H., corresponding to the 2nd of Tirmah, 1287 [1908], the number of the casualties was less than that stated in most books on history. It says: —From the Cossacks two persons, from the *Majlis* 53 persons, two persons according to the judgement of the Cossacks. From the office to Bagh-e Shah, three of the mercenaries of the Cossacks were killed. 43 to 48 persons were jailed, 16 killed and 27 were wounded. The bombardment destroyed Zillus-Sultan building, partly; the complete building of the Adharbayjan Society; the whole building of the *Majlis* and Aminuddawlah Park. As is said, they are going to close up the gun-barrel at 3 to the sunset: Aqa Sayyid 'Abdullah, Malikul Mutakallimin, Director of *Sur Israfil*, **Sayyid**

Jamal. Plundered: The house of **Zillus-Sultan** completely, Adharbayjan Society completely, the *Majlis* completely including beams and boards, Aminuddawlah garden completely." *Tarikh-e Muasor-e Iran*, Book 6, p. 256, doc. No. 28, Muasseseyeh Pazduhesh wa Mutalaateh Farhangi [The Establishment for Research and Cultural Studies].

125. *Sahifeye Imam*, vol. 1, p. 260. Once again he used the statement: —Ïe deeds which he did cannot be explained. This would be known in the other world. In this world we cannot understand. We cannot understand what a beast he was!" Ibid., vol. 4, p. 147. The above expression is about **Muhammad Rida Pahlavi**. The only difference between the two is that the beastliness of **Muhammad 'Ali Mirza** is for granted and which is known to all in this world.

126. 4th Isfand.

127. 3rd Khordad.

128. Corresponding to 27th Feb.

129. 28th Farvardin.

130. **Baqir Aqili**, *Ruz Shimar-e Tarikh-e Iran*, vol. 1, p. 47.

131. **Amir Bahadur, Shapshal Rusi, Mafakhirul Mulk, Aminul Mulk, Muqtadirul Mulk** and **Mujallalus-Sultan**.

132. The two preachers were: **Malikul Mutakallimin** and **Sayyid Jamaluddin**. The journalists were: **Sayyid Muhammad Rida Shirazi**, director of *Musawat*, **Sultanul Ulama Khurasani**, director of *Ruhul Quds*, **Mirza Jahangir Khan**, director of *Sur Israfil* and **Sayyid Hasan Taqizadeh**, who was neither a preacher nor a journalist, though, apparently, an opposer of the Court.

133. The other three were: Ali **Bick, Muwaqqarus-Saltaneh** and **Iftikharul Mulk**.

134. **Amir Bahadur**, 12 Khordad, 1287 [1908]. *Ruz Shemar-e Tarikh-e Iran*, vol. 1, p. 48.

135. About ten o'clock in the morning of 15th Khordad, 1287 [1908].

136. **Jalaluddawlah, Alauddawlah, Muinuddawlah, Amir Nizam and Sardar Mansur**.

137. Ibid, p. 49.

138. 22nd Khordad.

139. The first of Tir, 1287 [1908].

140. **Shaykh Fadlullah Nuri**, son of **Mulla 'Abbas Tabarsi**, was born on the 2nd of Dhul-Hijjah, 1259 A.H. in Kajur village of Nur township. He had his preliminary studies in Iran, then he travelled to Najaf to complete his studies. He attended the classes of great teachers like **Shaykh Radi al-e**

Khidir, **Mirza Habibullah Rashti** (a student of **Shaykh Murtada Ansari**), **Sayyid Muhammad Hasan Mirza Shirazi**, etc. Obtaining the degree of *ijtihad*, he returned to Iran, where he played an active role in the Tobacco Prohibition. He was one of the theorists of the Constitutional uprising, while it was shaping. But at last, when the Constitution was put to practice, he had difficulties with it concerning its legality. Lastly, on the 12th of Rajab, 1328 A.H. he was convicted of backing legitimacy and was martyred.

Among his works are: *Sharh-e Maqasid*, covering his articles, letters and statements published during his taking sanctuary in Shah Abdul Azim; *Tahrim-e Mashrutiyyat*, explaining his preliminary agreements and later disagreements with Constitutionalism; *Tadhkiratul Aqil wa Irshadul Jahil*, in defiance of the policy of Constitutionalism. Concerning this latter book there is dispute about whether it is really his or ascribed to him. Some historians have a double-feeling regarding him, but the majority praise him for his frankness, exposing his beliefs and insisting on his ideas, and take him to be fond of religion.

141. —Adharbayjan, which has always been supporting Islam, was the pioneer in every question, vanguard in doing away with injustice. Adharbayjan worked so hard in the early Constitutional movement under the leadership of **Sattar Khan** and **Baqir Khan** ...” *Sahifeh-ye Imam*, vol. 11, p. 173.

Also addressing the members of Jihad-e Sazandagi in Tabriz, he said: —You were in the front line. During Constitution and after you were at the head of the *mujahids* you have numerous *mujahids*, you have **Khiyabani**, you have **Sattar Khan** and **Baqir Khan**.” Ibid., p. 178.

142. For further information concerning how they were exiled and the names of the exiled, look up *Fighting Muhammad Ali Shah–Documents of the Activities of the Freedom-Loving People in Istanbul*, with the help of **Iraj Afshar**, Tehran Farhang-e Iran Zamin, 1359 [1980], p. 14.

143. Of **Dekhow**‘s wonders was that the head of a cow was entangled in a barrel. He suggested to cut the head of the cow. The head dropped inside the barrel. Then he told them: Now break the barrel. The cow‘s head and barrel are ironic symbols for planning according to **Dekhow**‘s method.

144. **Dr**. **Sayyid Jafar Shahidi** (oral memoirs).

145. Nizamuddin Ubaydullah Zakani, a poet in the 8th century A.H., died in 772 A.H. (1370 or 1371 A.D.), was a critic wise, gnostic, orator and poet who used the language of poetic satire to expose double-facedness in all political, social and religious aspects. He was born in Qazvin, and he lived in Shiraz, Tabriz and Baghdad for a while. His works are: *Diwan-e Ashar*,

Akhlaqul Ashraf, Rishnameh, Resaleye Sad Pand, Ta'rifat or *Dah Fasl, Dilgusha, Falnameh, Ushshaq Nameh* and *Mush-u-Gurbeh*. This last book is the most famous of his works, by which he is often known.

146. –**Mr. Carter** is also one of those who have got no heavenly education. If you had heard that within these days he went to the church once to invoke for their (the hostages) release. Do know that his invocation is like those of **Muhammad Rida** [Shah] who used to go to Mashhad and invoke. This is like one of the parables of one of our sages, **Ubayd of Zakan**, who said: _Good news! The cat has become pious.' This is the question." *Sahifeyeh Imam*, vol. 10, p. 245.

The above passage refers to the occupation of the USA's Embassy by the _Students Following the Line of the Imam', and Mr. Carter's invocation in the church for the release of the hostages. This is one of his most gnostic speeches which showed, before and after it, how the powers forget the human beings and think only of their interests. It warns the naive people not to be deceived by the outward appearance and judge by it. It also disclosed that the sarcastic critic, *Ubayd Zakani*—whom many of the *faqih*s disliked—was, to him, a wise man in sentimental wordings: —ne of our sages."

147- —…Hisjudgement reminded me of the book *Mush-u-Gurbeh*. Today it is a valuable and instructive book. It demonstrated the very want for sovereignty, as well as exposing the Powers at time of might and at time of weakness, and portrayed their trickery. In this book of *Mush-u-Gurbeh* the cat spreads the salat-carpet, to show that he was performing the *salat* and has repented and asked **Allah**'s forgiveness, to the effect that: _I will never do anything', and thus those helpless mice were deceived and brought him food and the like, but he, then, jumped and seized five of them on the spot …" *Didgah ha wa Rahnemudhayeh Imam Khomeini dar Masail-e Farhangi*, p. 238.

148- *Ruz Shimar-e Tarikh-e Iran*, vol. 1, p. 56.

149- The name of the shooter was **Karim Dawatgar**, who, on the 9th of Daymah, 1287 [1908] shot at the Shaykh in front of the house of **Adudulmulk**. Seeing himself surrounded, he shot at his own mouth, but he did not di.e. The Shaykh forgave him, and he later joined the Punishment Committee to which he became the second victim.

150- On the 30th of Farvardin, 1288 [1909] hail, as large as a hazelnut, poured down, within five minutes, all the fruits of the trees in Zanjan and its villages. In that year not a single fruit was seen in that locality.

151- On the 20th Isfand the sky was pierced, the Sepahdar Dam of Qazvin broke and destroyed all the cultivation, and water entered the town causing much casualties and property losses.

152- There were many terroristic events, the most distinguished among them were the assassinations of **Shaykh Fadlullah** on the 9th of Daymah, 1287 [1908], **Mirza Masud Shaykh al-Islam**, on the 16th of Farwardin, 1288 [1909], **Iftikharul Ulama Shaykh Ghulam Husayn**, leader of the *salat* and **Aqa Sayyid Ismail Mujtahid**, on the 2nd of Ordibehesht, 1288.

153- **Howard Bascroil** was born in 1885 and finished his study in Princeton University in 1907. He came to Iran and taught history in Memorial School. Then, at request of some students, he taught Intentional Rights, too. When the National Assembly was bombarded, the heart-rending scenes of killings and plunderings roused his anger and, despite the warnings of the headmaster and the American Consul, he hurried to help the injured, joining the ranks of the Constitutionalists, and on the 31th of Farwardin, 1288, he manly gave his life in the war. Look up *Qiyam-e Adharbayjan and Sattar Khan*, by **Ismail Amirkhizi**.

153/1- It is a loose narration from the **Prophet (s)**.

154- While the Islamic Revolution was getting mature, ‗the north and the south‗ had given its place to ‗the political east and west‗, though the slogan of ‗Neither Eastward nor Westward‗ has three more meanings, which shall be referred to in other chapters. However, one of its evidences is the juristic rule ‗Negation of the Way‗, but it is certain that the Imam‗s serious attention to this fundamental slogan was positively affected by the contemporary history of Iran and the world of Islam.

154/1- Look up: *Tarikh-e Bidari-ye Iraniyan,* by **Nazimul Islam Kirmani**.

154/2- The members of this body were: **Barnosky, Churchil, Muwaththaquddawlah, Wuthuquddawlah, Musharus-Saltanah, Ibrahim Hakimul Mulk and Husayn Quli Nawwab**.

154/3- *Tarikh-e Bidariy-e Iraniyan*, p. 506.

155- *Dorna* [Crane] is the name of a *halal* bird which flies in group. Their playfullness in the sky is sightly: Sometimes they fly in the shape of a triangle, sometimes in a complicated form. That is why when a handkerchief is twisted so as to beat someone with it like a whip, it is called *dorna* or *torna*. During the rule of the Qajaris, the game of Shah-and-Vizier played in the coffee shops, was called *Dorna*: By drawing lots a person would be the Shah and he would appoint the Vizier and the Executer, then somebody would volunteer to obey the Shah and bear the strikes of the *Dorna*, and sometimes, up to 200 strikes. Of course, the Shah himself would name the number of the strikes according to the endurance of the beaten, because if the beaten became the Shah he would avenge himself on the former Shah's hands and feet for the *Dornas'* he had to endure at the orders of the former Shah. It was rather a brutal game, but it could exhaust the youths' energies. It also conveyed the message that it seems that the Shah had nothing to do but to issue beating orders. The Shah-and-Wazir game played by the youngsters was kinder than the Dorna game played by the elders. It was called *torrah'* game. Sometimes the Shah would command his fellow-players to go home and bring for the Shah some eatables. It also appears that the children's Shah game was a mirror reflecting the reality, because the Shah, in all games, was always the subject of right, priviledged, self-indulgent, without feeling any responsibility.

156- *Kawthar*, vol. 2, p. 544.

In the year 1919 **Wuthuquddawlah** signed a draft agreement according to which two million Pounds were to be given to Iran as a loan, and the organization of the Iranian army was to be entrusted to Britain. **Ahmad Shah** refused to sign it. But by saying: —You have taken the lists", he referred to the fact that in the World War II the Allied Forces prepared a list of the wanted persons and exerted pressure upon the government to have the persons on the list admitted to the National Assembly. It is painfully regretted that it so happened.

157- The historians who look for the facts in the heart of the events do not believe this expression to be uttered by the Shaykh, and if it is the silent tongue of the situation, it will have a deeper meaning.

158- Oral history. The concept is from **Shaykh Ja'far** and the phrasing is from the writer.

159- A speech addressed to the *ulama* and the university people on 27/9/1359 [1980]. *Sahifeh-ye Imam*, vol. 13, p. 211. In this speech there are advices for the university people as well as for the theological *hawzahs*. He referred to **Sharif Imami**, a university graduate, as an example of an unrefined person, and from the theological *hawzahs* he referred to **Shaykh Ibrahim Zanjani**. Undoubtedly, mentioning these two names from two scientific centers was not disregarding the relations of these two (persons) to freemasonry.

160- These two incidents happened on the 4th of Murdad, after 8 days of sieging the house of **Shaykh Fadlullah.**

161- —Apparntly we arrived in Tabriz in Shaban, 1323 [1945]. This time we secretly met our very close political friends and engaged in political affairs and activities against despotism and advocating freedom." *Zendegi-ye Tufani, the Memoirs of Sayyid Hasan Taqizadah,* p. 46.

162- 18 Shahrivar, 1288 [1909].

163- —The Constitution had two stages: 1. The stage before **Rida Khan**'s coup d'état. At that time the situation was such that the Iranians and the Muslims could not suggest the establishment of a Muslim government. Therefore, in order to lessen the injustice of the despotism of the Qajar dynasty and before it, they decided to accept the exacted law and the sultanate in the form of a Constitutional Sultanate ..." A press-interview with the German, French, Italian and Spanish journalists, on 19/8/1357 [1978]. *Sahifeh-ye Imam,* vol. 3, pp. 94-97.

164- A press-interview with the German TV, Channel 2. Ibid., p. 31.

165- —In Khomein, in the school of the late **Aqa Shaykh Jafar** I started learning." *Hudur* magazine of Khordad, 1370 [1991], p. 5.

166- *Hijab* is obligatory for the Muslim women. So, picturing a Muslim woman, without observing the least limits of *hijab* acceptable by religion, cannot be shown on the TV in the Islamic Republic. But showing films including non-Muslim women actresses who stir no sexual desire, is not prohibited, according to the Imam's *fatwa.* But how much of their bodies should not be naked and exposed to the eyes, needed the opinion of the experts. So, those who objected the opinions of the experts continued asking him for *fatwas* on the subject. When it was known that some of the questions were put forth by those who were more fanatic than the religious law, and some others were so ailing that every ordinary picture could arouse them, he could deduct from *Usul* and *fiqh* such a *fatwa* that the artists issued their *fatwas,* approving the delicacy and artfulness of his *fatwa.*

167- *Tajwid* is the science of how to recite the *Quran* more correct and more beautiful.

168- The original text is in Arabic.

169- *Sahifeh-ye Imam,* vol. 12, p. 136.

170- —The new schools refer to teaching places other than old-fashioned one-class schools and the theological schools. The said schools, which were established in the days of **Mirza Taqi Khan Amir Kabir**, were abolished after deposing him, though there remained a few number of national schools which were founded by charitable people who offered their houses and accepted to provide for keeping them running, until in the days of **Ahmad Shah** when the government allowed the Ministry of Education to allot a budget to them and to establish other schools by hiring places for them, where primary subjects were taught in schools of six classes, from one to six. Before **Amir Kabir** and even after him, constructing schools was regarded of the unbecoming deeds, accusing those who do that of trying to turn the children away from religion and to ruin them ..., while those who built schools and bequeathed them to the theological studies, were approved, praised and endearsed." *Tarikh-e Ijtimai-ye Tehran dar Qarn-e Sizdahum*, vol. 1, pp. 302 and 304.

171- Probably it was the newly established school named Ahmadiyyeh. *Sargudhashtha-ye Widzeh as Zindagiy-e Imam Khomeini*, vol. 3, p. 9.

172- Translating the concept of this *hadith* is quite difficult, unless it is literally translated.

173- **Imam Khomeini (S.)**, *Chehel Hadith*, p. 47.

174- That is, from the gum to the tips of the teeth.

175- Look for knowledge even in China.

176- ‒So give thou good tidings to My servants who listen to the speech, then follow the best of it". The *Quran, surah Az-Zumar*: 17-18.

177- *Tafsir-e Sureyeh Hamd*, Hijrat Publication, 1st ed., p. 24.

178- Of course, when he was in exile, in Najaf, writing books, the Iraqi type-setters were not acquainted with cursive handwriting and found difficulty in reading it. So, somebody had to rewrite it in clear *naskh* script. One day a student of him, from Isfahan, wrote something in *naskh* script. When the Imam (S.) saw that, he remained gazing at it for a while, then, smiling, he said to him: ‒Aren't you an Isfahani?" The penman, who could not realize a kind of praise is hidden behind that question, thought that he had committed a mistake, lowered his head and said nothing. The Imam continued: ‒Most of good penmanship is from the Turks, whether in Iran or in the world. In the Ottoman Turkey there were forerunners in good penmanship." *Dar Sayeyeh Aftab*, by **Muhammad Hasan Rahimiyan**, 4th ed., p. 234.

179- Before the establishment of the ICPIKW, the late **Haj Ahmad Aqa** [the Imam's son] had realized that such judgments would turn to be so valuable that their original texts should be preserved. So, many of the tableaus are reproduction copies of his handwritings.

180- His handwriting, before being beautiful, is legible, and before being legible, it has spirit. It is good, but not the most beautiful.

181- *Tafsir-e Sureyeh Hamd*, p. 32.

182- The late **Haj Sayyid Ahmad Aqa**: ‒He had exercises in broad and high jump in his childhood and had both his hands and a leg broken because of these sports. More than ten spots in his head had broken and there were a few cracks in his forehead. *Pa beh Pay-e Aftab*, vol. 1, p. 81.

183- The number of the casualties of that war was estimated even up to thirteen and a half million, but the number of the wounded and injured was out of count, especially that chemical gases were plentifully used in this war.

184- The First World War, which started in 1914 and lasted till 1918, began on the pretext of the murder of the Austrian Crown Prince by a Serbian, causing Austria and Serbia to spring at one another. Germany backed Serbia in the war. France, Britain and Russia, in the form of a defensive triangle attacked Germany. The Ottomans, for complicated reasons, were dragged into the war. Bulgaria, by way of supporting the Ottomans, came to the arena. Then Belgium, Romania, Greece, Italy, Portugal, Finland, Hungary, and from the farthest sides of the world, Japan and the USA joined in. When the war ended there appeared a new system of international relations, in which the world of Islam was dissected into pieces and wounded, and played a sentimental role. The USA became the rival of the Russian Empire, Britain and France.

185- *Ittilaat* newspaper of 17/10/1356 published an article under the title: —Red and Black Reactionary", in which **the Imam (S.)** and other religious authorities were insulted. On 19th of Day demonstrations were held in Qum. The demonstrations were bloodily suppressed at the orders of **Muhammad Rida Shah**.

186- *Kawthar*, vol. 1, p. 324.

187- In the year of 1502 A.D., **Shah Ismail Safavi**, for the first time after the arrival of Islam into Iran, established an independent and powerful government in the greater part of the Iranian plateau, announcing Shiism to be the official religion of the country. Form the beginning of the establishment of this government, the Ottomans showed hostility to it and waged wars against it.

188- Before that, under the rule of Al Buyeh and the local government of the Sarbedaran of Khurasan, a Shiite government had been established, but not as powerful as the Safavid government, nor in a land as large as theirs.

189- *Tarikh-e Rawabit-e Kharejiy-e Iran*, by **Abdur-Rida Hushang Mahdawi**, p. 343.

190- Ibid., p. 345.

191- Three weeks before the war, he became 18 years old and was crowned. He was twelve [thirteen] years old when the leaders of Constitutionalism dethroned his father, who was against Constitutionalism and had bombarded the *Majlis* at the intrigue of the Russians, and throned him instead, and, until reaching legal age, **Adudul Mulk**, the chief of the Qajar clan, was appointed as the regent. 1327 A.H. [16/6/1909]. *Tarikh-e Rawabit-e Khareji-ye Iran*, by **Hushang Mahdawi**, p. 336.

192- Ibid., p. 350.

193- The first defeat was by the British, and the second, more painful, was by the Ottomans, for the sake of whom they had entered the war.

194- **Hienriche von Rois** and **Count le Qonti**.

195- This was just one cause, there are other causes, which will gradually be referred to within later chapters.

196- —Heart speaks to Heart" is a Persian proverb which probably is a translation of a *hadith* from **the Imam as-Sadiq** (*a*) to the effect that if you want to know how much someone likes you, see how much you like him.

197- **Mrs. Zahra Mustafawi** quoted the Imam to have said that when he was 15 or 16 years old he used to shoulder a rifle, and, at times of possible attack on Khomein, he ascended to the roof and the tower and got ready to defend Khomein, while his mother was worried about him.

198- *Sahifeh-ye Imam*, vol. 12, p. 136.

199. In the middle years of Qajarian government, some ruffians, like **Nayeb Husayn Kashani**, resorted to violence in between Qum and Isfahan. And in the late days of the Qajarians, others like **Rida Jawzani**, **Rajab Ali Zahzumi** and **Zallaqi**, besides some of the remaining followers of **Nayeb Husayn Kashani**, disturbed security in those regions and horrified the people. Look up *Khaterat-e Abdullah Bahrami*. *Khaterat-e Izamul Wizareyeh Qudsi*, and refer to the semi-official newspaper *Iran* in the years 1295-1299 S.H. [1916-1920].

200. *Sahifeh-ye Imam*, vol. 10, p. 136.

201. A believing Muslim is not allowed, under any conditions, to put an end to his own life, because he believes that **Allah** has provided for every problem tens of solutions. As regards the voluntary suicidal operations in wars, and which are regarded as couragious deeds, are allowed only if they direct a severe blow at the enemy, or save a life from death.

202. This story is a reconstruction of several similar stories which some people of Khomein remember from their fathers.

203. Ibid., vol. 16, p. 92.

204. It is a saying from **the Prophet** (*s*).

205. Ibid.

206. The *Quran, Surah Maidah*: 32.

207. Ibid., *Surah Tawbah*: 111.

208. *Sahifeh-ye Imam*, vol. 16, p. 92.

209. **Mirza** is not a separate name. It is used as a prefix to other names. Probably he was called just **Mirza** in order to mislead the local enemies.

210. *Kalimat-e Qisar*, p.162. (By induction one can get from this sentence that the intention is not only those religions which do not give head to the imposed realities of the imposed wars, rather it mostly means that any impression of the religion which disregards the reality of the war is incomplete).

211. It is also said that every Sunday he used to go to the bath house, because the water of the reservoirs [into which people used to wash themselves] got dirty on Fridays, and was changed with fresh water on Saturdays, and on Sundays it was fresh.

212. **Hujjat al-Islam Sirajuddin Musawi**: –The grave of the Imam's mother is in Qum. I have seen her gravestone and recited the *Fatihah* for her." *Hudur* Quarterly Magazine, No.19, Spring 1376.

213. *In Aineyeh Daneshwaran*, **by Muhammad Yazdi Husayni**, published in Tehran in 1353 A.H., there is a brief biography of him, written by himself as follows, with a slight alteration by the writer: —Hewas born in 1320 A.H. and till 1339 A.H. when he was 19 years old, he did not leave his birthplace."

214. Quoted from *Comiteyeh Mujazat*, a thesis for M.A. in history, by **Muhammad Muqaddas**, in Islamic Free University, Tehran Branch, p. 133.

215. *Tarikh-e Mashrutiyyat dar Iran*, by **Hasan Ma'asir**, Ibn Sina Publication, vol. 1, p. 44.

216. *Ruz Shemar-e Tarikh-e Iran*, by **Baqer Aqili**, vol. 1, p. 29.

217. Ibid., pp. 144 and 145.

218. *Asrar-e Tarikhi-ye Comiteyeh Mujazat*, by **Jawad Tabrizi** Kawiyan Press, 2nd ed., p. 59.

219. *Khaterat-e Sadr al-Ashraf*, by **Muhsin Sadr**, Wahid Publication, vol. 2, p. 223.

220. *Asrar-e Tarikhi-ye Comiteyeh Mujazat*, pp. 82 and 83.

221. Ibid., p. 85.

222. According to a conversation with the late **Haj Ahmad Aqa** in 1369 [1980].

223. The amounts paid by **Wuthuquddawlah** are different in different sources. The above sums are the least amounts.

224. *Tarikh-e Muasir-e Iran*, Book one, Entesharateh Muasseseyeh Pzduhesh wa Mutala'at-e Farhangi, pp.149, 150. In the same page, the late **Sayyid Muhammad**, son of the late **Behbahani**, is quoted to have said that the other murdurer was an Indian.

225. *Yadegar* magazine, 1st year, No. 2, 1323, p. 51.

226. One of the great *ulama* of Tehran. He played a role in the event of prohibiting the tobacco, and died in 1318 A.H.

227. The police announced that the time of the assassination was 10.20.

228. Ibid., p. 151.

229. Ibid., p. 155.

230. *Comiteyeh Mujazat*, thesis by **Muhammad Muqaddas**, p. 180.

231. When the people of Iraq asked the **Imam Husayn (*a*)** to come to their land to undertake the leadership of the *ummah*, he sent his cousin, **Muslim ibn Aqil** to al-Kufeh in order to investigate the situation. **Ubaydullah ibn Ziyad**, sent by **Yazid**, came to the Kufeh, too. One night **Hani ibn Urwah**, one of the most loyal friends of **Muslim**, invited **Ubaydullah** to his house, telling **Muslim** to hide behind a curtain, and when he heard him caughing, he was to come out and with his sword cut off **Ubaydullah**'s head. But despite **Hani**'s several coughings, **Muslim** did not appear. When **Ubaydullah** returned home, **Hani** asked why he didn't attack, the answer bore the meaning that a Muslim fights face to face, and does not kill by surprise.

232. I found no transmitted document.

233. *Ittilaat* newspaper, No. 20623, Saturday, 11 Adhar, 1374 [1995], p. 6. *Yadnameh An Kuchak-e Buzurg*.

234. **Sayyid Abdur-Rahim Khalkhali, Sayyid Mahdi Afjei, Husayn Parviz, Shaykh Husayn Tehrani, Shaykh Ahmad Sigari and Musawat.** *Tarikh-e Enqelab-e Jangal*, p. 69.

235. Ibid., p.68.

236. Ibid., p.69.

237. Lenin.

238. *Kawthar*, vol. 1, pp. 507-508.

239. Oral history.

240. Someone by the pseudonym —Muhammad Taqi Haj Bushehri" had a different explanation for this change of name: —Durig the twenty-years reign (of Rida Khan's government), which used to rename some of the towns and regions, when the Trans-Iranian Railway was extended to Sultan-abad, they changed its name with a pure Persian, i.e. Arak. The railway of that town, which had been improved by another Sultan, could not be inaugurated. The Sultans want untouched (things)." *Ruhullah Musawi Khomeini: Childhood, Boyhood and Youth. —Perspective*" magazine (abroad), No. 5, autumn 1367 [1988], p. 26.

241. *Farhang Muin* [Muin Dictionary], quoting *Atharul Ajam* [The Works of the Non-Arabs].

242. —Aak was built in 240 A.H. by **Yusuf Khan**, known as **Gurji**, in the south-east of Farahan Plain." *Farhang Muin*, vol. 5, p. 114.

243. **Ali Akbar Wilayati**: *Tarikh-e Rawabit-e Kharejiy-e Iran–Dawreyeh Awwal-e Mashruteh* [The History of Iran's Foreign Relations–The First Period of Constitutionalism]. Political and International Studies Department, p. 45.

The losses caused by the Russians, Ottomans and the British to the towns of Iran were very much. Tabriz bore the biggest losses amounting to 80 kurur tumans. [1 kurur = 500000 tumans]. 60 kururs by the Russians and 20 kururs by the Ottomans were the losses afflicted on this town. The second afflicted region was Kurdistan with 33 kururs caused by the Ottomans. Arak was the third. Tehran, after Isfahan and Malayer, bore 4.1 kururs of losses. As to the more losses caused by the British and the Germans to the towns of Iran no information is available. Similarly we know little about the properties and wealths confiscated by the British and the Germans from the businessmen. A single item of it amounted to 5,137,612 Ottoman Pounds.

244. **The Imam (s)** had said: —Itwas the second day of my settling in the school when I saw there a young boy behaving warmly and attractively. I asked what his name was. **A Mirza Muhammad Husayn**, I was told. It was then that I got acquainted with him." **Dr. Mahmud Burujerdi**, *Ganjineyeh Dil*, ICPIKW, p. 84.

245. **Ayatullah Pasandideh**: —Hestudied *al-Mutawwal* under the late **Shaykh Muhammad Ali Burujerdi**, continued studying logic under **Haj Shaykh Muhammad Gulpaygani**, and started taking lessons on *Sharh-e Lumeh* under the late **Aqa Abbas Araki**." *Khatirat*, p. 51.

246- *Kashf-e Asrar*, **Imam Khomeini**, Azadi Publication, p. 34.

247- I could not trace the name of this Egyptian scholar.

248- Belonging to the Establishment of Cultural Research and Studies, affiliated to **Bunyad-e Mustadafan wa Janbazan**.

249- Ibid, under the name of Kamareh, in 31/1/1299, the texts were not classified.

250- Ibid, No. 2- 4/390.

251- Ibid, the 12th of Adhar.

252- The majority took the opinion of the above two *ulama* in respect of **Taqizadeh** to be *takfir*.Thus, **Shaykh Abdullah Mazandarani** wrote an extensive letter to Haj Muhammad Ali Tajer Badamchi Tabrizi, saying: —The judgement which we two had issued concerning Taqizadeh, and which was concurrently issued, was not *takfir*. Whoever ascribed *takfir*, it was a more li.e. Actually the judgement was corruption of his political conduct, which was contrary to the kingdom's Islam." *Habl al-Matin* [magazine], Calcutta, the 18th year, No.15, 28 Ramadan, 1328, the 3rd of October, 1910, pp. 20, 21.

This letter, bearing a deep expression of the deviations of the Constitutional movement, admits that —The procedures and offences of Taqizadeh, denoting his corrupt conduct, were all documented fundamental and decisive, and certainly the original secret Tehran Society was either established by him, or he had a principal part.

253- The story of his martyrdom had been related by **Husayn Laleh** in the chapter concerning **Comiteyeh Mujazat**.

254- Another narration says that he went to the bathroom and performed a *ghusl*.

255- From several quotations I obtained the common result that that very speech was so catching and its topic was so circulated over the tongues that it seemed as if **Ruhullah** was a professional orator. The late **Muhammad Ali Araki**, who was elder than he, was then taking his lessons in Arak, but had not been acquainted with **Aqa Ruhullah**, remembered things, in the corner of his memory, about that speech. From his expression one may gather that he continued delivering speeches on the *minbar*. Probably the repetition of the first speech among the students made him think that there were many speeches. **Ayatullah Araki** says in this respect: —Aqa Khomeini lived in Arak for a while studying in the *hawzah* of Arak. He was even delivering speeches on the *minbar*. At that time I was not acquainted with him." *Particular Accounts*, vol. 6, p. 11.

256- *Sahifeh-ye Imam*, vol. 21, p. 102. After the victory of the Islamic Republic it was decided to revise the school text books. In rewriting the book of history for the third year of the secondary school, quoting documents about the late Behbahani allowing the people to take asylum in the garden of the British Embassy, there is an expression to which the above expressions are some sort of answers.

257- 15th of the month of Dey.

258- Once, when his blood-pressure fell to 5, and his doctors could improve it a bit, he tried to raise to prepare himself for the *salat*, but one of his doctors said: —You are a *mujtahid* in *fiqh*, and I am in medication. To my *fatwa*, movement is *haram* for you." *Imam dar Sangar-e Namaz*, published by ICPIWK, p. 36. The doctors knew his being a *muqallid* in this respect, so they dared to express their medical instructions in the form of a decree. Yet, the same physicians, in the presence of other *mujtahid*s, had to express their medical instructions in the form of a request or a suggestion. Witty ones used to say that the one who regards *taqlid* a condition for being rational; he himself must first be a *muqallid*.

259- The original *hadith* is in Arabic.

260- —Scince is light. Allah flings it in the heart of whom He will."

261- *Sahifeh-ye Imam*, vol. 5, p. 155. The Imam's statements to a group of the physicians in Qum dated: 16/12/1357. On the same day he delivered another speech to another group of physicians, in which he repeated the same ideas.

262- The third of Isfand, 1299.

263- The coup d'état forces consisted of 2500 Cossack soldiers, eight cannons and 18 heavy machine guns. *Tarikh-e Rawabit-e Khareji-ye Iran*, **Abdur-Rida Hushang Mahdawi**, p. 369.

264- *Az Sayyid Diya ta Bakhtiyar*, **Masud Behnud**, p. 20.

265- Ibid.

266- *Ruz Shemar-e Tarikh-e Iran*, **Baqir Aqili**, vol. 1, p. 145.

267- *Tarikh-e Rawabit-e Kharejiy-e Iran*, Ali **Akbar Wilayati**, pp. 66-67.

268- *Kalimat-e Qisar*, p. 78.

269- *Az Sayyid Diya ta Bakhtiyar*, p. 25.

270- *Ruz Shemar-e Tarikh-e Iran*, vol. 1, p. 101.

271- Ibid.

272- 28th Murdad, 1332.

273- —**Dr. Musaddiq** came to power, but he did mistakes. He wanted to serve the country but he committed mistakes. One of the mistakes was that when he came to power he did not get rid of this [**Muhammad Rida Pahlavi**] to put an end to the matter. It was not difficult for him at that time, as the army was in his hand, all powers were in his hand, and this [the Shah] was worthless at that time. At that time this man had no power, as he obtained later. He was weak at that time and was in his claw, but he was careless. Another carelessness was his dissolution of the *Majlis*, forcing everyone of the deputies to resign. When they all resigned a legal way was opened for the Shah. That is, as there was no *Majlis*, the Shah had the right to appoint the prime minister, and the Shah did appoint the prime minister. This was a mistake on the part of the Dr., and as a result, this man was brought back to Iran. As it was said: **Muhammad Rida Shah** went and **Rida Shah** came back." *Sahifeh-ye Imam*, vol. 3, pp. 34-40.

274- *Ruz Shomar-e Tarikh-e Iran*, vol. 1, p. 102.

275- In the Islamic thought, martyrdom is not for keeping alive a good name, rather it is for keeping alive a good path. It may often happen that a martyr be sacrificed, but not with a good reputation in the darkness of the ignorance of his time.

276- His dispraises of **Dr. Musaddiq** and some other nationalists, even of **Ayatullah Kashani**, I take them to be a warning to the policies of the politicians, not a denial of their personalities. The following expressions deserve contemplation: —Dring the uprising of **Kashani** and **Dr. Musaddiq**, whose political front was stronger, in a letter to **Kashani**, I wrote that it was necessary to pay full attention to the religious side of the uprising. But, instead of strengthening the religious aspect and giving it priority to the political aspect, he did the contrary such that he became the Speaker of the *Majlis*. This was a mistake. I wanted him to work for religion, not that he

should become a politician." *Dar Justojuy-e Rah– Shakhsiyyatha*–p. 23.

277- 27th Isfand, 1299.

277/1- The first hemistich of this couplet might be: —Youwished me old age, O father, come,"

278- *Sahifeh-ye Imam*, vol. 9, p. 81.

279- *Ruz Shemar-e Tarikh-e Iran*, vol. 1, p. 383.

280- Ibid, p. 384.

281- Ibid, p. 104.

282- Surah an-Nisa: 102.

283- At that time **the Imam (s)** thought the disarmament to be a plot planned by the foreigners. Fifty seven years later, he, in Paris, said: —Il **Rida Shah**'s era (i.e. before **Rida Shah**) the nation had powers. Actually, they, too, were aggressive, but they were a support for the kingdom. They were disarmed by the order of the foreigners ..." *Kawthar*, vol. 2, p. 176.

284- **Dr. Ali Shariati**, who was an enlightened believer, seriously believing in the comprehensiveness of Islam, referring to *Nowruz*, said: —Nowruz has always been endeared in the eyes of the Magi, in the eyes of the Zoroastrian priests, in the eyes of the Muslims and in the eyes of the Shiah Muslims. All took it to be dear to them, and with their own tongues talked about it. Even the philosophers and the scholars who said: _Nowruz is the first day of creation ...' What a wonderful legend! More wonderful than reality! By the way, isn't it that everybody feels that the first day of Spring is the first season, Farwardin the first month and *Nowruz* the first day of creation? If **Allah** had in one day created the world, undoubtedly that day must have been this *Nowruz*. Undoubtedly Spring is the first day of creation. **Allah** has never started the world and the nature in autumn, winter or summer. Undoubtedly, on the first day of Spring the greenery began growing, the rivers ran, the buds sprouted up and the blossoms opened, that is *Nowruz*.

Undoubtedly, the soul was born in this season and love appeared on this day, and the sun rose for the first time on the first *Nowruz*, and time had started with it.

Islam, which wiped off all kinds of nationalism and changed the traditions, bestowed more lustre upon *Nowruz*. It bound it and, with a strong support, protected it against the danger of fading away during the Islam of the Iranians. Choosing Ali (*a*) as a successor and also as an executor in Ghadir Khum, both happened at this season, and what a surprising coincidence! *Kawir*, Dr. Ali Shariati, p. 264.

285- The religious minorities put their own Scripture instead of the *Quran*.

286- Something like the Santa Claus game, which is probably an imitation of this, or probably this is an imitation of that.

287- *Kalimat-e Qisar*, p. 104.

288- Tautologic.

289- —Bjeh Sultan is the most famous mountain in Khomein, among 30 other mountains. Its fame is not because of huge physical body; rather it is because of some cultural aspect. Bujeh is the promised place for the gathering of all the people of Khomein and the nearby villages, except the women, on the 13th day of *Nowruz*. In old times it was the place for the meetings of the rogues, and in near past it was the meeting place for the athletic and enlightened youths for sports and discussions." *Nameyeh Kamareh*, vol. 1, p. 300.

290- *Surah Taha*: 55.

291- **Ayatullah Khalkhali**: The Imam said: —After the migration of **Ayatullah Hairi** from Arak I consulted the *Quran*, the said *ayah* appeared. I said to myself: My growing, life and death will be in Qum." *Ganjineh-ye Dil*.

292- **Dr. Mahmud Burujerdi**: —After *Nowruz* of the year 1340 A.H, and after the travel of the Great **Ayatullah Hairi** to Qum, accompanied by my grandfather, and his decision to establish a theological *hawzah* in Qum, my father, together with two other persons, accompanied the Imam to Qum in a post carriage. They wanted to help in the establishment of the theological *hawzah*, being his fellow travellers prove their close friendship. The relationship of the two families started from that time." *Ganjineh-ye Dil*, p. 84.

Ayatullah Pasandideh: ―From Arak he came to Khomein, then he travelled to Qum." *Tarikh-e Shafahi*. As **Ayatullah Pasandideh** remembers very well the moments of his return to Khomein for the New Year, by considering both sayings, perhaps it can be possible to conclude that on the 14th of Farwardin, with the intention of accompanying his friends, he left Arak to Qum.

293- *Ruz Shemar-e Tarikh-e Iran*, vol. 1, p. 106.

294- Those which will come from now on till the end of the chapter:

a. They are not all of Iran's important events of those days. They are, in a way, a part with a trace in his works.

b. We try to sit behind his eyeglasses and look at any event in the same way with which we believe he used to look at it. So, these matters are the writer's personal impressions about his mental engagements.

c. Attempts are made to locate evidences denoting the time in which he had probably thought about it, so that the reader may imagine the chronic order of the events. However, we have but to follow up the development of each subject up to the last opinion of the late deceased.

295- *Surah Rad*: 12.

296- *Sahifeh-ye Imam*, vol. 19, pp. 247-248. This was one of his gnostic and political speeches, delivered on 9/9/1364 on the occasion of the anniversary of the birthday of **the Prophet (s)** and the birthday of the Imam **as-Sadiq (a)**.

297- This legend is differently related for different people.

298- The Arabic text is: ―Wulidtu fi zaman-e malikil adil."

299- *Sahifeh-ye Imam*, vol. 19, p. 248.

300- The same meanings are related in different wordings.

301- **Safiyuddin Ardabili** was born in 650. His lineage goes up to the Imam **Musa al-Kazim**. **Shaykh Safi** was a Sufi, or, in other word, he was a gnostic. He had followers in every corner of the world of Islam. After his death, his son, **Sadruddin** took his place (735-794). After **Sadruddin** his son, **Khwajah Ali,** undertook the leadership of the Sufis. He died in Palestive in 830. **Shaykh Ibrahim** sat in his father's place. After him **Shaykh Junayd**, his youngest son, undertook the leadership of the Sufis. He was invited to the court of **Uzun Hasan**, the powerful ruler of Aq Quyunlu. He married **Uzun Hasan**'s sister. Ten thousand of **Uzun Hasan**'s army became Sufis and of his followers. **Jahan Shah**, the ruler of Adharbayjan, was afraid of him, and incited **Sherwan Shah** to fight him. **Shaykh Junayd** was killed. His son, **Shaykh Haydar**, succeeded him. **Shaykh Haydar** ordered his followers to wear, instead of the Turkish cap, red caps made of

12 pieces after the 12 Imams. For this reason, the group with him was called _Qizilbash'. In 893 **Sherwan Shah** killed this son, too. When **Shaykh Haydar** was killed, his son, **Ismail**, was one year old. His father's followers respected him. At the age of 13, with the cultural support which he inherited from his fathers, and with the support of the followers of his grandfathers, he did a big act. He conducted many wars with the local rulers and forced them to submission. He participated in five big wars. In one of them, by the name of _Chaldiran', he was defeated by **Sultan Salim**, the Ottoman Caliph. Those wars had two results: The first was the establishment of a single sovereignty in the wide land of Iran, the other result was the establishment of Shiism as an official creed, which was (formerly) the fire under ashes, and which was not officially recognized for fear of the fanatic Sunni *ulama* and rulers.

302- *Sahifeh-ye Imam*, vol. 2, p. 252, dated 9/8/1357.

303- 1155-1211 A.H.

304- *Kawthar*, vol. 1, p. 616.

305- *Sharh-e Hal-e Rejal-e Siyasi-ye Iran*, vol. 3, pp. 246-257.

306- *Kawthar*, vol. 2, p. 544.

307- —From the beginning when **Rida Khan** came and made a coup d'état till now that—thank **Allah**—victory was obtained, along these fifty years—which probably were the hardest on the nation of Iran—if they were not more felonious than all the former kings, they were more treacherous. Possibly someone may say that **Agha Muhammad Qajar** was a criminal like these. But **Agha Muhammad Qajar** was not a traitor like these. It is not in the history that **Muhammad Khan Qajar** had given up the interests of his own kingdom for the sake of another kingdom. He was criminal, yes, but he was not a traitor. Likewise, all the former kings were criminals, were bad, but they were not traitors, like this corrupt man. No one of Iran's kings was traitor like him. They, the father and the son, betrayed this kingdom time and again such that we cannot know them in a short time." *Sahifeh-ye Imam*, vol. 6, p. 203.

308- *Kawthar*, vol. 2, p. 296.

309- —The biggest evidence proving his extraordinary moral weakness is his forming the *harem* in which he kept hundreds of women under permanent and temporary marriage contracts, as well as maid servants." *Tatawwur-e Hukumat dar Iran bad az Islam*, **Muhit Tabatabai**, p. 95.

310- Gulestan in 1228 A.H. and Turkamanchai in 1243 A.H.

311- **The Akhbariyyun** (tradition-addicts) are vis-a-vis the **Usuliyyun** (the Fundamentalists). The **Akhbariyyun** believe that the **Akhbar** (the traditions) received from the immaculates (*a*) are sufficient to deduct from them the precepts. The Fundamentalists believe that the original sources of *fiqh* are: the *Quran*, the *Sunnah* (Traditions), unanimity and reason.

312- *Tarikh-e Jamee Bahaiyyat* (New Masonry). **Bahram Afrasiyabi**, Entesharat-e Sukhan, p. 26.

313- 1250 A.H.

314- Aqasi (Aghasi).

315- 1254 A.H.

316- *Tarikh-e Kamil-e Iran*, p. 514

317- *Kawthar*, vol. 1, p. 75.

318- Ibid., p. 445.

319- He refers to the simple operations on the tonsils and the appendix of **Muhammad Rida Pahlavi** for which they ordered foreign surgeons.

320- *Kawthar*, vol. 1, p. 26.

321- *Iran dar Dawreyeh Saltanat-e Qajar*, **Ali Asghar Shamim**, p. 115.

322- Probably he had come to Tehran, before **Nasiruddin Shah**, to attend to the affairs.

323- It is not exaggeration to say that the majority of the Iranian physicians, concerning theoretical and practical knowledge, not only have nothing less than the physicians of the West, they are even in a higher level in respect of some specialties. Nevertheless, in the medical management there are grave weaknesses, to one of which the Imam referred in his speech on 17/6/1358. He said: ―The operation on the tonsils is an easy one… What does it tell the world that someone who is put, by force, at the head of a kingdom, and is known to be the Shah of the kingdom, when this Shah finds no Iranian physician to be fit to conduct an operation on his tonsils. What an insult to Iran‗s medicine and to the Irani physicians! What a treason to the Irani nation to be introduced to the world that in the entire country there is not a single physician capable of operating on tonsils!… How much does this assist imperialism? How much will this disgrace the dignity of our nation?… We do have good doctors, but our brains have become westernized. This is true of the very physicians, too. When you consult them they themselves tell you: You have to go to Europe… Unless our people get out of this westernization, they will never get their independence." Look up *Sahifeh-ye Imam*, vol. 9, pp. 59-66.

324. **Khusrow Mu'tadid**: ―Late in the Safavid rule, the Armenians of Isfahan established a printing house with Latin and Armenian characters for printing their religious books."

325. Introduction to *Waqayi-e Ittefaqiyyah* newspaper, by the late Professor **Muhammad Ismail Ridwani**, vol.1, published by the National Library of the Islamic Republic of Iran.

326. The first issue of *Ruznamcheyeh Akhbar-e Darul-Khilafeyeh Tehran*, Friday, the 5th of Rabi ath-Thani, 1267 A.H. In the next issue the name of *Ruznamcheh* was changed to *Ruznameyeh Waqayi-e Ittefaqiyyah*.

327. *Dastanhai az Zindagani-ye Amir Kabir*, **Mahmud Hakimi**, Daftar-e Nashr-e Farhang-e Islami, p.124.

328. From Rabi al-Awwal, 1268 to Rabi'uth-Thani, 1296. *Amir Kabir and Iran*, p. 334.

329. **Imam Khomeini**'s statements to a group of the personnel and the students of Shiraz University and the group of the physicians of the Islamic Traditional Medicine on 17/4/1358. *Sahifeh-ye Imam*, vol. 8, p. 78.

330. With a slight alteration. *Zindagani-ye Mirza Taqi Khan Amir Kabir*, **Husayn Makki**, Tehran, 1360, Bungah-e Tarjumeh wa Nashr-e Kitab, p. 123.

331. *Surah ash-Shuara*: 224-225.

332. *Sahifeh-ye Imam*, vol.12, p.115.

333. Ibid., vol.19, p.248.

334. Refer to *Fitneyeh Bab*, by Dr. **Abdul Husayn Nawai**.

335. Once, when preaching the followers of **Bab**, wearing erotic make-up, she removed her veil and uttered the following obscene words: —O companions, these days are counted of the interval days. Today all the religious obligations are entirely dropped. *Sawm* and *salat* are useless... So, do not make useless efforts. Let your women have sexual intercourse on a common principle... for which no punishment and no torture will befall you." *Tarikh-e Jami-e Bahaiyyat*, p. 114.

336. *Sahifeh-ye Imam*, vol. 1, p. 96.

337. *Qibleyeh Alam*, **Husayn La'l**, Tehran, Dunyay-e Kitab, 2nd ed., p. 304.

338. Ibid., p. 666.

339. **Muhammad Ghaffari**, the son of **Mirza Buzurg**. Later he was known as **Kamalul Mulk**. He was born in 1264 A.H. in Kashan. After finishing his primary school he was admitted to Darul Funun [Polytechnic Institute]. After three years he became a skillful painter. With the help of his father he found his way into the Court of **Nasiruddin Shah**, and within seven years he completed the nice tableau in the Salon of the Mirrors. At the beginning he was favoured by the Shah as he acquainted him with painting technology. After the death of the Shah in 1313 A.H. he went to France

where, for five years, he was acquainted with the European artists. In the negotiations of **Muzaffaruddin Shah**, in his second trip to Europe, with him, he returned to Iran, but owing to the courtiers' ignorance of arts, he went, this time, to the holy shrines (in Iraq) where he remained for two years and painted _Karbala Square'. He once again returned to Iran, and joined the rank of the Conservative Constitutionalists in the Court. He established Kamalul Mulk school where he educated a good number of his disciples, all of whom admired his character. Just to remain committed to his beliefs and not to be polluted with the corruptions of the court of **Rida Khan,** he went to Neyshabur in 1307 (S.H.). In 1319 (S.H.) he died and was buried next to **Attar**'s tomb.

He is one of Islam's luminaries who gave life to painting, creating more than two hundred valuable artistic works, of which only some survives. He also had a hand in other arts, such as sculpture, music, rug-weaving and tile-work. Regarding his ethical perfections it suffices to relate that one day **Sardar Mutamad Ganjehi**—one of his followers—threw a stone which hit him in the eye and blinded him, but he never talked to anybody about it, until **Sardar Mutamad** himself related it.

For further information about his life, refer to: *Yad-Namehyeh Kamalul Mulk,* with the help of **Darab Behnam Shabahang**, **Ali Dehbashi,** and to *Tarikh-e Hunarhay-e Milli wa Hunarmandan-e Irani,* by **Abdur-Rafi Haqiqat**.

340. *Sahifeh-ye Imam*, vol. 9, p. 10.

341.One of the most complicated thoughts of **the Imam Khomeini (a)** is that, despite his being a gnostic and a lover of beauty, he was always worried lest the artificiality in some architecture and tile-works in diverse buildings, whether holy or otherwise, should alienate man from the spirit of religion. The following expressions are worth attention in this respect: —Ourduty today, before everything else, is to offset the many centuries' propaganda of the foreigners and the agents of imperialism. The imperialistic experts, with perfect forgery and tricks, and under the pretext of loving Islam and orientalism, drew thick curtains on the luminous complexion of Islam, trying to show Islam's beauty only in architecture, paintings, high buildings and fine arts, and imposing the despotic and anti-Islamic governments of Ummaids, Abbasids and Ottomans, under the name of Islamic caliphate, upon the society, concealing the real features of Islam behind these curtains such that today it is difficult for us to be able to make the human societies, and even the Muslims, understand the Islamic government and its basic, political, economic and social organizations. We must try to remove the curtain from the several centuries' venomous propaganda of the foreigners. You, young generation, have the duty of wakening the westernized from their sleep, and expose the calamities of the antihumanistic governments and their agents, and explain to the societies, especially the children of Islam, the type of the Islamic government, which, regrettably, had a short life, yet it could throw light on the method of Islam in guardianship and governor. So you are to press more your ranks." *Sahifeh-ye Imam*, vol. 1, p. 152.

342. *Chehel Sal Tarikh-e Iran*, **Iraj Afshar**, Asatir Publication, vol. 3, pp. 802-803.

343. The origin of the story was short, but its marginal notes were so numerous that so far more than 80 books have been written down about it, and uncountable articles have referred to it, besides hundreds of analyses and hundreds of poems describing it are left behind. Nevertheless, many unsaid things are still to be said. Look up: *Shuresh bar Imtiyaznameyeh Regie*, by **Faridun Adamiyyat**. *Qarardad Regie*, by **Shaykh Hasan Karbalai**. *Naqsh-e Mujtahid-e Fars dar Nehdat-e Tanbaco*, by **Muhammad Rida Rahmati**. *Sadeyeh Tahrim Tanbaco*, by the attention of **Musa Najafi** and **Rasul Jafariyan**.

344. 1306 A.H.

345. On the 28th of Rajab, 1308 the agreement, which was in 15 chapters, was signed by the Shah, and **Gerald Talbut** was introduced as the owner of the Concession.

346. —Perhaps it can be said that in the 19th century tobacco was the most important industrial cultivation of Iran." *Bazarganan*, **Huma Natiq**, Tus Publication, 1373, p. 73.

347. _Makasib' is a collection of religious laws and regulations about different kinds of transactions. Ever since childhood Muslims are somewhat acquainted with the necessary ones of these laws and regulations. Despite the fact that for some decades _Makasib' did not develop in proportion to the new concepts and economic subjects, yet it still covers the most advanced instructions for transaction which have two securities for carrying them out: One of the securities is the legal authority, and the other better one is the religious beliefs.

348. A few number of the people tried to show that the factor of the disturbances was the Russian Embassy. To prove that they also collected documents. Others believed that the Russians tried more to convince the Shah to cancel that agreement. Had this been done at the hands of the people and the *ulama*, the people would have dared to announce the covenants of Turkamanchay and Gulestan to be *batil*, too.

349. The Shah received five hundred thousand bounds as a bribe. When the Agreement was cancelled he refunded nothing of the said amount.

350. *Tahrim-e Tanbacu, the First Negative Resistance in Iran,* **Ibrahim Teymuri**. Kitabkhaneyeh Suqrat, p.78.

351. The late **Mirza Muhammad Hasan (Mirza Shirazi)**, was a disciple of the late **Shaykh Murtada Ansari**, the *taqlid* authority of the Shiite. After the death of his tutor in 1291 A.H., he moved his teaching sessions, in a complicated struggle against the British imperialism, to the city of Samirra'. In his *fiqh* class he educated many students. **Shahid Aqa Mustafa**, father of **Imam Khomeini (*a*)**, was one of them. He died on the 8th of Shaban, 1312 A.H. in his 82nd year of age. Rumours said that he was poisoned.

352. The Regie Agreement was for fifty years.

353. *Tahrim Tanbacu,* **Haj Shaykh Reda Zanjani,** published by the Permanent Book Exhibition, 1365, pp. 75-83.

354. *The Holy Quran,* addressing **Moses (*a*)** and his brother **Aaron (A.H.),** says: ─Go to Pharaoh, surely he has become tyrannical. Speak to him softly, haply he may be mindful or fear."(20: 43-44).

355. The 1st of Jumada al-Ula, 1309 A.H., 12/9/1270 S.H., (3/12/1891).

356. **Itimadus-Saltanah** also testified: ─Ou of the 20 *kururs* of the Iranian subjects [a kurur = half a million], at least five *kururs* are addicted to tobacco, and among these there are persons who daily pay one q*iran* for cigarette or tobacco. "

Bazarganan, **Huma Natiq,** dus Publication, 1373, p. 74.

─O£ourse the consumption of cigarettes, in proportion to other kinds of tobacco products, was much less. The consumption of the tobacco was 2,250,000 Tabriz *mans,* and the consumption of cigarette tobacco was 30,000 *mans.*" Ibid. p. 75.

357. ─The rogues and the raffians broke their pipes and piled them in front of the Company's building, and, by reviling and abusing the Company (Regie), they shouted out: _We drink wine openly and in public, and we are afraid of no..., but our lips will never touch the pipe unless **Aqa Mirza** makes it *halal.* We drink wine putting our hope in **Sahib az-Zaman** [the 12th Imam]. But what hope we have in smoking the pipe?'" *Tahrim Tanbacu,* **Ibrahim Teymuri,** p. 106.

358. ─Amng the *ulama* of Tehran, **Aqa Sayyid Abdullah Behbahani** did not follow **Mirza Ashtiyani,** saying: _I am not a *muqallid* but a *mujtahid.* Secondly, this judgement which is ascribed to **Mirza Shirazi,** is it a decree or a *fatwa*? If it is a decree, it must be between the claimant and the

www.ingramcontent.com/pod-product-compliance
Lightning Source LLC
Chambersburg PA
CBHW021706120626
46545CB00004B/1433

defendant in a pleading. But if it is a *fatwa*, it must be universal, and it is compulsory in respect to the *muqallids,* not in respect of a *mujtahid.'* Anyhow, he did not cooperate with the others." *Muqaddameyeh Tarikh-e Bidari-ye Iraniyan,* **Nazim al-Islam Kirmani,** p. 22, Also: *Sharh-e Hal-e 'Abbas Mirza Malikara,* by **'Abdul-Husayn Nawai,** Shirkat Sahami Chap, 1325, p. 162.

In some other references are other names of those who did not accept the decree which was almost unanimously accepted by the people. **Faridun Adamiyyat** writes: —Among the *ulama* group there were persons (whether because of the nature of the decree of prohibition, or because of their connection with the government or with the Regie Company, or because of selfishness, or any other motive, hidden or manifest) who did not see that they should follow that *fatwa.* Among these persons in Tehran were **Sayyid Abdullah Behbahani, Sayyid Ali Akbar Mujtahid Tafrishi** and **Zahir al-Islam,** the leader of the Friday salat, whom we know, particularly **Behbahani** who smoked a cigarette in the Ottoman Embassy, and remained till the end in the opposition against the public ..."

Shuresh bar Imtiyaznameyeh Regie, **Faridun Adamiyyat,** Tehran, Entesharat-e Payam, 1360, p. 77.

359. *Sahifeh-ye Imam,* vol. 18, p. 136.

360. **Haj Mirza Hasan** or **Muhammad Hasan Ashtiyani** (1248-1319 A.H) was a disciple of **Shaykh Murtada Ansari**. After obtaining the degree of *ijtihad* in 1282, he came to Tehran and played an important part in the Tobacco Uprising.

361. —The number of the casualties was seven and the wounded were twenty, as reported." *The Revolution of Iran,* by **Edward Brown,** p. 52.

362. **Faridun Adamiyyat** says: —The supposition of liquidating the Regie Co. was born in the Shah's mind and thought, and it was manifest for the first time late in the month of Muharram, 1309.... The Shah even in his cable to the government of Adharbayjan said: I am busy with that and I will have talks with the Company, or, if **Allah** wills, we will completely stop it and be relieved.' We also [knew] that it was **Amin as-Sultan** who changed the Shah's opinion, but the difference between the tastes of the Shah and the Chancellor remained intact.'" *Shuresh bar Imtiyaznameyeh Regie,* **Faridun Adamiyyat,** Tehran, Payam Publication, 1360, p. 69.

363. A number of people wore shrouds, and some of the theology students carried swords. When **Nayibus-Saltanah** signed with his hand to the cannos stationed around Ark, and threatened the people to massacre them, a theology student brought out his sword from under his *aba* and

hurled it at him. He was not injured, but fell into the mud. Refer to: *Tahrim Tanbacu,* **Muhammad Rida Zanjani**, p. 193.

364. –Tehran, to the Excellencies and great elites of the House of Caliphate (may **Allah** double their prestige), the good tiding of cancelling the Tobacco Concession caused much thanksgivings, hope and praying for His Imperial Majesty the Shahanshah, may **Allah** perpetuate his kingship. By the will of **Allah,** the Exalted, and by the kind royal grace, the hands of the foreigners will be completely short of Iran. **Muhammad Hasan al-Husayni**." *Tarikh-e Bidari-ye Iraniyan,* as related in *Tarikh-e Rawabit-e Khareji-ye Iran,* **'Ali Akbar Wilayati**, p. 409.

365. Ibid., p. 411.

366. The father of **the Imam (*a*)**.

367. **Aqa Mustafa** was martyred on 1/8/1356, and the speech was delivered on 10/8/1356.

368. In high gnostic stages, one is not attached to anything except **Allah**. In higher stages, one's attachment to all things increases: –There is no objection in being attached." It is an answer to a prescribed question in this respect. But it also has two other clearer meanings which drew more attention at his time: one was expressing his attachment to those whom he felt to be real servants of Islam and humanity, and the other was to be giving the answer to those who were not pleased with expressing his attachment.

369. *Kawthar,* vol. 1, p. 300.

370. By _enlightened' he often meant the graduate thinkers.

371. Ibid., pp. 304-305.

372. **Mirza Yusuf Ashtiyani** (1227-1303 A.H.), an honest Qajari personality.

373. Ibid., pp. 303-306.

374. *Alawi and Safavid Shiism* is the title of a book written by **Dr. 'Ali Shariati**, in which two impressions of the concept of Shiism are posed facing each other. In this book the names of some *ulama* of that period are stated to be the *ulama* of Safavid Shiism.

375. Some writers could not analyze the scientific, artistic, intellectual, juristic and philosophic flourishing which coincided with the Safavid rule. They did not pay attention to the fact that the seeds of the growth of the rich Shiite culture had been scattered, and that had it not been for the Safavid rule, the sturdy tree of Islam could spread its shade over many other lands from this rich itellectual, juristic, philosophic and gnostic base. They tried to find all their hopes in Shiism in the Safavid rule. They praised that rule, and, consequently, they did not regard the deviations of this dynasty to be

diversions on its part. For this reason they, in order to completely deny the content of the book *The Alawi and Safavid Shiism,* they actually refused this kind of classifications and said that Shiism cannot be sorted. But **the Imam** (*a*) announced that there are, today, two impressions about Islam: The impression of an understanding which **Muhammad (*s*)** offered, and the Islam which is desired by the American politicians. So, presenting a pure Muhammadan Islam vis-a-vis the American Islam can be an answer to those who took the plan of placing the Alawi and the Safavid Shiisms vis-a-vis each other to be originally invalid. By careful scrutinizing and studying the works of the **Imam (*a*)** one can easily gather that he was quite disgusted with the Safavid Shahs, while he highly esteemed most of the *ulama* of that period, such as what he said in this very speech about the close relation of those *ulama* to the Court, which he described to be a self-sacrifice and struggle, not that they believed the Safavid government was the desired one and so they neared it and cooperated with it.

376. Ibid., p. 304.

377. It was not yet time for him to say: —he Shah must go!", but most of those who played a role in the struggle knew his real viewpoint. In a more exact word, the spirit of this speech attracted the attention of the majority to the dissolution of the system of kingship.

378. **Hatif Isfahani**.

379. In this same speech he refers to the services of tens of other fighting *ulama*, including: —The question of Iraq was delivered by **Mirza Shirazi the Second,** this great man, this distinguished man, this man of high position in knowledge and action. He saved Iraq. He issued the decree of *jihad,* and sent them …The tribes came to him and he issued the order of *jihad.* They fought and gave casualties; they sacrificed themselves to make Iraq independent. Had it not been for him, we would have now been enslaved, we would have now been a part of the British colonies. It was because of the serious diligence of the *ulama.* Deporting the *ulama* of Iraq to Iran was because of their opposition to the regime. The late **A Sayyid Abul-Hasan**, the late **Aqa Naini,** the late **Shahrestani**, the late **Khalisi,** were exiled from Iraq to Iran because they spoke against what they wanted, against the regimes, for this reason they were exiled and sent to Iran. We ourselves had witnessed that." Ibid., pp. 307-308.

380. *Tarikh-e Tabari.*

381. This concept has been repeated in his statements so that no doubt may befall its being a judgement:

- —If the *faqih* slips, if he does even a venial sin, he will fall off the position of guardianship."

- —The *faqih* does not want to impose despotism on the people. If a *faqih* tried to be tyrant, he would not be a guardian any more.

- —It is the *faqih*'s guardianship which stops dictatorship. If the *faqih*'s guardianship is not there, there will be dictatorship."(*Kalimat-e Qisar—Pithy Aphorisms*, p. 119).

382. **Anushirwan** the Just, **Shah Abbas** the Paradise Dweller and **Nasiruddin** the-Already-Martyr are great in the eyes of the small persons, but in his eyes they are small. He, in accordance with the *Fiqhi* rule of Befriending and Dissociating—not like Traditionists' manner, but according to the gnostic method—strongly renounced them.

383. **Nasiruddin Shah**'s assassination took place on the 17th of Dhulqadah, 1313 A.H. at half an hour afternoon.

384. History in its philosophic concept, because in the terminology of historians, less than a generation belongs to the present, not to the history, whereas **the Imam (a)** used to look, with an interpretive eye, at the far-away pasts, which the historians named before history', as both present and history. The stories of the peoples of **Idris**, **Noah**, **Ibrahim** and other prophets (*a*) as well as other peoples, in the look of the one who knows the *Quran*, are all history as much as if they were a moment before. However, in the field of politics, when he referred to history, he paid attention to its technical and current concept.

385. Due to the fact that the late Imam was born in the time of the rule of **Muzaffaruddin Shah**, and as we had been following up his points of view about him and his two successors, along his life from his birth till his youth, we refrain form retelling the events of that era.

386. Refer to **Abdullah Mustawfi**, *Sharh-e Zindagani-ye Man*. **Muzaffaruddin**, who lived in Tabriz, after the death of his father, tried to find excuses for not going to the Capital. But, under the pressure of his retinue, he arrived in Tehran on the 25th of Dhulhijjah 1313 A.H. (the 18th of Khordad, 1275 S.H.).

387. In some countries, the 13th story number is written 12+1.

388. **Sayyid Ahmad Kasrawi**, son of **Haj Mir Qasim**, was born in Tabriz in 1269 S.H. He was extraordinarily talented. He quickly learnt the Arabic language and literature. He got knowledge of the English, French and Russian languages, too. He turned to essay writing. His articles, which concerned social, historical and religious questions, were published in a newspaper called *Parcham*. The context and the sentence-construction of his

articles were somewhat novel. He attached great importance to the country's history and literature. He tried to exclusively use Persian words. His works along his life amounted to some seventy books and essays. The following books are his better known ones: *Good and Bad, The Path of Deliverance, Shiism, Sufism, Bahaism, About History, The Law of Justice, Ten Years in the Department of Justice, Constitution the Best form of Government* and *The History of Iran's Constitution.* His style was frank, sharp and fanatic, as he had completely fanatic personality. In his youth he was a zealously religious person, and in his older ages he was a fanatic with a fanciful creed. He very well knew a part of the country's historical anatomy and literature, but the majority of men of opinion believe that he was alien to the culture and the religion of his country. Consequently, he took the superstitions which had entered religion to be parts of it, and regarded some religious delicacies to be superstitions. On the 20th of Isfand, 1326, when he was summoned to the Court to answer to some of his insults, on the way he was assassinated by two members of Fadaiyan-e Islam [Devotees of Islam].

389. *Mafatih al-Jinan* is a book found in most of the houses of the Shiite—one copy of it, at least. The text of this book is a rippling sea of nice supplications and deep gnostic prayers, some of which have political aims (not conventionally) according to the Imam's opinion. Its literary expressions and its deep and elevated contents indicate that these invocations are nice interpretations of the Glorious *Quran* uttered by the Imams of guidance. The everyday repetition of some of them does not create boredom, rather it is animating, filling the heart with love, the mind with elevation and creating divine fervour, love and vividity, deepening even more the religious beliefs. In its margin, however, there are writings which, on the first look, do not seem to be in harmony with the text at all. (The text is in Arabic and the margin is mostly Persian. The nicety of supplication is reciting it in Arabic.) Although what is in the margin is narratives from the pure Imams, yet, as these narratives need to be explained, and as they are not explained in this book, but they are presented for practical application by way of encouraging the reader, some readers, before being eager to fly by reading them, in the unlimited heaven of gnosticism and thoughts, they plunge into the thoughts of material profit and loss.

390. *Sahifeh-ye Imam*, vol. 12, p. 240.

391. Ibid.

392. During the war imposed by Iraq on Iran, old people also went to the front and behind the front. Someone of them used to tell the boys behind the front some jokes. This one was among his jokes, and the boys used to retell it

to their ditch-mates. A fighter narrated: ―I an operation, while the mortar-shells were raining down, I noticed my ditch-mate wants to say something. By hard attempts I could bring my ear near his mouth. He was relating that joke, then he said: _Beware! If a shell of these hits your head, it will throb till morning.' Moments later a splinter stroke his head. Consoling him, I said to him: _It's Ok, it will only throb till morning.' He smiled, turned towards Karbala, greeted [**the Imam al-Husayn**] and closed his eyes. When I took his body to the quarters and uncovered his head to see the splinter, I saw four scars of a sword on his head."

393. According to the *fatwa*s of the Imam and the present leader of the Revolution, striking the head with sword is contrary to the *Shar*.

394. *Sahifeh-ye Imam*, vol. 21, p. 41, dated 12/7/1367.

395. **Imam Khomeini:** ―Know that the state of consent [*Rida*] is other than the state of reliance [*tawakkul*]. Rather it is loftier than that, because _the reliant' looks for his goodness and well-being, and demands from **Allah**, whom he knows to be the doer of good, to grant him good and well-being. _Consent' means annihilating one's will in **Allah**'s will, demanding nothing for one's self. A gnostic person was asked: ―What do you want?" He said: ―I want not to want." His want was the state of _Consent'.

396. When the **Imam ar-Rida (*a*)** arrived in Neyshabur (the city from which the fathers of **Ruhullah** moved to Kashmir), there arrived, from various parts of Iran, scholars, pen in hand, to register the Imam's talks. The historians say that the number of the pen-in-hand persons was between four thousands and twenty thousands. Some of them had written the Imam's talks with golden water. Probably that is why his speeches were called *Silsilatudh-Dhahab* [The golden series]. Or it maybe that the source of the *hadith* was like a chain till the fountainhead. The *hadith* went like this: ―I heard my father who heard his father who heard his father...." The narrators thus continue till they reach **the Prophet (*s*)**, who had said that he heard from **Gabriel** who said from **Allah**: ―*La ilaha illallah* is my fortress. Whoever entered it would be secured against my Punishment."The sentence finished. All were surprised at hearing one of the most evident principles of Islam. After a while of silence during which they were engaged in thinking, he continued: ―Entering this fortress is conditional, and _I' am one of its conditions." This short *hadith* was delivered in the difficult conditions of _dissimulation' (a Shiite way for facing the tyrannical governments), as a guidance for the nation. The original text of the *hadith* is stated in more than twenty books, including *Uyun Akhbarir-Rida*, vol. 2, p. 153.

397. *Safinah al-Bihar,* vol. 2, p. 446, extracted from *Pishwayan Islam,* **the Imam Musa ibn Jafar (*a*) by Aqiqi Bakhshayeshi.**

398. Socrates the Wise used to say: —Iam not a scholar, I am a philosopher." That is: I love knowledge. At a time, a philosopher, according to Socrates, got a meaning higher than a scholar.

399. This concept was, of course, used in the same sense before him, and the great *ulama* used to call themselves *talabah'*, but by way of praising knowledge, not themselves.

400. No source refers to how he was acquainted with him, but **Aqa Ruhullah** might have used the same trick used by the students. Whenever they wanted to have a talk with some great personality, they used to wait for him to stand for the greeting *salat* or any other *salat,* and they tried to find a place next to him and tried to finish their *salat* a little earlier than he. After finishing the *salat,* usually one turns to the one sitting next to him and shakes hands with him, and it will be a good chance to exchange few greeting words while shaking hands, as a chance for starting a conversation. However, now as we read his book *Adabus-Salat,* we notice that he crosses off this idea, because he believes that the *salat* is a meeting with **Allah,** the Exalted, and cannot be an excuse for meeting someone else. But if we accept perfectibility in him, this method of getting acquainted, or some other methods, cannot be improbable in his youth.

401. —Aso the late **Mudarris** (may **Allah** be pleased with him), I had met him. He was one of those who stood against injustice, against that tyrant from Sawadkuh, **Rida Khan**, the lawless. He was in the Parliament. The *ulama* sent him to Tehran as a first-class scholar. He arrived in Tehran by a carriage. A trustworthy man related that he had bought the carriage, and probably he himself drove the horse up to Tehran. There he hired a modest house, which I frequently visited, and met him there. *Sahifeh-ye Imam,* vol. 1, pp. 255-266.

402. The session No. 202, Thursday, 24th Muharram al-Haram, 1329 A.H. inviting the deputies to unite in the objective, though different in tastes. *Mudarris in Five Legislative Terms of the Parliament,* vol.1, with the assistance of **Muhammad Turkman,** p.10.

403. That which is surprising is that in 1363 A.H. he suspended three teaching days just to give answers to the incredulities of someone who was struggling in the crisis of killing questions. *Hudur,* 3rd year, No. 4, *Philosophy in Imam Khomeini's Time.* **Ali Akbar Diyai,** p. 69.

404. **Imam Khomeini:** —Il Tehran **Mudarris** was the first deputy. He alone stood against despotism and delivered speeches. Other personalities,

such as **Malikush-Shuara**, supported him, but it was he who stood talking against the unjust acts of that man, **Rida Khan**. At that time the Russian government sent an ultimatum to Iran, and its soldiers proceded to Qazwin. They wanted something from Iran (I do not remember now what it was; it is in history). It meant almost capturing Iran. They said that it must be accepted by the Parliament. It was presented to the Parliament, and all the deputies were perplexed what to do. A foreign magazine wrote that a *ruhani* (an *Alim*) with trembling hands, mounted the rostrum and said: ‗Now that we are to be annihilated, why should we ourselves do it to ourselves?' So, he stood in the opposition. The others found courage and backed him, and the ultimatum was rejected, and they could do noting.'" *Sahifeh-ye Imam,* vol. 1, p. 261.

405. **Muhammad Turkman**, *Mudarris in Five Legislative Terms of the Parliament,* vol. 1, p. 69. Under the title: —Sesion No. 326, Saturday, 30th Dhul Hijjah, 1329 A.H." In this session, **Mudarris** was elected as a member of the Fifth Section of the Parliament, by which the author ends the Second Term. By page 73 he begins the Third Term without referring to the ultimatum or **Mudarris**'s speech. But in the book's preface page ‗q' he refers to a point; from both items one can infer that the author does not authorize the original text of the speech as published in some sources. Notice: —B.Concerning another question referred to at the beginning (speeches, writings …of **Sayyid Hasan Mudarris**) in respect of **Mudarris**'s opposition to the ultimatum of the Tzarist Russia in the Second Term of the Parliament (though stating the source) is not right. The opposer who was praised by the American **Morgan Shuster**, without stating his name, was **Shaykh Muhammad Khiyabani**, not **Mudarris**."

406. At last, the government of Iran, which saw itself weak, accepted the ultimatum on the first of Muharram, 1330 A.H. on the 2nd day of Muharram, **Nasir al-Mulk**, the Regent of the junior king **Ahmad Shah**, resolved the Parliament and cancelled all the national organizations by announcing a martial court government. *Kawthar,* vol. 2, p. 56, footnote No. 17.

407. Speech No. 51, 8th Aban, 1357 A.H., Paris, Neauphle-le-Château, *Kawthar,* vol. 2, p. 56.

408. **Shuster** was ousted from Iran. In America he wrote a book under the title *Iran's Suffocation,* uncovering the allegiances of authorities and nobilities, and the insolences of Russia, as well as the slyneses of the British statesmen. At the same time he praised the popular struggles and the immature, enthusiastic and anti-imperialistic feelings of some religious and national leaders. In that ultimatum Russia had three demands:

1. Dismissing the American **Morgan Shuster**.

2. Employing the foreigners with the permission of the Russians and the British.

3. Refunding the expenditure caused by sending the Russian army to Iran.

The Armenian **Yeprim Khan**, who was the head of the Police, suggested that five deputies, with full authorities, should give their opinion in respect of the Russian ultimatum. These five deputies were: **Sayyid Hasan Mudarris, Fahimul Mulk, Sardar Asad Bakhtiyari, Shaykh Ibrahim Zanjani** and **Said al-Atibba**. At last, **Wuthuquddawlah**'s cabinet accepted the context of the Russian ultimatum, on the 28th of Adhar, 1290 S.H., with the support of the deputies. Particular events caused this period of the history to be complicated. For example: When the Russians sent the ultimatum to the Iranian government, many of the *ulama,* in the holy places (in Iraq), decided to wear fighting uniforms in defence of the country and to go to Iran. **Akhund Mulla Kazim Khurasani** and **Shaykh Abdullah Mazandarani** were among the most notable *ulama* of that time, who moved to Iran. But on the 21st of Adhar 1290, **Akhund Mulla Kazim Khurasani** died in doubtful circumstances, and a 3-days general mourning was announced.

409. Ruhaniyyat (Ruhaniyyun).

410. *Nehdat-e Imam Khomeini*, vol. 1, p. 316.

411. _Women and Elections' of a series of discussions titled: _What do We Know of Islam?', by **Zayn al-Abidin Qurbani, Muhammad Shabestari, Ali Hujjati Kirmani, Abbas Ali Amid Zanjani** and **Husayn Haqqani**. In this book the two lines of westernization and Islamization are very clearly facing each other, but the conception of that day's writers of women's right in elections and their arguments in some instances are exactly contrary to their today's opinions.

412. *Kalimat-e Qisar*, p. 210.

413. *Sahifeh-ye Imam*, vol. 4, p. 70.

414. **Hairi,** the grand child of the late **Ayatullah Hairi**: —He did not take the monthly allowance, thus he was brave in expressing his opinion." *Tarikh-e Shafahi.* (Others said that he did take it. From these two sayings one may infer that he sometimes did and sometimes did not.)

415. In one of the narrow alleys near Baharistan Square, there still is a plate denoting the existence of a clinic under the name of the Charity Establishment of the Imam al-Jawad (*a*). This clinic was the very house of **Ayatullah Shahabadi**, which **Ruhullah** used to knock at its door whenever he came to Tehran, and perhaps he had slept in it more than twenty nights.

416. From Rajab of 1340 to 1355 A.H.

417. Although a few number of the westerners were sufficiently acquainted with the philosophy of Islam, yet the current course in the West kept most of the westerners away from this philosophy, and most of our West-visitors were also incapable of understanding their own philosophic resources. The following expressions describe such a situation:

—They did such in order to educate our brains in such a way that if we wished to be something we write a book which must begin with the name of one of them so that they would buy it... If our young men want to buy a book, if it is by **Marx** or by **Lenin**, buyers are numerous, but if it is by **Avicenna**, no, despite the fact that all of them cannot understand a single page of the **Shaykh Avicenna**, but since he is from the orient, not from the West, hence they did not hear the name of **Mulla Sadra** at all, nor they heard of our **Mulla Hadi**, while the names of all of their personalities are there. They do not know what our books are." *Sahifeh-ye Imam*, vol. 9, p. 9.

418. In Arak, too, his desire to get acquainted with the new science of medicine prompted him to look for somebody to teach him French, but the conditions were not convenient for that.

419. The principle of evolution is a requisite for religiosity. But its manner has always been under discussion. **The Imam (*a*)**, in pursuit of **Mulla Sadra** and **Mulla Hadi Sabzawari**, believed that evolution was essential. He taught —the Essential Movement", and he very much expanded upon the expression taken from a poem by **Mulla Hadi**:

The requisite of wisdom and care

Is to take every possible to a goal.

That is, **Allah**'s wisdom and His care decide that all beings should reach their own goals, and, while getting nearer to their goals, they complete their evolution.

420. The Month of Shahrivar, 1346 S.H.

421. Another one of his teachers in astronomy was **Haj Shaykh Ali Akbar Yazdi,** known by the name of **al-Hakim'**. —*Philosophy in the Time of Imam Khomeini" Hudur* magazine, Khordad, 1371 S.H., p. 68. Ali **Akbar Diyai**.

422. *Gulhay-e Bagh-e Khatirah,* 2nd ed., p. 8, altered.

423. Many of the Muslim astrologers did not believe in the Ptolemaic system, such as **Khajah Nasiruddin Tusi**.

424. *Surah* 62: 5.

425. *Surah* 56: 75-76.

426. *Qunut* is a non-compulsory action in the *salat*, performed in the second *rakah*, by raising the palms of the hands upwards and reciting some invocations.

427. Surah 88: 17-20.

428. ―We are closer to him than his jugular vein (50: 16)."

429. These sorts of his mental engagements during the days when he used to teach philosophy can be deducted from his writings, and this part is drawn in his speeches. Even during his old age and the maturity of his thoughts, these arguments can be traced in his writings. However, sometimes man's smallness in respect to the bigness of the galaxies was a topic, then the triviality of the solar system and the galaxies in respect of **Allah**'s greatness was the topic. But the developed man with sufficient knowledge of philosophy and gnosticism, was, in his view, the center of existence. The clearest evidence of that is in his writing *Rah-e Ishq*, which is a gnostic letter written on the 5th of Khordad, 1363 S.H. Read this: ―My daughter (addressing **Fatimah**), conceit and self-admiration are of complete ignorance of one's humility and of Allah's greatness. If a little attention is paid to the greatness of the creation according to little knowledge which man could acquire despite his scientific progress, he would realize his humility and all the solar system and the galaxies, in respect to his little understanding of **Allah**'s greatness. He would, then, be ashamed of his conceit, selfishness and self-admiration, and he would comprehend his ignorance ...Man, who thinks himself to be the center of creation—though the perfect man is so—in the eyes of other creatures he may not be so, since the undeveloped man is not so. _The likeness of those who were charged with the Torah, yet they did not observe it, is as the likeness of the ass...' (62: 5). This is related to the scientific progress minus refinement. Such men are described to be _as cattle, nay, they are worse in astraying"' (7: 179). *Rah-e Ishq*, pp. 26, 27.

430. A *hadith*.

431. If understanding, feeling, knowing, conceptualization, meaning and verbal text are placed in a generality called knowledge, then knowing any subject can either occur automatically and without learning, in this case it is a kind of understanding called _intuitive knowledge', or to know we need to be taught, in which case it is called _acquired knowledge'. Of course, this classification of intuitive and acquired knowledge is, philosophically, still arguable.

432. *Sahifeh-ye Imam*, vol. 18, p. 79.

433. In former pages the meaning of: ―The legs of the rationalists are wooden" had been briefly said. It is also a part of the answer to this question.

434. ―When there comes the help of Allah, and victory, and you see the people entering the religion of Allah by companies, then glorify your Lord‗s praise and beg Him forgiveness. Surely He is Oft-Returning!" (110: 1-3) When the mind cannot fully understand the meaning of _tawwab‗ (oft-returning), cannot but to take it to mean _accepting repentance‗, which is not incorrect, but it is a low understanding of the final concept.

435. When we have (in the next volume) the honour of visiting Najaf with him, we will see how firmly, patiently and fearlessly he forbore the vacancy of his [martyred] son.

436. *Kawthar*, vol. 1, pp. 297, 298.

437. *Az Sayyid Diya ta Bakhtiyar*, **Mas'ud Behnud**, p. 67. Many of the historians doubt the question of **Rida Khan** accompanying **Ahmad Shah** in this travel.

438. 10th of Bahman, 1315 S.H.

439. *Hadith-e Bidari*, p. 26.

440. ―In the year 1324 S.H., when the late **Ayatullah Burujerdi**, because of his slight illness, came from his town Burujerd, to Tehran for medical treatment, due to the extensive efforts of **Imam Khomeini**, the way was paved for **Ayatullah Burujerdi** to move to Qum and take in his hand the leadership of the *hawzah* and to be the *marja* of the Shiite." *Imam Khomeini dar Aine-ye Khatirah-ha*, Ali **Dawani**, p. 15.

441. After finishing the building of the Khan School, an orderly program was arranged for it, including teaching the English language… When he saw that, he said: ―If one knows a language one is a man, if one knows two, one is two men, if one knows three, one is three men." *Hawzah* magazine, 1373 S.H., p. 167. Despite the fact that the above expression goes back to a thousand years, but the young students heard it for the first time from him.

442. The assertions of **Ayatullah Burujerdi** (beginning with discussions on *Usul* up to the discussions on supposition) within the years of 1364 and 1369 A.H.

443. **The Prophet (s)** had no son. The Arabs of the Era of Ignorance thought that when **Muhammad (s)** dies he will have no (male) offspring. But **Allah** said: ―We have given you the Kawthar" [plenty]. It was so, and the twelve Imams were his offspring from his daughter, **Fatimah (a)**, who continued the path of the Prophet. Now, millions of million people, in whose veins **Fatima**‗s blood runs, are proud of their grandfather, **Muhammad (s)!**

444. **Imam Khomeini**‗s wife.

445. **Mrs. Zahra Mustafawi** said: —I was the elder brother of **Aqa Muhammad Sadiq Lawasani, Aqa Haj Sayyid Ahmad Lawasani**, who suggested the proposal of marriage to the **Imam (a)**.

446. **Mrs. Zahra Mustafawi**: —As far as I remember, the answer did not reach the **Imam (a)**, because **Aqa Thaqafi** himself wanted it and waited for an affirmative reply from his daughter."

447. *Kalimat-e Qisar*, p.207.

448. In her identity card her name was **Khadijah**, inside the house she was called **Quds Iran**, on the tongues of her father, mother and the relatives she was sometimes **Qudsi Khanum** and sometimes **Qudsi-jan**.

449. He did tell, once or twice, his dreams, including his dream about **Mirza Kuchak Khan**.

450. He did this for two reasons: a practice in preventing extravagance, and not bothering the servants and the others.

451. About 25 years before his departure. Perhaps the Summer of 1341 S.H.

452. **Mrs. Zahra Mustafawi**: —Her name was **Muluk**, but as her father was the treasurer of **Nasiruddin Shah**, she was known as **Khazin al-Muluk**.

GLOSSARY

A

aba: A (loose) cloak; a cloak-like (woolen) wrap.

adhan: Call for the *salat*; certain words recited loudly when it is time for performing the *salat*.

akhund: A Persian epithet indicating the man who wears the special uniform of the *talabah,* consisting of the turban, the outer and the inner gowns, and *aba*.

Alim: A scholar, particularly in *fiqh* and religious matters.

al-Masjid al-Aqsa: The great Islamic mosque in Jerusalem. It was the first *qiblah* for the Muslims before turning to Mecca.

andaruni: The part of a house confined to the family, compared with the *biruni* which is the part confined to the guests and the strangers.

arak tree: A nice-smelling tree whose branches are cut into some 10 cm pieces, lacerated and used as tooth-brushes.

ashrafi: An old Iranian gold coin.

ashura: The tenth day of the Hijri month of Muharram on which **the Imam Husayn (a)**, the grandson of **the Prophet (s)**, was martyred by the order of **Yazid**, son of **Mu'awiyah**.

ayah: A verse of the *Quran*, being the smallest unit of it.

Ayatullah: The highest religious rank bestowed upon the *mujtahid* who is highly versed in religious precepts.

B

Baqi: The cemetery in al-Madinah, Arabia, in which four of the Shiite Imams are buried.

batil: Invalid.

baqiyyatullah: The epithet of the 12th Imam of the Shiite.

basij: Militia forces.

Basmillah: Short form for: *Bismillahir-Rahmanir-Rahim* [In the name of Allah, the Beneficent, the Merciful].

biruni: The section of a house allocated to the guests and strangers.

bi'thah: The sending of **the Prophet (s)** by Allah with the mission of Islam.

C

chador: A veil or mantle worn by Persian women to cover their whole body and dress.

charandu parand: Nonsense; fiddle-faddle.

charshanbeh suri: the last Wednesday before Nowruz.

charuq: A kind of shoes for men and women in Iran.

D

da'ifah: The delicate sex. It refers to a woman.

dua: Invocation words addressed to **Allah** requesting him to respond to them.

dugh: Yoghurt thinned with water.

dunya: The lowest world in which we live.

F

faqih: An expert in religious teachings.

farsakh: A distance measure of 6 kms.

fasiq: The one who commits cardinal sins and insists on the small ones.

fatihah: 1. The recitation of *surah* of *al-Fatihah* once, and the surah of al-Ikhlas three times, sending its heavenly rewards to some dead person (s). 2. The mourning gathering held on behalf of a deceased person to recite the *Fatihah*.

fatwa: A decree issued by a *mujtahid* giving his opinion on some religious matters.

fiqh: The science handling religious precepts and deducting them from their detailed reasons.

fitr: The first day of the month of Shawwal, which is a feast after the end of the fasting days of Ramadan.

G

galush: Rubber shoes worn over the ordinary shoes to protect them against water and mud.

Ghadir: Literally, a pool. The name of a place near Mecca where **the Prophet (s)** stopped the pilgrims on his return from his last *hajj*, to announce Ali ibn Abi Talib (*a*) as his successor after him.

ghayb: Whatever is invisible from man; the information known only to **Allah**.

giweh: A kind of men's shoes made of hand-knitted cotton thread.

Ghusl: A ritual wash of the whole body.

H

hadith: The Prophet's traditions relating his deeds, utterances and assertions.

Haftsin: Lit. Seven —Ss; seven eatables whose names start with the letter "S", arranged on a *sufreh* on the *Nowruz* day.

haj Aqa: An epithet of respect given to a man who has visited Mecca.

haji: The man who goes on pilgrimage to Mecca is called the *haji.*

hakim: A physician; a philosopher or a wiseman.

halal: Anything which is religiously neither *haram* nor *makruh.*

haram: The prohibited; whatever is stated by the Islamic law to be prohibited or not allowed.

harem: The women household of a man; the section of a Muslim's house in which his women live.

hawzah: the schools for teaching religious and relevant subjects with their teachers and stuff.

hijab: The veil and, or, the *chador*, or the *aba* worn by the women.

I

iftar: Breakfast of the fasting; the food eaten to break the fasting.

ijtihad: The process of deducting religious judgments from their relevant evidences and principles.

imam Jumah: The leader of the congregational noon *salat* on Fridays.

imamzadeh: The shrine of an offspring of the Shiite Imams.

inshaallah: Lit. —fl Allah willed!", God willing; If God will(s). It is said whenever a Muslim says he intends to do something.

isha: Some time after the *maghrib* [sunset]; the meal at night [supper]; the *salatul isha*, the *salat* which is to be performed after *salatul maghrib.*

ishraq: Illumination; intuition; spiritual insight.

istikan: A glass tea-cup slim in the waist, with a capacity of some 1.5 to 3 ounces.

J

jabr and ikhtiyar: Fatalism and volition; predetermination and self-determination; determinism and free will.

jihad: Fighting in defence of one's religion and against the enemy.

jiweh: Mercury.

Jumah: Friday.

K

kabab: Minced meat, or small pieces of meat, seasoned and roasted on skewers.

Ka'bah: A sacred place in Mecca to which all Muslims, wherever they may be in the world, turn their faces during their *salat*s.

Karbala: A sacred city in Iraq where the **Imam Husayn (*a*)** is buried, and the Shiite from all over the world travel to visit it.

Kawthar: Abundance; the name of a water spring in Paradise.

kharwar: About 300 kgs.

khums: One-fifth of the surplus of one's incomes, which is to be distributed among the needy ones, according to **Allah**'s order.

kifai: The religious duty imposed on every Muslim, unless a number of them undertook to carry it out, in which case the others are exempted.

kursi: Lit. a chair; in Iran it is a rather large table under which usually a brazier with lit coal is put, and on it a thick blanket is spread. It is placed in the middle of the room, and the household sit around it, covering their legs with blanket, during cold winter season.

kurur: 500,000; half a million.

L

labbadeh: Long outer garment for men.

M

maghrib: The early time after sunset; the time for performing *salatul maghrib*; the west.

mahkameh: Law court.

majlis: A meeting; the Parliament.

makasib: Pl. of maksab, i.e. a profession; a branch of the *fiqh* subjects concerning the *halal* and *haram* jobs.

makruh: Anything which is religiously disapproved.

maktab: The old-fashioned non-official schools for children.

man: A weight of about 3 kgs.

marja': The *mujtahid* to whom is referred in religious questions as an authority.

masjid: Mosque; a place built by the Muslims for worship.

Masjid an-Nabi: The Mosque in which **the Prophet (*s*)** is buried in al-Madinah.

mata': Any worldly material which is transitory compared with spiritual things which are eternal.

minbar: A structure made of wood or bricks, with several steps, on which a speaker sits to deliver a speech.

miswak: A tooth-brush made of the branches of a tree called *arak-tree*, with a nice smell.

mudhdhin: The one who loudly recites the *adhan*, telling the Muslims that it is time for performing the *salat*.

muqallid: The Muslim individual who follows the religious instructions of a *mujtahid*.

mujahid: The one who fights for the sake of religion, *jihad*.

mujtahid: The *faqih* who reaches the rank of *ijtihad* and becomes an authority to issue Shar'i fatwas.

mulla: Teacher of religious law; an *akhund*.

musalla: Place allocated for the people to perform the daily *salats*.

Mustadaf: Oppressed; one under oppression; weak.

N

naskh: A form of handwriting with which the *Quran* is printed.

nazmiyyah: An old name for the police; the police department.

Nowruz: The first day of the Persian year = 21st March.

Q

qaba: A long garment with open front, worn by men.

qiran: An old Persian metal coin; the old Persian monetary unit.

qiblah: It is the *Ka'bah* which the Muslims have to face during the *salats*. It is in Mecca.

qimah: A kind of broth made of beans, meat and tomatoes.

qunut: An invocation recited in the *salat* with the palms of the hands raised before face.

qur'ah: Casting lots.

qurban: Sacrifice.

R

rial: A Persian metal coin; monetary unit.

ruhani: See Ali*m*.

ruhaniyyun: See *ulama* (*ulema*).

ruznameh: Daily newspaper.

S

sajdah: Prostration with the legs folded under the body and placing the forehead on the ground, during the *salat.*

salat: An act of worship with particular rites. All Muslims are to perform the *salat*s five times a day and night.

salatul layl: A supererogatory *salat* performed during the last part of the night.

samanu: A kind of porridge made of wheat-sprouts. It is commonly cooked some days after the *Nowruz.*

salawat: Sending blessings on **the Prophet (s)** and his offspring.

sawm (or **siyam**): Fasting.

Sayyid: A suffix added to the names of the male offspring of **the Prophet (s)** to denote that he is of them.

senjed: Sorb; service.

serkeh: Vinegar.

shabih(eh) khani: A play popularly acted to show the tragedy of the massacre of the Imam Husayn (*a*) and his family and companions on the Ashura

shahi: An old Persian metal coin.

sharbat: Any *halal* sweet (cold) drink.

shar': The revealed, or canonical, law of Islam.

Shari'ah: The revealed, or canonical, law of Islam.

siffah: A platform built by the Prophet (*s*) in Masjid an-Nabi for the poor who had no place to live in.

sighah: The text of the marriage contract. In Iran it has also become a term denoting temporary marriage.

sizdah bedar: The 13th day of the first month of the year. The people in Iran spend it out of doors.

sunbul: An ear of wheat.

sur: A banquet.

T

Tabarra: Renouncing attachment to the enemies of the progeny of **the Prophet (s)**.

tabarruk: Seeking blessing from something.

tajwid: Reciting the *Quran* in a resonant tone.

tafsir: Exegesis of the *Quran.*

talabah: A student of theology and the Islamic law.

Taq Kasra: Ctesiphon.

taqlid: Imitation; performing the religious *fatwas* of a *marja*.

taqwa: God-fearing; protecting oneself against **Allah**'s wrath and seeking His proximity by complying with His commands.

tasht: A shallow basin for washing clothes.

tarhim: A mourning gathering in which the *fatihah* and the *Quran* are recited as a blessing to the deceased soul.

Tawalla: Adhering to and loving **the Prophet**'s progeny.

tawaf: Going around the *Kabah* as a ritual act.

tawhid: Monotheism; believing in the one God.

tuman: A Persian currency.

U

ulama (ulema): (Pl. of *Alim*) Scholars.

ulul-azm: The prophets who brought laws: **Noah, Ibrahim, Moses, Jesus** and **Muhammad**.

ummah: A nation

W

wafur: Opium-smoking pipe.

wajib: Duty; anything one has to do.

wilayat al-faqih: The rule of the *faqih* who possesses the required conditions and abilities for governing a country.

Z

zakat: A tax to be paid by every Muslim on certain kinds of his properties.

zar: Agriculture; cultivation.